THE TERRESTRIAL ECOLOGY
OF ALDABRA

THE
TERRESTRIAL ECOLOGY
OF ALDABRA

A ROYAL SOCIETY DISCUSSION

ORGANIZED BY D. R. STODDART
AND T. S. WESTOLL, F.R.S.

HELD ON 16 AND 17 MARCH 1977

LONDON
THE ROYAL SOCIETY
1979

Printed in Great Britain for the Royal Society
at the
University Press, Cambridge

ISBN 0 85403 111 1

First published in *Philosophical Transactions of the Royal Society of London,*
series B, volume 286 (no. 1011), pages 1–263

Published by the Royal Society
6 Carlton House Terrace, London SW1Y 5AG

CONTENTS

[Two plates; one pullout; one microfiche inside back cover]

CONTENTS

Phil. Trans. R. Soc. Lond. B. **286**, 3–10 (1979)
Printed in Great Britain

[3]

Aldabra and the Aldabra Research Station

By D. R. Stoddart
*Department of Geography, Cambridge University,
Downing Place, Cambridge, U.K.*

This introductory paper describes the history of the Royal Society's involvement with Aldabra since 1966. After an initial expeditionary phase in 1967–9, the Society built the Aldabra Research Station and planned a series of scientific studies centred on the giant tortoise. A revised place-name map of the atoll is provided to serve as background to the discussion.

The Royal Society's involvement with Aldabra dates from 1966, when on behalf of the Southern Zone Research Committee Dr C. A. Wright of the British Museum (Natural History) and I were attached to a B.B.C. and Ministry of Defence party going to the atoll to study the feasibility of constructing an air staging post there. As a result of that visit and subsequent discussions, the Society convened a conference of interested scientific and conservation bodies in January 1967, at which it was concluded that the proposed developments were incompatible with the preservation of the ecology of Aldabra. In April 1967 the Society prepared a memorandum which stated that 'if development takes place at Aldabra the loss to science will be permanent', and argued that the major contribution that the study of the atoll could make to science could only be made by its total preservation for long-term studies. Thus began what came to be known as 'the Aldabra affair' (Stoddart 1968a, b).

In anticipation of a Government decision to build the staging post, the Society began a major expedition to Aldabra in August 1967. In the event this lasted until September 1969, and involved some 50 people and about 14 man-years of field investigation. Its initial aim was to make as full an inventory as possible of the terrestrial and marine features of the atoll before development began. Its methods were thus necessarily rapid and aimed at speedy results, and large collections were made, especially of plants and invertebrates, which continue to provide material for study. In addition the Expedition was concerned to document distributions of plants and animals and to estimate population levels, especially in the airfield area at the eastern end of Grande Terre. But within a few months of the start of the Expedition (in November 1967) the Government abandoned its defence proposals, and it became possible to plan the study of Aldabra in a more comprehensive manner.

The Society then decided to build a small Research Station on the atoll, to provide for longer-term scientific research, and the Aldabra Research Committee was set up under the chairmanship of Professor T. S. Westoll, F.R.S., to coordinate this work. In August 1968 Professor Westoll, Dr M. E. D. Poore of the Nature Conservancy, and I visited Aldabra, chose a site for the Research Station, and laid out a preliminary plan of the buildings. We afterwards went on to Mahé and discussed with the Government of Seychelles the practical problems that would be faced during construction.

The first Director, the late Lt Cdr G. R. Lush, R.N., M.B.E., was responsible for building the Station during 1969–71. It proved a much longer and more difficult process than originally envisaged, but at the end of the day the Society had a large, sturdy and well equipped centre for research. It included main laboratory and accommodation blocks, additional living quarters, stores, a workshop and boatshed, generators giving continuous power, and both rainwater tanks and solar stills (figure 2). In addition there is a network of field huts around the atoll. The whole complex was declared open on 30 June 1971. Most of the cost of building and operating the Station has been carried by the Society's Parliamentary Grant-in-Aid, though with additional support from the National Academy of Sciences, the Smithsonian Institution, and the World Wildlife Fund. In addition to the actual construction the Society was also concerned with other safeguards. The lease of Aldabra from the Seychelles Government had been held for many years by Mr Harry Savy of Mahé. Mr Savy had been extremely cooperative throughout our earlier involvement, and in August 1971 the Society was able, with generous financial help from Mr Christopher Cadbury, to take over the lease itself. This runs to 1985, with optional extension. Efforts were also made to define adequate conservation measures for the atoll under the laws of the British Indian Ocean Territory, of which Aldabra formed a part from 1966 to 1976.

FIGURE 1. The Aldabra Research Station from the northwest.

Thus, when the first Discussion Meeting on Aldabra was held in March 1969 (Westoll & Stoddart (eds) 1971), most of our knowledge was of a preliminary or indeed reconnaissance kind. The Expedition itself was still continuing, and the work of building was soon to slow down the pace of scientific research for several months. Once the Station was complete, however, a new programme began under guidelines adopted by the Aldabra Research Committee in 1970 and revised in 1973. These called for the completion of certain types of inventory work already begun (for example on the plants and insects), for basic surveys in geology and geomorphology, and for the establishment of a meteorological station which now operates to World Weather Watch standards. They also specified a series of priorities in scientific research, the most important of which was the study of the tortoise population, initially concentrating on population dynamics, distribution and movement. Studies of land birds, including several of the passerines as well as the flightless white-throated rail, came second, followed by an array of other terrestrial topics. The existence of this scale of priorities was not intended to inhibit other types of study, notably on the marine ecology in which a start had been made during the Expedition (Stoddart & Yonge (eds) 1971), but the Committee took the view that if such wide-ranging studies were to be manageable they also had to be managed. Finally the Natural Environment Research Council financed the establishment of an Aldabra Data Unit housed in the Department of Zoology, British Museum (Natural History), under the direction of J. F. Peake, to standardize field observation and to organize and make accessible the results (Peake, Sinclair & Lomas 1978).

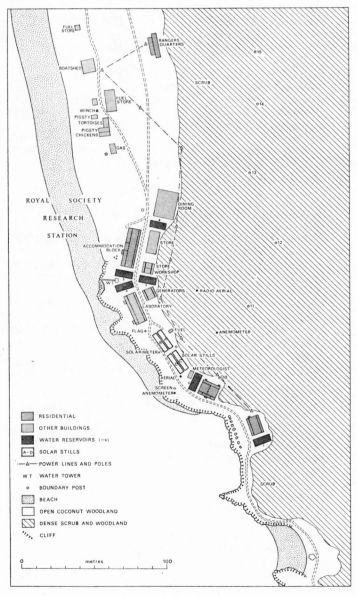

FIGURE 2

TABLE 1. STAFF AND VISITORS AT THE ROYAL SOCIETY ALDABRA RESEARCH STATION,
FEBRUARY 1969 TO MARCH 1980

name	institution at time of visit	time	field
Alexander, Dr H. G. L.	Department of Natural Sciences, South London College	Aug. 1971–Aug. 1972, Jan.–Mar. 1978	land crabs
Anderson, F. F.	The Divinity School, Duke University, U.S.A.	June–Oct. 1976	goats
Blackmore, Dr S.	Station staff	Dec. 1976–Nov. 1977	administrative officer
Blackmore, Mrs P. J. M.	—	Dec. 1976–Nov. 1977	
Bone, D. G.	Station staff	Sep. 1971–Dec. 1972	administrative officer
Bone, Mrs Sally Elisabeth	—	Sep. 1971–Dec. 1972	
Bourn, D. M.	Department of Zoology, University of Oxford	Dec. 1972–Sep. 1974	tortoise population dynamics
Braithwaite, Dr C. J. R.	Department of Geology, University of Dundee	June–Sep. 1969	geology
Bruce, Dr A. J.	East Africa Marine Fisheries Research Organisation, Zanzibar	Feb. 1972	Crustacea
Bruce, R. W.	Department of Zoology, University of Glasgow	Oct 1975–Aug. 1976, Nov. 1977–Jan. 1978	parrot fish
Busby, J. P.	Edinburgh College of Art	Jan.–Mar. 1974	wildlife painting
Butterfield, M. R.	Station staff	May 1975–Apr. 1976	meteorologist
Cause, Cpl. R.	Royal Engineers	Oct. 1969–Feb. 1970	station construction
Chelazzi, Dr G.	Istituto di Zoologia, University of Florence, Italy	Jan.–Mar. 1979	orientation and migration of coenobites and *Nerita*
Chivers, I. G.	Institute of Oceanographic Sciences, Bidston Observatory	May–June 1975	tide gauge installation
Coe, Dr M. J.	Department of Zoology, University of Oxford	Sep. 1974, July 1978	tortoises
Cowx, W. D.	Station staff	Mar. 1978–Mar. 1980	officer-in-charge
Dale, P. F. and student party	Department of Geography, University of Cambridge	June–Aug. 1970	topographical survey
Diamond, Dr A. W.	Department of Zoology, University of Aberdeen	Mar.–Sep. 1969	sea bird ecology
Donaldson, A.	Department of Botany, University of Durham	Oct. 1972–June 1973	terrestrial and freshwater algae
Edwards, G.	Anglia Television Ltd	Sep.–Nov. 1970	cine-photography
Edwards, Ms Kimberly	—	July 1975–Nov. 1976	scientific field assistant
Forbes-Watson, A. D.	National Museum, Nairobi, Kenya	Sep.–Oct. 1974	land birds
Forster, G. R.	The Marine Laboratory, Plymouth	Mar. 1971, Nov. 1977–Jan. 1978	long line fishing
Frazier, Dr J. G.	Department of Zoology, University of Oxford	June 1969–June 1970	tortoise behaviour and ecology
Fricke, Dr H.	Max Planck Institut, Seewiesen, F.R.G.	July–Sep. 1975	anemone fish
Fricke, Mrs Simone	—	July–Sep. 1975	
Frith, C. B.	Station staff	Apr. 1972–Apr. 1973	junior staff scientist; land birds
Frith, Dr Dawn W.	Department of General Education and Science, Brooklands County Technical College	Aug. 1971–Aug. 1972	terrestrial invertebrates
Gallsworthy, J. M.	Station staff	Oct. 1975–Jan. 1977	station director
Gaymer, Dr R. D. T.	Department of Zoology, University of Bristol	June–Sep. 1969, June–Aug. 1970	tortoise marking

TABLE 1 (*cont.*)

name	institution at time of visit	time	field
Gibson, Dr C. W. D.	Station staff	Nov. 1976–Jan. 1979	staff scientist: tortoise/vegetation interaction
Gibson, Mrs Julie	Department of Zoology, University of Oxford	Nov. 1976–Jan. 1979	tortoise feeding
Gibson, T. S. H.	—	May 1975–Apr. 1976	scientific assistant
Gillham, Dr Mary E.	Department of Extra-Mural Studies, University College of South Wales and Monmouthshire	Feb.–May 1970	seabird/vegetation interaction
Gould, Ms Margaret S.	Department of Zoology, Duke University, U.S.A.	June 1976–Sep. 1977	goats
Griffin, D. J. H.	Royal Society	Aug.–Sep. 1973	administrative visit
Grinter, J.	—	Feb.–June 1969	assistant
Hartnoll, Dr R. G.	Department of Marine Biology, University of Durham	Feb.–Mar. 1979	land crabs
Hemmen, G. E.	Royal Society	Apr. 1970	administrative visit
Hill, Dr M. G.	Department of Zoology, Imperial College	Nov. 1976–Nov. 1978	coccid/plant relationships
Hnatiuk, Dr R. J.	Station staff	Feb. 1973–Oct. 1974	senior staff scientist/ director: vegetation
Hnatiuk, Dr Sarah	—	Feb. 1973–Oct. 1974	spp. distribution on lagoon islets
Huxley, C. R.	Sub-department of Ornithology, British Museum (Nat. Hist.)	Aug. 1973–Apr. 1976	flightless rail
Johnston, D. R.	Royal Engineers	Oct. 1969–June 1970	station construction
	Station staff	Apr. 1973–Nov. 1975	station engineer
Kennedy, Dr W. J.	Department of Geology, University of Oxford	June–Sep. 1969	geology
Klopfer, Prof. P. H.	Department of Zoology, Duke University, U.S.A.	Dec. 1976–Jan. 1977	goats
Klopfer, Mrs Martha	—	Dec. 1976–Jan. 1977	
Lawson, D.	Station staff	Mar. 1978–July 1979	meteorologist
Lewis, Prof. D.	Department of Botany, University College, London	Aug. 1971	*Pemphis* heterostyly
Lush, Lt Cdr G. R.	Station staff	Oct. 1969–June 1971	station director
Lush, Mrs Janet H.	—	Oct. 1969–June 1971	
Lythgoe, Dr J. N.	M.R.C. Vision Unit, School of Biology, University of Sussex	Feb.–Mar. 1971	photography/visual pigments of reef fishes
Merton, L. F. H.	Department of Botany, University of Sheffield	Aug.–Sep. 1973, July–Sep. 1974	vegetation
Mole, L. U.	Royal Society	Sep.–Oct. 1969, Oct.–Dec. 1972, July–Oct. 1975 July 1976, Jan.–Mar. 1978	administrative visits
Morrison, R. C.	Station staff	Apr. 1977–Mar. 1978	meteorologist
Muntz, Dr W. R. A.	Laboratory of Experimental Psychology, University of Sussex	Feb.–Mar. 1971	visual pigments and schooling of coral fishes
Nelson, Dr J. B.	Department of Zoology, University of Aberdeen	Jan.–Mar. 1974	sea birds
Newberry, Dr D. McC.	Department of Zoology, Imperial College	Nov. 1976–Jan. 1979	coccid/plant relationships
Niedzwiedzki, P. S.	Station staff	Dec. 1976–Nov. 1977	senior staff scientist/ director: fat storage in lizards

TABLE 1 (*cont.*)

name	institution at time of visit	time	field
Niedzwiedzki, Mrs Margaret A.	—	Dec. 1976–July 1977	
Peake, J. F.	Department of Zoology, British Museum (Nat. Hist.)	Sep.- Oct. 1974	administrative visit
Peet, C. J.	Station staff	Mar. 1976–Sep. 1977 Apr. 1978–Mar. 1980	scientific assistant officer-in-charge
Penny, M. J.	The Wildfowl Trust, Slimbridge	Mar.–June 1969	wading birds
Pettigrew, J. J.	Meteorological office	Apr. 1976–Apr. 1977	meteorologist
Phillipson, Dr J.	Department of Zoology, University of Oxford	Apr. 1977	primary productivity
Polak, T. A.	Churchill College, Cambridge	July–Sep. 1978	station engineer
Polunin, N. V. C.	Department of Zoology, University of Cambridge	July–Oct. 1975	reef fishes
Porteous, Dr A.	Department of Mechanical Engineering, University of Glasgow	May–June 1970	solar still installation
Potts, Dr G. W.	The Marine Laboratory, Plymouth	Nov. 1977–Jan. 1978	predatory fishes
Potts, Dr M.	Department of Botany, University of Durham	Nov. 1974–June 1975	blue-green algae
Povey, D. I.	Station staff	June 1977–Mar. 1980	station engineer
Prŷs-Jones, O. E.	Department of Applied Biology, University of Cambridge	Oct. 1976–Jan. 1977	land birds
Prŷs-Jones, Dr R. P.	Sub-department of Ornithology, British Museum (Nat. Hist.)	July 1974–Feb. 1977	land birds
Pugh, Dr D. T.	Institute of Oceanographic Sciences, Bidston Observatory	May–June 1975	tide gauge installation
Reinboth, Prof. R.	Institut für Zoologie, Johannes Gutenberg-Universität, F.R.G.	July–Aug. 1975	sex changes in fishes
Renvoize, S. A.	Royal Botanic Gardens, Kew	May–June 1975	coccid/plant relationships
Reville, B. J.	Department of Zoology, University of Aberdeen	Jan. 1976–Jan. 1978	sea birds
Robertson, Dr D. R.	Smithsonian Tropical Research Institute, Panama	July 1975–Jan. 1976	reef fishes
Rutter, Prof. A. J.	Department of Botany, Imperial College	Apr. 1977	coccid/plant relationships
Schmidt, Dr H.	Zoologisches Institut der Universität Heidelberg, F.R.G.	Oct.–Nov. 1975	sea anemones
Shapiro, Dr D. Y.	Department of Zoology, University of Cambridge	July–Oct. 1975	sex changes in fishes
Shapiro, Mrs Milbrey	—	July–Oct. 1975	
Sinclair, Ms Amanda J.	Department of Zoology, British Museum (Nat. Hist.)	Sep.–Oct. 1974	data processing
Sloan, Dr N. A.	Department of Zoology, Queen Mary College	Nov. 1977–May 1978	echinoderms
Smith, A.	Station staff	Oct. 1969–Apr. 1971	station construction
Smith, Mrs Kathleen	—	Oct. 1969–Apr. 1971	
Smith, G.	Station staff	June 1970–May 1971	station engineer
Snow, Dr D. W.	Sub-department of Ornithology, British Museum (Nat. Hist.)	Sep.–Oct. 1974	land birds
Spaull, Dr V. W.	Station staff	Oct. 1973–May 1975	staff scientist: soil and freshwater invertebrates
Stevens, Dr J. D.	The Marine Laboratory, Plymouth	Nov. 1977–Nov. 1978	sharks
Stevenson, J. A.	Station staff	Aug. 1970–Apr. 1972	junior staff scientist
Stickley, H. C.	Station staff	Feb. 1971–Apr. 1973	station engineer

TABLE 1 (*cont.*)

name	institution at time of visit	time	field
Stoddart, Dr D. R.	Department of Geography, University of Cambridge	Apr. 1970, July 1976, Dec. 1976, Apr. 1978, July 1979	administrative visits and accompanying President of Seychelles
Swingland, Dr I. R.	Department of Zoology, University of Oxford	Jan. 1975–Nov. 1976	tortoise population dynamics
Taylor, G. C. M.	Meteorological Office	Mar. 1976–Nov. 1977	meteorologist
Taylor, Dr J. D.	Department of Zoology, British Museum (Nat. Hist.)	June–Sep. 1969, Aug.–Oct. 1973	intertidal ecology
Topliffe, F. W.	Station staff	Oct. 1972–July 1975	station director/ administrative officer
Topliffe, Mrs Lorise C.	—	Oct. 1972–July 1975	data processing
Trudgill, Dr S. T.	Department of Geography, University of Bristol	June–Sep. 1969, Mar.–May 1971	limestone solution/ soils
Turner, G. C.	Meteorological Office	Nov. 1977–Nov. 1978	meteorologist
Vannini, Dr M.	Istituto di Zoologia, University of Florence, Italy	Jan.–Mar. 1979	orientation and migration of coenobites and *Nerita*
Walker, J.	Station staff	Dec. 1975–July 1977	station engineer
Walker, Mrs Marilyn	—	Dec. 1975–July 1977	
Waloff, Dr Nadia	Department of Zoology, Imperial College	Apr. 1977	coccid/plant relationships
Whitelaw, J. J.	Station staff	Jan. 1977–Mar. 1978	staff scientist: rats
Whitton, Dr B. A.	Department of Botany, University of Durham	Mar.–Apr. 1973, Dec. 1974–Jan. 1975	blue-green algae
Wickens, Dr G. E.	Royal Botanic Gardens, Kew	July–Sep. 1974	vegetation
Wilderspin, R. C.	Meteorological Office	Jan. 1975–Mar. 1976	meteorologist
Williams, Dr Carol A.	Department of Geodesy and Geophysics, University of Cambridge	June–Aug. 1970	gravity measurements
Wilson, J. R.	Station staff	Apr. 1973–Oct. 1974	junior staff scientist: waders
Wilson, Mrs Jane R.	—	Oct. 1973–Oct. 1974	
Wood, Dr D.	Station staff	Sep. 1971–June 1972	director: phenology
Wood, Mrs Jane	—	Sep. 1971–June 1972	
Woodell, Dr S. R. J.	Department of Botany, University of Oxford	Jan.–Mar. 1974	pollination and seed dispersal
Woodell, Mrs Rebecca	—	Jan.–Mar. 1974	coucals

Allowing for funding difficulties and logistic delays, research proceeded smoothly. In addition to the 14 man-years represented by the Expedition, a further 34 man-years were invested from 1970 to March 1977, giving a total to that date of nearly 50 man-years. A list of investigators during phases I–VI of the Expedition was given by Stoddart (1971 *a*, table 2), and this is brought up to date and extended to March 1980 in table 1. Aldabra is now among the best known oceanic islands and coral atolls on Earth. More than this, the work has confirmed the initial judgement of the Southern Zone Research Committee and the Aldabra Research Committee that Aldabra is a scientific resource of unique interest and importance. The core of its significance lies, of course, in the population of some 150 000 giant tortoises living in remarkably undisturbed conditions. But it has also become apparent that the interest resides not only in the study of individual components of the ecosystem but in the elucidation of the often complex linkages between them and of the relations between the biota and a variety of environmental factors varying on different spatial and temporal scales.

The time when the Royal Society will cease to have prime responsibility for operating the Research Station and conserving the atoll is now approaching. Under present plans it is hoped to hand over these functions to another body by March 1980. The independent Republic of Seychelles, which came into being in June 1976 and which has sovereignty over Aldabra, continues to show great interest in the project and an awareness of both the potentialities and the difficulties of maintaining the atoll as a resource for science. We hope that this meeting will not only demonstrate some of the new insights into the terrestrial ecology of Aldabra gained over the last decade, but will also help to provide a basis for sound conservation measures in the future.

A brief introduction to the major features of the topography and ecology of Aldabra has been given by Stoddart (1968b), and will not be repeated here. Location on the atoll itself, however, still remains something of a problem. A revised version of the place-name map published in 1971 is reproduced as a pullout at the end of this publication.† It represents a cooperative effort by Aldabrans, notably R. J. Hnatiuk, S. Hnatiuk, I. R. Swingland and R. Prŷs-Jones, largely coordinated by G. C. M. Taylor, and it should serve as a background to the papers that follow.

I cannot close this brief introduction without a word of acknowledgement. The Society's initial involvement in Aldabra and the decision to build the Research Station largely resulted from the interest of the late Lord Blackett, of Sir Ashley Miles, and of the late Sir David Martin. The subsequent management of Aldabra affairs – often seemingly a thankless task – has been guided by Professor T. S. Westoll as chairman of the Aldabra Research Committee, and by other senior Committee members, notably Dr F. C. Fraser, Professor D. Lewis and Professor W. H. Thorpe. The Station itself has been in the hands of a succession of Directors: the late Lt Commander Lush, Dr David Wood, Dr Roger Hnatiuk, Mr Fred Topliffe, Mr John Gallsworthy, and Mr Paul Niedzwiedzki. The whole operation has been serviced by the Royal Society's office staff, notably by Mr L. U. Mole, Mr D. J. H. Griffin and Mr G. E. Hemmen, all of whom have spent varying periods on the atoll. But above all, thanks are due to our long line of visitors and residents on Aldabra. Our Europeans and Americans have worked in lonely, difficult and occasionally hostile conditions to achieve the results we are about to discuss, and whatever they have done has been made possible by the strength, loyalty and good humour of Antonio Constance (Mazarin), Harry Charles, and Georges Larue and our other Seychellois Aldabrans. In spite of what has been done over the last 10 years, however, I think it will be felt at the end of this Discussion that even in so simple a system as that of Aldabra we have now only reached the stage where the truly interesting questions can be defined, and I hope it will be possible to look forward to several decades more of continuing research and conservation on this remarkable island.

REFERENCES (Stoddart)

Peake, J. F., Sinclair, A. & Lomas, S. 1978 Data recording. In *Coral reefs: research methods* (ed. D. R. Stoddart & R. F. Johannes), pp. 123–137. Paris: Unesco.

Stoddart, D. R. 1968a The Aldabra affair. *Biol. Conserv.* 1, 63–69.

Stoddart, D. R. 1968b The conservation of Aldabra. *Geogrl J.* 134, 471–485; discussion 485–486.

Stoddart, D. R. 1971a Scientific studies at Aldabra and neighbouring islands. *Phil. Trans. R. Soc. Lond.* B 260, 5–29.

Stoddart, D. R. 1971b Place names of Aldabra. *Phil. Trans. R. Soc. Lond.* B 260, 631–632.

Stoddart, D. R. & Yonge, C. M. (eds) 1971 Regional variation in Indian Ocean coral reefs. *Symp. zool. Soc. Lond.* 28, 1–584.

Westoll, T. S. & Stoddart, D. R. (eds) 1971 A discussion on the results of the Royal Society Expedition to Aldabra 1967–8. *Phil. Trans. R. Soc. Lond.* B 260, 1–654.

† Some contributors to this volume use names from the 1971 map.

Phil. Trans. R. Soc. Lond. B. **286**, 11–23 (1979)
Printed in Great Britain   [11]

Long-term climatic change in the western Indian Ocean

By D. R. Stoddart† and R. P. D. Walsh‡

† *Department of Geography, University of Cambridge, Downing Place, Cambridge, U.K.*
‡ *Department of Geography, University College, Swansea, U.K.*

Analysis of rainfall records for stations on Mahé (Seychelles), Mauritius, Minicoy and Amini Divi (Laccadives), and other western Indian Ocean stations, shows substantial fluctuations in mean annual rainfall over the past 100 years, with high rainfalls at the beginning of this century, at about 1930, and at the present day, with troughs during 1915–20 and 1940–50. Overlapping series of more recent records for Aldabra, Assumption and the Iles Glorieuses also suggest substantial variations, and the existence of these is supported by episodic historical records. The consequences of such changes for the land biota of Aldabra, especially for the giant tortoises, are discussed, and brief reference is made to other types of evidence for climatic change on the atoll.

Introduction

Detailed climatic records have only been maintained at Aldabra since late 1968, though some rainfall data are available for earlier years (Stoddart & Mole 1977). Figure 1 shows that the atoll is located in the driest sector of the western Indian Ocean. Since 1968 it has become apparent that the variability of climate and especially of rainfall from year to year has major significance for the flowering and fruiting of plants, and hence for the feeding and breeding of insects, birds and reptiles. In reconstructing the development of the terrestrial ecosystem, therefore, it is important to determine the range of historical fluctuations in climate, as well as the direction and scale of changes over recent geological time.

In this paper we first use historical records for a number of western Indian Ocean stations to establish a regional view of climatic periodicities over the last century; secondly, we discuss and extrapolate the instrumental record on Aldabra itself; and thirdly, we suggest some biological consequences of the variations to which we draw attention, on a time-scale extending into the late Pleistocene.

Climatic changes at western Indian Ocean islands
Annual Rainfall

Figures 2 and 3 show 10 and 20 year running means of annual rainfall over the past 80–100 years for six island locations in the western Indian Ocean. Three (Amini Divi, Minicoy, Pamban) are situated in the northern Indian Ocean between 8 and 12° N; Mahé is an equatorial station at 4° S; and Tananarive (Madagascar) and the Royal Alfred Observatory (Mauritius) are southern Indian Ocean stations between 18 and 21° S.

All the stations display considerable fluctuations over the period of record, and these are summarized (together with Zanzibar) in terms of 'rainfall epochs' in table 1. The epochs are based on the Seychelles record as identified from the annual deviations from the 1901–30 normals, although the magnitude and timing of epochs on different islands vary considerably.

In the northern Indian Ocean, Minicoy and Amini Divi were characterized by low rainfalls before 1905, higher rainfalls from 1905 to 1937, lower rainfalls from 1938 to 1958, and markedly higher rainfalls since 1959. The trends at Pamban are less clear, with high rainfalls before 1905 and from 1923 to 1937, and lower rainfalls from 1905 to 1922 and since 1938. Pamban does not show a recent increase. At Mahé, Seychelles, in the equatorial Indian Ocean, the changes in annual rainfall are dramatic in terms of scale, periodicity and consistency. High rainfalls

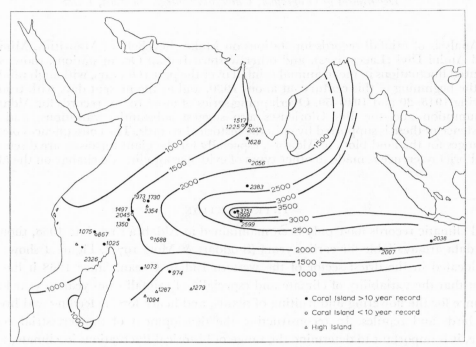

FIGURE 1. Distribution of mean annual rainfall (millimetres) over the Indian Ocean from coral island data.

occurred before 1905, from 1923 to 1937, and since 1959; markedly lower rainfalls characterized the intervening 1905–22 and 1938–58 epochs: Aspin (1976) has already drawn attention to the scale of these variations since 1941. The changes are of the order of 500 mm, or 20% between each period, and all are statistically significant at the 99% confidence level. Similar fluctuations are indicated by the unfortunately shorter and broken record at Zanzibar (interrupted by a change of site), although here the peaks and troughs appear to occur a few years later than in Seychelles. Long series of rainfall data are not available for other equatorial stations, but records are available for five stations since 1931. Table 2 summarizes the results and shows that marked increases in rainfall have occurred along the equatorial east coast of Africa, at the northern tip of Madagascar, and in the Comores. In the cases of Garissa and Diego Suarez the increases were exceptionally high (35–36%) and even greater than those at Mahé.

In the southern Indian Ocean, the long Mauritius record at the Royal Alfred Observatory (which after its record ceased in 1959 was extended by cross-correlation with that at the nearby Pamplemousses S.I.R.I. station) displays interesting trends, recently confirmed by Morales (1977) for the nearby Pamplemousses Garden station. The underlying trend from 1875 until the 1930s is markedly positive. Very low rainfalls occurred in the early part of the record and recurred in the late 1930s and 1940s, with a series of drought years from 1947 to 1951. Rainfall

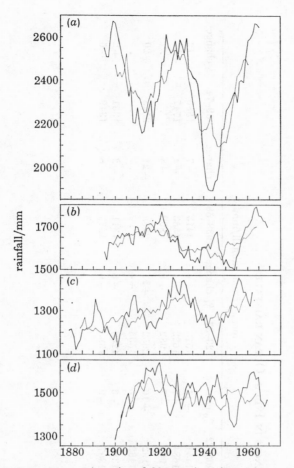

FIGURE 2. Annual rainfalls: 10 year (———) and 20 year (———) running means for (*a*) Mahé, (*b*) Minicoy, (*c*) Mauritius and (*d*) Amini Divi.

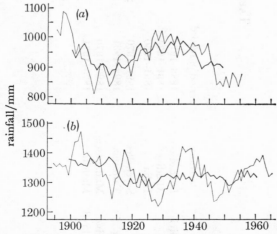

FIGURE 3. Annual rainfalls: 10 year (———) and 20 year (———) running means for (*a*) Pamban and (*b*) Tananarive.

TABLE 1. CHANGES IN INDIAN OCEAN RAINFALL

station	territory	period of record	mean annual rainfall/mm									
			–1904	1905–22	% change	1923–37	% change	1938–58	% change	1959–74	% change
Amini Divi	Laccadives	1889–1974	1310	1454	+11	1513	+4	1413	–7	1580	+12
Minicoy	Maldives	1891–1974	1593	1684	+6	1622	–4	1553	–4	1747	+12
Pamban	India	1891–1960	975	908	–7	982	+8	899	–8	.	.
Mahé	Seychelles	1891–1970	2600	2192	–16	2652	+21	2105	–21	2528	+20
Zanzibar	Tanzania	1892–1931	1560	1482	–5	1535	+4	.	.	.	.
Tananarive	Madagascar	1890–1970	1342	1385	+3	1280	–8	1311	+2	1331	+2
Royal Alfred	Mauritius	1875–1971	1202	1307	+9	1383	+6	1273	–8	1349	+6

has again been higher since 1952. Brooks (1919), using earlier records from 1853 to 1879, showed that the early marked upward trend in Mauritius rainfall dated back to at least 1853. He calculated the average increase in annual rainfall over the period 1853–79 to be 14.7 mm a^{-1}, or approximately 400 mm over the 27 year period. The Tananarive record, which dates from 1890, shows no really marked changes, although the 10 year running means show the existence of relatively minor rainfall peaks around 1903, 1918, 1938 and 1960, with intervening troughs. There has been a recent increase in rainfall, though this is much less marked than in the equatorial areas.

TABLE 2. RECENT RAINFALL CHANGES IN THE EQUATORIAL INDIAN OCEAN REGION

station	territory	lat. S and long. E	rainfall/mm 1931–60	1961–73	% change
Garissa	Kenya	0° 25′ 39° 40′	280	378	+35
Dar-es-Salaam	Tanzania	6° 29′ 39° 18′	1043	1168	+12
Diego Suarez	Madagascar	12° 17′ 49° 18′	915	1248	+36
Grande Comore	Comoro Is	11° 42′ 43° 14′	2639	2714	+3
Mayotte	Comoro Is	12° 49′ 45° 17′	1170	1283	+10

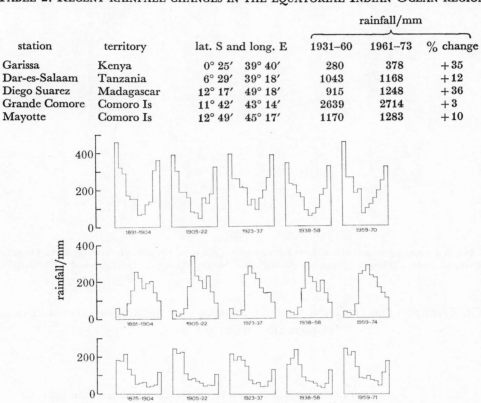

FIGURE 4. Changes in rainfall régimes at (a) Minicoy, (b) Mahé, and (c) Mauritius.

Seasonality and occurrence of dry periods

Changes in rainfall régime at Minicoy, Mahé and Mauritius are shown in figure 4; 10 year running means of the mean number of dry months (less than 4 in or 102 mm) per annum and 20 year frequencies of dry periods of different durations for the same three stations are shown in figure 5 and table 3.

At Minicoy, the most marked feature is the absence of the normal secondary maximum of rainfall in October during the recent 1959–74 period, when the markedly increased annual rainfall has been concentrated into the summer period. Thus, interestingly, lengths of drought were longer in the wetter than the drier epochs, although the mean number of dry months did not change significantly during the period of record. At Mahé, most of the increase in rainfall in the wetter epochs occurred in the summer months. Markedly longer droughts characterized

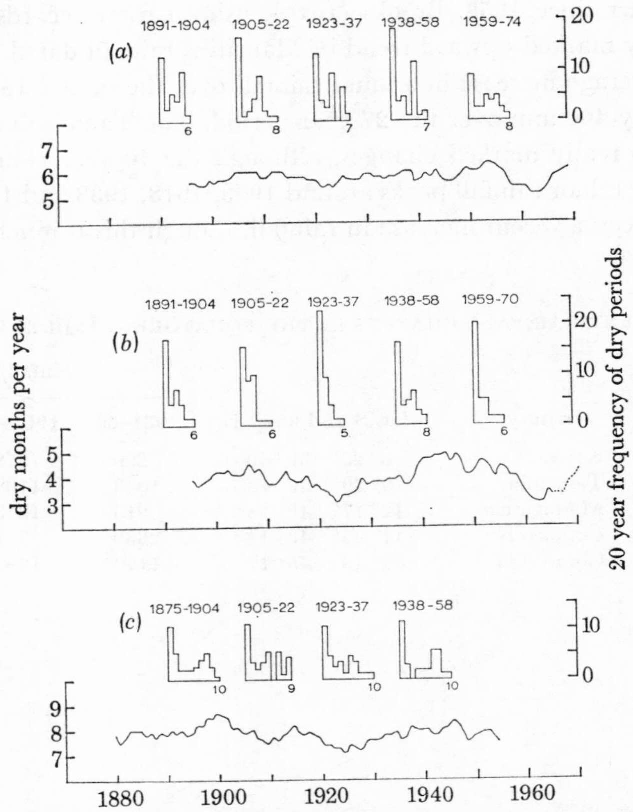

FIGURE 5. Ten year running means of number of dry months (102 mm) per annum (curves) and 20 year frequencies of dry periods of different durations (histograms) for (*a*) Minicoy, (*b*) Mahé and (*c*) Mauritius.

TABLE 3. TWENTY YEAR FREQUENCIES OF LENGTHS OF DRY PERIODS OF DIFFERENT DURATIONS IN DIFFERENT RAINFALL EPOCHS

		length of dry period (successive months each with less than 102 mm)										mean number of dry months
station	period	1	2	3	4	5	6	7	8	9	10	per year
Minicoy, Laccadives	1891–1904	12.9	2.8	5.7	4.3	10.0	1.4	—	—	—	—	5.71
	1905–1922	16.7	1.1	2.2	4.4	8.9	2.2	1.1	1.1	—	—	5.83
	1923–1937	13.3	4.0	2.7	9.3	0.0	6.7	1.3	—	—	—	5.14
	1938–1958	18.1	3.8	4.8	1.0	11.4	1.0	1.9	—	—	—	6.00
	1959–1974	8.8	2.5	2.5	5.0	3.8	5.0	2.5	1.3	—	—	5.50
Mahé, Seychelles	1891–1904	17.2	4.3	7.2	4.3	1.4	1.4	—	—	—	—	4.00
	1905–1922	15.5	8.9	10.0	1.1	1.1	1.1	—	—	—	—	4.00
	1923–1937	22.6	9.3	4.0	1.3	1.3	1.9	—	—	—	—	3.26
	1938–1958	16.2	3.8	4.8	6.7	2.9	1.9	—	—	—	—	4.57
	1959–1971	20.0	5.0	5.0	1.7	1.7	1.7	—	—	—	—	3.50
Royal Alfred, Mauritius	1875–1904	10.7	5.4	2.0	2.0	2.0	2.7	4.0	5.4	2.7	0.7	8.10
	1905–1922	11.1	3.3	2.2	3.3	5.5	0.0	5.5	1.1	4.4	—	7.50
	1923–1937	10.6	4.7	2.4	3.5	1.2	4.7	3.5	1.2	1.2	1.2	7.47
	1938–1958	11.4	2.9	0.0	1.9	1.9	1.9	5.7	5.7	1.2	1.2	7.87
	1959–1974					no comparable data						—

the very dry 1938–58 epoch. The mean number of dry months per year ranged from 4.00 in the two early epochs, down to 3.27 in the wet 1922–37 period, to as high as 4.52 in the dry 1938–58 period, declining to 3.50 since 1959. At the Royal Alfred Observatory, the two wet epochs are characterized by longer wet seasons. In the wet 1922–37 epoch, rainfall was markedly higher in April and May (at the end of the wet season); in the recent 1959–71 wet period, most of the increase in rainfall was accounted for during the early part of the wet season in November and December. Significantly longer droughts occurred in the dry 1875–1904 and 1938–58 periods than in the wetter 1923–37 epoch.

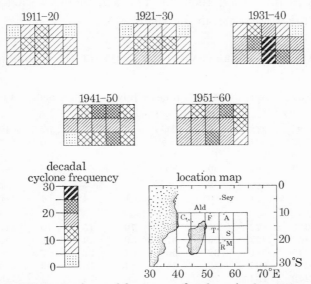

FIGURE 6. Changes in the spatial distribution and frequency of cyclones in the southwest Indian Ocean 1911–60.

Tropical cyclones

Milton (1974) examined changes in cyclone frequency for the main hurricane belts of the world, including those of the Indian Ocean. In both the Bay of Bengal and the southwestern Indian Ocean, there have been marked fluctuations since 1890. In the Bay of Bengal, peaks occurred around 1900 and from 1920 to 1950, with troughs from 1900 to 1910 and since 1950. In the southwestern Indian Ocean, similar peaks and troughs are evident, although they occur about 10 years later than in the Bay of Bengal.

By using charts of cyclone tracks compiled by Chaussard & Laplace (1964), changes in the spatial distribution of cyclones in the southwest Indian Ocean between 10 and 25° S were plotted for 5° squares of latitude and longitude during each decade from 1911 to 1960 (figure 6). There are marked spatial changes in cyclone frequency. The general increase in frequency in the 1930s was concentrated in the central Madagascar, Tromelin, and Mauritius–Réunion squares and the area off the southeastern coast of Madagascar. In the decade 1941–50, the main area of cyclone activity shifted north into the Farquhar and Agalega squares, although frequencies remained high in the Mauritius–Réunion area. The 1951–60 period was characterized by a marked increase in cyclone frequency over southern Madagascar and in the adjacent ocean areas off the southern eastern and western coasts of the island. Clearly local spatial shifts in cyclone tracks are as important as regional changes in cyclone frequency in this sector of the Indian Ocean.

18 D. R. STODDART AND R. P. D. WALSH

Mechanisms of change

The changes in rainfall here identified can be related to known variations in atmospheric circulation and associated changes in ocean currents and sea surface temperatures. These variations have been of different character in different sectors of the Indian Ocean.

The sustained increase in Mauritius rainfall from 1853 until the 1930s can be directly correlated with a marked southward shift in the location of the intertropical trough at the height of the southern summer in January (Lamb & Johnson 1959), from a mean position of $5\frac{1}{2}°$ S in 1850–89 to $10\frac{1}{2}°$ S in the period 1900–39. This shift may also account for the increased cyclone frequency in the Mascarenes in the 1930s.

TABLE 4. ALDABRA: MONTHLY RAINFALL (in millimetres)

	Jan.	Feb.	Mar.	Apr.	May	June	July	Aug.	Sep.	Oct.	Nov.	Dec.	total for year
1949	—	—	—	—	—	2	26	0	0	0	13	57	—
1950	95	219	423	272	6	24	0	16	37	10	23	67	**1192**
1951	92	60	—	221	46	—	13	32	0	7	70	—	—
1952	160	306	29	250	13	18	4	0	—	—	—	—	—
1953	—	—	54	67	30	38	—	—	—	—	—	—	—
1958	92	101	40	36	2	2	9	8	4	2	45	40	**381**
1959	102	199	6	1	0	1	1	4	4	0	19	12	**349**
1967	—	—	—	—	—	—	—	—	—	3	147	5	—
1968	12	28	133	72	21	38	70	15	10	117	57	85	**547**
1969	153	147	152	394	176	37	39	14	19	12	55	57	**1254**
1970	48	85	140	211	32	30	34	26	7	21	13	56	**700**
1971	245	57	286	193	35	66	14	19	9	6	90	202	**1220**
1972	225	15	112	162	28	100	55	75	4	13	26	240	**1055**
1973	261	287	263	57	57	48	81	25	22	34	9	78	**1221**
1974	291	115	381	346	50	29	52	32	2	1	19	149	**1467**
1975	131	163	111	167	77	41	16	15	15	3	92	136	**966**
1976	358	177	261	87	67	64	65	35	5	0	17	104	**1241**
n	14	14	14	15	15	15	15	15	14	15	15	14	**12**
mean	162	140	171	169	43	36	32	21	9	8	46	92	**966**

The recent marked increase in rainfall and the disappearance of the double maximum at Minicoy and Amini Divi may result from the failure of the northern hemisphere intertropical trough to advance as far north over the Indian subcontinent as formerly. A second factor, noted by Sana (1974), may be a decrease in strength of the southwest monsoon winds, with a parallel decrease in the strength of monsoon-driven currents. When the monsoon is strong (as during 1930–59), cool upwelling water from the Somali coast arrives in the Laccadives in midsummer, and the consequent reduced sea surface temperatures lead to a decline in evaporation and rainfall until the current weakens in the autumn. Since 1960 the current has often not been as strong as formerly: sea surface temperature and midsummer rainfall have increased, giving a single rather than a double rainfall peak. A third possible factor is the decline in cyclone frequency in recent years, giving a reduction in autumn rainfall and also accounting for the occurrence of longer dry periods in recent years.

Changes in rainfall over the equatorial Indian Ocean are complex and cannot yet be fully explained. There has, however, been a shift towards the equator of the subtropical high pressure belts in recent years, with the restriction of the intertropical troughs to narrower zones on either side of the equator (Lamb 1966, 1974). This has resulted in increased rainfall in the equatorial belt and markedly decreased rainfall over most of the rest of the tropics. The earlier peaks in rainfall noted in the Seychelles before 1905 and from 1923 to 1937 are more difficult to explain. The southward shift in the January position of the southern intertropical trough to a position of 10° S by the 1930s may account in part for the decline in rainfall after 1905, but the 1923–37 peak remains unexplained.

An important factor in explaining rainfall trends in the western Indian Ocean is that of sea surface temperatures, ocean currents, and upwelling and advection of cool water off the East African coast south of the equator at the height of the northwest monsoon in January and February. In 1963–4 the International Indian Ocean Expedition noted two areas of very warm water (27–29 °C) separated by a tongue of cold water (17–20 °C) off the East African coast (Lamb 1966). Changes in the strength of the northwest monsoon and in the location of cold and warm water areas will have marked consequences on rainfall. Changes in cyclone frequency in the Bay of Bengal can be directly related to changes in sea surface temperatures (Frost 1966). It is generally accepted that sea surface temperatures of at least 26–28 °C are necessary for cyclone development, and shifts of the magnitude of those identified in the western Indian Ocean could be of critical importance in controlling cyclone frequency. The lower temperatures of 1900–29 and 1960–4 account for the lower frequency of cyclones in those years, and the higher temperatures of 1930–59 explain the higher cyclone frequency of that period. Comparable changes have been identified in the Caribbean area, where more data are available (Walsh 1977).

CLIMATIC CHANGE AT ALDABRA

The rainfall records for Aldabra (table 4 and figure 7) and for adjacent islands are short and discontinuous. Good records date only from 1968. All that can be said about rainfall trends at Aldabra is that compared with the 12 year mean, 1950 was reasonably wet, 1951–3 relatively dry, 1958 and 1959 extremely dry, 1968 dry, and the years 1969–76 rather wet. However, analysis of such limited data is clearly inconclusive as regards longer term trends.

Extrapolation of trends, based on cross-correlation of existing Aldabra data (1950, 1958–9, 1968–76) with the corresponding annual data of other Indian Ocean stations with much longer records, was attempted, with mixed results (table 5). Reasonable positive correlations were obtained between Aldabra rainfall and that of Amini Divi and Minicoy in the Laccadives, and a strong negative correlation (−0.80) emerged between Aldabra and Mauritius rainfall. This was expected: Aldabra (10° S), like the Laccadives (10° N), is relatively equatorial and hence has higher rainfall when the intertropical troughs are more confined to equatorial latitudes; high rainfalls in Mauritius (20° S), on the other hand, occur when the intertropical trough migrates further from the equator. Extrapolating from these relations, one would expect that the present rainfall on Aldabra is considerably higher than that of the period 1930–60. One would also expect Aldabra to have been markedly wetter in the mid-nineteenth century, when Mauritius rainfall was low and the intertropical trough in January was located near 5½° S.

On the other hand, correlations were very low between the rainfall at Aldabra and at other much closer Indian Ocean stations. Thus the correlation with Seychelles was −0.13, with Diego Suarez −0.14, and with the Iles Glorieuses (the closest meteorological station to Aldabra) only +0.01. These may be explained in terms of the very localized nature of rainfall and rainfall-producing mechanisms both in the tropics in general and the western Indian Ocean in particular.

2-2

These include: (1) the precise position of the intertropical troughs during any one summer; (2) the relation between the exact longitudinal positions of the recently discovered cross-equatorial low-level jets (Findlater 1969) and rainfall patterns in the area in any one summer; and (3) the spatial distribution and extent of cold and warm bodies of water off the East African coast, particularly in the southern hemisphere summer. Also, it should be stressed that the lack

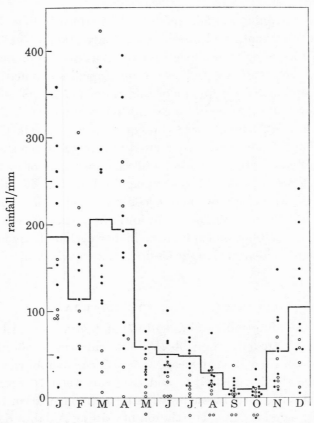

FIGURE 7. Monthly rainfalls at Aldabra (open circles 1949–59; closed circles 1967–76).

TABLE 5. ALDABRA RAINFALL: CORRELATIONS WITH THE ANNUAL RAINFALL OF OTHER
INDIAN OCEAN STATIONS

location	territory	lat. and long.	no. of years overlap	correlation coefficient	rainfall since 1961 as % of 1913–60 mean
Amini Divi	Laccadives	11° 07′ N 72° 44′ E	10	+0.33	+7
Pamban I.	India	9° 16′ N 79° 35′ E	8	+0.53	+1
Minicoy	Laccadives	8° 18′ N 73° 00′ E	10	+0.30	+9
Garissa	Kenya	0° 25′ S 39° 40′ E	6	−0.63	+35
Mahé	Seychelles	4° 37′ S 55° 27′ E	6	−0.13	+20
Dar-es-Salaam	Tanzania	6° 29′ S 39° 18′ E	7	−0.24	+12
Aldabra		9° 22′ S 46° 28′ E	*	*	*
Agalega		10° 30′ S 56° 00′ E	6	−0.70	ND
Isles Glorieuses		11° 30′ S 47° 20′ E	8	+0.01	ND
Grande Comore	Comoro Is	11° 42′ S 43° 14′ E	6	+0.48	+3
Diego Suarez	Madagascar	12° 17′ S 49° 18′ E	8	−0.14	+36
Mayotte	Comoro Is	12° 49′ S 45° 17′ E	8	+0.67	+10
Tananarive	Madagascar	18° 54′ S 47° 32′ E	6	−0.13	+5
Royal Alfred	Mauritius	20° 06′ S 57° 33′ E	7	−0.80	+3

of correlation between *annual* data at two locations does not preclude the existence of *longer-term* correlations between rainfall trends at the two stations.

An alternative, simpler, and perhaps more conclusive way of estimating recent changes in rainfall at Aldabra is to examine general spatial patterns of change in the Indian Ocean. It is almost certain that the rainfall of Aldabra since 1960 has been considerably above that of the 1931–60 normal, since all stations in the region recorded an increase in this period (table 5),

TABLE 6. ALDABRA RAINFALL (millimetres) 1949–59 AND 1967–76

period	Jan.	Feb.	Mar.	Apr.	May	June	July	Aug.	Sep.	Oct.	Nov.	Dec.	year
1949–59	108	177	110	141	16	14	9	10	9	4	34	44	676†
n_1	5	5	5	6	6	6	6	6	5	5	5	4	—
1967–76	192	119	204	188	60	50	47	28	10	10	53	111	1075†
n_2	9	9	9	9	9	9	9	9	9	10	10	10	9
change	+84	−58	+96	+47	+44	+36	+38	+18	+1	+6	+19	+67	+399

† Annual mean calculated from sum of monthly means.

and the locations nearer to Aldabra markedly so. This inference is supported by the limited Aldabra data available (table 6). Broad comparisons with long-term trends in the Seychelles and Zanzibar suggest wet phases around the turn of the century, from 1922 to 1937, and since 1960, and markedly drier phases in the intervening periods. Both the Aldabra record and shorter-period records form a larger number of stations in the equatorial Indian Ocean appear to confirm the last two of these phases, namely the dry phase of the 1930s, 1940s and 1950s and the considerable increase in rainfall since 1960. Lastly, and more tentatively, much higher rainfalls in Aldabra around the middle of the nineteenth century are indicated by correlation with the Mauritius records and the documented evidence of the intertropical trough lying much closer to the equator at that time.

There is only fragmentary direct evidence for such changes at Aldabra and nearby islands before the first modern records in 1949. In 1878, goats were reported to have died on Cosmoledo because of lack of rainfall (Rivers 1878). Spurs (1891, p. 48) reported a fall of 6 in (152 mm) of rain in 24 h at Aldabra during a cyclone (the most recent daily maximum is 166 mm on 7 April 1969), but Abbott (1893, p. 760) commented that in spite of this 'sometimes many months elapse during which not a drop of rain falls'. Abbott himself (1893, p. 761) recorded monthly totals of 0 in October, 0 in November, and 15 in (381 mm) in December 1892. Voeltzkow (1897, p. 75) cites the same figures but gives the year as 1895, the time of his own visit. Baty (1895) stated that no rain fell at Astove and Cosmoledo from June to November 1895, or at Aldabra for two months before 17 November 1895. Dupont (1907) gives monthly figures for October 1906 to January 1907. The total fall in this period was 866 mm, which compares with the recent October–January mean of 352 mm, but 73 % of the total came in the month of January, with 636 mm (recent January maximum 358 mm), presumably from a hurricane. These scattered figures are at least consistent with the inferences given above. It might also be noted that in the late 1930s, D. Vesey-FitzGerald (1942), a very experienced ecologist, estimated the annual rainfall of Aldabra as only 15 in (less than 400 mm).

SOME IMPLICATIONS

If, as seems likely, mean annual rainfall has fluctuated at Aldabra between *ca.* 500 and *ca.* 1500 mm over a period of decades, the consequences for geomorphology and especially land biota will have been considerable. Thus there is evidence in the surface features, especially in the platin, that freshwater pools have been much more extensive in the past than at present (Stoddart *et al.* 1971, p. 60). Abbott (1893, pp. 760 and 763) suggested that large dead trees with trunks up to 2 ft (60 cm) in diameter on Picard indicated former wetter conditions, and Grubb (1971, p. 355) considered that climatic change might have been responsible for the extensive death of *Guettarda* trees along the south coast. There is scope for analysis of growth conformations and tree rings in some of the larger trees and shrubs on Aldabra, to see if any periodicities are revealed. Cogan *et al.* (1971, p. 322) comment also on the effect of dry years on the insect fauna. But the most obvious effect may well have been on the tortoises. Bourn (1977) has shown a direct relation between breeding behaviour and rainfall, and elsewhere in this volume Stoddart & Peake (1979) summarize historical evidence of fluctuations in the tortoise population.

On a longer time scale, linkages become more speculative. Braithwaite *et al.* (1973, p. 330) suggested a higher rainfall than at present during the last glacial maximum, forming submarine solution grooves and buttresses along the north coast (and perhaps also the 6 m deep karren on Ile Esprit). Arnold (1976, p. 113), on the other hand, proposed that extended drought in the late Quaternary may have led to lizard extinctions through a reduction in habitat diversity. Simulations of late Pleistocene climate, however, suggest no marked divergence either in wetness or dryness in this sector of the Indian Ocean (CLIMAP 1976; Manabe & Hahn 1977), and certainly the effect of sea level change alone, through water table fluctuation, would probably have outweighed purely climatic effects on the local biota.

Nevertheless, speculative as these comments are in the longer term, our analysis has suggested that any interpretation of the present terrestrial ecosystem on Aldabra must take account of considerable climatic fluctuations over the lifespan of the dominant organisms now inhabiting the atoll.

REFERENCES (Stoddart & Walsh)

Abbott, W. L. 1893 Notes on the natural history of Aldabra, Assumption and Glorioso Islands, Indian Ocean. *Proc. U.S. natn. Mus.* **16**, 759–764.

Arnold, E. N. 1976 Fossil reptiles from Aldabra Atoll, Indian Ocean. *Bull. Br. Mus. nat. Hist. (Zool.)* **29**, 85–116.

Aspin, D. 1976 Rainfall in the Seychelles 1941 to 1970. *Weather* **31**, 47–56.

Baty, S. C. E. 1895 *A report on the Aldabra and Cosmoledo groups of islands.* Mahé: Government Printer.

Bourn, D. 1977 Reproductive study of giant tortoises on Aldabra. *J. Zool., Lond.* **182**, 27–28.

Braithwaite, C. J. R., Taylor, J. D. & Kennedy, W. J. 1973 The evolution of an atoll: the depositional and erosional history of Aldabra. *Phil. Trans. R. Soc. Lond.* B **266**, 307–340.

Brooks, C. E. P. 1919 The secular variation of rainfall. *Q. Jl R. met. Soc.* **45**, 233–248.

Chaussard, A. & Laplace, L. 1964 Les cyclones du sud-ouest de l'Océan Indien. *Mém. Met. Nat.* (Paris), no. 49.

CLIMAP Project Members 1976 The surface of the Ice-Age earth. *Science, N.Y.* **191**, 1131–1137.

Cogan, B. H., Hutson, A. M. & Shaffer, J. C. 1971 Preliminary observations on the affinities and composition of the insect fauna of Aldabra. *Phil. Trans. R. Soc. Lond.* B **260**, 315–325.

Dupont, R. P. 1907 *Report on a visit of investigation to St Pierre, Astove, Cosmoledo, Assumption and the Aldabra Group.* (51 pages.) Mahé: Government Printer.

Findlater, J. 1969 A major low-level air current near the Indian Ocean during the northern summer. *Q. Jl R. met. Soc.* **95**, 362–380.

Frost, R. 1966 Major storms in West Pakistan in September in relation to the Mangla Dam project. *Met. Mag.* **95**, 57–63.

Grubb, P. 1971 The growth, ecology and population structure of giant tortoises on Aldabra. *Phil. Trans. R. Soc. Lond.* B **260**, 327–372.

Lamb, H. H. 1966 Climate in the 1960s: changes in the world's wind circulation reflected in prevailing temperatures, rainfall patterns and the levels of the African lakes. *Geogrl J.* **132**, 183–212.

Lamb, H. H. 1974 *The current trend of world climate – a report on the early 1970s and a perspective*. University of East Anglia Climatic Research Unit, Research Publication 3.

Lamb, H. H. & Johnson, A. I. 1959 Climatic variation and observed changes in the general circulation. *Geogr. Annlr* **41**, 94–134.

Manabe, S. & Hahn, D. G. 1977 Simulation of the tropical climate of an Ice Age. *J. geophys. Res.* **82**, 3889–3911.

Milton, D. 1974 Some observations of global trends in tropical cyclone frequencies. *Weather* **29**, 267–270.

Morales, C. 1977 Rainfall variability – a natural phenomenon. *Ambio* **6**, 30–33.

Rivers, F. 1878 Letter to Chief Civil Commissioner, Seychelles, 11 December 1878, on a visit to Aldabra. Seychelles National Archives, Letter book (outward), 1878–1880, B 37.

Sana, K. 1974 Some aspects of the Arabian Sea summer monsoon. *Tellus* **26**, 464–476.

Spurs, J. 1891 Report on Aldabra to T. Risely Griffiths, Esq., Administrator of Seychelles Islands, Port Victoria, Seychelles, July 19, 1891. *Colonial reports – annual, no. 40: annual reports for 1899 and 1890: Mauritius*. (50 pages.) London: H.M.S.O.

Stoddart, D. R. 1971 Rainfall on Indian Ocean coral islands. *Atoll Res. Bull.* **147**, 1–21.

Stoddart, D. R. & Mole, L. U. 1977 Climate of Aldabra Atoll. *Atoll Res. Bull.* **202**, 1–21.

Stoddart, D. R. & Peake, J. F. 1979 *Phil. Trans. R. Soc. Lond.* B **286**, 147–161 (this volume).

Stoddart, D. R., Taylor, J. D., Fosberg, F. R. & Farrow, G. E. 1971 Geomorphology of Aldabra Atoll. *Phil. Trans. R. Soc. Lond.* B **260**, 31–66.

Vesey-FitzGerald, L. D. E. F. 1942 Further studies of the vegetation on islands in the Indian Ocean. *J. Ecol.* **30**, 1–16.

Voeltzkow, A. 1897 Einleitung: Madagaskar, Juan de Nova, Aldabra. *Abh. Senckenb. naturf. Ges.* **21**, 1–76.

Walsh, R. P. D. 1977 Changes in the tracks and frequency of tropical cyclones in the Lesser Antilles from 1650 to 1975 and some geomorphological and ecological implications. *Swansea Geogr.* **15**, 4–11.

Phil. Trans. R. Soc. Lond. B. **286**, 25–34 (1979)   [25]
Printed in Great Britain

Temporal and spatial variations in precipitation on Aldabra

By R. J. Hnatiuk†

The Royal Society Aldabra Research Station, Seychelles

Analysis of hourly rainfall data from Aldabra has indicated that the atoll influences its own weather as recorded at the Research Station on Ile Picard. The strength of this local influence varies with the season and may be related to the relative temperature difference between lagoon surface water and the atmosphere above it. The direction and strength of the prevailing wind may also be of some importance. The rôle of the semi-diurnal atmospheric pressure waves is not clearly evident at all times but is most prominent during the early hours of both wet and dry seasons. Its effect may also be present in the slight increase in rain frequency during the late afternoon of the trade wind seasons.

The trans-atoll variations in rainfall amounts confirm the earlier reports of non-synchronous rainfalls. There is some indication of seasonal variation of rainfall at different points around the atoll relative to that received at the Research Station. The northwest and southwest parts of the atoll may receive more rain than the northeast or west central parts.

The study of precipitation on small oceanic islands has attracted attention for some time. Wiens (1962) collated reports from Pacific islands which suggested that atolls were too low to produce orographic rain and too small to affect the time of rainfall, but that maximum falls occurred at the time of maximum atmospheric instability: early morning and afternoon. A contrary opinion was expressed by Riehl (1954) who stated that even small islands affected their local weather. The controversy continued when Lavoie (1963) studied nearly 9 years of precipitation records from the atoll of Eniwetok and concluded that that atoll exerted no detectable influence on the meteorological records obtained there. Kiser, Carpenter & Brier (1963) and Brier & Simpson (1969) extended the studies of island precipitation in another direction by looking for causes for the observed diurnal patterns in rainfall recorded from island stations.

The systematic recording of meteorological phenomena from Aldabra began relatively recently and the synopsis of the first year of detailed records is to be found in Farrow (1971), with subsequent longer term summaries by Stoddart & Mole (1977). The regional setting of precipitation patterns for Aldabra was established by Stoddart (1971) and modified by Stoddart & Mole (1977).

This paper analyses nearly 7 years of hourly rainfall records from Aldabra with the view to describing small scale patterns and to seeing whether they relate to features of Aldabra. It also examines rainfall records from several points around the atoll to see if any pattern is evident in the spatial distribution of rainfall.

Diurnal variations
Data and Methods

The data for diurnal rainfall came from 6 years and 11 months of strip chart records (January 1968 to December 1974, excluding March 1968 for which there were no records) made on a

† Present address: The Western Australian Herbarium, Department of Agriculture, George Street, South Perth, Australia, 6151.

British Meteorological Office Dines Tilting Siphon recording rain gauge. The gauge was situated on Ile Picard on the west coast of the atoll. At first it was at Settlement at a site moderately protected by tall *Casuarina* and *Cocos* trees (Farrow 1971) but in 1970 it was moved to a less sheltered site at the new Research Station about 1 km south of Settlement (Stoddart & Mole 1977).

Initial processing of the data was done at the Department of Nuclear Physics, Oxford University, by using a special, computer-assisted, semi-automatic system for digitizing rainfall charts of the British Meteorological Office. The resulting monthly summaries consisted of hourly totals of rainfall for each day, the monthly totals for each hour, and the total for the whole month. The few records which proved difficult to analyse by computer were visually checked and either manually analysed or rejected if unanalysable. In total, 2490 records out of a possible 2557 (i.e. 97.4%) were available and acceptable for analysis.

The data were analysed for monthly amounts and frequency of rainfall without regard to hour of occurrence (figure 1), and then for hourly amounts and frequency without regard for month (figures 2 and 3, respectively). Because of the pronounced seasonality in precipitation on Aldabra, the data were separately analysed for trade wind (May–October) and monsoon (November–April) seasons (figures 2 and 3), using the season definition of Farrow (1971) to allow direct comparisons with his results.

Two further reductions of the data, which each simultaneously took account of hourly and monthly variations, resulted in the summary of diurnal patterns of rainfall amount (figure 4) and rainfall frequency (figure 5). The isopleths in these latter two figures mark the periods where values were 25% greater or less than the individual monthly means. The centring of the diagrams on December and January followed the practice of Troll (1958) for stations south of the equator.

All analyses were based upon rainfall events defined here as either the amount or the occurrence of rain not less than 0.1 mm during a 1 hour block of time. Thus if two distinct showers occurred within one hour block, they were recorded as a single occurrence and their sum was the amount for that hour. Furthermore, if one shower spanned the division between two consecutive hour blocks then an occurrence was recorded for each hour and the amount falling within each hour contributed to the amount for that hour. The numerically overriding influence of seasonal variation was removed by expressing variation in each hourly mean from its respective monthly mean. All times are expressed as local time which equals G.M.T. plus 3 h.

Results

Variations in monthly rainfall (figure 1) indicated the strong seasonality in precipitation with both frequency and amount reaching a peak during the 'wet season' from about December to April inclusive. These results were consistent with those of Farrow (1971) and Stoddart & Mole (1977).

Diurnal variations in rainfall amount (figure 2), without regard for season, showed a strong tendency for most rain to fall between 10h 00 and about 15h 00 with a relatively minor peak between 23h 00 and midnight. Periods of relatively little rainfall occurred between 07h 00 and 09h 00 and again from 21h 00 to 23h 00. There was a general decrease in rainfall amount from 15h 00 until 23h 00 and also from 05h 00 to 08h 00.

The diurnal variation in frequency of rainfall without regard to season (figure 3) resembled that shown by amount of rainfall, but with a less marked pattern as none of the extremes exceeded 25% of the mean. The period of greatest frequency was between 14h 00 and 15h 00 which was slightly later than the peak in rainfall amount. A weak, broad, secondary maximum occurred in the hours before dawn. Frequency of rainfall was least between 08h 00 and 09h 00, and 20h 00 and 23h 00, somewhat similar to the periods of lowest rainfall amounts.

An indication of the influence of season upon the diurnal pattern of rainfall was included in figures 2 and 3. The monsoon season was defined as the months of November to April while

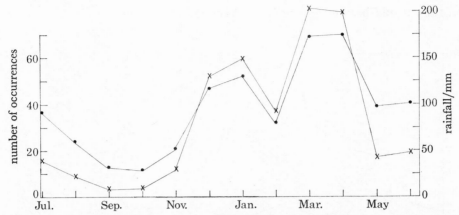

FIGURE 1. Mean monthly amount (×), and frequency (•) of rainfall at the Picard, 1968–74.

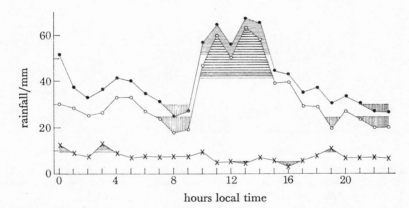

FIGURE 2. Hourly mean amounts of rainfall at the Picard, 1968–74: •, total; o, monsoon season November to April; ×, trade wind season May to October. Horizontal shading represents more than 25% of the mean; vertical shading less than 25%.

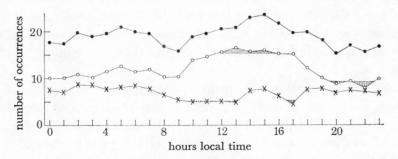

FIGURE 3. Hourly mean number of occurrences of rainfall at the Picard, 1968–74: •, total; o, monsoon season November to April; ×, trade wind season May to October. Shading as in figure 2.

the trade wind season was May to October. This division followed that of Farrow (1971) in order to make easy comparison with his data. Rainfall amount (figure 2) for the monsoon season closely followed the pattern of the curve for the whole year. Amounts less than **25 %** of the mean occurred from 07 h 00 to 09 h 00 and greater than **25 %** of the mean from 10 h 00 to 15 h 00. The trade wind season, however, was markedly different. There was no midday peak in rainfall amount during the trade wind season, and there were only small peaks during the early morning and just after sunset. Also at this season there was a tendency for especially low amounts of rain at midday and in the late afternoon.

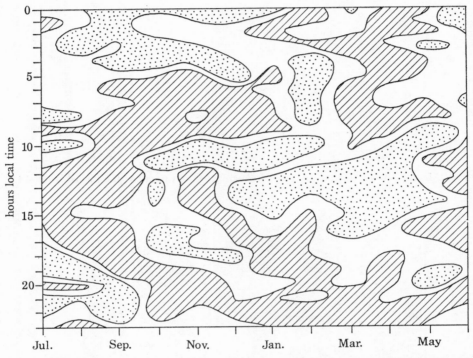

FIGURE 4. Isopleth diagram of rainfall amount at the Picard, 1968–74. Diagonal shading marks time periods that received less than 25 % of the appropriate monthly mean rainfall; dotted areas mark the periods receiving greater than 25 % of the monthly mean rainfall.

Rainfall frequency during the monsoon season (figure 3) showed a bimodal pattern with greatest frequencies near sunrise and midday to mid-afternoon. These peaks appeared to be slightly later in the day than the corresponding peaks in the amount of rainfall (figure 2). The trade wind frequency curve is subdued with only three minor extremes exceeding ±**25 %** of the mean. There is a maximum at 02 h 00–03 h 00 and there are minima at 12 h 00–13 h 00 and near 17 h 00.

Figures 4 and 5 provide a further refinement on the relation between diurnal and seasonal patterns of rainfall. There were two major periods of maximum rainfall frequency (figure 5). One was between about midnight and 07 h 00 during the months of August–October (November), and the other was from about 09 h 00 to 17 h 00 during the months of October–April. During November–February there was a midday depression in frequency from about 12 h 00 to 15 h 00. The period with the least frequency of rain occurred in the morning daylight hours during July–November (December). The frequency of rain at other times showed no discernible pattern.

The isopleth diagram of rainfall amount (figure 4) showed extended periods of heavy rainfall during the midday and post-midnight periods similar to the pattern seen for rainfall frequency. There also was an extensive period of dry conditions between the two major peaks in rainfall amount. It appeared that the midday maximum during the wet season was surrounded by a particularly dry period. Such an encircling feature was not prominent in the frequency isopleth. There was a slight development of a post-sunset maximum in both frequency and amount of rain during the trade wind season.

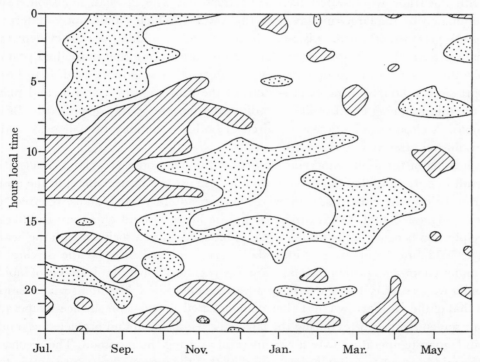

FIGURE 5. Isopleth diagram of rainfall frequency at the Picard, 1968–74. Shading as for figure 4 but with frequency in place of amount.

There were several other differences between the isopleth diagrams for frequency and amount of rainfall. The midday period of rain extended later in the season on the rainfall amount diagram (April), i.e. rainfall frequency appeared to decrease more rapidly than amount as the trade wind season approached. The afternoon 'dry' period was more extensive and continuous on the amount than on the frequency diagram. The post-midnight maximum during the late trade wind season was concentrated on the frequency diagram during August and September between midnight and 07h 00, while on the amount diagram it was spread broadly over August–December and rarely extended later in the day than 05h 00.

The amplitude of the diurnal variation in rainfall was found to be large. On the rainfall frequency diagram it ranged from +135 to −100 % of the monthly mean values while on the amount diagram it ranged from +35 to −100 % of the monthly means.

Discussion

The most prominent feature seen in the pattern of rainfall on Aldabra is the strong influence of season of the year upon both the frequency and amount of rainfall. Rain is both most frequent and most abundant during the monsoon season, which extends from about December to April (figures 1, 4 and 5). The seasonal fluctuations in rainfall correspond to the regular alternation between the southeast trade winds and the equatorial low pressure trough.

The second most prominent feature of rainfall on the atoll is that it exhibits clear diurnal patterns. These patterns are seen to be influenced by season of the year even after bias caused by the numerically larger values of rainfall amount and frequency during the monsoon season compared with the trade wind season have been removed. The diurnal, monsoon, rainfall pattern is dominated by the large midday peak (figures 2–5) which should not be interpreted as indicating the presence of a heated island effect. No similar midday peak is evident in the one year's data presented by Farrow (1971) for Aldabra, indicating that individual years can differ considerably from the mean of several years. A smaller, secondary peak is to be seen during the pre-sunrise hours during both seasons of the year (figures 2 and 3) and may be evidence of the rain inducing effect of the semi-diurnal atmospheric tide described by Brier & Simpson (1969). A close examination is required of both the midday rainfall peak and the possible semi-diurnal atmospheric tide effects.

The daily heating of the atoll's land rim may cause the often observed cloud streets. These appear to result in only restricted falls of rain that are usually out to sea where, in the absence of heating from below, the cloud base is lowered with resultant rain. Malkus, referred to by Farrow (1971), suggested that clouds produced by the heated island effect are less likely to result in precipitation because of the raising of cloud base level also associated with the heating. The lagoon on Aldabra could, by providing both heat and moisture, be the driving force causing the midday monsoon peak in rainfall. Riehl (1954) has shown that transfers of moisture and heat from a water surface to the overlying air occurs only when the water surface temperature exceeds that of the air. Farrow (1971) has demonstrated that lagoon surface temperatures can exceed air screen temperatures during the late trade wind season and predicted as much as 4 °C excess in lagoon temperature over air temperature during the monsoon. The mechanism for causing the midday peak in rainfall, then, could be that the increased moisture supply to the air may result in taller clouds than those produced by the heated island alone. Such taller clouds might then be sufficient to produce precipitation over the atoll. If Aldabra's lagoon is responsible for the midday monsoon peak in rainfall, then the state of the oceanic tide can be expected to be an important factor in modifying its influence. Lagoon waters are expected to be warmest when low tide in the lagoon corresponds with the midday period (i.e. neap tides). Heaviest and most frequent midday falls should be expected at this time also. A detailed study of rainfall pattern in relation to the state of the tide would be rewarding on Aldabra but it would be difficult because of the complex pattern of the flow and ebb of the tide in the shallow lagoon.

The rôle of the semi-diurnal atmospheric tides, which are so prominent a feature of tropical regions, in influencing rainfall has been the subject of some controversy. Lavoie (1963) discounted them as being too weak to cause any rainfall. Brier & Simpson (1969), however, have proposed a mechanism whereby the force of the atmospheric tide, acting upon only limited areas, can be demonstrated to be sufficient to stimulate rain. The hypothesis is that convergence associated with the atmospheric tide will stimulate rainfall near sunrise and sunset. The diurnal rainfall analysis for Aldabra shows a broad, pre-dawn peak in rainfall frequency and amount, but a pre-sunset peak is only scarcely detectable during the trade wind season. The isopleth diagrams (figures 4 and 5) help to resolve the problem by indicating that there is a tendency for the midday peak to extend into the late afternoon peak if the July–September data are merged with the October–December data as was done to produce figures 1 and 2.

It is useful to note here that the demonstration of a relation between hour of rainfall and the semi-diurnal atmospheric tide for Aldabra will not be a simple task. A summary of the monthly mean hour of occurrence of the pressure maxima and minima for September 1973 to October 1974 at the Research Station showed a steady drift in the mean hour of the morning minimum from 06h 42 in September 1973 to 03h 30 in January 1974. During the same time the afternoon minimum shifted from 18h 16 to 16h 06 while the time of the maxima changed virtually not at all. These observations do not show the constancy of phase hour of the atmospheric tide reported by Lavoie (1963) and Brier & Simpson (1969). If the time of occurrence of pressure extremes is always as changeable as noted here it could account for the broadness of the pre-sunrise rainfall peak but could also make difficult the proof on Aldabra of a relation between rainfall and the semi-diurnal atmospheric tide.

One further, final point which may be incidental but is worth noting in relation to rainfall patterns on Aldabra is that the midday peak during the monsoon (figure 4) corresponds roughly to the period of time when monthly mean hourly air screen temperatures (Hnatiuk, unpublished data) equal or exceed 28 °C. Also, the months of greatest rain correspond to the months when open ocean surface temperature equals or exceeds 28 °C (Farrow 1971).

Conclusion

Several factors are acting simultaneously to produce or modify rainfall on Aldabra. Some of these are seasonal factors, local heating of the lagoon and atoll rim, regional storms, ocean tides as they affect lagoon temperature, the force and direction of the prevailing wind, and the semi-diurnal atmospheric tide. At any time one or more of these factors may gain the ascendancy while at another time a different combination may predominate. On average it appears that the seasonal alternation between trade wind and monsoon régimes are most prominent while the heating of the lagoon and the atoll land rim and the semi-diurnal atmospheric tides are next in importance. The other factors act to modify these by either reinforcing or counteracting the tendency to rain, as the case may be.

TRANS-ATOLL VARIATIONS

Methods

Totalizing rain gauges were established at eight out-stations around the coast of the atoll. They were located at semi-permanent camps which were visited periodically by various workers who could maintain records. For most of the period of recording reported here, it was not practicable to make regular visits to all sites.

The gauges, except one at Passe Houareau which was of standard Meteorological Office construction, each consisted of a plastic 1 gallon (5 l) holding tank, immersed where possible in soil or rocks, connected directly to a plastic receiving cylinder. The holding tank contained a layer of oil sufficient to form a thin layer over water caught and so to reduce, as far as possible, water loss through evaporation.

The locally made gauges were subject to systematic errors. Light showers were unlikely to be adequately recorded through evaporation of the small quantities of water caught on the sides of the warm walls of the gauges. Small water droplets would also tend to remain on the top of the oil and be lost through evaporation. On the few occasions when the oil in the holding tank solidified, exposing an open water surface, some evaporation could have occurred, although the low temperatures at the time and the relatively high humidity would have reduced the rate and quantities involved. All of these factors would act to reduce the measured quantities of rain.

At each location, the gauges were sited in the most open area available, and away from over-hanging foliage. The gauges at Anse Polymnie and Passe Houareau were the most sheltered, having *Casuarina* and *Cocos* trees 10–15 m tall within 20 m. At Dune D'Messe, two gauges were installed, one on the dune in the lee of the trade winds, and one on the exposed sea coast. The dune site appears to have been a sheltered one relative to the coastal one and to the Research Station.

The records have been summarized by comparing the data from each station to the data for the similar time interval extracted from the daily rainfall records kept at the Research Station. The out-station data have been expressed as percentages of the Research Station rainfall and are shown in table 1.

TABLE 1. RECORDINGS OF TOTAL RAINFALL AROUND ALDABRA
AS USED IN THE PRESENT STUDY
(Trade wind season is May–November; monsoon season is December–April.)

station	duration	no. of days	no. of recordings	rainfall†	rainfall for trade wind season†	rainfall for monsoon season†
Passe Houareau	5 April 1973–3 February 1975	669	74	90	65	102
Anse Mais	3 July 1973–27 February 1975	604	38	140	215	117
Cinq Cases	13 May 1973–9 October 1974	514	22	95	152	76
Dune d'Messe						
exposed	2 May 1973–6 May 1974	369	16	137	142	129
sheltered	10 February 1973–6 May 1974	450	13	61	39	80
Dune Jean-Louis	30 June 1973–8 September 1974	435	16	105	98	107
Anse Polymnie	9 November 1973–7 August 1974	196	25	134	121	135
Anse Gionnet	15 April 1974–19 October 1974	187	4	141	121	153
Anse Takamaka	28 February 1974–9 August 1974	162	7	114	63	122

† Expressed as a percentage of that at Ile Picard during the equivalent period.

Results

The duration and number of records for each site are given in table 1. Three sites had records covering less than one year and especial caution was necessary in evaluating them.

The data on spatial variation in rainfall are presented in table 1 as a summary of all records and also for the wet and dry seasons separately. The wet season was defined as the period December–April and the dry season as May–November, based on the long-term averages in Stoddart & Mole (1977).

The most obvious result found in table 1 was that there was heterogeneity in rainfall across the atoll in any season. Anse Mais, Anse Polymnie, Dune d'Messe (exposed) and Anse Gionnet consistently received more rain in all seasons than did the Research Station, while Dune Jean-Louis received about the same amount. Passe Houareau and Cinq Cases at the eastern end of the atoll, showed distinct but opposite seasonal variations in rainfall relative to the Research

Station. Cinq Cases received nearly 50 % more dry season rain than the Research Station while Passe Houareau received only 65 % as much. During the wet season Cinq Cases received only 76 % as much rain as Research Station but Passe Houareau received virtually the same amount. The dune site at Dune d'Messe was consistently drier than Research Station but was driest during the trade wind season.

The original data indicated that rainfall was heavy from moderate tropical depression 'Bernardette' at Research Station, Anse Polymnie, Anse Gionnet, Dune d'Messe, Dune Jean-Louis and Anse Takamaka. At Passe Houareau only 50 % and at Cinq Cases only 36 % as much rain was recorded as at Research Station over the period of the storm.

Discussion

Simultaneous records of rainfall at Passe Houareau and Settlement were first made by Farrow (1971). Subsequently, one year's records were collected by J. Frazier at Dune Jean-Louis (Stoddart & Mole 1977). Farrow's short run of observations served to show that rainfalls were not synchronous at the two ends of the atoll. Frazier's data indicated that yearly totals at two widely separated points on the atoll could differ by nearly 30 %. Stoddart & Mole (1977) concluded that higher rainfall totals at Dune Jean Louis were due to more frequent rainfall and not heavier falls than at Ile Picard.

The summary of all data now available supports Farrow's original observation that rainfall is variable across the atoll. Trans-atoll variation needs to be separated into that portion due to local factors and that due to regional ones. There does not appear to be any reason for expecting systematic patterns resulting from regional causes, because Aldabra is small in relation to the surrounding relatively empty and open ocean. The search for local patterns in rainfall on Aldabra, therefore, should be directed towards finding systematic trends for relative excesses and deficiencies that are correlated with geographic position around the atoll.

The trend of rainfall at Research Station is for most of the rain in any year to come from only a few heavy falls (90 % of rain days have less than 15 mm recorded (Stoddart & Mole 1977)). The data from regional storm 'Bernadette' indicate that even heavy falls are not necessarily recorded everywhere on the atoll at one time. Therefore it seems necessary to conclude that many years of simultaneous records will be needed before any trans-atoll patterns can be detected among the large apparently chance variations of a regional origin.

References (Hnatiuk)

Brier, G. W. & Simpson, J. 1969 Tropical cloudiness and rainfall related to pressure and tidal variations. *Q. Jl R. met. Soc.* **95**, 120–147.
Farrow, G. E. 1971 The climate of Aldabra Atoll. *Phil. Trans. R. Soc. Lond.* B **260**, 67–91.
Kiser, W. L., Carpenter, T. H. & Brier, G. W. 1963 The atmospheric tides at Wake Island. *Mon. Weath. Rev.* **91**, 566–572.
Lavoie, R. L. 1963 Some aspects of meteorology of the tropical Pacific viewed from an atoll. *Atoll Res. Bull.* **96**, 1–80.
Riehl, H. 1954 *Tropical meteorology.* (392 pages.) New York: McGraw-Hill.
Stoddart, D. R. 1971 Rainfall on Indian Ocean coral islands. *Atoll Res. Bull.* **147**, 1–21.
Stoddart, D. R. & Mole, L. U. 1977 Climate of Aldabra Atoll. *Atoll Res. Bull.* **202**, 1–21.
Troll, C. 1958 Climatic seasons and climatic classification. *Orient. Geog.* **2**, 141–165.
Wiens, H. J. 1962 *Atoll environment and ecology.* New Haven, Conn., and London: Yale University Press.

Phil. Trans. R. Soc. Lond. B. **286**, 35–45 (1979)   [35]
Printed in Great Britain

Surface lowering and landform evolution on Aldabra

By S. T. Trudgill

Department of Geography, University of Sheffield, Sheffield S10 2TN, U.K.

Aldabra landforms are the result of the karstification of carbonate rocks distributed on surfaces which have been exposed to erosion for varying lengths of time. Morphometric analysis (which is of interest in both geomorphological and botanical contexts) suggests that the most well developed karst features (closed depressions) occur on what appear to be the oldest surfaces. Morphology also varies with lithology. Measurements of present-day erosion rates suggests that weakly cemented rocks and the most soluble mineral components are eroding most rapidly. The evolution of a dissected morphology is related to lithological heterogeneity in coralline rocks or, in the case of the more homogeneous rocks, to the short residence time of waters on the rock surface (the more rapidly dissolving mineral grains eroding faster). Dissolution also proceeds in fresh water pools, but this may be offset by precipitation in some cases. The surface is mostly case hardened, except under deep organic soils where erosion rates are much higher than in other areas. A mean erosion rate measured at 0.26 mm/a appears to make it feasible that large erosional features, such as the lagoon, could have been formed during periods of emersion as suggested by research workers who have hypothesized that an atoll shape may be substantially derived by subaerial weathering.

Introduction

The aim of the work undertaken on Aldabra was to examine the relation between landform and surface age (as described by geological work by other authors). An attempt was also made to account for variations in the degree of surface dissection with reference to lithological variation and erosional environment. Broad correlative inferences have been made based on geological information and selected examples of morphometric analysis. Detailed studies of erosion rates were undertaken in order to give insight into the process mechanisms involved. Furthermore, information on landform evolution and nature is of interest in terms of the plant and animal ecology of the island and also in the wider context of the evolution of atolls in general.

Aldabra is situated in the western Indian Ocean at 9° S and 46°E. The stratigraphy, evolution and surfaces of the island are described by Braithwaite *et al.* (1973) and earlier geomorphological work is summarized by Stoddart *et al.* (1971). Limestone erosion processes are described by Trudgill (1976*a*) and also in Trudgill (1972, 1976*b*). Palaeosols and other terrestrial sediments are described by Braithwaite (1975). Other work on the island is summarized in Westoll & Stoddart (1971).

Surface morphometry, lithology and surface age

Two major surfaces exist on Aldabra, one at approximately 8 m above present sea level and one at 4 m (Stoddart *et al.* 1971; Braithwaite *et al.* 1973). They appear to have formed in successive periods of emersion since about 80000 a B.P. The upper 8 m surface is cut almost exclusively in Aldabra Limestone but the 4 m terrace and associated lagoonward surface is cut in both Aldabra Limestone and the older Takamaka Limestone. Some morphological contrasts between the two areas are illustrated in figures 1 and 2 and in table 1.

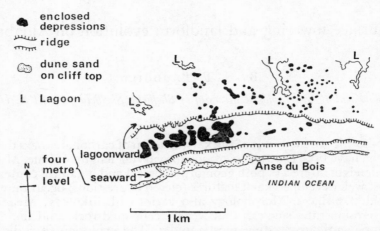

FIGURE 1. Enclosed depressions, from air photographs 040, 039 and 038, Dune Jean-Louis area.

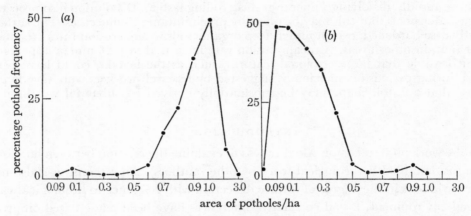

FIGURE 2. Frequency of potholes of given sizes on (a) the 8 m ridge and (b) the lagoonward 4 m level.

TABLE 1. MORPHOMETRIC PARAMETERS IN AIR PHOTOGRAPH STUDY QUADRAT, DUNE JEAN-LOUIS, ALDABRA (SEE FIGURES 1 AND 2)

parameters†	ridge	4 m level (lagoonward)
study area (A)/km²	1.887	3.108
number of pits (n)	14	98
density of pits† (n/A)/km⁻²	7.4192	31.53
sum of area of pits (A_P)/km²	0.2664	0.2849
% area covered by pits (% A_P)	14.1	9.1
indices of pitting		
(1) i.a.p.‡		
$\dfrac{\text{area}}{\text{area of pits}}$	7.083	10.9091
(2) i.c.p.§		
$\dfrac{\text{% area covered by pits}}{\text{number of pits}}$	1.008	0.0929

† After Williams (1966, 1969, 1971).

‡ The lower the number the higher the area occupied by pits.

§ The lower the number the more complex and pitted the surface (the complexity of the surface being proportional to the number of pits but inversely proportional to the area of pits).

It can be seen that the 8 m ridge is characterized by the presence of a few large depressions whereas the lagoonward 4 m surface has a large number of small depressions. Takamaka Limestone is found at the base of some of the larger depressions in Aldabra Limestone and it is not necessarily clear whether a depression represents an erosional feature or an area where deposition was lacking initially. However, it is reasonable to suggest that the surface which has been exposed for the longest period of time, the 8 m surface, has a better developed karst surface with the development of larger depressions.

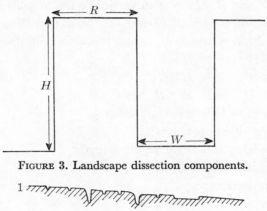

FIGURE 3. Landscape dissection components.

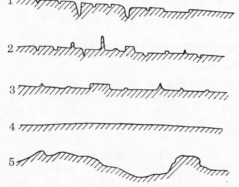

FIGURE 4. Relief classes recognized in morphometric analysis on Aldabra: 1, general surface with negative departures; 2, general surface with negative and positive departures; 3, general surface with positive departures; 4, general surface with no departures; 5, no general surface.

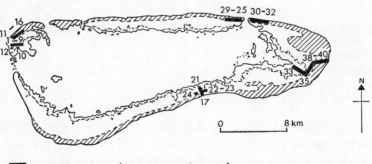

FIGURE 5. Location of quadrats for ground morphometric analysis.

The 8 m ridge often has a characteristic pavé form (Stoddart *et al.* 1971) whereas the younger surfaces appear to be more closely dissected (champignon) or to have a smooth (presumably pre-existing) surface. In order to have some basis on which to substantiate possible genetic arguments it is useful to be able to describe the landforms in some standard way other than by the use of the terms pavé, platin and champignon. Accordingly, detailed study areas were chosen as representative of various landform types, geology and surface age. In each area landform parameters were measured in accordance with the scheme illustrated in figure 3. The parameters used are H, W and R. H refers to vertical relief amplitude, R to the width of the upstanding intervening portion (residual) between potholes and W to the width of the pothole. The existing morphological terms can be given more precise definition using these parameters:

(1) champignon $H > W$ and $H > R$;
(2) pavé $H \leqslant W$ and $H \leqslant R$;
(3) platin $W \gg H$ and $W \gg R$.

Relief classes were also identified (figure 4) as follows:

(1) general surface, negative departures;
(2) general surface, positive and negative departures;
(3) general surface, positive departures;
(4) general surface, no departures;
(5) no general surface.

TABLE 2. MORPHOMETRIC INDICES FOR ALDABRA QUADRATS

(a) geology	no. of quadrats	$\bar{H}$	A_P	D	I_P	I_C	C	V	P
Aldabra Limestone	20	1.78	33.2	0.11	14.8	10.6	4	90	7
Picard Calcarenite	9	0.74	51.5	0.40	2.2	6.7	29	24	47
Takamaka Limestone	10	0.85	61.9	0.36	6.4	12.2	56	22	22
(b) surface									
8 m ridge	11	1.45	25.2	0.08	18.8	6.3	0	89	11
4 m terrace (seaward)	9	0.70	43.3	0.18	3.6	16.0	44	56	0
4 m terrace (lagoonward)	19	0.51	58.1	0.37	8.0	9.2	44	50	6

TABLE 3. RELIEF CLASSES, NUMBER OF OBSERVATIONS IN EACH CLASS

relief class	1	2	3	4	5
Aldabra Limestone	4	11	1	3	0
Picard Calcarenite	6	7	1	9	0
Takamaka Limestone	0	2	0	1	1
8 m ridge	1	6	2	1	1
4 m terrace (seaward)	3	5	0	0	0
4 m terrace (lagoonward)	6	9	1	9	0

Forty 10 m × 10 m quadrats were laid out in the study areas (figure 5). These were selected with bias according to ease of access and to represent different rock types and surfaces. Thus the exercise was not a statistical one and in making any inferences this should be borne in mind. The morphometric parameters H, W and R were measured in the field and the general relief class was identified. From the measurements taken the following indices were computed (after the work of Williams 1966, 1969, 1971):

(1) $\bar{H}$, average (mean) depth of potholes;
(2) A_P, percentage area occupied by potholes;

(3) D, density of potholes (number/m²);

(4) I_P, index of pitting $= \dfrac{\text{(total area)}}{A_P}$;

(5) I_C, surface complexity index $= \dfrac{A_P}{\text{(number of potholes)}}$.

The percentage of quadrats occupied by champignon (C), pavé (V) and platin (P) were also noted. The data for rock types and surfaces are summarized in tables 2 and 3.

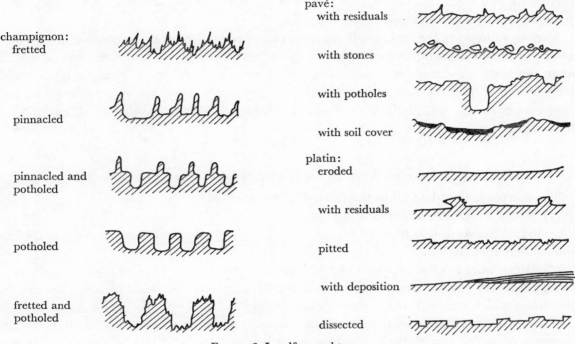

FIGURE 6. Landform subtypes.

Although some of the definition of morphology in the field is necessarily subjective, especially in terms of the edges of potholes, this morphometric approach is felt to be preferable to a completely subjective approach to landform evaluation. One problem is that areas which may appear to be dissected champignon by visual evaluation may be classified as pavé on morphometric grounds as shallow dissected areas are not detected as champignon. A pavé area (morphometric definition) can have a small amount of dissection where the depth of pothole is equal to the width of intervening residual. However, given this qualification and the statistical limitations of the data, it is nevertheless possible to make some inferences from the morphometric data:

(1)   Pothole depth appears to vary independently of lithology and be more related to surface age.

(2)   The Takamaka Limestone and Picard Calcarenite examples studied have a greater area of potholes, a greater density of potholes and are more pitted than the Aldabra Limestone examples studied.

(3)   While on the air photograph scale there appear to be a few large pot-holes on the 8 m ridge, at the 10 m quadrat scale there appear to be a few, narrow and very deep potholes (especially east of Anse Var).

(4) The area occupied by potholes and the density of potholes is greatest on the 4 m (lagoon-ward) surface but the seaward 4 m terrace is more pitted than the other surfaces.

(5) The 8 m ridge has the most complex surface.

Some broad generalizations can be made about the surfaces. The greatest dissection appears to occur on the younger (4 m) surface but this is often associated with a platin surface. This can be interpreted as fresh erosion in a differential manner upon a pre-existing planar surface. The modal pothole depths of the champignon measured was 1.2 m. On the older (8 m) surface there were two modes measured, one at 0.45 m and another at about 4 m. A few very deep potholes occur on an otherwise subdued surface.

Various subtypes of the main landform types can be recognized and it is possible that further work will be able to correlate these more closely with geology and erosional environment as well as to establish the nature of any possible influence upon vegetation. Such subtypes could include fretted, pinnacled or potholed champignon, pavé with residuals, loose boulders and stones or potholes, and platin with residuals, pitting, deposition, erosion or dissection (see figure 6).

Erosion processes and the evolution of a dissected surface

The morphometric data allow the following two inferences to be made:

(1) Rocks which are apparently lithologically relatively homogeneous can give rise to a dissected surface as well as those which are lithologically heterogenous and can be expected to show differential erosion.

(2) Differential erosion appears to be rapid at first but, from the evidence of the older surfaces, a subdued relief evolves (assuming that the initial starting point is a planar surface in all situations, which may well not necessarily be the case).

If these inferences are true then it remains to understand the nature of differential erosion processes occurring on relatively homogeneous rocks and to establish how this may become self-limiting over time. In order to elucidate the erosion processes which may be involved, erosion rates were measured on contrasting lithologies and in contrasting environments. Again, this is not a statistical exercise, for practical reasons. A micro-erosion meter method (High & Hanna 1970) was used to measure erosion rates. This has the advantage that accurate measurements of surface lowering may be gained in a short time though there exists the possible disadvantage that the measurement probe may disturb the surface of less well consolidated rocks unless extreme care is taken. The meter consists of a micrometer dial gauge mounted on a tripod framework resting upon three reference studs which are inserted into the rock surface. Successive micrometer measurements of the height of the rock surface relative to the studs gives an accurate indication of the rate of surface lowering of the rock provided that the studs are adequately protected between times of measurement. The results are summarized in table 4.

These data are displayed in figure 7 and it is clear that the results differ not only in their mean value but also in their ranges. The Aldabra limestone shows a wide range, as is to be expected for a heterogeneous rock composed of corals, shells and sand-sized material. The calcarenite (2) shows a wide range of erosion rates. This accords with morphometric observations but does not account for the processes involved. It is, however, clear that where lithological components are juxtaposed then marked differential erosion could occur. One additional comment on the method is that the most rugged topographies do not provide the best surfaces for the use of the micro-erosion meter and therefore data on this type of area are lacking. However, it still remains to account for the differential erosion of the calcarenites.

It is felt that, in part, differential erosion could be due to the dislodgement of calcarenite grains subsequent to the dissolution of cement, rather than an even dissolution of the whole surface. Often a point cement may exist, possibly with a more readily soluble mineralogy (aragonite or high magnesium calcite) than the grains themselves (low magnesium calcite).

TABLE 4. MICRO-EROSION METER RATES AND LITHOLOGY

limestone	dominant mineralogy	erosion rate/(mm/a)	
		mean	range
(1) Aldabra Limestone	aragonite and high magnesium calcite	0.11	0.09–0.62
(2) Picard Calcarenite	low magnesium calcite	0.35	0.09–0.530
(3) Picard Calcarenite	high magnesium calcite and aragonite	0.51	0.49–0.60
(4) Takamaka Limestone	low magnesium calcite	0.10	0.09–0.11

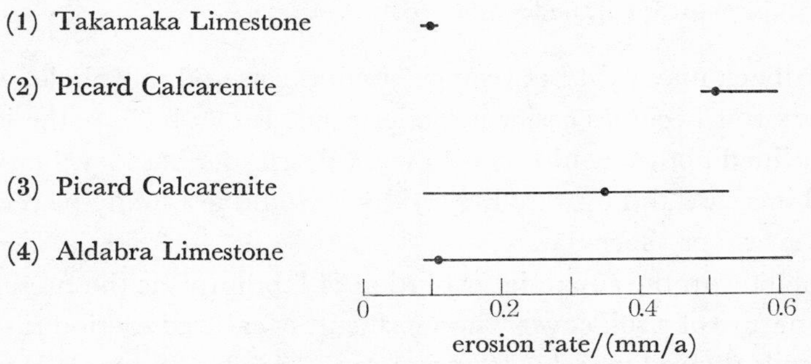

FIGURE 7. Ranges of measured erosion rates with lithology: •, mean value; ——, range

Alternatively, a more soluble grain with a less soluble cement may be involved. The problem is to establish how this mechanism finds expression at a slightly larger scale. Here it is possible that the short residence time of rain water on a subaerially exposed surface may contribute to the exaggeration of differential erosion of grain and cement, possibly also linked to variations in surface porosity and therefore in water penetration. Any minute depression would retain water and encourage the dissolution of the carbonate material present, whereas slightly upstanding areas would shed water more rapidly. This could become a self-reinforcing process. The rate of dissolution would be more important than the final equilibrium solubility where short residence time of water was involved. The more slowly dissolving minerals would gradually be left as upstanding while the most rapidly dissolving minerals would be preferentially eroded, leaving small eroded areas. After this initial phase, waters would subsequently collect preferentially and for a slightly longer time in the eroded areas. Dissolution of all mineral constituents would become progressively more equal in these areas. Thus flat floored pools may form. Alternatively, if the nature of the surface that was evolving encouraged the rapid runoff of waters then residence time would be kept low and differential erosion would be encouraged. This would require the mineralogical constituents involved to have different rates of dissolution, irrespective of final solubility levels.

Experiments were undertaken on the dissolution uptake of calcium and magnesium by rain waters running off subaerial surfaces and collecting in fresh water pools.

The results suggested that runoff waters were high in calcium concentrations, often approaching saturation; however, they were low in magnesium content. Magnesium content only rose after water residence in fresh water pools. This suggests that in a mixed magnesium–calcium system, short residence time will lead to differential erosion but that during a longer residence time both magnesium and calcium would come into equilibrium and that the mineralogical constituents would be dissolved equally. The evenness of the surface would increase in long residence time situations where equilibrium levels were comparable and the ruggedness would increase in short residence time situations where the dissolution rates were most disparate.

TABLE 5. CALCIUM AND MAGNESIUM LEVELS (milligrams per litre)
IN RAINWATER RUNOFF

water type	CaCO$_3$	MgCO$_3$
rainwater	10 (u)	19 (u)
rainwater runoff in pool soon after shower	100 (s)	12 (u)
semi-permanent rain water collecting pool	80 (s)	63 (u)

(s), saturated; (u), undersaturated.

Given that a feedback may exist between erosion process and morphology then the evolution of some of the landforms becomes easier to understand. It can be hypothesized that eventually the progression outlined above would tend to work down to a base level at which time pothole coalescence would increase and upstanding residuals would gradually be removed. This type of hypothesis is, however, very speculative.

One additional factor in the subaerial evolution of landforms is the presence or absence of a soil cover and the nature of a soil cover where present. Measured erosion rates under deep, acid (pH 6.5) organic soils showed very high erosion rates (5.5–20.4 mm/a). However, the bedrock is not case hardened and is very soft: some surface disturbance by the measurement probe may have occurred. Nonetheless, given this qualification it would still appear that erosion is very rapid under these soils. Erosion under shallow organic soils, which are essentially accumulations of leaf litter, is comparable with subaerial soil-free rates at 0.09–0.13 mm/a (the mean rate for soil free areas being 0.26 mm/a). Erosion under soils with a high carbonate content was slight and some deposition was even indicated at some sites. The fact that soils are spatially limited in their extent makes these data quantitatively unimportant when considering influence on differential erosion on a small scale. Again, a feedback may exist in that hollows may encourage soil accumulation and the feedback would further encourage deepening if the soil was organic and acid or it would limit erosion if the soil was high in carbonates, as many of the soils occurring on the pavé areas may have a high carbonate content this could have some effect upon the lack of differential erosion in these areas.

LONG-TERM SPECULATIVE EXTRAPOLATIONS OF EROSION RATES AND THE
EVOLUTION OF ALDABRA

The works of MacNeil (1954) and Flint et al. (1953) suggest that an atoll shape may be derived from subaerial weathering during times of emersion as much to the initial peripheral growth of corals. The work of Braithwaite et al. (1973) also stresses the importance of erosional events in the evolution of Aldabra. Although it is a somewhat unwarranted extrapolation it is tempting to convert the erosion rates measured over 2 years on Aldabra to rates per thousand years in order to investigate the feasibility of the rôle of subaerial weathering in the evolution of the atoll shape of Aldabra. It is a speculative extrapolation simply because it makes the assumption that the climate of the 2 year measurement period can be equated with past climates and also that the data are statistically representative, neither of which is true. However, order of magnitude estimates are possible.

The measured micro-erosion meter rates are higher than that suggested by Stoddart *et al.* (1971) of 0.05 mm/a. This was, however, based on assumptions of rainfall and calcite solubility and constancy of conditions over the atoll. Given these difficulties with the data it is probably best to work with minimum and mean estimates of erosion rates and to qualify carefully the interpretations thus gained. This is a reasonably valid procedure in the absence of any better information.

The summary of the evolution of Aldabra is given in Braithwaite *et al.* (1973) with some possible and one definite date for certain events. Given these dates it is possible to surmise that emersion periods of 80000, 27000 or 5000 years could have been involved at stages of the island's history. Extrapolations of erosion rates for these periods are given in table 6.

TABLE 6. EXTRAPOLATIONS OF EROSION RATES (metres) FOR EMERSION PERIODS

emersion period/a ...	80000	27000	5000
erosion rates/(mm/a)			
(1) 0.09 (min.)	7.2	2.43	0.45
(2) 0.26 (mean)	40.80	13.77	2.55

If emersion was subsequent to 27000 years and submersion was at around 5000 years a time span of 14000–22000 years is possible. A lagoon some 3.6–5.7 m deep could have formed during this period (using the mean rate) and 0.76–1.1 m using the lowest rate. This does not prove that the lagoon was formed subaerially, it simply does not go against MacNeil's theory and appears to make it feasible.

If the lagoon was formed subaerially, some further problems remain. The most significant is that subaerial surfaces appear to be characteristically dissected. However, evidence, especially from the Cinq Cases area, suggests that present subaerial weathering is dissecting a pre-existing planar surface, not a pre-existing dissected surface. If it is assumed that the pre-existing surface is an emersed old lagoon floor then it can be suggested that the lagoon morphology was formed by marine planation rather than subaerial weathering. This is in accord with other geological and morphological evidence from Aldabra. Since marine planation is largely a lateral process rather than a vertical one, data on shoreline retreat are more pertinent than data on subaerial lowering. Erosion rates measured on Aldabra give a range of 1–3 mm/a for a seaward coast (increasing with exposure) and a rate of about 2–3 mm/a for the lagoon (Trudgill 1976c). This gives rates of the order of 1–3 m/ka. It is not clear when sufficient time periods of marine planation that would be necessary to evolve the lagoon could have occurred. As Braithwaite *et al.* (1973) observe, features of only 15 m could have evolved in the last 5000 years at present sea level. The previous period of submergence appears to have been extensive and existing for possibly 125000–80000 a B.P. or later, giving a possible time span of around 45000 years. At 3 m/ka a lateral planation rate of 155 m is possible.

The questions this type of speculation raises must, of necessity, often remain substantially unanswered and there are few concrete arguments either way. However, it can be suggested that both subaerial and marine erosion have played some part in the evolution of the lagoon. Whatever the erosional environment, however, it can certainly be suggested that the atoll shape could have been formed by one or other erosional process. Central erosion, rather than peripheral coral growth, would appear to be feasible but the time periods and processes involved are as yet unclear.

Conclusions

Erosional events have been important in the evolution of Aldabra as stressed by Braithwaite et al. (1973). Extrapolation of present day erosion rates is speculative but appears to make it feasible that large scale erosional features could have been formed during the possible time periods available. These erosional events left three primary land surfaces at the present day. They are the higher 8 m ridge and a seaward 4 m terrace and its lagoonward equivalent. The 8 m ridge, on the scale of morphology detectable on air photographs, appears to show a relatively well developed karst morphology with the occurrence of some large broad shallow closed depressions together with a few narrow and very deep (often tidal) potholes. On the ground, a subdued relief occurs. A large number of small potholes and a dissected surface is found on the other levels. Within any one given surface, morphology can be related to lithology though the contrasts between the surfaces for any one lithology are greater than the contrasts between the lithologies on any one surface. Heterogeneous rocks (often coralline) display marked differential erosion, which is to be expected. Apparently homogeneous rock also shows a dissected surface and also measurable differential erosion rates. These appear to be linked to mineralogy and it is hypothesized that a short residence time of rain water on a subaerial surface would emphasize differences in dissolution rate leading to a feedback between erosion rate and morphology.

The field work was made possible by the Royal Society and the N.E.R.C. I should like to thank Dr C. J. Braithwaite, Dr J. D. Taylor and Dr W. J. Kennedy for help in the field and Dr C. J. R. Braithwaite, Dr D. Briggs and Dr D. R. Stoddart for comments on the manuscript.

References (Trudgill)

Braithwaite, C. J. R. 1975 Petrology of palaeosols and other terrestrial sediments on Aldabra, western Indian Ocean. *Phil. Trans. R. Soc. Lond.* B **273**, 1–32.

Braithwaite, C. J. R., Taylor, J. D. & Kennedy, W. J. 1973 The evolution of an atoll: the depositional and erosional history of Aldabra. *Phil. Trans. R. Soc. Lond.* B **266**, 307–340.

Flint, D. E., Corwin, G., Dings, M. C., Fuller, W. P., MacNeil, F. S. & Saplis, R. A. 1953 Limestone walls of Okinawa. *Bull. geol. Soc. Am.* **64**, 1247–1260.

High, C. J. & Hanna, F. K. 1970 A method for the direct measurement of erosion on rock surfaces. *Br. Geomorph. Res. Grp, tech. Bull.* 5.

MacNeil, F. S. 1954 The shape of atolls: an inheritance from subaerial erosion forms. *Am. J. Sci.* **252**, 402–427.

Stoddart, D. R., Taylor, J. D., Fosberg, F. R. & Farrow, G. E. 1971 The geomorphology of Aldabra Atoll. *Phil. Trans. R. Soc. Lond.* B **260**, 31–65.

Trudgill, S. T. 1972 Quantification of limestone erosion in intertidal, subaerial and sub-soil environments with special reference to Aldabra Atoll, Indian Ocean. *Trans. Cave Res. Grp. G. B.* **14**, 176–179.

Trudgill, S. T. 1976a The subaerial and subsoil erosion of limestones on Aldabra Atoll, Indian Ocean. *Z. Geomorph.*, suppl. **26**, 201–210.

Trudgill, S. T. 1976b Rock weathering and climate: quantitative and experimental aspects. In *Geomorphology and climate* (ed. E. Derbyshire), ch. 3. Wiley.

Trudgill, S. T. 1976c The marine erosion of limestones on Aldabra Atoll, Indian Ocean. *Z. Geomorph.*, suppl.
  26, 164–200.
Westoll, T. S. & Stoddart, D. R. (organizers) 1971 A discussion on the results of the Royal Society expeditions
  to Aldabra, 1967–1968. *Phil. Trans. R. Soc. Lond.* B **260**, 1–654.
Williams, P. W. 1966 Morphometric analysis of temperate karst landforms. *Irish Speleol.* **1**, 23–31.
Williams, P. W. 1969 The geomorphic effects of groundwater. In *Water, Earth and Man* (ed. R. J. Chorley).
  London: Methuen.
Williams, P. W. 1971 Illustrating morphometric analysis of karst with examples from New Guinea. *Z. Geomorph.*
  15, 40–61.

Phil. Trans. R. Soc. Lond. B. **286**, 47–66 (1979)   [47]

Printed in Great Britain

Terrestrial faunas and habitats of Aldabra during the late Pleistocene

By J. D. Taylor†, C. J. R. Braithwaite‡, J. F. Peake† and E. N. Arnold†

† *Department of Zoology, British Museum (Natural History), Cromwell Road, London SW7 5BD, U.K.*

‡ *Department of Geology, University of Dundee, Dundee DD1 4HN, U.K.*

[Plate 1]

Far from being fixed and unchanging, the islands and land areas of the western Indian Ocean are in a dynamic state; the most important variable, apart from tectonic activity, has been the rise and fall of sea level as a consequence of late Pleistocene glacial advances and retreats. Geological studies at Aldabra show that there have been great variations in the land area of the atoll, the topography, and the height above sea level. Moreover, the land has been completely submerged on at least two occasions. Fossil tortoises, crocodiles, lizards, birds and snails illustrate, if fragmentarily, the pattern of colonization and extinction on the Atoll. Although the earliest terrestrial deposits represent vegetated sandy cay habitats colonized by crocodiles, iguanas, petrels, tortoises and snails, the later deposits indicate dissected rocky substrates with meagre soil formation and scrub vegetation more similar to present day Aldabra. However, both the lizard and snail faunas indicate that considerable faunal change has occurred.

Introduction

The faunas and floras of oceanic islands have long excited biologists interested in both evolution and biogeography. The publication of MacArthur & Wilson's *The theory of island biogeography* (1967) emphasized the growing interest in the dynamic nature of island biotas, with both short-term studies and the examination of historical records revealing patterns of colonization and extinction on islands which conform, more or less closely, with their models. However, with few exceptions, it is rare to find any evidence of the long-term history of the fauna on an oceanic island. Atolls in particular, by virtue of their mode of formation by subsidence, rarely reveal any of their previous history from a study of the surface deposits, and what fragmentary evidence is available concerning the history of the land biota of atolls has come from a few boreholes (Ladd 1958; Leopold 1969). It was therefore of some interest when, during the geological survey of the slightly elevated atoll of Aldabra in the western Indian Ocean, Braithwaite, Taylor & Kennedy (1973) discovered a series of fossiliferous terrestrial deposits within a dominantly marine, late Pleistocene rock sequence.† The importance of these deposits to the understanding of the present day fauna of the Atoll was underlined when it was demonstrated that the giant tortoises must have colonized the atoll on at least three separate occasions. It is the purpose of this paper to show that this pattern of colonization and extinction extends to a number of other fossil groups.

In this paper we describe the fossils and sediments from a variety of fragmentary deposits distributed throughout the Aldabran rock sequence. We attempt to reconstruct the palaeo-

† Incidentally, Sir John Fryer collected a sample of these rocks from Bassin Cabri in 1908 which he clearly recognized as of terrestrial origin. The fossils were reported upon by Dr Bullen-Newton of the British Museum (Natural History), but the information was not incorporated into Fryer's (1911) report on the geology of the atoll.

environments which these represent and discuss the significance of the fossils in relation to the faunal history of Aldabra and the biogeography of the area in general. The field work upon which this study is based was carried out by J. D. Taylor in 1969 and 1973, and by C. J. R. Braithwaite in 1969.

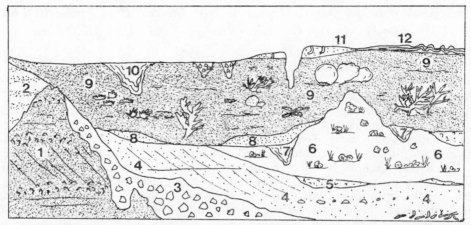

FIGURE 1. Stratigraphic model for Aldabra showing the general relations of terrestrial and marine rock units. Lateral scale approximately 10 km, vertical scale 9 m. Bed thickness not to scale. 1, Esprit Limestones; 2, 3, Esprit Phosphorites; 4, Picard Calcarenites; 5, Post-Picard Calcarenite 'soils'; 6, Takamaka Limestone; 7, post-Takamaka Limestone 'soils'; 8, hard marine calcarenites; 9, Aldabra Limestone; 10, post-Aldabra Limestone solution pits and fillings; 11, crab burrowed calcarenites; 12, stromatolites.

GEOLOGICAL HISTORY AND PHYSICAL SETTING OF ALDABRA

Aldabra Atoll (lat. 9° 24′ S, long. 46° 20′ E) is 34 km long and 14.5 km wide, with islands 0.25–5 km wide and 155 km² in area. It is one of a group of slightly elevated coralline islands lying to the north of Madagascar which form the subaerial tips of individual sea-mounts rising 4000–4500 m from the abyssal floor of the Somali Basin.

The Pleistocene surface geology has been described by Braithwaite *et al.* (1973), and the geomorphology by Stoddart, Taylor, Fosberg & Farrow (1971); only the essential features are outlined below. The exposed rocks reveal a complex series of erosional and depositional events which consist of shallow-water marine limestones, limited terrestrial calcarenites, calcareous soils and cavity-fills, and phosphorites. These deposits occur in association with, or are separated by, erosional surfaces which were produced by subaerial solution–dissection or by marine planation of the limestones. The nature of the geological events recognized and of the depositional processes is such that no single deposit is found over the entire area of Aldabra. Some deposits are, and perhaps were, merely a few centimetres thick, and occupy areas of only a few square metres.

The major sedimentary units and the events affecting Aldabra are shown diagrammatically in figure 1. The oldest sediments exposed are marine calcarenites (1), the Esprit Limestones. The deposition of these was followed by a period of emergence with subaerial erosion and the subsequent accumulation of the Esprit Phosphorites (2, 3). The next recorded event was a marine regression, culminating in the deposition of terrestrial calcarenites and soils, the Picard Calcarenites (4, 5). These were covered by a transgression represented by the Takamaka Limestone (6), which is a marine calcarenite/calcilutite containing abundant calcareous algae.

A period of emergence followed, resulting in solutional erosion and the deposition of cavity-fill and other terrestrial deposits (7, 8). This regression may also be related to the deposition of beach sediments in the Passe Houareau area. Submergence about 125 ka B.P. (Thompson & Walton 1972) formed an extensive thick calcarenite, the Aldabra Limestone (9) containing abundant corals. Following this important marine interval there was emergence and erosion of the limestones, perhaps with the deposition of cavity-fill deposits. Submergence cut the +8 m and +4 m terraces interpreted by Braithwaite *et al.* (1973) as being produced by simple still-

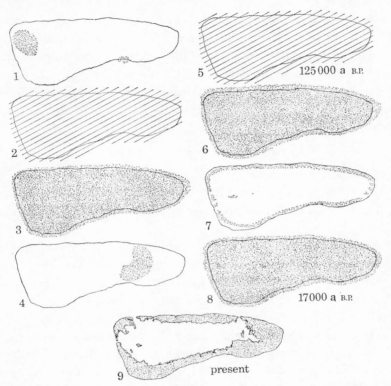

FIGURE 2. Diagrammatic representation of the sequence of possible land areas at various times in the history of Aldabra. Stippled areas, land; cross-hatched areas, complete marine inundation. Key events: 1, Picard Calcarenites; 2, Takamaka Limestone; 5, Aldabra Limestone; 7, The +4 m terrace; 8, The Wisconsin glacial minimum sea level.

stands of a sea level falling progressively from the last interglacial to the Wisconsin glacial maximum about 17 ka B.P. Evidence from other parts of the world shows, however, that this is a very poor record of this interval. Steinen, Harrison & Matthews (1973), and Bloom *et al.* (1974), describe 'reef terraces' on the emergent coasts of Barbados and New Guinea respectively. At the New Guinea site, as many as five depositional terraces were recorded, dated between 125 and 15 ka B.P., and apparently separated by erosion surfaces produced by periods of lowered sea level. There is no evidence on Aldabra of deposits of comparable ages, although the +8 and +4 m terraces are probably partly time-equivalent. However, both the peaks and the troughs of the oscillations in New Guinea and Barbados are thought to represent sea levels well below the present. Braithwaite *et al.* (1973) postulated that Aldabra had been tectonically stable in the late Pleistocene, but if the New Guinea and Barbados estimates of eustatic sea levels are correct, then Aldabra may well be emergent and the planation surfaces elevated.

Whatever the interpretation, it is clear that, after the deposition of the Aldabra Limestone, sea level fell, probably exposing a land area as large as the whole atoll (400 km²). A subsequent rise in sea level inundated the land with marine erosion, forming the +8 m terrace. A further fall in sea level, represented by the +4 m terrace, exposed a narrow fringe of low rocky islands of about 50 km² area encircling a large shallow rock-bottomed lagoon (at the end of the stand). Sea level then dropped again, with probable oscillations, down to about −120 m at the Wisconsin glacial maximum about 15 ka B.P. Aldabra would have stood at this time as a steep-sided, flat-topped rocky island about 120 m high and again about 400 km² in area. Extensive solutional erosion took place, probably accompanied by cavity-fill deposition. The subsequent post-glacial sea level rise reached its present level 3–5 ka B.P. (Stoddart 1976). The most significant result of this rise was the breaching of the present lagoon which would have reduced the land area by about 60%. The present situation is simply the latest event in this series; it is again notable for the extensive marine and terrestrial erosion taking place without significant deposition (Trudgill 1976 a, b). As one might expect, this appears to be true for all of the terrestrial or regressive intervals.

REGIONAL CONTEXT OF ALDABRA

Far from being fixed and unchanging, the islands and land areas in the western Indian Ocean are in a dynamic state. The most important variable, apart from tectonic activity, has been the rise and fall of sea level as a consequence of late Pleistocene glacial advances and retreats.

Most of the islands close to Aldabra, such as Cosmoledo, Astove, Assumption, Farquhar and Glorioso, are low coralline islands which would have been inundated during the last interglacial when sea level stood about 10 m higher than at present. However, the volcanic Comores, the granitic Seychelles and Madagascar are high islands, and would have been present as land during this period with relatively little change in area. By contrast during the last glacial maximum when sea level was considerably lower than at present, large areas of land now submerged as shallow platforms would have been emersed. These include the Seychelles, Amirantes, Nazareth, Farquhar and Zelee Banks, and Saya de Malha. This emergence would have produced a series of large islands with a total area of approximately 140000 km². Individual banks were quite large, the Seychelles Bank would have been about 43000 km² and Saya de Malha about 40000 km². These banks are largely uninvestigated at present, but coring may be expected to reveal terrestrial sediments or subaerial erosion surfaces produced during these emergent periods. Sea level changes have thus been of critical importance in determining the land areas available for colonization and continuing habitation by a terrestrial biota.

In addition to variations in the habitat and its area there have been significant changes in climatic conditions. The $^{16}O/^{18}O$ palaeotemperature records indicate a drop in the surface water temperatures of the Indian Ocean of about 8 °C (Emiliani 1971). This would have placed the islands of the Aldabra group outside the region of active coral growth. Rainfall and cloud cover were possibly also higher, and would have had direct effects upon vegetation and terrestrial habitats.

THE TERRESTRIAL DEPOSITS AND THEIR FAUNAS

Although some of the terrestrial sediments are bedded, most are in the form of irregular cavity-fill deposits. These are usually small in extent, isloated from one another, and thus difficult to correlate, or to place satisfactorily into a stratigraphic time sequence. Braithwaite

(1975) has described in detail the structure, petrology and mineralogy of the sediments, and Arnold (1976), van Bruggen (1975), and Harrison & Walker (1978) have described some of the terrestrial fossils.

Although the cavity-fill deposits are very common on Aldabra, those containing fossils are comparatively rare. In the case of vertebrate material, this is not surprising, but the patchy occurrence of terrestrial snails, which are more likely to be widely distributed, seems anomalous.

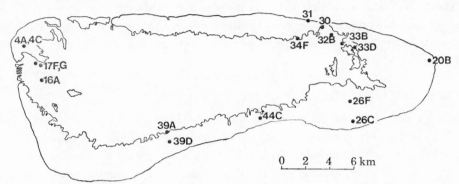

FIGURE 3. Location on Aldabra of the terrestrial rock sample sites mentioned in the text.

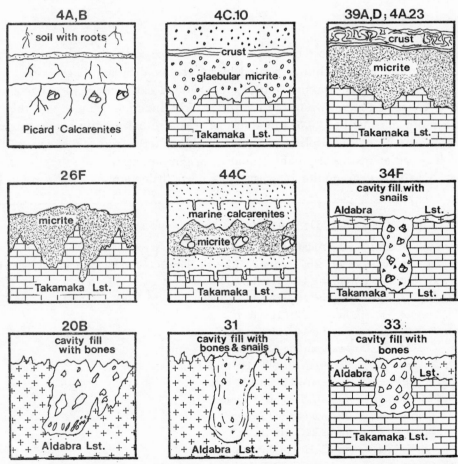

FIGURE 4. Diagrammatic representation of the stratigraphic positions of the various terrestrial deposits discussed in the text.

It may conceivably be attributed to preservational loss, but if this is the case there is no direct diagenetic evidence and it must have taken place before lithification. The nature of each terrestrial deposit, its sediment and contained fossils, and an environmental interpretation is outlined below in an approximate time sequence. The localities and stratigraphic positions of each deposit discussed are shown in figures 3 and 4 respectively. In the text, each deposit is referred to by grid reference and sample collection number. The present account is concerned only with those deposits for which there is substantive evidence (in the form of diagnostic fossils) of a terrestrial origin. The degree of refinement in the identification of the fossils varies considerably according to both the state of preservation and the morphological complexity of the animal group concerned.

The Picard Calcarenites

0635.0990, samples 4A1, 2; 4B4, 6, 12, 13, 20, 21, 22; 4C1, 2.

These deposits post-date the Esprit Limestones and Phosphorites, and are overlain by the Takamaka Limestone. The present exposures occupy an area of about 20 km² at the southern end of Picard (Bassin Cabri) extending to Iles Châlen. Evidence for a second island in the Point Lion area is given by Braithwaite *et al.* (1973) and there may have been others. The surface upon which the deposits rest is not seen, but probably included rocky pinnacles such as that now formed by Esprit.

Sediment

In the Bassin Cabri area, two sets of beds have been recognized, representing parts of the same major depositional cycle, but separated by an erosional break. The lower, thicker, and more extensive unit consists of about 3 m of cross-bedded calcarenites in which the laminae dip gently (5–7°) in a general westerly to southwesterly direction. The top of this rock unit consists of a more massive bed, 0.5–1 m thick, of a coarse calcarenite containing abundant moulds of rootlets with oxidized plant remains, moulds of terrestrial snails, and partly articulated bones. The sediment was originally of marine origin but, apart from the post-depositional solution or alteration of aragonite bioclasts, has been little modified. The micritic matrix

---

DESCRIPTION OF PLATE 1

Some fossil terrestrial snails from the Aldabra deposits.

FIGURE 1. Silicone rubber cast of *Tropidophora* sp. from the Picard Calcarenites. Actual height 14.4 mm

FIGURE 2. *Tropidophora* sp. from site 44C. Height 21.6 mm.

FIGURE 3. *Tropidophora* sp. from site 44C. Height 15.9 mm.

FIGURE 4. *Otopoma flexilabris* from site 31. Height 16.2 mm.

FIGURE 5. *Tropidophora* sp. from site 44C. Height 21.9 mm.

FIGURE 6. *Tropidophora* cf. *aspera* from site 34F. Height 31.8 mm.

FIGURE 7. *Cyathopoma* cf. *pauliani* from site 26F. Height 5.1 mm.

FIGURE 8. *Rachis aldabrae* from site 4A. Height 19.7 mm.

FIGURE 9. *Neritina* sp. from site 44C. Height 12.6 mm.

FIGURE 10. Silicone rubber internal cast of '*Succinea*' from the Picard Calcarenites. Height 6.0 mm.

FIGURE 11. *Melampus* sp. from site 44C. Height 12.3 mm.

FIGURE 12. Ellobiid from site 44C. Height 3.9 mm.

FIGURE 13. *Truncatella* cf. *guerini* from site 26F. Height 6.9 mm.

FIGURE 14. Moulds of *Tropidophora* and rootlets in the Picard Calcarenites.

PLATE 1. For description see opposite.

present in some areas may have been introduced by infiltration (by rainwash) or by mixing by animal activity.

These lower calcarenites were cemented and subjected to solutional erosion for an unknown period before the deposition of a group of soils now restricted in occurrence to a small area at Bassin Cabri. The sediments in these are 10–15 cm thick and occur in three distinct layers. The lowest layer is a fairly homogenous biomicrite packed with ostracods and, towards the top, Foraminifera. It is burrowed and penetrated by rootlet tubules, but filled cavities suggest that it may have been lithified before deposition of the unit above. This is a thin (5–15 mm) white calcarenite and rests upon a well defined erosion surface. It contains fragments of calcareous algae, mollusc shells, Foraminifera and echinoderms, but also includes some chips of bone. There is again evidence of lithification before deposition of the uppermost sediment, a dense brown–white micrite with an anastomosing network of tapering fractures and a crude lamination. This contains abundant ostracods, Foraminifera and moulds of terrestrial snails, together with occasional burrows. The lower part also contains numerous, possibly faecal, pellets.

The fauna

Mollusca. The uppermost bed of the lower calcarenite unit contains abundant moulds of a terrestrial prosobranch snail belonging to the genus *Tropidophora* (plate 1, figure 1) but impossible to identify with certainty to species level.

In the thin soils from the upper sequence, moulds of the small pulmonate snail '*Succinea*' were abundant. Patterson (1975) has demonstrated the impossibility of making specific identifications of this family from shell material alone, but extrapolating from her work it might be expected that the species here belongs to the genus *Quickia*, which is represented by endemic species on Indian Ocean islands.

Vertebrata. All of the vertebrate material recovered came from the lower calcarenite unit.

(1) Tortoise bones are abundant in the upper part of the calcarenite and occur as individual disarticulated bones or, in the Bassin Cabri area, as eroded but probably once complete articulated skeletons. In addition, a lower horizon of the calcarenites in the La Gigi area, about 30 cm above low water level, contained large numbers of shell fragments and other bones which appeared on the outcrop as slot-like moulds. The tortoise bones are indistinguishable from those of *Geochelone gigantea* (Schweigger).

(2) Two teeth thought to belong to *Crocodylus niloticus* (Laurenti) were found in the upper part of the calcarenite in the Bassin Cabri area.

(3) Three pieces of maxilla, two pieces of dentary and a single tooth found at Bassin Cabri were identified as derived from an iguanid lizard *Oplurus*, resembling *O. cuvieri* (Gray). The animals had an estimated body size from snout to vent of about 170 mm.

(4) Many disarticulated bird bones were found at Bassin Cabri. Of these, 15 were identifiable and were ascribed to a species of *Pterodroma*, a gadfly petrel.

(5) A single bone, the distal end of a humerus of a duck described as a new genus *Aldabranas* (Harrison & Walker 1978) and resembling a shelduck.

Environmental interpretation

The sedimentological evidence shows that this deposit represents a prograding sand-cay rising to probably not more than 2 m above sea-level. This was probably extensively vegetated, but the component sediment was not modified and a true soil was not developed. The cay was colonized by tortoises, iguanas and crocodiles with the ground-nesting gadfly petrel probably seasonally abundant (figure 5). The large prosobranch snail *Tropidophora* was extremely abundant, but the heavy shells are resistant to erosion and large numbers could have accumulated over a considerable period. It belongs to a group of species which are characteristic of open dry habitats, such as might develop upon the upper parts of sand cays.

The estimated area of present outcrops (20 km²) was probably inadequate to support the terrestrial vertebrate fauna described. The evidence for a second land area which may have been continuous with the Bassin Cabri islet has been noted, and perhaps the proto-Aldabra platform bore one or two large, or a number of smaller, sand-cays.

FIGURE 5. Sketch impression of the general habitat during the formation of the Picard Calcarenites.

The abundant ostracods and 'Succinea' in the upper soil sequence indicate at least seasonal flooding of a moist, low, grassy habitat, the desiccation cracks suggest perhaps periodic drying of the sediment. The thin marine intercalation may have resulted from a storm influx. Such an environment is not inconsistent with the continuing existence of beach ridges and dune sands similar to those described above, and analogous facies mosaics may be seen in present-day Andros and parts of the Florida Everglades.

The Takamaka deposits

The next group of deposits all post-date the deposition and cementation of the Takamaka Limestone and are believed to pre-date the accumulation of the Aldabra Limestone. However, within these time limits the deposits are not necessarily contemporaneous.

0635.0990, samples 4C10, 11.

This deposit is exposed in a mound in the Bassin Cabri area approximately 20 m long and rising 1.5 m above the general erosion surface. The base of this outcrop is made up of Takamaka Limestone which has a solution-fretted upper surface, with the cavities filled with a fine-grained friable terrestrial sediment.

Sediment

The fine-grained grey–orange sediment consists of amorphous micritic glaebules 0.03–0.3 mm in diameter, with occasional lithoclasts. Glaebules are oval or subspherical in shape, and areas in which they are well-defined grade laterally into dense micrite. Burrows and rootlet moulds are common. This sediment is overlain by a yellow–brown laminated crust which passes gradationally into a paler unlaminated sediment containing large (up to 1 mm) concentrically zoned glaebules bound by a sparry calcite cement. A 'bird's-eye' fabric of spar-filled spaces is common.

Fauna

The lower glaebular soil has yielded an abundant fauna of terrestrial snails: *Truncatella* cf. *guerini*; *Streptostele nevilli*; *Cyathopoma* sp.; and four other unidentified pulmonates.

Environmental interpretation

The sediment gives little information about environmental conditions, other than that the land was rocky with an irregular topography with soils accumulating in cavities. The possible climatic implications of the concentric glaebules have been discussed elsewhere (Braithwaite 1975). The precise mechanism of formation of these bodies is not fully understood, but it may be linked to a marked seasonal variation in rainfall. The gastropod fauna is composed entirely of small species. *Streptostele* and *Cyathopoma* are forms which are associated with an accumulation of leaf litter and insulation from high temperatures. Such conditions are found in high scrub with a dense canopy which has been established long enough to develop a litter layer. *Truncatella* is a group which now has a wide distribution on the Atoll, but is typically found close to the sea; however, shells can be passively transported considerable distances.

3368.0545, sample 26F.

At this site, cavities in the irregular, fretted upper surface of the Takamaka Limestone contain an earthy brown filling.

Sediment

The sediment is poorly sorted and texturally disorganized, with cavities formed by differential compaction. Some parts consist of amorphous or concentrically zoned glaebules (0.1–0.5 mm) set in a sparry cement, others of apparently amorphous micrite. Burrows 1 mm in diameter are present containing ovoid faecal pellets.

Fauna

The site contains abundant terrestrial gastropods including: *Truncatella guerini*; *Tropidophora* sp.; *Assiminea* sp.; *Rachis aldabrae*; 'Succinea' sp.; *Gulella peakei*; and one unidentified pulmonate.

Environmental interpretation

The habitat at this site was an irregular rocky surface with soil accumulating in pockets. The diverse gastropod fauna suggests a wider range of habitats than in 4C10. The presence of *Succinea*, *Tropidophora* and *Rachis aldabrae* suggests open habitats varying from low vegetation with periodic flooding to drier habitats with open scrub. *Rachis aldabrae* is an arboreal species now frequently associated with *Euphorbia pyrifolia*, a shrub typical of 'edge' habitats. *Assiminea*, like *Truncatella*, is now found close to the sea. Thus there is again indirect evidence of transport of material from a number of different habitats. The presence of ovoid faecal pellets and burrows could indicate the presence of an organism associated with the breakdown of litter, similar to the millipede *Spirobolus* recorded from the Atoll today (Spaull 1976).

1858.1288 and 1858.0238, samples 39A, D.

At localities north of Dune d'Messe, the irregular fretted surface of the Takamaka Limestone is overlain by small patches of buff, friable, terrestrial sediments.

Sediment

Individual outcrops are quite variable. Some sediments contain uncompressed but poorly preserved rootlets and others abundant ovoid faecal pellets and burrows. In some cases they are overlain by up to 5 cm of a dense micritic laminated crust with discrete mamillated or pisolitic horizons. Numerous filaments are present within some sediments, which may be borings. Crusts and 'soils' contain terrestrial snails. In some cavities these early sediments are overlain by a fine-grained calcarenite with well preserved marine molluscs.

Fauna

The terrestrial sediments have yielded an extensive snail fauna, of which the most common members are *Tropidophora* and *Cyathopoma*, but it includes: *Tropidophora* sp.; *Otopoma flexilabris*; *Assiminea* sp.; *Cyathopoma* cf. *pauliani*; *Cyathopoma* sp.; *Rachis aldabrae*; *Gulella gwendolinae*; and *Gulella peakei*.

Environmental interpretation

The snail fauna from these samples is less restricted that for site 26F. The presence of *Tropidophora* and *Rachis* suggest patchy scrub or edge zone habitats, although van Bruggen (1975) comments that species similar to *Gulella peakei* are restricted to forest habitats in Africa.

0635.0990, sample 4A23.

A small outcrop in the Bassin Cabri area contained a sediment similar to 39A, D, and rested upon an irregular surface of Takamaka Limestone. It contained the following terrestrial molluscs: *Truncatella guerini*; *Tropidophora* sp.; *Otopoma flexilabris*; *Cyathopoma* cf. *pauliani*; *Cyathopoma* sp.; *Rachis aldabrae*; and *Gulella* sp. This is a similar fauna to 39A, D, although the presence of *Truncatella* indicates close proximity to the sea.

2633.0418, sample 44C.

This is a complex bedded deposit (figure 4) found in a small area immediately to the north of Dune Jean-Louis. It clearly overlies the Takamaka Limestone, but underlies, at least in part, the Aldabra Limestone.

Sediment

Borings in the planated Takamaka Limestone surface are filled by a hard fine-grained calcarenite containing *Halimeda*, lithothamnioid algae and some molluscan shell fragments. Overlying this is a soft light brown friable sediment which is basically micritic but which contains some indistinctly pelleted areas. In addition to abundant terrestrial molluscs there are rock fragments, and some areas are penetrated by laminated pedotubules, probably rootlets. The terrestrial sediment is overlain by a second hard, well cemented erosion surface, bored by *Cliona* and polychaetes, and encrusted by algae and Foraminifera.

Evidence from other sites around the atoll suggests that this deposit represents a brief terrestrial interlude during the deposition of the lowest part of the Aldabra Limestone. Unfossiliferous calcarenites in the Bras Takamaka area and beach deposits at Passe Houareau may be contemporaneous.

Fauna

The fauna recovered from the chalky soil consists of abundant terrestrial molluscs with *Tropidophora*, *Truncatella* and *Melampus* prominent: *Truncatella guerini*; *Tropidophora* sp; *Cyathopoma* sp.; *Neritina* sp.; and *Melampus* sp.

Environmental interpretation

The presence of abundant *Melampus* and *Truncatella* in this deposit indicates a close proximity to the sea. The abundant *Tropidophora* suggest a low dry scrub vegetation, with *Cyathopoma* suggesting patches of denser scrub, while the occurrence of *Neritina* means the presence of standing bodies of fresh water.

3143.1193, sample 30A; 3195.1173, sample 32B; 3318.1058, sample 33B.

At these three sites, deposits fill small cavities which cut the Takamaka Limestone, but are overlain by Aldabra Limestone. They yielded fragmentary bones of *Geochelone*. The sediments are dense and micritic with local crumb-like aggregates. Some areas contain well-preserved roots, and the sediment clearly functioned as a soil. Elsewhere, however, (32B4), there is evidence of extensive reworking during an intermittant deposition.

Post-Aldabra Limestone deposits

This series of deposits post-dates the Aldabra Limestone but probably includes sediments of widely differing ages within the 125 ka interval.

2928.1090, sample 34F.

This outcrop consists of the deposit filling a single cavity about 1 m deep and 1.5 m in diameter. This cuts both the Takamaka Limestone and about 30 cm of hard calcarenite believed to be a lower facies of the Aldabra Limestone.

Sediment

Large, commonly broken, shells of *Tropidophora* cf. *aspera* are the dominant element in this sediment. They are contained within a dark brown micritic sediment with micropellets and scattered larger grains. Rootlets preserved in calcite are common.

Fauna

The fauna extracted from this deposit consists of an abundant and diverse association of terrestrial molluscs. The large ribbed shells of *Tropidophora aspera* are the most conspicuous elements, but some of these shells were packed with hundreds of smaller shells, which also occurred, less commonly, in the matrix. Species found were: *Truncatella guerini*; *Tropidophora* cf. *aspera*; *Cyathopoma* cf. *pauliani*; *Cyathopoma* sp.; *Assiminea* sp.; *Rachis aldabrae*; *Gulella gwendolinae*; *Gulella peakei*; *Gulella insulicola*; *Gulella* sp.; and five other unidentified pulmonates.

Environmental interpretation

The occurrence of the large *Tropidophora* in this sediment in closely packed masses could represent accumulation over a number of years, or an aestivating group which died within a particular solution cavity. Similarly, the smaller species, by virtue of their high density and unbroken appearance, may have used the larger dead shells as refuges. Their general paucity in the matrix sediment suggests that this may have been added at a slightly later date, possibly by rainwash, but clearly the loosely aggregated mass became colonized by higher plants and penetrated by their roots. The fauna in general indicates a wide range of habitats from well developed, open wood and scrub with litter formation and insulation, while the presence of *Rachis aldabrae* indicates open or 'edge' habitats, and *Truncatella* the proximity of the sea.

3005.1225, sample 31.

This deposit fills a solution pipe 2 m deep and 0.5 m in width, penetrating the Aldabra Limestone and exposed on the 3.5–4 m high cliffs. The sediment can be seen to be crudely bedded with laminae draped against pit margins.

Sediment

The sediment is a pale, friable, highly porous calcarenite with visible rootlet moulds. It has a poorly sorted heterogeneous texture, the smaller fraction consisting of 0.15 mm diameter round or irregular glaebules, probably of faecal origin, with a few which are concentric. The coarser fraction consists of lithoclasts and bioclasts which include abundant coral and *Halimeda* fragments and bones. Rootlets are not common, but algal filaments are abundant between the grains. There is no obvious precipitated cement.

Fauna

This deposit has yielded a single bone of *Geochelone* as well as abundant but mostly fragmentary terrestrial snails, *Otopoma* being the most common. They include: *Truncatella guerini*; *Otopoma flexilabris*; *Cyathopoma* cf. *pauliani*; '*Succinea*' sp.; *Rachis aldabrae*; *Streptostele nevilli*; and *Gulella gwendolinae*.

Environmental interpretation

At least some of the elements in this fauna indicate open habitats with at least seasonal moist conditions; *Streptostele* and *Cyathopoma* are, however, associated with denser scrub and litter development. Periodic, perhaps seasonal, sediment increments are also indicated by the crudely bedded nature of the deposit. The wetter periods were probably characterized by the growth of filamentous algae and the activity of the organisms producing pellets.

4025.0930, sample 20B, Point Hodoul.

In the Point Hodoul area there is an unusually large number of pipe-fill deposits. These can be seen in the cliff line penetrating the Aldabra Limestone, but about 200 m inland in an area of land-enclosed tidal pools, many such deposits have been exposed as residual pinnacles, and bones derived from them litter the present pool floors.

Sediments

The pipe-fill deposits consist of brown earthy sediment containing abundant, but largely comminuted, bones and limestone fragments. The matrix has an open friable texture and consists in general of pellets (0.1 mm diam.), sometimes grouped into crumb-like aggregates, and structureless micritic areas cut by tapering shrinkage fractures. Intraclasts similar to the host soil are common and indicate more than one cycle of deposition. Tubules of rootlets and small burrows are common. The bones range in size from tiny fragments 8–10 mm in diameter to unbroken limb elements, but they often occur as densely packed aggregates of small splinters. The cement in general is a clear granular calcite but local inclusions suggest that an early stalagmite-like cement may have been present. In a few samples small areas of a late dahllite cement are present.

Fauna

A large and diverse vertebrate fauna is present within these deposits:

(1) Abundant tortoise bones similar to *Geochelone gigantea*.

(2) Many bones of crocodiles identical with *Crocodylus niloticus* are present; these include pre-maxillae, maxillae, jugals, frontals, parietals, teeth, vertebrae and osteodermal scutes. The bones seem to have been derived from animals 2.33–2.4 m in length, smaller in general than adults in normal mainland populations but dwarf assemblages are known (Cott 1961). The sample may, of course, be biased.

(3) Lizard bones are common in some of the deposits and six species have been recognized. These are reported upon in more detail by Arnold (1976) and are summarized below.

Iguanidae:
Oplurus cf. *O. cuvieri* (Gray)
7 bones, total length of animal estimated at 570–680 mm.

Gekkonidae:
Geckolepis cf. *G. maculata* Peters
54 bones, general estimated size 90–100 mm from snout to vent.
Paroedura cf. *P. stumpfii* group
598 bones, animals estimated snout to vent length 90–100 mm.
Phelsuma sp.
4 fragments, distinct from *P. abbotti* (Stejneger) present on Aldabra today. Estimated size of animal from snout to vent 50 mm.

Scincidae:
'*Scelotes*' sp.
437 bones similar to those of *S. johannae* Gunther and *S. valhallae* Boulenger from Glorioso.

Mabuya maculabris (Gray)

18 bones from animals with an estimated snout to vent length of 80–95 mm.

(4) A single bone was found, the distal end of a right metatarsus 17–7 mm long, typical of *Dryolimnas cuvieri*, the rail (Harrison & Walker 1978).

(5) In addition to these vertebrate remains occasional broken fragments of the snails *Tropidophora* and two specimens of *Cyathopoma* were recovered from the matrix.

FIGURE 6. Sketch impression of the general habitat at the time of the formation of the Point Hodoul cavity-fill deposits (20B).

Environmental interpretation

It is clear that at the time of formation of these deposits, the Point Hodoul area was rocky, intensely pot-holed, and close to the sea (figure 6). The densely packed aggregations of bones are suggestive of winnowing and concentration by flowing water, indicating a high rainfall. However, fragments are angular and unworn, and this indicates that transport was minimal. Both tortoises and crocodiles could have fallen into open pits and been trapped. This is a frequent occurrence with the tortoises on Aldabra today, but does not account for the very high concentration of bone fragments nor for the level of breakage and lack of even partial articulation. The lizard bones appear to be concentrated in particular cavities and are unlikely to have accumulated by pit-fall trapping. It is possible that they represent the food residue of some predator; such situations are known from the West Indies where accumulations of small vertebrate fossils have been attributed to the activities of owls (Etheridge 1965). No owl bones or the remains of any other comparable predator have been found at Point Hodoul or elsewhere on Aldabra, but both very small and very large bones are rare, and it may be significant that a high proportion of the individuals represent nocturnal species. No owls are present on Aldabra today, but the Barn owl *Tyto alba* (Scopoli) has become extinct there since 1906 (Benson & Penny 1971).

The presence of crocodiles suggest a sea level close to or slightly higher than at present, with subaerial solution producing a few relatively large pits rather than the highly irregular, delicately fretted, surface characteristic of coastal areas today. A higher rainfall may be indicated.

3380.1028, sample 33D.

Scattered around the atoll are a fairly large number of small resistant pinnacles of cavity deposits which are distinguished by their pinkish red–brown colour. The pipes containing these deposits cut both the Takamaka Limestone and the Aldabra Limestone. Ilot Rose (33D) is a typical example of such deposits.

Sediment

The rock is a breccia with a light brown to pinkish red–brown earthy matrix enclosing bone fragments, limestone blocks, travertine fragments and other lithoclasts. In section the matrix is micritic, but it is almost entirely pelleted. A few areas have a crudely laminated structure which may be algal.

Fauna

These deposits contain abundant fragments of bone, all the identifiable pieces of which seem to be *Geochelone gigantea*.

Environmental interpretation

These sediments may be compared with those forming on the atoll at the present day in solution pits inhabited by the crab *Cardisoma carnifex* (Herbst). In these pits tortoise bones may be derived from animals which fall in accidentally, and tufa and limestone blocks may become detached from pit margins. However, in the Ilot Rose deposits, bones are disarticulated and broken to a degree which the activities of the crustacean scavengers does not adequately explain. There is further the important point that modern *Cardisoma* pits commonly contain few bones. The sediments are unbedded and, if incremental, have been subject to a re-working which obscures increment boundaries.

PRESENT DAY ENVIRONMENTS

Aldabra today is a series of rocky islands surrounding a large central lagoon. The limestones are intensely dissected and soil accumulation is generally limited to cavities and depressions within the rock surface. Sand dunes and perched beach deposits are small in extent and are only significant along the south coast. The Atoll is generally covered by a low scrub vegetation with varying density of cover, open areas of coastal turf being present along the southern and easterly shores. The lagoon shores are fringed with dense mangroves.

The terrestrial flora comprises 190 species, of which 44 are believed to have been introduced by man and 18 are endemic. Most plants are coastal bush or supralittoral forms, many of them widespread palaeo- and pantropical varieties. A small but significant proportion are derived specifically from the Afro-Oriental and Madagascar regions.

Among the land fauna those forms which are potentially fossilizable include the giant tortoise

Geochelone gigantea and three species of lizards. The latter comprise two geckos, *Phelsuma abbotti* Stejneger and *Hemidactylus mercatorius* Gray, and a skink, *Cryptoblepharus boutonii* (Desjardins). The bird fauna includes 14 species of breeding land birds with two endemic species (Benson & Penny 1971), 14 regular migrant waders, and 10 species of breeding sea birds. The terrestrial snail fauna consists of 14 species, most of which are rather small.

TABLE 1. DISTRIBUTION OF FOSSIL REPTILES AND BIRDS IN THE ALDABRA TERRESTRIAL DEPOSITS

	4C1,2	4C10	26F	39A,D	4A23	44C	30A	20B	33D	34F	31	present
reptiles												
Geochelone gigantea (Schweigger)	*				*	*	*			*		*
Crocodylus niloticus Laurenti	*							*				
Oplurus cf. *cuvieri* (Gray)	*							*				
Paroedura sp.								*				
Geckolepis cf. *maculata* Peters								*				
Mabuya cf. *maculabris* (Gray)								*				
Scelotes sp.								*				
Phelsuma sp.								*				
Phelsuma abbotti (Stejneger)												*
Hemidactylus mercatorius (Gray)												*
Cryptoblepharus boutoni (Desjardins)												*
Birds												
Pterodroma sp.	*											
Aldabranas sp.	*											
Dryolimnas cuvieri (Pucheran)								*				*

       marine incursion   marine incursion

DISCUSSION

Although the position of the sea relative to the land, and hence the land area, of Aldabra has been constantly changing with time, the major events affecting the terrestrial biota were the complete inundations of the Atoll by the sea. These occurred during Takamaka Limestone times, later during the deposition of the Aldabra Limestone (125 ka B.P.) and possibly in post-Aldabra Limestone times (100–80 ka B.P.) during the formation of the + 8 m terrace. On each of these occasions the terrestrial biota must have been completely eliminated. The data on the fossil terrestrial fauna are summarized in tables 1 and 2 and arranged in an approximate time sequence. The fossil terrestrial gastropods provide the best evidence of habitat type and they divide into four clear groups:

(1) Maritime habitats in close proximity to the sea with snails just above storm levels: *Truncatella* and *Assiminea*.

(2) Open habitats, with freshwater flooding and standing fresh water: '*Succinea*' and *Neritina*.

(3) Open habitats, consisting of thick grass, open scrub or edge habitats: *Tropidophora*, *Rachis aldabrae*, *Otopoma flexilabris* and *Gulella gwendolinae aldabrae*.

(4) Denser scrub, providing insulation, tending towards a closed canopy with some soil development and moist conditions: *Cyathopoma*, *Streptostele nevilli*, *Gulella peakei*, Ereptinae.

The Picard Calcarenites, interpreted as originating on a low sand cay, represent a habitat of small importance on Aldabra today, and were probably similar to some existing low atolls. By contrast, all of the other deposits indicate dissected rocky substrates, meagre soil formation perhaps concentrated by rain-wash, and scrub vegetation, features which probably differed very little from Aldabra today. Evidence of cave systems, groove and buttress structures and other erosional features (Braithwaite *et al.* 1973; Barnes *et al.* 1971) indicates that at times the rainfall was probably higher than that of the present day.

The present biota of the atoll has colonized Aldabra since 80–100 ka B.P., previous terrestrial faunas having been eliminated by marine inundation. During this period, since the last high sea level stand, the land area of Aldabra has undergone quite drastic changes in size, the most

TABLE 2. DISTRIBUTION OF FOSSIL MOLLUSCA IN THE ALDABRA TERRESTRIAL DEPOSITS

	4C1, 2	4C10	26F	39A, D	4A23	44C	30A	20B	33D	34F	31	present
terrestrial												
Truncatella guerini A. & J. B. Villa		*	*		*	*		*		*	*	*
Tropidophora – small	*		*	*				*				*
Tropidophora – medium					*							
T. cf. *aspera* (large) Potiez & Michaud										*		
Otopoma flexilabris Sowerby				*						*		
Cyathopoma cf. *pauliani* F. Salvat			*	*				*		*	*	*
Cyathopoma sp.		*	*	*	*					*		
Assiminea spp.		*	*							*		*
Rachis aldabrae Martens		*	*	*						*		*
'Succinea' cf. *Quickia*	*	*									*	*
Streptostele nevilli H. Adams		*									*	*
Gulella gwendolinae aldabrae van Bruggen		*	*								*	*
Gulella peakei van Bruggen		*	*							*		
Gulella insulicola van Bruggen										*		
Gulella sp.					*					*		
Pulmonate sp. A		*								*		
Pulmonate sp. B		*										
Pulmonate sp. C										*		
Unidentified species	3	2	1	1						3	1	
Gastrocopta microscopica Nevill												*
Lamellaxis gracilis Hutton												*
Kaliella sp.												*
freshwater												
Neritina sp.							*					
Bulinus bavayi (Dautzenberg)												*
littoral fringe												
Ellobiacea							*			*		*

marine incursion   marine incursion

recent being the breaching of the lagoon perhaps 5 ka ago. Aldabra, in common with low atolls but in contrast to the higher igneous islands of the Indian Ocean (which have not been submerged since their formation), exhibits a low degree of endemism, with a vegetation consisting largely of maritime lowland species. Faunal size is about what might be expected for an atoll the size of Aldabra, and Peake (1971, fig. 9) has shown for terrestrial molluscs a clear distinction in faunal size that exists between the high and low islands of the western Indian Ocean.

The main point to emerge from this study is that in the history of Aldabra there has been considerable faunal turnover, with periods of extinction followed by recolonization, the most spectacular of the colonists being the giant tortoise. Two problems emerge: first the origin of the faunal propagules and secondly the method of dispersal.

The data from Aldabra provide a salutary warning of interpreting past distributions from the present, but it is possible that faunal turnover on higher islands is not as great as on small remote atolls. Within the fossil fauna of Aldabra it is possible to see affinities with Madagascar (in birds, reptiles and some terrestrial molluscs) and with other islands such as the Comores (reptiles and molluscs); some forms have widespread island distributions while others have African mainland affinities. It is interesting that the Atoll is not completely dominated by present day African and Madagascan taxa. This may be attributable to the presence during some of Pleistocene time of other land areas of considerable size. There is a considerable literature concerning methods of dispersal, but many accounts appear to reflect subjective judgements regarding the probability of successful dispersal by a particular method. Nevertheless, whatever methods are employed, they are obviously successful. As Peake (1969) has emphasized, no particular method must be considered exclusive to any taxon. In the case of island faunas, much attention has been paid to methods of dispersal in the Pacific region, where there is a wide variety of island types with varying degrees of isolation and a range of taxa which have successfully colonized islands. Three methods of dispersal, namely by wind, birds and sea, have received the most attention.

Peake (1969) and later Vagvolgyi (1975) have analysed terrestrial molluscan faunas from the Pacific and found that a large proportion of island snails are small in size, and that the more isolated islands are colonized by the smaller species. The basic conclusion of these observations is that aerial dispersal by wind is a major mechanism. The molluscan fauna of Aldabra is predominantly small and therefore, extrapolating from the Pacific, many species probably arrived by wind dispersal. Constant wind movements are not required. The main problem could be that of becoming airborne in strong winds and storms, with then a very slow rate of descent, even in light winds. Dispersal by birds is often cited, but its importance is very difficult to assess; species which are frequently found upon birds' feathers have sticky mucus, for example *Vitrina pellucida* (see review by Rees 1965). Marine dispersal of molluscs by rafting can be considered for those species which are frequently found in littoral habitats, and are thus resistant to seawater. In the operculate taxa, the operculum isolates the snail from the surrounding medium, and it is possible to consider these and even the large thick shelled *Tropidophora aspera* as perhaps being dispersed by sea. In the case of the reptile fauna, seaborne dispersal is the only obvious mechanism.

The giant tortoise has had an almost continuous presence in the terrestrial deposits, and has obviously managed to colonize the Atoll on at least three occasions. In historical times the tortoise was present in vast numbers on other western Indian Ocean islands (Rothschild 1915), but was extinct everywhere except on Aldabra by about 1830 (Stoddart & Peake 1979, this volume). Recolonization from higher islands such as the Seychelles, Comores, or northern Madagascar would have been feasible, but ocean current considerations suggest that Madagascar would have been the most likely origin (see Arnold 1979, this volume). Tortoises are extremely buoyant, and on Aldabra today they frequently make excursions on to the shore to feed upon intertidal debris. It is not unusual at high spring tides in mangrove areas to see tortoises floating around. Grubb (1971) has pointed out that the distribution of tortoises of the *Geochelone* group on isolated islands in the Indian Ocean, Galápagos, Celebes and West Indies clearly indicates that they are able to survive trans-oceanic crossings better than any other large tetrapod. The remains of *Crocodylus niloticus* present in the Picard and Point Hodoul deposits represent two successful colonizations of Aldabra. Crocodiles were probably eliminated either by the higher sea level stand which cut the + 8 m terrace, or by the restriction of habitat consequent upon the depressed sea level of the last glacial maximum. Crocodiles are present today on the East African coast and in Madagascar, and were once found upon both the Comores and the Seychelles. They became extinct in the Seychelles only at the end of the eighteenth century and, according to Lionnet (1970), early visitors to the islands found them abundant, some occurring far out to sea. Marine transport of crocodiles is well known. Wood-Jones (1909) for example, records two *Crocodylus porosus* which had made a trans-oceanic journey of 965 km (600 miles).

The iguana *Oplurus* was present during deposition of the Picard Calcarenites and the Point Hodoul terrestrial sediments and had obviously made more than one colonization. However, apart from this species, we have no record of lizards other than those in the extensive Point Hodoul fauna. Here, at least six species of lizard of Comoran or Madagascan affinities had managed to colonize the Atoll after the high sea level stand of the Aldabra Limestone. The pipe-fill deposits in which they are contained are truncated, possibly by the + 8 m but certainly by the + 4 m terraces, and these high sea level stands were probably responsible for the extinction of the lizards. None of the six species named is present on the Atoll today. By contrast, Williams (1969), considers that the four species of *Anolis* lizards found now on the small island north of Bimini (Bahamas) represent a residual concentration from their former extent over the now submerged Great Bahamas Bank during the last glaciation. As has been mentioned before, tortoises and crocodiles can make trans-oceanic voyages by virtue of their natural buoyancy. Lizards, on the other hand, although they appear able to disperse relatively easily, obviously require some form of rafting. Successful colonization of oceanic islands by lizards must necessarily be rare events (Williams 1969).

At present, large rafts of floating vegetation, consisting mainly of bamboo, are fairly frequent arrivals at Aldabra. Their provenance is unknown, but northern Madagascar could be considered a likely source. The distance from northern Madagascar to Aldabra is approximately 420 km and, with surface currents running in a fairly constant northwesterly direction at 0.5–1.0 m/s, the journey time to Aldabra could be as short as 3–9 days. Although no vertebrates have yet been found on such rafts, the number examined before or upon arrival is small.

We are grateful to the Royal Society for the opportunity of working at Aldabra, and to the Royal Society staff both in London and on the Atoll for assistance in many ways. Dr C. J. O. Harrison and Mr C. A. Walker kindly provided information on the fossil bird material, Mr P. Auber helped with the preparation of the fossil mollusca, Mr P. Richens and Ms K. Way took the photographs.

References (Taylor *et al.*)

Arnold, E. N. 1976 Fossil reptiles from Aldabra Atoll, Indian Ocean. *Bull. Br. Mus. nat. Hist. (Zool.)* **29**, 85–116.

Arnold, E. N. 1979 Indian Ocean giant tortoises: their systematics and island adaptations. *Phil. Trans. R. Soc. Lond.* B **286**, 127–145 (this volume).

Barnes, J., Bellamy, D. J., Jones, D. J., Whitton, B. A., Drew, E. A., Kenyon, L., Lythgoe, J. N. & Rosen, B. R. 1971 Morphology and ecology of the reef front of Aldabra. *Symp. zool. Soc. Lond.* **28**, 87–114.

Benson, C. W. & Penny, M. J. 1971 The land birds of Aldabra. *Phil. Trans. R. Soc. Lond.* B **260**, 417–527.

Bloom, A. L., Broecker, W. S., Chappell, J. M. A., Matthews, R. K. & Mesolella, K. J. 1974 Quaternary sea level fluctuations on a tectonic coast. New ^{230}Th/^{234}U dates from the Huon Peninsula, New Guinea. *Quat. Res.* **4**, 185–205.

Braithwaite, C. J. R. 1975 Petrology of palaeosols and other terrestrial sediments on Aldabra, western Indian Ocean. *Phil. Trans. R. Soc. Lond.* B **273**, 1–32.

Braithwaite, C. J. R., Taylor, J. D. & Kennedy, W. J. 1973 The evolution of an atoll: the depositional and erosional history of Aldabra. *Phil. Trans. R. Soc. Lond.* B **266**, 307–340.

van Bruggen, A. C. 1975 Streptaxidae (Mollusca, Gastropoda: Pulmonata) from Aldabra Island, western Ocean. *Bull. Br. Mus. nat. Hist. (Zool.)* **27**, 157–175.

Cott, H. B. 1961 Scientific results of an enquiry into the ecology and economic status of the Nile crocodile (*Crocodilus niloticus*) in Uganda and Northern Rhodesia. *Trans. zool. Soc. Lond.* **29**, 211-350.

Emiliani, C. 1971 The amplitude of Pleistocene climatic cycles at low latitudes, and the isotopic composition of glacial ice. In *The late Cenozoic glacial ages* (ed. K. K. Turekian), pp. 183–197. New Haven: Yale University Press.

Etheridge, R. 1965 Fossil lizards from the Dominican Republic. *Q. Jl Fla. Acad. Sci.* **28**, 83–105.

Fryer, J. C. F. 1911 The structure and formation of Aldabra and neighbouring islands – with notes on their flora and fauna. *Trans. Linn. Soc. Lond.* **14**, 397–442.

Grubb, P. 1971 The growth, ecology and population structure of giant tortoises on Aldabra. *Phil. Trans. R. Soc. Lond.* B **260**, 327–372.

Harrison, C. J. O. & Walker, C. A. 1978 Pleistocene bird remains from Aldabra Atoll, Indian Ocean. *J. nat. Hist.* **12**, 7–14.

Ladd, H. S. 1958 Fossil land shells from western Pacific atolls. *J. Palaeont.* **32**, 183–198.

Leopold, E. B. 1969 Miocene pollen and spore flora of Eniwetok Atoll, Marshall Islands. *Prof. Pap. U.S. geol. Surv.* 260–11, pp. 1133–1185.

Lionnet, J. F. G. 1970 *A short history of the Seychelles.* Victoria: Saint Fidèle.

MacArthur, R. H. & Wilson, E. O. 1967 *The theory of island biogeography.* Princeton, New Jersey: Princeton University Press.

Patterson, C. M. 1975 *Quickia aldabrensis* (Mollusca, Gastropoda: Pulmonata, Succineidae), a new species of land snail from Aldabra Atoll, western Indian Ocean. *Bull. Br. Mus. nat. Hist. (Zool.)* **27**, 176–185.

Peake, J. F. 1969 Patterns in the distribution of Melanesian land mollusca. *Phil. Trans. R. Soc. Lond.* B **255**, 285–306.

Peake, J. F. 1971 The evolution of terrestrial faunas in the western Indian Ocean. *Phil. Trans. R. Soc. Lond.* B **260**, 581–610.

Rees, W. J. 1965 The aerial dispersal of mollusca. *Proc. malac. Soc. Lond.* **36**, 269–282.

Rothschild, W. 1915 On the gigantic land tortoises of the Seychelles and Aldabra–Mascarene group with some notes on certain forms of the Mascarene group. *Novit. zool.* **22**, 418–422.

Spaull, V. W. 1976 The life history and post-embryonic development of '*Spirobolus*' *bivirgatus* (Diplopoda: Spirobolida) on Aldabra, western Indian Ocean. *J. Zool., London.* **180**, 391–405.

Steinen, R. P., Harrison, R. S. & Matthews, R. K. 1973 Eustatic low stand of sea-level between 125,000 and 105,000 B.P.: Evidence from the sub-surface of Barbados, West Indies. *Bull. geol. Soc. Am.* **84**, 63–70.

Stoddart, D. R. 1973 Coral reefs: the last two million years. *Geography* **58**, 313–323.

Stoddart, D. R. 1976 Continuity and crisis in the reef community. *Micronesica* **12**, 1–9.

Stoddart, D. R., Taylor, J. D., Fosberg, F. R. & Farrow, G. E. 1971 Geomorphology of Aldabra Atoll. *Phil. Trans. R. Soc. Lond.* B **260**, 31–65.

Thompson, J. & Walton, A. 1972 Redetermination of chronology of Aldabra Atoll by ^{230}Th/^{234}U dating. *Nature, Lond.* **240**, 145–146.

Trudgill, S. T. 1976*a* The marine erosion of limestones on Aldabra Atoll, Indian Ocean. *Z. Geomorph., Suppl.* **26**, 164–200.

Trudgill, S. T. 1976*b* The subaerial and subsoil erosion of limestones on Aldabra Atoll, Indian Ocean. *Z. Geomorph. Suppl.* **26**, 201–210.

Vagvolgyi, J. 1975 Body size, aerial dispersal, and origin of the Pacific land snail fauna. *Syst. Zool.* **24**, 465–488.

Williams, E. E. 1969 The ecology of colonization as seen in the zoo geography of Anoline lizards on small islands. *Q. Rev. Biol.* **44**, 345–389.

Wood-Jones, F. 1909 The fauna of Cocos-Keeling Atoll, collected by F. Wood-Jones. *Proc. zool. Soc. Lond.* **1909**, 132–160.

Phil. Trans. R. Soc. Lond. B. **286**, 67–77 (1979) [67]
Printed in Great Britain

The soils of Aldabra

By S. T. Trudgill

Department of Geography, University of Sheffield, Sheffield S10 2TN, U.K.

The soils of Aldabra are of patchy distribution, consisting of pockets of either accumulated organic matter or of biogenic mineral detritus. The soils are shallow (10–20 cm) but locally deeper and more extensive soil covers do occur. Organic covers occur under well established *Casuarina* stands and mineral soil covers occur on the floors of rock basins or where sands are present. The organic soils originate from leaf litter, with local increments of faecal material and bird remains. The mineral soils are primarily carbonate and are derived mechanically from carbonate rocks, from windblown bioclastic carbonate grains or from terrestrial sediments. Solution residues and phosphatic particles also contribute to these soils.

Attempts are made to cross-correlate existing soil information, and several organic and carbonate soil types can be recognized. These are: shallow organic (including litter, pellet and guano varieties); deep organic; calcarenaceous bioclastic soils; brown (silt or silt loam) carbonate soils (including a phosphatic variety) and a widespread organic brown carbonate soil.

The soils may be slightly acid but are mostly circumneutral or alkaline; high salinity may occur in coastal locations. Phosphate levels are usually low.

Insufficient profile data are available at present to define soil type in any rigorous way and the spatial distribution of soil types is only scantily known.

Introduction

The purpose of this paper is to review and consolidate the existing work on Aldabra soils. Of particular interest are (1) the establishment of a classificatory framework which may be of use to other research workers, (2) the origin of the soils and (3) their ecological significance. The paper considers terrestrial soils. Marine (mangrove) soils are not discussed. The formation of palaeosols and other terrestrial sediments is discussed by Braithwaite (1975). These are not discussed here, except where they influence present day soils.

The extent of well developed soils on Aldabra is limited. The soils are often little more than leaf litter mixed with fragments of carbonate rock and show only rudimentary horizonation. As such they may be viewed as immature. They have a discontinuous distribution and are often shallow (of the order of 10–20 cm and frequently as low as 1–2 cm in thickness).

The carbonate rocks which are the commonest soil parent materials are relatively pure, insoluble residues, commonly being in the region of 1–2 % by mass, only locally rising to 10–20 %. Carbonate dissolution thus leads to only slow formation of residual soils. Often only unaggregated and unconsolidated carbonate sediments or phosphatic sediments form the skeletal grains of the soil material. The soils are generally carbonate rich and mostly alkaline or circumneutral, though slightly acid soils do occur.

Variations in the types and amounts of organic and mineral matter can be used to differentiate soil types. At the present state of knowledge it is not possible to ascribe the soils to soil series in any consistent manner. A soil series can be defined as a group of profiles with similar successions of horizons developed in lithologically similar parent materials. Assignation to a series thus involves an extensive study of complete soil profiles to ascertain whether they have similar characteristics. A type profile should be described so that the series can be consistently recognized in the field. This type of information is not yet available for many parts of the island. Much of the area would be classified as 'rock dominant' in terms of many soil mapping

TABLE 1. ANALYTICAL METHODS USED

(1) Carbonates: Collins calcimeter.
(2) Loss on ignition on carbonate free sample (acid washed); percentage given as of whole sample.
(3) pH: laboratory pH meter, 1:2.5, in distilled water.
(4) Phosphate: colour comparator with the use of ammonium molybdate on an $NaHCO_3$ extract of fresh soil, results as PO_4 (extractable, not total, phosphate).
(5) Colour: Munsell Colour, soil colour chart.

TABLE 2. HORIZON NOMENCLATURE USED IN PROFILE DESCRIPTION

L	Litter layer. Plant remains recognizable.
F	Fermentation layer. Plant remains partly decomposed.
H	Humus layer. Plant remains mostly unrecognizable.
A	Mixed mineral–organic horizon.
Ah	A horizon with large proportion of humus material.
B	Mineral horizon, altered by weathering/pedogenesis.
B(ca)	Calcareous B horizon.
C	Parent material, unconsolidated material.
R	Parent material, bedrock.

TABLE 3. SELECTED DATA FOR SOIL TYPES

	soil type†	location	vegetation	rock type‡	soil depth cm	soil colour	pH§	carbon-ates	per-centage organic	phos-phate mg/g
1	OS	Takamaka	*Ficus*	Takamaka Lst.	10	10 YR 3/3	7.2	11.5	36.7	0.0
2	OS	Middle Camp	*Casuarina* and shrubs	Aldabra Lst.	10	10 YR 5/2	7.5	17.0	56.4	0.1
3	OS	Middle Camp	*Casuarina* and shrubs	Aldabra Lst.	10	10 YR 4/2	6.5	3.5	73.6	0.01
4	OSP	Takamaka	*Thespesia*	Takamaka Lst.	10	10 YR 3/3	7.4	2.0	48.5	0.0
5	OSG	Gionnet	—	Aldabra Lst.	10	2.5 YR 6/2	7.0	19.0	76.0	1–5
6	OD	Middle Camp	*Casuarina*	Aldabra Lst.	20	10 YR 5/2	7.4	19.0	77.0	0.5–1.0
7	OD	Picard	*Casuarina*	Aldabra Lst.	20	5 YR 3/2	6.4	0.3	99.7	0.8–0.9
8	OD	Picard	*Casuarina*	Aldabra Lst.	20	5 YR 2/2	7.1	0.7	90.3	0.8–0.9
9	OD	Middle Camp	*Casuarina*	Aldabra Lst.	20	7.5 YR 4/2	7.5	27.5	76.9	<0.1
10	OD	Picard	*Casuarina*	Aldabra Lst.	25	7.5 YR 3/2	7.6	8.0	49.5	0.1
11	CA	Dune Jean-Louis	—	dune sand	10	7.5 YR 8/0	7.9	82.0	0.9	tr.
12	CB	Middle Camp	*Casuarina* and shrubs	Aldabra Lst.	5	10 YR 7/1	7.2	50.5	15.1	1.0
13	CB	Gionnet Camp	sparse shrubs	Aldabra Lst.	10	2.5 YR 6/2	8.0	14.0	29.1	1.0–0.5
14	CB	Dune Jean-Louis	sparse shrubs	Takamaka Lst.	10	10 YR 3/3	8.0	93.0	4.0	0.4
15	CP	Picard	—	Aldabra Lst.	20	5 YR 3/3	8.0	41.0	0.0	1–5
16	CO	Middle Camp	*Casuarina* and shrubs	Aldabra Lst.	10	10 YR 6/3	8.2	22.5	36.2	0.0
17	CO	Dune Jean-Louis	shrubs	Takamaka Lst.	15	10 YR 6/3	7.5	4.0	20.8	0.0
18	CO	Dune Jean-Louis	shrubs	Takamaka Lst.	15	10 YR 5/3	7.9	16.0	41.1	0.5
19	CO	Dune Jean-Louis	shrubs	Takamaka Lst.	15	10 YR 2/2	7.6	8.0	54.8	0.1–0.5

† For notation, see text, pp. 69–70.
‡ Lst. = Limestone.
§ Analysis for horizon 5–10 cm above bedrock.

procedures since it is often the case that over 50 % of any given area is a bare rock surface. This approach is, however, not particularly helpful and in current definitional terms the soils which do exist fall into the rendzina (or U.S.D.A. Rendoll) category. This is a shallow soil, dominantly of one mixed mineral–organic horizon and occurring over calcareous bedrock. The horizon is of high base status. A broader definition is currently in use in Britain which allows for the presence of a B horizon. Typically, however, the soil has an A/C or A/R profile (the horizon nomenclature used is given in table 2). A broad soil survey approach would not be particularly helpful unless conducted at a large scale mapping level. It is only possible to use the existing works and attempt to cross-reference their partial observations. Baker (1963) has identified soil groups, as has Piggott (1968), with reference to soils in the Seychelles. Hnatiuk (Hnatiuk & Merton 1979, this volume, and personal communication) has undertaken a description of soil types in a botanical context as do Merton *et al.* (1976, and Merton's field notes). Trudgill (1972) has suggested a grouping of soil types, based on pedological and geomorphological observations.

Existing soils information is based on surface observations and sampling of profiles for a variety of purposes. The field work of Merton was based on the collection of soil profile data and samples under contrasting vegetation types. The sample data are discussed below and summarized in the tables. Hnatiuk (Hnatiuk & Merton 1979, this volume, and personal communication) discusses the existence of the soil series recognized by Piggott, namely (1) the Farquhar series (a soil formed on windblown sand, with or without a shallow organic horizon, overlying a slightly lighter colour sand and underlain by a transitional zone merging into unaltered sand); (2) the Shioya series (a soil formed on water-lain sand with an A horizon merging into lighter coloured sand) and (3) the Desnoeufs series (a phosphatic humus soil formed from bird excreta, fish waste and bird remains). Saline soils are seen in the bottoms of summer flooded basins. Trudgill (1972) recognized a shallow organic soil (0–10 cm) and a deep organic soil (10–30 cm) and calcareous mineral soils, with or without organic horizons. A proposed scheme of soil types is outlined below, by amalgamating all the existing work. It should be stressed that this is an interim scheme, based on a limited number of examples of soils. It is emphasized that cross-correlations can only be reliably checked by further field work. Moreover, care should be taken not to confuse terrestrial sediments and palaeosols (Braithwaite 1975) with the more recently formed soils under discussion here. The groupings suggested below are based on field observations of profile nature and upon laboratory analysis. They are not based on any speculations as to the origin of the soils. The analytical techniques are listed in table 1, the horizon nomenclature is given in table 2, and selected profile and analytical details are given in table 3. The occurrences of the soils on the island are given in a section after the profile descriptions, though this information is partial.

ALDABRA SOILS – AN INTERIM IDENTIFICATION OF TYPES

The main types are as follows (with shorthand notation):

(1) *Organic soils* (O)   (i) shallow (0–10 cm) (OS)
                                  + pellet variety (OSP)
                                  + guano variety (OSG)
                             (ii) deep (10–30 cm) (OD)

(2) *Carbonate soils* (C)   (i) calcarenaceous (CA)

           (ii) brown carbonate (CB)

              + (humic) phosphatic variety (CP)

              + cavity fill variety (CF)

         (iii) organic brown carbonate (CO)

3. Other sedimentary (S) types with little or no pedological organization or plant growth:
 – organic (algal) sediments (SA)
 – carbonate sediments in enclosed basins (SM).

The details of each soil type are given below. The ranges of data given are not necessarily exclusive limits, but represent commonly found ranges in the samples studied.

(1) *Organic soils*

These are accumulations of litter on rock surfaces. The litter may show varying degrees of decomposition. If the bedrock is not well consolidated, lithoclastic and bioclastic fragments of rock (1–10 mm in size) may be mixed in the lower layers of the soil, but not as a distinct horizon. Other than rock fragments or gastropod shells, no substantial mineral matter is present. The profile commonly consists simply of decomposing litter passing abruptly to case hardened bedrock, or in the case of deeper, more acid soils, merging distinctly into soft, non-case hardened limestone. Subdivisions can be made according to the depth of the soils and the origin of the organic matter:

(i) *Shallow organic soil*

Depth of up to 10 cm. Typically occurring under stands of mixed scrub in pockets and small patches, but occasionally more extensive. Accumulations of gastropod shells may be present.

General profile:

depth/cm	horizon†	description and analytical data‡
0–5	L	Litter from shrubs. pH 6.5–7.0
5–10	F	Merging to partly decomposed leaves. Some humus; pH 7.0–8.0; colour, 10YR 3/3–5/2; carbonates, 15–20 %; organic matter, 50–80 %§; phosphate, 0.1–0.5 mg/g. Sharp boundary.
10+	R	Limestone (usually case hardened).

Pellet variety. The soil is of faecal pellets of millepedes/orthopterans.

General profile:

depth/cm	horizon	description and analytical data
0–5	L	Invertebrate faecal pellets. pH: 6.5–7.0.
5–10	F	Merging to partly decomposed pellets. pH 7.0–7.5; colour, 10YR 3/3; carbonates, 0–10 %; organic matter, 40–60 %; phosphate, (no data available). Sharp boundary.
10+	R	Limestone (usually case hardened).

† Horizon nomenclature is given in table 2.
‡ Methods are given in table 1.
§ Any balance is soluble non-carbonate plus acid insoluble residue.

Guano variety. Present-day accumulation of guano, fish and bird remains. Usually confined to nesting colonies on lagoon islands; (see also under brown carbonate soils, (humic), phosphatic variety (CP), but more organic and fresher than this).

(ii) *Deep organic soils*

A rather more well developed soil, usually of depth 10–30 cm and possessing a well marked humified layer. Occurring in pockets and also in blankets, especially under stands of *Casuarina*; also under *Ficus*. Mostly over non-case hardened rock, occasionally over sand.

General profile:

depth/cm	horizon	description and analytical data
0–2(5)	L	Needles and cones of Casuarina. Merging to
2(5)–10	F	decomposing needles and cones of *Casuarina*.
10–30	Ah	Merging to mixed humus and limestone particles in varying proportions. pH 6.5–7.5; colour, 5YR 3/2 (more calcareous) to 7.5 YR 4/2 (more humic); carbonates, 0.5–30 %; organic matter, 50–90 %; phosphate, 0.1 mg/g. Variability in data due to differing proportions of humus and limestone particles. Distinct boundary.
30 +	C	Unconsolidated bedrock, not case hardened, or if so then not to the extent of subaerially exposed surfaces. Brown stained (by humus and/or iron); for 1–5 cm merging into soft bedrock limestone,
	R	no brown staining.

(2) *Carbonate soils*

These soils are dominantly composed of carbonate particles, though some organic matter may be present, either as a discrete surface horizon and/or as an intimate fraction within the soil. Most profiles have an horizon of unconsolidated mineral matter passing to bedrock. The soils can be subdivided according to texture, the presence or absence of surface organic horizons and of reddish (phosphatic, humic) material.

(i) *Calcarenaceous carbonate soils*

Present on uncemented carbonate sand (calcarenite) and is differentiated from unaltered sand by the presence of a humus stained layer next to the surface.

General profile:

depth/cm	horizon	description and analytical data
0–1	L	Litter (of grasses or shrubs). Merging to
1–2	H	decomposed humus (with root mat if under grass vegetation). pH 6.0–6.5. Distinct boundary.
2–4	A/Ah	Humus stained carbonate sand, whitish/humus and some sand, grey. pH 8.0/7.0–7.5; colour, 7.5 YR 8/0; carbonates, 80–95 %; organic matter, 2–10 %; phosphate, trace. Texture, coarse – fine sand. Distinct boundary.
4 +	C	Unaltered sand.

Two important erosional/vegetational situations can be distinguished:

(*a*) *Grassland. Fimbristylis* and *Sclerodactylon* present. Relatively stable and not prone to erosion while vegetation root mat is intact.

(*b*) *Shrub. Tournefortia, Scaevola, Guettarda* (occasionally some *Casuarina, Cocos*) present. Relatively unstable, often only loose litter on sand surface. Prone to erosion unless H and A layers are well developed, but, lacking a root mat, is more sensitive than above.

(ii) *Brown carbonate soils*

These soils possess dominantly brown (brown, 10YR 5/3; reddish brown, 2.5YR 5/4–4/4 or greyish brown, 10YR 5/2) carbonate horizons. The texture is predominantly silty (sandy silt, silt and silt loam). There is little or no organic matter present, unless it is a minor proportion of intimate humus.

General profile:

depth/cm	horizon	description and analytical data
0–20	B	Brown silt or silt loam, occasionally laminated, mostly apedal. pH 7.5–8.0; colour, 10YR 5/3–5/2; carbonates, 50–95%; organic matter, 0–5%; phosphate, 0.2–0.8 mg/g. Sharp boundary.
20+	R	Case hardened rock, often with layered deposition (whether layers pre-date soil formation or are consequent upon soil formation is not evident).

Humic phosphate variety. These soils have a relatively high phosphate content and are often reddish brown (2.5YR 5/4–4/4). There is little or no discrete surface humus but the soils may have a relatively high content of intimate humus (but still having the appearance of a dominantly mineral soil). This is probably analogous to the Desnoeufs series of Piggott (together with the fresher, guano variety of the shallow organic soil).

General profile:

depth/cm	horizon	description and analytical data
0–10(20)	B(ca)	Reddish brown or brown silt or silt loam. Apedal. pH 7.5–8.0; colour, 2.5YR 5/4–4/4; carbonates, 10–60%; organic matter, 15–30%; phosphate, 1–2 mg/g (merging locally with terrestrial sediment of greater age of 5–20% phosphate; latter present in fills in solution pipes but often, in practice, difficult to distinguish). Distinct boundary.
10(20)	R	Case hardened bedrock, often stained reddish brown and often with layered deposition (whether layers pre-date soil formation or are consequent upon soil formation is not necessarily evident).

Cavity fill variety. Coincident with unlaminated soils and cavity fills recognized by Braithwaite (1975). This is a deep (1–2 m) sedimentary deposit in solution pits, not a surface soil. *Cardisoma* crabs may be present. Little or no horizonation evident (but may support vegetation and therefore of interest). pH 8.0; colour, 5YR 7/3; carbonates, 40%, organic matter, 0.0; phosphate, 5–20%.

(iii) *Organic brown carbonate*

The most developed soil on Aldabra in terms of horizonation. Possesses a discrete surface organic horizon and a discrete mineral horizon together with a mixed A horizon. Widely occurring, possibly in need of further differentiation.

General profile:

depth/cm	horizon	description and analytical data
0–2	L	Litter. Merging to
2–10	F/H	decomposing litter (H usually very small). Merging to
10–12	A	mixed humus and carbonates. pH 7.5–8.0; colour, 10YR 6/3; carbonates, 5–20 %; organic matter, 20–40 %; phosphate, 0.1–0.5 mg/g. Distinct/merging boundary.
12–20	B(ca)	Silt or silt loam mineral soil, mostly apedal. pH 7.5–8.0; colour, 10YR 3/3; carbonate, 75–95 %; organic matter, 0–5 % or 10 %; phosphate, 0.2–0.8 mg/g. Sharp boundary.
20+	R	Case hardened limestone.

(3) *Other sedimentary types*

These are materials showing little or no pedological organization and are usually simply sedimentary accumulations in flat or gently concave areas often seasonally or temporarily filled with water. They may comprise organic (usually algal) remains (pH 7.5; colour, 5YR 4/2; carbonates, 10–20 %; organic matter, 70–80 %; phosphate, 0.1 mg/g), or they may be mineral (pH 7.0–7.5; colour, 10YR 7/1; carbonates, 50 %; organic matter, 15 %; phosphate, 1 mg/g). These latter probably merge to Hnatiuk's saline soils. Here, further field work is needed to clarify the distinction between possible terrestrial saline soils and semi-tidal saline soils (such as occur in the southeast of the island inland from the lagoon).

The occurrence of the soil types

(1) *Organic soils*

(i) *Shallow organic*

Widespread, but often occurs in scattered patches in the localities where present. Largely under mixed scrub and also under *Pemphis*. Mostly on champignon but also on other surfaces.

Pellet variety. Local scattered occurrence, open or closed scrub.

Guano variety. Mostly on lagoon islands.

(ii) *Deep organic*

Largely confined to *Casuarina* stands (north and west coast); also under *Ficus* (Takamaka).

(2) *Carbonate soil*

(i) *Calcarenaceous*

Largely coastal locations (south, west and east coast) (also on Michel and other pocket beaches facing the lagoon); shrub/eroded form on unstable dunes.

(ii) *Brown carbonate*

Widespread in location but patchy in occurrence; most common on platin areas and also in some shallow basins elsewhere.

(*Humic*) *phosphatic variety*. Mostly confined to lagoon islands.

Cavity fill variety. Confined to larger solution pits in champignon.

(iii) *Organic brown carbonate*

Most widespread of all, especially on pavé (but also on other surfaces) and under mixed scrub. Often patchy but sometimes relatively continuous covers with only a few rock outcrops appearing through the soil cover.

(3) *Other (sedimentary) soil types*

Organic confined to pool floor, many localities.

Mineral mostly common on SE platin area.

Also in SE (Cinq Cases) semi-tidal area merging to marine saline sites (mangrove soils occur on lagoon fringes; see MacNae (1971)).

TABLE 4. ACID (HCl) INSOLUBLE RESIDUES OF EXAMPLES OF ALDABRA SOIL PARENT MATERIALS

site	parent material	percentage
Dune Jean-Louis	solution pipe sediment	18.34
Middle Camp	solution pipe sediment	9.86
Anse Var	*Platygyra* coral (Aldabra Limestone)	8.31
Picard	Calcarenite	4.97
Anse Var	*Goniastrea* coral (Aldabra Limestone)	4.73
Passe Gionnet	Aldabra Limestone, shelly	3.20
Dune Jean-Louis	*Halimeda*, Aldabra Limestone	2.97
Sylvestre	bioclastic phosphate	2.83
Esprit	Esprit phosphorite	2.38
Picard	Aldabra Limestone, coralline	2.37
Cinq Cases	laminated terrestrial sediment	2.21
Esprit	Esprit phosphorite	2.11
Dune Jean-Louis	Aldabra Limestone, shelly	1.99
Anse Var	Aldabra Limestone, calcarenite	1.70
Cinq Cases	laminated terrestrial sediment	1.45
Picard	solution pipe sediment	1.16
Passe Houareau	Takamaka Limestone, algal	0.83
Anse Var	Aldabra Limestone, calcarenite	0.71
Anse Var	Aldabra Limestone	0.58
Dune Jean-Louis	Aldabra Limestone	0.42
West Channels	Calcarenite	0.19

THE ORIGINS OF ALDABRA SOILS

There are six possible sources of soil constituents, four mineral and two organic.

(1) Chemical rock weathering, yielding an insoluble residue.

(2) Mechanical weathering/erosion and deposition, yielding either sand grains or larger rock fragments.

(3) Terrestrial sediments (other than carbonate rocks from marine sources) as described by Braithwaite (1975).

(4) Extra-island sources: atmospheric dry fallout (such as volcanic dust) and solutes.

(5) Leaf litter.

(6) Animal faecal and detrital material (bodies, feathers).

While the proportions of these constituents will vary with locality, some generalizations can be made about their relative importance for the whole island. Data for the acid insoluble residues of examples of Aldabra rock types (table 4) suggest that the rocks and terrestrial sediments fall into three broad categories: (1) very pure (less than 1 % acid insoluble residue); (2) moderately pure (1–5 %) and those with significant proportions of insoluble residue (5–20 %). The data can be summarized as follows with reference to rock types:

(1) 0.1–1.0 %. Calcarenites. Takamaka limestone (algal micrite).

(2) 1–5 %. Some solution pipe sediments; calcarenite pockets, some shell and coral rich portions of Aldabra Limestone; Esprit phosphorites.

TABLE 5. CALCULATION OF THE PRODUCTION OF ALDABRA SOILS
BY THE ACCUMULATION OF SOLUTION RESIDUE

limestone	acid insoluble residue (%)	erosion rate mm/a	centimetres of residual soil produced in	
			1000 a	10 000 a
Aldabra				
Limestone	0.83	0.10	0.83	8.3
Picard	4.97 (max.)	0.39	1.94	19.4
Calcarenite	0.19 (min.)	0.39	0.07	0.7
generalized figures				
(1)	0.1	0.05	0.01	0.1
	2.0	0.05	0.10	1.0
(2)	0.1	0.26	0.03	0.3
	2.0	0.26	0.52	5.2

(1)   Estimated erosion rate (Stoddart et al. 1971).
(2)   Mean erosion rate (Trudgill 1976).

(3) 5–20 %. Some solution pipe and phosphatic sediments. Assuming that the dissolution of rock material in acid is pertinent to natural soil-forming processes it can be suggested that the solution pipe sediment (which is of spatially limited distribution) is liable to produce thick soils but that most of the limestones will make a much smaller contribution to soil formation. In the latter case a very long time would have to elapse before a distinctive residual soil could be built up. Given the measured erosion rates of subaerially exposed Aldabra limestones (Trudgill 1976; 1979, this volume), surface lowering rates per 1000 years can be estimated. Assuming the weathering of a cube of rock, and the formation of residue in situ, then the percentage residues can be used to calculate probable depths of residual soil formation (table 5).

It can be seen from table 5 that in terms of the conservative estimates of erosion rates and time periods and of the lowest insoluble residues, only a thin skin of residual soil can be expected to have formed. However, the time scale involved since the last emersion is probably longer than 10000 a and possibly as long as 27000 a B.P. (Braithwaite et al. 1973). Given this possible time, and taking the higher figure for insoluble residue, it would appear possible for a residual soil of a few centimetres thick to have accumulated in situ. Given the possible focusing effects of runoff waters, sedimentary accumulations could be much thicker locally in basins. Since emergence appears to have been periodic it is possible that the ages of different emerged surfaces could be reflected in the depths of accumulation of residual soil.

The organic soils are essentially derived from leaf litter *in situ*. The thickness of the organic horizons is related to the decomposition rates of the litter. The presence of calcium tends to stabilize humus decomposition. This gives rise to a nutrient rich mull humus, the stable calcium humates aggregates accumulating to give the thickness of the soil. Sand grains, rock fragments and terrestrial sediments form dominant mineral sources. Extra-island sources, such as volcanic dust are, as yet, undetected sources of soil constituents. Animal faecal and detrital material are only of local importance and not a widespread dominant soil constituent.

TABLE 6. SOME ASPECTS OF VEGETATION–SOIL RELATIONS, SELECTED DATA
(from data and samples of L. F. Merton)

sample	vegetation	pH, A horizon	depth of litter/cm	depth of A horizon/cm	A horizon CaCO₃(%)	A horizon K/(mg/g)	Na mg/g	NaCl equivalent mg/g
1	Casuarina	7.2	1.0	5.0	9.8	0.65	4.3	10.6
2	Casuarina	7.6	1.0	5.0	59.0	0.30	51.8	132.0
3	Guettarda	7.7	2.5	6.5	35.0	0.70	2.1	5.4
4	Guettarda	8.7	1.0	2.0	43.0	0.50	2.6	6.5
5	Pemphis	6.6	1.0	3.0	8.0	0.10	0.1	0.3
6	Pemphis	7.6	4.5	3.0	14.0	3.05	77.5	197.4
7	Pemphis	8.3	1.0	5.0	22.0	0.42	0.8	2.0
8	Pemphis	6.6	2.0	12.0	8.0	0.38	1.8	4.6
9	Euphorbia, Acalypha, Pemphis	7.9	2.0	7.0	30.0	0.35	11.0	28.0
10	Acalypha, Cyperus	7.1	1.0	3.0	4.5	0.39	0.7	1.7
11	Pandanus, Ficus	7.8	1.0	3.0	5.0	0.35	1.1	2.8
12	Ficus	8.0	0.0	0.5	19.0	0.35	1.0	2.6
13	Thespesia	7.9	1.0	2.0	38.8	0.38	2.1	5.2
14	open ground	7.7	1.0	2.0	8.5	0.40	2.9	7.4
15	'coastal scrub'	8.6	1.0	2.0	42.0	0.60	2.9	7.4

ECOLOGICAL INTERRELATIONS

The soils of Aldabra are important as a rooting medium for herbaceous ground flora and for a proportion, but not all, of the shrubs and trees. Some of the woody vegetation is actually rooted in the rock stratum and not in the surface soil. Their roots penetrate through solutionally opened crevices and cavities into terrestrial or marine sediments. Nevertheless, the chemical and physical properties of the surface soils which have been described will be edaphic considerations relevant to all the herbaceous and to a proportion of the tree and shrub vegetation. Furthermore, it may be observed that many of the soils do not bear much relation to underlying geology. The nature of the vegetation cover is just as important a factor in determining the nature of the soil.

Some data on some aspects of vegetation–soil relations are presented in table 6. The salinity (NaCl) data are calculated from sodium data.

Since only the dominant shrub vegetation is given in table 6 then the influence of shrub vegetation on soil type is more apparent than the influence of soil type on herbaceous vegetation. The thickest organic horizons occur where *Casuarina* and also, to a lesser extent, *Pemphis* occur. The *Pemphis* litter appears to be more acid than that of other plants. Some soils appear to be relatively highly saline. These appear to be largely related to proximity to pocket beaches (e.g. Anse Var) or to location on the exposed southeast coast.

In addition, the highly alkaline soils (pH 8 and above) may present some nutritional problems in terms of elements which are less soluble at high pH (such as iron, manganese, zinc and phosphate). Moreover, in the shallow soils of open structure, water retention is likely to be low. It should be possible to specify these limiting factors more precisely in the light of further analyses.

CONCLUSIONS

Three primary sources account for the bulk of Aldabran soils: (1) mechanically derived carbonate fragments (lithoclastic grains of cemented limestones and bioclastic grains of organic skeletal material), (2) chemically derived solution residues and (3) leaf litter. Phosphates, faecal material and terrestrial sediments are of local importance as soil parent materials. The nature of the tree and shrub vegetation has considerable influence upon the nature of the organic soils. Estimates of weathering rates and data on acid insoluble residues suggest that it is possible for a residual soil of the order of 2–10 cm thickness to have been formed during the latest emergence time of Aldabra which has lasted to the present day. The presence of deeper organic soils tends to be coincident with a lack of case hardening of the subsoil rock surface, but case hardening appears to be present under all other soil studied. The degree of mixing of organic and carbonate mineral matter varies considerably. The relative amounts and dispositions of organic and mineral matter can be used as a basis for the grouping of soil profiles into organic, carbonate and intermediate soil types, but further work is necessary over the whole atoll before the full nature and extent of the soils can be determined.

The assistance of the Royal Society and the N.E.R.C. made the field work possible. The help in the field of Dr C. J. R. Braithwaite, Dr J. D. Taylor and Dr W. J. Kennedy are gratefully acknowledged. The British Geomorphological Research Group made a grant towards the cost of the soil analyses which were undertaken by Mr G. Ulmanis and Miss J. Crosland. Dr D. J. Briggs, Dr D. R. Stoddart, Dr R. J. Hnatiuk and Dr C. J. R. Braithwaite are thanked for criticism of the manuscript. Some of the data have been derived from the soil samples and field notes of Dr L. F. H. Merton (deceased).

REFERENCES (Trudgill)

Baker, B. H. 1963 Geology and mineral resources of the Seychelles Archipelago. *Geol. Surv. Kenya Mem.* **3**, 106–110; 126–127.

Braithwaite, C. J. R. 1975 Petrology of palaeosols and other terrestrial sediments on Aldabra, Indian Ocean. *Phil. Trans. R. Soc. Lond.* B **273**, 1–32.

Braithwaite, C. J. R., Taylor, J. D. & Kennedy, W. J. 1973 The evolution of an atoll: the depositional and erosional history of Aldabra. *Phil. Trans. R. Soc. Lond.* B **266**, 307–340.

Hnatiuk, R. J. & Merton, L. F. H. 1979 A perspective of the vegetation of Aldabra. *Phil. Trans. R. Soc. Lond.* B **286**, 79–84 (this volume).

Merton, L. F., Bourn, D. M. & Hnatiuk, R. J. 1976 Giant tortoise and vegetation interactions on Aldabra Atoll, I. *Biol. Conserv.* **9**, 293–304.

Piggott, C. J. 1968 A soil survey of the Seychelles. *Tech. Bull. Land Resources Division, Dir. Overseas Surv.*, no. 2. Tolworth, Surrey.

Stoddart, D. R., Taylor, J. D., Fosberg, F. R. & Farrow, G. E. 1971 The geomorphology of Aldabra Atoll. *Phil. Trans. R. Soc. Lond.* B **260**, 31–65.

Trudgill, S. T. 1972 Process studies of limestone erosion in littoral and terrestrial environments, with special reference to Aldabra Atoll. Ph.D. thesis, University of Bristol.

Trudgill, S. T. 1976 The subaerial and subsoil erosion of limestones on Aldabra Atoll, Indian Ocean. *Z. Geomorph.*, suppl. **26**, 201–210.

Trudgill, S. T. 1979 Surface lowering and landform evolution on Aldabra. *Phil. Trans. R. Soc. Lond.* B **286**, 35–45 (this volume).

Phil. Trans. R. Soc. Lond. B. **286**, 79–84 (1979)   [79]
Printed in Great Britain

A perspective of the vegetation of Aldabra

By R. J. Hnatiuk†‡ and L. F. H. Merton§||

† The Royal Society Aldabra Research Station, Seychelles
§ Botany Department, The University, Sheffield, U.K.

1. Introduction

Several accounts are now available about the vegetation, or portions of it, of Aldabra (Fryer 1910–12; Vesey-Fitzgerald 1942; Stoddart & Wright 1967; Stoddart 1968; Fosberg 1971; Grubb 1971 and Hnatiuk & Merton 1979). Most of these reports derive from short periods of observation, which, while adequate for general description, are generally insufficient to permit much synthesis. The work of Grubb (1971) is an exceptional case in so far as it shows fine perception of the factors affecting vegetation within his particular study area. The presence of the Royal Society Aldabra Research Station has been fundamentally important in permitting many researchers the opportunity to study Aldabra both in detail and for extended periods of time. The result has been that a more complete understanding of the vegetation is now possible. It is our objective to present some of this synthesis, even if in doing so we largely highlight the voids in our knowledge.

2. Mosaics in the vegetation patterns

One of the most striking features of the vegetation of Aldabra is the complex spatial patterning it shows. A large part of this mosaic pattern appears to be due to the fragmentated nature of the habitats for plants provided by the underlying limestone substrate. The origin of the pattern must lie in the combined effects of the pattern of growth shown by the original organisms producing the limestone and the subsequent erosional and depositional patterns superimposed on these structural ones after the coral and algae had died. The parallel rows and fields of more or less circular patterns of various sizes that can be similarly seen in living parts of the reefs on Aldabra and on other atolls as on dry land on Aldabra, lend support to the idea that the present day vegetation patterns are controlled by the patterns found on the original reefs.

In our classification of Aldabra's vegetation (Hnatiuk & Merton 1979), the patterns of the vegetation that are related to spatial distribution and fragmentation of the vegetation have not been used as criteria as they were in the classification of Fosberg (1971). We believe that a clearer understanding of the vegetation is to be had by excluding the spatial pattern from the classification and only bringing it in in the descriptive notes. Our units may be subdivided by using criteria of spatial pattern if, for example, plant density or spacing were of importance to habitat studies.

Another aspect of the mosaic nature of the vegetation is that caused by changes that occur to only selected elements of the vegetation. For example, if *Cyperus niveus* can develop as a continuous mat only under a scrub canopy and then the scrub dies and decays, leaving the

‡ Present address: Western Australian Herbarium, George Street, South Perth, Australia 6151.
|| Deceased.

Cyperus, which having become established, persists, then the usual association of this sedge as an understorey to scrub is seen to have an apparent exception at such a site if little trace of the original scrub remains. Many other examples of this sort could also be given.

The distribution patterns of individual species across the atoll add yet another dimension to the vegetation mosaic. Some of the species patterns appear to be substrate controlled (e.g. *Pemphis*, and many of the Tortoise Turf species) while others, especially in relation to their frequency of occurrence, appear to be related to colonization patterns (e.g. *Passiflora, Scaevola, Polysphaeria, Coptosperma nigrescens, Sophora tomentosa*). Vigorous, opportunistic species that invade certain disturbed habitats (e.g. *Cyperus ligularis, Sporobolus virginicus*) add yet more complexity to the mosaic of species and vegetation.

3. STRATIFICATION OF THE VEGETATION

The classification of Aldabra's vegetation presented by Hnatiuk & Merton (1979) is based upon criteria of the overstorey only. In general, understorey vegetation is not very well developed on Aldabra with a few important exceptions: herbs beneath *Cocos* and *Casuarina* (partly maintained by plantation management); shrubs beneath *Cocos* and *Casuarina* (a slow invasion of coconut groves by Mixed Scrub and an invasion of Mixed Scrub by *Casuarina* are the important immediate causes); the 'Mixed Scrub' understorey in Takamaka Grove where it appears that sufficiency of water has permitted some scrub species to overtop others that is not generally seen elsewhere on the atoll (e.g. *Dracaena* and *Polysphaeria* in the understorey); and extensive *Cyperus niveus* and *C. dubius* mats beneath some areas of Mixed Scrub.

4. DYNAMIC INTERRELATIONS IN THE VEGETATION

That vegetation is a dynamic element in the landscape is hardly questioned by anyone, but the inclusion in a classification of variability due to the passage of time is difficult and little agreement is to be found on criteria or methods for doing so. Nevertheless, its existence cannot be ignored if the units of the classification are to be understood and evaluated. While the present paper does not allow a detailed presentation of the information now accummulating, a few of the findings will be summarized here because they help to build a synthetic view of part of the Aldabran ecosystem.

The source regions for the Aldabran flora have been determined by Renvoize (1971, 1975) as primarily the surrounding land areas flanking or lying within the Indian Ocean. The unpublished work of one of us (R.J.H.) indicates that viable propagules of a large number of species (about 50) not found on Aldabra are washed onto its beaches in a period of 20 months and others are accidentally or deliberately introduced by man. Many germinate, but only a few produce viable seed and spread. Thus there is a potential for continual accretion of new species to the flora. Most of these potential additions to the flora, even excluding those brought in by man, appear to arrive on the west coast of the atoll. Studies of local distribution maps for each species in the Aldabran flora (S. H. Hnatiuk & R. J. Hnatiuk, unpublished) show that within the atoll there is a geographic variation unrelated to vegetation type, represented by areas adjacent to passes (and also facing the north and west) being rather different from the rest of the atoll, perhaps reflecting the preferential sites of introduction of many species. Dispersal within Aldabra appears to be readily accomplished for many species with the aid of seed-eating animals such as birds and tortoises (S. Hnatiuk, personal communication). The animals themselves appear to be helping to shape the vegetation as for example the apparent destruction of shrubs and spread of grassland in the south and east of the atoll caused by the activities of the large tortoise population (Hnatiuk *et al.* 1976, Merton *et al.* 1976). And finally, the variation in climate from year to year (Stoddart & Mole 1977) with periods of exceptionally dry years broken by relatively wet ones, must severely affect the kinds of plants that can establish on Aldabra.

The interaction between all these factors means that the vegetation of the atoll is in a constant state of flux, as new disturbances destroy part of the existing vegetation. The vegetation that follows disturbances such as a cyclone, drought, or excessive grazing and browsing, may bear little relation to what existed before because new species may be present that were not there when the previous vegetation became established. Thus a new balance between species will be struck that will not necessarily be the same across the whole atoll. Chance factors like the distribution of viable seed and the state of the climate during and following a disturbance, may play a very large rôle in determining the pattern of species and vegetation. The hypothesis of catastrophic events being the main driving force in shaping vegetation may apply to Aldabra with the added nuance that the 'raw materials' for rebuilding following each catastrophe may be continually changing.

The relevance of these ideas on change to Aldabra's vegetation is that we shall be unlikely ever to produce a satisfactorily complete classification of Aldabra's vegetation that is entirely understandable in terms of the then existing physical environment, and that is neither a classification of habitats nor of floristic distribution patterns. Thus the rapid spreading of such species as *Casuarina* and *Passiflora* that can drastically alter the structure of the vegetation soon make obsolete a necessarily static image of vegetation in a classification based solely upon the plants as seen at one time. This does not negate the value of the classification, because if it is found 'good' it will greatly help in understanding the functioning of the Aldabran ecosystem as it currently exists, and may even help to predict some of the changes that will occur if certain habitat factors are changed (e.g. if grazing pressure increases or decreases).

5. Life forms in the Aldabran flora

Fosberg's classification of Aldabra's vegetation finds particular use in indicating some of the potential vegetation types that could develop on Aldabra and thus the vegetation of the atoll can readily be compared to that of other atolls. Another system of classification which can be usefully applied to show the relationship of Aldabra to other areas of the world is the life-form system of Raunkiaer (1934). Table 1 shows the life-form spectrum for Aldabra in comparison with Raunkiaer's 'Normal Spectrum' for the whole world, and also for some other atolls, and tropical islands.

Aldabra's spectrum differs from the Normal Spectrum by a relatively high proportion of chamaephytes, low proportions of hemicryptophytes, and cryptophytes, and about the same amount of phanerophytes as in the Normal Spectrum. In Raunkiaer's terms then, the 'plant climate' of Aldabra is a chamaephyte climate. His findings indicate the chamaephyte climate to occur in cold, polar regions. However, in none of his data for the chamaephyte type is there an example that also has relatively high values for phanerophytes.

In order to assess the significance of the Aldabran spectrum, a survey was made of some other

82 R. J. HNATIUK AND L. F. H. MERTON

atolls for which species lists were available and for which life forms could be determined. The results are listed in table 1 together with spectra from the Seychelles and coastal Jamaica. From these data it can be seen that the coral atoll spectra differ from those of the large tropical islands in that chamaephytes predominate in the former and not the latter. Among the atolls, the one with the most similar spectrum to that from Aldabra is Diego Garcia, also a 'raised' atoll. The sand cay atolls of the Hawaiian Islands have high proportions of chamaephytes but somewhat lower levels of phanerophytes although this latter life form is still the second most common one on the sandy cays.

TABLE 1. LIFE-FORM ANALYSIS FOR THE FLORA OF ALDABRA

leaf size ...	lepto	nano	micro	meso	macro	mega	sum	% of total	Normal Spectrum[1]
life-form									
phanero-	3	8	38	36	6	0	91	48	46
chamae-	8	18	11	6	1	0	44	23	9
hemicrypto-	0	4	3	6	0	0	13	7	26
liane	0	2	5	6	0	0	13	7	—
thero-	3	7	11	4	0	0	25	13	13
parasite	0	1	0	1	0	0	2	1	—
crypto-	0	0	1	0	0	0	1	0.5	6
sum	14	40	69	59	7	0	**189**		
% of total	7	21	37	31	4	0			

life-form	Diego Garcia[2]	Laysan[3]	Lisianski[4]	South East[5]	North[5]	Grass[5]	Seal[5]	Little N.[5]	'combined'[5]	Seychelles[6]	coastal Jamaica[7]
phanero-	41	32	33	25	18	20	20	25	22	61	75
chamae-	43†	54	61†	60†	82†	70†	80†	75†	71†	6	10
hemicrypto-	—	3	—	—	—	—	—	—	—	12	2
liane	—	—	—	—	—	—	—	—	—	—	7
thero-	9	11	6	10	0	10	0	0	5	16	5
parasite	—	—	—	—	—	—	—	—	—	—	—
crypto-	5	—	—	—	—	—	—	—	—	5	0
sum	121	37	18	20	11	10	10	4	55	—	—

References: (1) Raunkiaer (1934), p. 428; (2) Fosberg & Bullock (1971), spp. list, data are percentage of total; (3) Ely & Clapp (1973), spp. list, data are percentage of total; (4) Clapp & Wirtz (1975), spp. list, data are percentage of total; (5) Amerson, Clapp & Wirtz (1974), data are percentage of total; (6) Raunkiaer (1934), p. 428, data are percentage of total; (7) Asprey & Loveless (1958), data are percentage of total.
  † Chamaephytes and hemicryptophytes combined because of difficulty in distinguishing them from available information.

Raunkiaer attributes a predominance of chamaephytes to a plant response to unfavourable conditions, particularly water supply and temperature. The tropical atolls may generally have an unfavourable water supply owing to either low rainfall or porous soil and thus the chamaephyte form may be selected for. The absence or low level of geophytes contrasts the atoll's spectra with those often found in continental semi-arid areas. The relatively high phanerophyte proportions, especially on the raised atolls, may indicate the relation of the atolls to the tropical region where phanerophytes are supposed to be predominant if moisture permits.

The evergreen and deciduous nature of the vegetation is an important element in its characterization, especially on a world-wide scale. However, in the semi-arid tropics the characteristic feature in this respect is variability, in response to the irregular oscillations of wet and dry years.

Asprey & Loveless (1958) attempted an analysis of coastal vegetation in Jamaica on the basis of the plant response under 'average' conditions. Not enough is known of Aldabra's climate to state what conditions are average. However, after 21 months' continuous observation including two dry seasons it has been possible to tentatively classify the flora in terms of 'evergreen', 'deciduous', and 'intermediate' (table 2). From this analysis it is seen that over half of the flora is evergreen, while less than a third is deciduous and only a small proportion falls in the intermediate category. Evergreenness and deciduousness are distributed between leaf-size categories more or less in proportion to that in the whole flora, for example, there are nearly half of the species in each leaf size class that are evergreen and under a third are deciduous. Among the life-form classes, however, the proportions are different from those in the whole flora, e.g. 67 % of phanerophytes are evergreen and only 22 % are deciduous.

TABLE 2. AN ESTIMATE OF EVERGREENNESS AND DECIDUOUSNESS IN THE ALDABRAN FLORA

(Numbers represent percentages of total flora.)

leaf size ...	lepto	nano	micro	meso	macro	sum
evergreen	4	11	22	20	2	50
deciduous	2	6	12	8	0.5	28.5
indeterminate	2	5	3	3	1	14

life-forms ...	phanerophyte	chamaephyte	hemicryptophyte	liane	therophyte	parasite	cryptophyte
evergreen	32	14	6	3	0	1	0
deciduous	11	2	0	3	12	0	0.5
indeterminate	5	7	0.5	1	0	0	0

Only 18.5 % of the flora has divided leaves and of these 63 % are phanerophytes, 17 % lianes, 11 % chamaephytes, 6 % therophytes, and 3 % hemicryptophytes. Of the 35 species with divided leaves, 57 % have microphyllous leaflets, 26 % nanophyllous, 23 % mesophyllous, 11 % leptophyllous, and only 3 % megaphyllous leaflets.

We are indebted to D. Bourn, S. Renvoize, V. Spaull, I. Swingland, G. Wickens, and S. Woodell for critically reading early drafts of the paper. Special mention is necessary for the detailed help and encouragement given by S. H. Hnatiuk, J. F. Peake, and D. R. Stoddart. We gratefully thank the Botany School, Oxford and the Western Australian Herbarium, Perth for all of their generous assistance and access to resources.

REFERENCES (Hnatiuk & Merton)

Amerson, A. B., Clapp, R. B., & Wirtz II, W. O. 1974 The natural history of Pearl and Hermes Reef. *Atoll Res. Bull.* **174**, 1–306.
Asprey, G. F. & Loveless, A. R. 1958 The dry evergreen formations of Jamaica. Part III. *J. Ecol.* **46**, 547–570.
Clapp, R. B. & Wirtz II, W. O. 1975 The natural history of Lisianski Island. *Atoll Res. Bull.* **186**, 1–196.
Ely, C. A. & Clapp, R. B. 1973 The natural history of Laysan Island. *Atoll Res. Bull.* **171**, 1–361.
Fosberg, F. R. 1971 Preliminary survey of Aldabra vegetation. *Phil. Trans. R. Soc. Lond.* B **260**, 215–227.
Fosberg, F. R. & Bullock, A. A. 1971 List of Diego Garcia vascular plants. *Atoll Res. Bull.* **149**, 143–160.
Fryer, J. C. F. 1910–12 The structure and formation of Aldabra and neighbouring islands with notes on their flora and fauna. *Proc. Linn. Soc. Lond. Zool.* (2) **14**, 397–442.
Grubb, P. 1971 The growth, ecology and population structure of giant tortoises on Aldabra. *Phil. Trans. R. Soc. Lond.* B **260**, 327–372.
Hnatiuk, R. J. & Merton, L. F. H. 1979 The vegetation of Aldabra: a reassessment. *Atoll Res. Bull.* (In the press.)

Hnatiuk, R. J., Woodell, S. R. J. & Bourn, D. M. 1976 Giant tortoises and vegetation interactions on Aldabra atoll. II. Coastal. *Biol. Conserv.* **9**, 305–316.
Merton, L. F. H., Bourn, D. M. & Hnatiuk, R. J. 1976 Giant tortoises and vegetation interactions on Aldabra atoll. I. Inland. *Biol. Conserv.* **9**, 293–304.
Raunkiaer, C. 1934 *The life forms of plants and statistical plant geography.* Oxford: Clarendon Press.
Renvoize, S. A. 1971 The origin and distribution of the flora of Aldabra. *Phil. Trans. R. Soc. Lond.* B **260**, 227–236.
Renvoize, S. A. 1975 A floristic analysis of the western Indian Ocean coral islands. *Kew Bull.* **30**, 133–152.
Stoddart, D. R. 1968 The conservation of Aldabra. *Geogrl J.* **134**, 471–486.
Stoddart, D. R. & Wright, C. A. 1967 Geography and ecology of Aldabra atoll. *Atoll Res. Bull.* **118**, 11–52.
Stoddart, D. R. & Mole, L. U. 1977 Climate of Aldabra Atoll. *Atoll Res. Bull.* **202**, 1–21.
Vesey-Fitzgerald, L. D. E. F. 1942 Further studies on the vegetation of islands of the Indian Ocean. *J. Ecol.* **30**, 1–16.

Phil. Trans. R. Soc. Lond. B. **286**, 85–97 (1979)   [85]

Printed in Great Britain

Speculations on seed dispersal and the flora of the Aldabra archipelago

By G. E. Wickens

Herbarium, Royal Botanic Gardens, Kew, Richmond, Surrey, U.K.

The 263 angiosperm non-marine taxa now recognized for the islands of the Aldabra archipelago consist of 176 native taxa, of which 43 are endemic to the islands, and 87 cultivated plants and weeds that have been introduced by man, of which 4 are no longer extant. A number of so-called introduced plants, such as *Casuarina equisetifolia* and *Cocos nucifera*, could be native, for they are well known strand species. Sites that are likely landing places for the establishment of sea-borne plant propagules are also likely places for human settlement, especially if there are shade and/or food trees already established. The status of these plants is therefore uncertain.

The endemic taxa are mainly of Madagascan and African affinities, as are also many of the inland, non-endemic, native taxa. The strand flora, however, generally have a wider, Indo-Pacific distribution.

Wind dispersal, as is to be expected from the prevailing winds, is ineffective, whereas sea dispersal, although effective, provides problems of successful establishment. It is estimated that a minimum buoyancy period of 5 or $7\frac{1}{2}$ days in sufficient for propagules to reach Aldabra from Madagascar or Africa respectively.

Dispersal by birds, despite the apparent shortage of suitable seed- or fruit-eating migrant birds, can be accounted for by the successful introduction of 1 taxon every 400 years. With a probability of 1 in 10^6 an annual migrant population of only 2500 birds is necessary.

The evolution of the flora followed the final emergence of Aldabra from beneath the sea some 80 000 years ago. The establishment of the strand flora was then followed by the less salt-tolerant inland flora. This flora must have been well established before the arrival of the giant tortoise in order to provide for its own regeneration as well as being able to withstand the requirements of the tortoise for shade and food. The establishment of the lagoon mangrove flora followed the breaching of the land rim some 4000–5000 years ago.

1. Introduction

The islands of the Aldabra archipelago consist of Aldabra, Assumption, Cosmoledo and Astove. The geographical affinities of the floras of the western Indian Ocean have already been investigated by Renvoize (1971*a*, 1975). There are four means of transport by which propagules are able to reach an island: by wind, sea, birds and man. Before dealing with each it must be emphasized that our present knowledge of long-distance dispersal is still very meagre. Positive evidence of an actual incident, especially over long distances, is difficult to obtain. The uncritical encyclopaedic work of Ridley (1930) is still the major source of information. A more modern, scientific appraisal is given by van der Pijl (1972), while the problems of island dispersal and biology are discussed by Carlquist (1974).

2. The flora

At present 2 pteridophyte and 263 angiosperm taxa, excluding the marine angiosperms, are recognized for the flora now being prepared by F. R. Fosberg and S. A. Renvoize; these are shown in table 1 (see microfiche), together with notes on their status, distribution and probable method of dispersal. The status of some plants, whether native or introduced, remains uncertain and is unlikely to be resolved to everyone's satisfaction.

(a) Weeds and cultivated plants

Weeds are regarded as species generally associated with the activities of man, and are usually associated with cultivation, habitation and waste places. All are characteristically widely dispersed species.

Although some plants may be regarded as weeds elsewhere it does not automatically follow that they behave as such on Aldabra. Thus on Aldabra the pantropical *Trianthema portulacastrum*, which elsewhere is often a weed of cultivated ground, is only known from a small islet in the lagoon, where it may have been brought by birds or possibly by the sea.

A number of species which may have originally been introduced as weeds of cultivation are now widely distributed throughout the islands, so that their original status as weeds is somewhat obscured. Such plants are *Sida acuta*, *S. rhombifolia*, and *Stachytarpheta* spp. Two weeds of cultivation, *Synedrella nodiflora* and *Tridax procumbens*, now abundant at Settlement on Aldabra, were not recorded during the 1968 survey and are therefore believed to be recent introductions.

Some species man has deliberately introduced for shade, food or ornament. A number of these are also well known strand species, dispersed naturally by the sea, for which a sandy beach provides a suitable habitat. A sandy beach is also suitable for settlement and cultivation, especially if there are trees already present to provide shade and possibly food.

The solitary specimen of *Erythrina variegata* at Settlement on Aldabra is presumed to have been deliberately planted. Near Anse Anglais and on Middle Island it is believed to be native. The species is largely sea-dispersed but is also deliberatly planted as an ornamental (Muir 1937; Verdcourt in Gillett *et al.* 1971). Viable seeds are occasionally found along the strand. Similarly *Terminalia catappa* on Aldabra and possibly the solitary tree of *Hernandia nymphaeifolia* at Settlement on Astove may not necessarily have been planted by man; viable fruits of the former and seeds of an unidentified species of *Hernandia* have been found on the Aldabra shore, evidence as to the possibility of natural dispersal.

The status of *Casuarina equisetifolia* is uncertain and further complicated by the widespread planting for shelter after settlement by Europeans and the ease by which it can become naturalized. An early description of Aldabra by a Captain Laing of the *Lord Castlereagh* in December 1815 records the eastern end of Middle Island as 'being elevated, and covered with very high trees, for at least a mile in extent, that may be seen 8 or 9 leagues [38 or 43 km] from the deck of a moderate-sized ship' (Horsburgh 1841). This description could equally apply today. The tall trees are undoubtedly *Casuarina*. The evidence suggests the presence of *Casuarina* on Aldabra before European occupation. However, there is always the possibility, however unlikely, that it could have been accidentally introduced by itinerant fishermen or Arab voyagers. *Casuarina* is a characteristic member of the Indo-Pacific strand flora, indigenous in the Seychelles (Sauer 1967) and Madagascar. The seed is winged and can be effectively wind dispersed over short distances, as is evident from its natural spread on Aldabra, although its introduction by wind dispersal, except possibly by cyclones, appears unlikely. Additional evidence for regarding *Casuarina* as a native species is suggested by its association with some of the endemic land birds. If it was introduced then a number of bird species must have undergone a truly remarkable habitat shift, or alternatively, have colonized the island and speciated following the introduction (C. B. Frith 1977, personal communication). Sauer (1967) suggests rafting of the seeds or fruit as a possible mode of dispersal. Bird dispersal is another possibility since the seeds are eaten by the locally endemic subspecies of the Malagasy Turtle Dove, Malagasy White Eye and the Red-headed Forest Fody (Benson & Penny 1971). All three species have affinities with Madagascar but this does not necessarily imply that Madagascar was the source area for *Casuarina* on Aldabra even though the distance involved is well within the limits imposed by speed of flight and passage through the digestive system. If *Casuarina* has been established on Aldabra for a long time then it would be expected that there might be some very old trees present. The absence of any old specimens can be accounted for by the devastation caused by hurricanes, such as that of 1889, when all the tall trees were laid low (Spurs 1892). Certainly a large number of tall trees on both Middle and South Islands were destroyed by the hurricane 'Georgette' of January 1968 centred over Madagascar.

The coconut is another characteristic strand plant that requires consideration, although the evidence for the possibility of it being native is extremely weak. The earliest reference in the literature appears to be that of Captain Moresby, who reported the presence of the coconut and other trees on Menai in 1822 (Moresby 1822; Horsburgh 1841; Bayne *et al.* 1970). Possibly these are the 12 trees observed by Baty (1896) on Mont Blanc, in which case they were clearly planted, being well away from the strand line.

The evidence from Astove is inconclusive. About 30 trees were planted in 1836 (Stirling 1843); whether these were in the form of a plantation or scattered along the shore is uncertain. Baty (1896) found two palms, which are marked on his sketch map. Baty's map is certainly suggestive of natural strand plants, although there is the possibility that one or both may have been planted. Later, lessees of the island established large plantations (Dupont 1907), a situation that has now obscured any possible hope of recognizing any recent natural introductions.

On Assumption, Baty (1896) recorded two palms at the site of the former settlement, of which one now remains (Stoddart *et al.* 1970), and four near the present Settlement, where there is now a large plantation. Apart from visits to capture tortoises, Assumption appears to have been uninhabited before the start of phosphate mining in 1908. The evidence here suggests a slight possibility that the coconut may have been native, but perhaps no longer extant in the wild.

The situation on Aldabra is confused and uncertain. Baty (1896) reports that the oldest trees on Ile Michel were planted some 40–60 years previously, followed by later plantings on Michel as well as on both West and South Islands. In the absence of any earlier references that status of the coconut on Aldabra must remain uncertain. In recent years nuts have been recovered from the sea shore, but whether they are of local origin, or are the survivers of long-distance dispersal from other islands, is not known.

Three species, *Oxalis* sp., the banana (*Musa* sp.) and the coco-de-mer (*Lodoicea maldivica*), have been noted in the early records of the islands but have not been seen in recent years, neither are there any herbarium records. The lime, *Citrus aurantifolia*, is believed to have disappeared in recent years.

(b) Endemic taxa

The endemic flora of the Aldabra archipelago consists of 43 taxa (25 % of the native flora), of which the majority, as may be expected, are derived from African–Madagascan stock (table 2, see microfiche). If we include all those taxa whose distribution extends to other islands in the Indian Ocean but not to the mainland of Africa, Madagascar or Asia, the total rises to 53.

Apart from the granite islands of the Seychelles, the other islands are of recent or fairly recent coral or volcanic origins. Their floras are of continental origin, the product of random long-distance dispersal by birds and ocean currents (Melville 1973).

According to the theories of MacArthur & Wilson (1967) and Simberloff (1974), the biota of any island consists of a dynamic equilibrium between the immigration of new species and the extinction of those already present. The differentiation of any endemic taxa that is likely to take place under such conditions is the product of the limited distribution of parental continental material and insular isolation.

To a biogeographer, endemism *per se* does not appear meaningful unless the taxa are analysed according to their genetic affinities. The 53 endemic taxa *sensu lato* present in the Aldabra archipelago are shown in table 2, together with their assumed relationship and continent of origin. For infraspecific taxa this is a straightforward analysis; at the species level, in the absence of any monographic treatment, the accepted relationship is generally the affinity assumed by the author of the species concerned. In instances where the author has referred to another Indian Ocean endemic species, then that too is examined for its continental affinities. The method is undoubtedly crude, but is considered sufficiently accurate for establishing the continent of origin.

The endemic status of a few taxa is uncertain. Perhaps in some instances the taxonomist concerned has been overcritical. In practice this does not matter for the purposes of this present exercise.

(c) *Native taxa*

Of the 176 native taxa, including endemics, only 5 are not found on Aldabra. However, for the purposes of this paper they will be treated as part of the Aldabra flora. The calculations given in the text are of such a general nature that a few additional taxa will not affect the conclusions.

3. DISPERSAL BY WIND

From December to March, during the season of the Northeast Monsoon, the winds are generally light and variable, while from May to September the southeast trade winds prevail, with average speeds of between 28 and 37 km/h (15–20 knots) (Passmore 1971). Such winds clearly do not favour the transport of propagules from Africa or Madagascar, whereas in the Galapagos Islands, where the winds are favourable, 31 % of the native flora is dispersed by wind (Porter 1976), compared with only 5% for Aldabra.

The average frequency of tropical cyclones in the Madagascar area is six or seven per year (Gentilli 1958; Boucher 1975). During the Monsoon season tropical storms breed and migrate over the Indian Ocean to the north and east of Madagascar. Some may cross the coast of Madagascar, but most recurve southwards and then move away to the southeast; some, such as hurricane 'Georgette', may be distinctly erratic in their course (Boucher 1975). With speeds of 100 km/h or more, hurricanes may be regarded as an effective means of transport for even quite large propagules, and although Aldabra may lie a little to the north of the belt of rather frequent hurricanes, these could nevertheless be regarded as a possible effective means of wind transport.

The low level (1–2 km), high-speed, westward-flowing jet streams observed by Findlater (1974) during the season of the southeast trade winds are not regarded as likely means of transport, partly because of the distances envolved in crossing the Indian Ocean, partly because of the smallness of the target area, but chiefly because of conspicuous absence of wind-dispersed taxa of Asiatic origin. The rarefied atmosphere and the intense cold of the jet stream are other factors that have to be considered.

The two families present whose propagules would appear to be best adapted for wind dispersal are the Compositae and Asclepiadaceae. In both cases the efficiency of the pappus is dependent upon dry conditions; the pappus is liable to collapse in moist air and is therefore regarded as unsuitable for transoceanic crossings. The paucity of native composites on Aldabra (3 species, of which 2 are sea-dispersed), is possibly a reflexion of the ineffectiveness of the pappus.

There are 4, possibly 5, native asclepiads on the islands. Since the terminal pappus readily disarticulates from the relatively large, flattened seed, the pappus is clearly effective over short distances only. The method of long-distance dispersal requires investigation.

The minute seeds of the orchids (3 species), and the spores of the pteridophytes (2 species) are generally accepted as being wind dispersed. For further discussion on the problems of wind dispersal see Wickens (1976).

4. Dispersal by sea

The currents of the southern Indian Ocean have been described by Passmore (1971). Throughout much of the southern Indian Ocean the currents are highly variable in direction. Although the Aldabra archipelago lies in the path of the predominantly westward flowing Equatorial Current, it may also be influenced by currents flowing northwards from the east coast of Madagascar, or north-eastwards from Africa.

According to Passmore (1971) the currents in the Aldabra area have an average speed of approximately 3.5 km/h (2 knots), so that it is theoretically possible for drift material to reach Aldabra from Madagascar in 5 days or Africa in $7\frac{1}{2}$ days.

(a) Strand vegetation

The dispersal of plant propagules by sea is well documented in the pioneer works of Guppy (1890, 1906, 1917). Of particular reference to the Indian Ocean are Guppy (1890) for Keeling Island, Muir (1937) for the coast of South Africa and Sauer (1961, 1967) for Mauritius and the Seychelles. Illustrations of many tropical drift seeds and fruits, together with a key for their identification, will be found in Gunn & Dennis (1976).

The experimental work of Guppy has adequately demonstrated that many propagules are capable of germination after floating in sea water for 6 or 7 weeks, or even longer, during which time the propagules could travel 1600 km, or further, with a surface current of 1.8 km/h (1 knot). As far as the strand flora of the Aldabra archipelago is concerned, a minimum buoyancy period of 7–10 days should suffice for propagules to drift from Madagascar or Africa under a favourable wind.

Considering the expanse of the Indian Ocean and the size of the islands therein, the efficiency by which strand plants are effectively dispersed is surprising. However, effective dispersal must not be confused with establishment. Hnatiuk & Merton (1976) have recorded the viable propagules of approximately 50 species collected over a period of 20 months from the beaches of Aldabra, yet not one of them is currently represented in the flora.

An example of the recent establishment of a widespread strand plant on Aldabra is the recent discovery, on an islet in the lagoon, of *Dodonaea viscosa*. According to Guppy (1917), the mode of dispersal in order of effectiveness is by granivorous birds, currents and man; wind is suggested as another possibility. The first method would appear to be the more probable in this particular instance.

Successful dispersal must be followed by successful establishment. Guppy (1890) has suggested that the predation of seedlings by land crabs could be responsible for the unsuccessful establishment of many strand plants (see Alexander 1979, this volume, for further discussion).

The strand flora of the Aldabra archipelago, with very few exceptions, consists of species that are widely distributed throughout the Indo-Pacific region, some even further afield. The small-seeded grasses and herbs generally have a more limited distribution, to the western Indian Ocean and the coastal regions of Africa and Madagascar. Their mode of dispersal is largely unknown. Possibly the propagules are dispersed by the muddy feet of birds, especially waders and other shore birds, although according to Moreau (1938) migrant waders may rest on the sea during transit and consequently wash off any adherent propagules. Falla (1960) appears to doubt whether viable propagules are able to adhere in sufficient quantities or for sufficient time for vagrant or migrant passerines to be effective distributers of propagules, but see later discussion on dispersal by birds.

Bor (1960) follows Ridley (1930) in suggesting that the seeds of *Lepturus repens*, *Paspalum distichum*, *Sporobolus virginicus* and *Stenotaphrum* sp. are protected from salt water and are dispersed by the sea, although the evidence for this, apart from their coastal distribution, is largely lacking. According to Sauer (1972) the propagules of *Stenotaphrum* become waterlogged and sink after 7–10 days. However, as far as Aldabra is concerned, this provides ample time for the spikelets to be effectively distributed by means of island-hopping across the Indian Ocean. Further experimental work is clearly required to determine the buoyancy period and the effect of salt water on germination of the strand grasses and herbs.

In table 1 the strand flora is classified either as 'strand' or 'lagoon'. The first are those species that are generally able to establish themselves along the exposed sea shore, the second are generally found in the less exposed inlets and sheltered lagoons, i.e. the mangroves and the low herbs of the mud flats. According to Macnae (1971), *Hibiscus tiliaceus*, which on Aldabra occurs at Anse Var, and on Astove at Grand Anse, is a species normally associated with the tidal flats to the landward side of mangroves; this is probably due to a confusion with *Thespesia populneoides*.

Macnae (1971) has also argued that the absence of mangroves on the Chagos archipelago can be taken as an indication that the mangroves must have migrated along the coast of Arabia to Africa and then to Aldabra rather than across the Indian Ocean; the possibility that suitable conditions for establishment may not exist on Chagos does not appear to have been considered.

Certainly other plants have managed to cross the Indian Ocean without difficulty. Thus *Calophyllum inophyllum*, which is present on the Chagos archipelago as well as Aldabra, is sporadically present along the east coast of Africa, a distribution in keeping with the westward peripheral distribution of an Indo-Pacific strand plant.

(b) Rafting

Such astute observers as Guppy (1890, 1906, 1917) and Muir (1937) have noted germinating seeds in holes and crevices on drift pumice and logs washed up by the sea and have deduced their transport across the oceans by such means. The seeds belong to those members of the strand flora that have small seeds which do not readily float, yet are capable of withstanding frequent immersions in the sea. They include *Portulaca oleracea*, *Sesuvium portulacastrum*, *Suriana maritima*, *Pemphis acidula*, *Scaevola taccada* and *Triumfetta procumbens*. Such circumstantial evidence requires the examination of drift material in mid-ocean for confirmation; it is perhaps difficult to imagine how the seeds could have become wedged with sufficient security from the very outset of the voyage to withstand the tossing and buffeting of an ocean voyage.

Floating islands of living plants suggest a more practicable mode of transport, not only for plant propagules, but molluscs, insects, etc., as well. Benson & Penny (1971) suggest that the white-throated rail (*Dryolimnas cuvieri*) and the Malagasy coucal (*Centropus toulou*), both poor fliers, may have travelled to Aldabra from Madagascar by rafting; certainly an island rather than a log would provide a suitable vehicle. Several large clumps of bamboo washed ashore on Aldabra in February 1968, after the hurricane 'Georgette' over Madagascar the previous month, furnish evidence for the availability of such transport, although unfortunately no examination was carried out to see what passengers they might have been carrying. There is also the possibility that the giant tortoise might have been transported by such means and, in turn, transported seeds via its digestive tract. Tortoise dung on Aldabra has been found to be a suitable medium for short-distance dispersal of many seeds and fruits.

TABLE 3. THE FEEDING HABITS OF THE BIRDS OF THE ALDABRA ARCHIPELAGO

class	status	piscivores	molluscivores	insectivores	omnivores	frugivores/ granivores
land	endemic	—	—	7 (1)	7	1
	resident	1	—	6	—	—
	migrant	—	—	14 (3)	—	—
	vagrant	—	1	7 (3)	—	1
shore	migrant	1	1	11 (5)	—	—
	vagrant	—	1	5	—	—
sea	resident	11	—	—	—	—
	migrant	7	—	—	—	—

Note: A number of land and shore birds are basically insectivorous but are known to eat seeds or berries on occasions. The number of species involved are shown in parentheses.

5. DISPERSAL BY BIRDS

An analysis of the feeding habits of all resident, migrant and vagrant birds recorded from the archipelago (table 3) has been complied from the reports of Gaymer (1967), Benson (1970 a, b), Benson & Penny (1971), Penny (1971), Penny & Diamond (1971), Diamond (1971), Stoddart *et al.* (1970) and Frith (1976). Supplementary information on their diet has been obtained from Collinge (1924–7), Bannerman (1930–51) and Drive Publications (1969). Although the eating of seeds and fruits cannot be taken as positive evidence of bird dispersal, it at least provides an indication of the possibility.

It would be wrong to presume that sea birds are of little importance as transporters of seeds to the archipelago; a few examples of sea birds eating fruits are recorded by Ridley (1930). Both Guppy (1890) and St John (1951) state that the anthocarps of *Pisonia grandis* are transported externally by sea birds, although the only reference regarding the association of birds on Aldabra with *Pisonia grandis* is a comment by Benson & Penny (1971) of the Pied Crow (*Corvus albus*) nesting therein.

Muir (1937) suggests that the fruits of *Triumfetta procumbens* are possibly dispersed by adhesion to the plumage of birds; and Guppy (1890) has reported finding the fruits attached to the feathers of boobies. Guppy has also recorded finding the seeds of *Caesalpinia bonduc* in the stomach of both frigate birds and boobies, while Fosberg (1978, personal communication) has identified *Ipomoea pes-caprae* in the stomach of a tern (*Gygis* sp.) from the Marshall Islands. Guppy considers sea birds an important agency for seed dispersal and suggests that *Pemphis acidula*, which is ill-adapted for sea dispersal, is transported by sea birds.

The diet of the waders and other shore-birds consists mainly of insects, molluscs and crustaceans, with seeds or berries forming a very minor part of their diet. Since they are non-perching, the seeds or fruits are either from the ground flora or windfalls. Their rôle in seed dispersal would appear to convey seeds in mud caked to their feet, although McAtee (1947) regards this as exceptional, seeds attached to the feathers being regarded as more likely, since the feet are usually very clean.

The land birds of the archipelago are mainly insectivorous. Only one species, the endemic Comoro blue pigeon (*Alectroenas sganzini minor*) appears to be entirely frugivorous. Another endemic, the Malagasy turtle dove (*Streptopelia picturata coppingeri*) is mainly frugivorous, feeding on fallen fruits and seeds and occasional insects.

A vagrant, mainly granivorous, turtle dove (*Streptopelia turtur*) observed by Frith (1974) feeding with a flock of *S. picturata* may represent a hitherto unsuspected normal source of seed transport. Although only one bird was seen, it is possible that this species may have been present in other flocks of *S. picturata coppingeri*, with which it may be readily confused. There may even be other species that were resident, migrant or vagrant, for which there are no records available (C. B. Frith 1976, 1977, personal communications).

The three other important fruit-eating birds are omnivorous and endemic. They are: the Malagasy bulbul (*Hypsipetes madagascariensis rostratus*), Malagasy white-eye (*Zosterops madagaspatana aldabrensis*) and the red-headed forest fody (*Foudia eminentissima aldabrana*). There are also six insectivorous migrants or vagrants that are known to eat seeds or fruits on occasions and may therefore be considered as possible infrequent vectors.

The results of this avifaunal analysis are, at first sight, puzzling. A considerable number of the inland flora (as distinct from the strand flora) have fruits or seeds that are believed to be dispersed by birds, yet their otherwise apparently suitable vectors are represented by subspecies endemic to Aldabra; the subspecies are said to have their origins in Madagascar (Benson & Penny 1971).

Seed dispersal and establishment, however rare, is a continuous process. Neither is it a one-way process, as can be seen from the example of *Tarenna trichantha*, once regarded as confined to the archipelago but during the past two decades there have been three records from the Comoros and the east coast of Africa, suggestive of a recent introduction to the mainland by birds. Indeed, there is undoubtedly a continuous exchange of genetic material between the archipelago and the mainland, and in both directions. The problem is to obtain proof to support the otherwise irrefutable circumstantial evidence.

It seems inconceivable that the numerous species present that have berries or drupes apparently suitable for bird transport should not have been eaten and transported internally by birds. A 500 km journey with a flight speed of 50 km/h and a 10 h ingestion/excretion rate, or permutations thereof, is not unreasonable. There is well documented evidence for such seed dispersal elsewhere: 77% of the flowering plants of the Galápagos Islands, for example, are dispersed by birds, involving a sea crossing of 800 km (Porter 1976). The alternative of sea transport for these inland species is untenable. Although there is little or no evidence to support the idea, it is suggested that the inland species have little or no salt tolerance compared with strand species. This is another aspect of the island flora where further research is required.

There is always the possibility of a few migrant birds flying high enough to reach the jet stream, and make very fast passages over long distances, perhaps attaining speeds of 160 km/h (R. K. Murton 1977, personal communication). This would, of course, be for westward flying birds.

Too little is known about the past distribution of the birds. The Pleistocene fossil record for Aldabra reveals the presence of an extinct duck, *Aldabranas cabri*, and a small procellarid, *Pterodroma kurodai* as well as the native rail, *Dryolimnas cuvieri* (Harrison & Walker 1978). The first two pre-date the final emergence of Aldabra while the rail possibly post-dates the emergence.

Are the present endemic species the result of vagrants that were unable to return to their homeland, or was there a regular movement of birds between Madagascar and the archipelago, and a gradual isolation? Is the isolation complete, or are there sporadic reinforcements from Madagascar? How effective are the migrant birds from the African mainland? Answers to these and other questions would lead to a deeper understanding of birds as dispersal agents.

At a very rough estimate the native flora contains 120 taxa that could have been introduced by birds, either internally or externally. The average rate of introduction and successful establishment over the 80 000 years since the archipelago was last exposed above the sea is approximately 1 taxon every 650 years. This compares with 7900 years for the Galápagos Islands and 20–30 000 years for the Hawaiian Islands (Porter 1976); these estimates, however, have not taken into account possible changes in land area with changes in sea level. A more conservative estimate for Aldabra to allow for past changes in the flora, based on the successful establishment of 200 taxa, would be at the rate of 1 taxon every 400 years.

Even if the probability of a bird successfully introducing a propagule in any one year was 1 in 10^6, then the migrant bird population required would be only 2500. Thus, the apparent paradox of a large bird-dispersed flora and no obvious active vectors can be simply explained by a very slow introduction over a long time. What we are unable to estimate are the number of introductions that have taken place for each successful establishment.

6. DISPERSAL BY BATS

The frugivorous fruit-bats are represented on Aldabra by the endemic *Pteropus seychellensis aldabrensis*, with the other subspecies in the Seychelles, Mafia Island and the Comoro Islands (Hill 1971). They are nocturnal creatures and very little is known about their behaviour on Aldabra. According to Ridley (1930) the fruit-bats are strong, if slow, fliers and have been observed a long way out to sea, although little is known about their migratory habits. They are known to feed on the flesh of such fruits as *Calophyllum*, *Eugenia*, *Ficus*, *Terminalia catappa*, etc., but do not swallow the hard seeds, although on occasions certain small seeds, such as those of *Ficus*, have been found in the intestines (van der Pijl 1957). They are regarded as very unlikely agents for long-distance dispersal as far as the flora of Aldabra is concerned.

7. Discussion

According to Braithwaite *et al.* (1973) the last emergence of Aldabra from beneath the sea took place during the mid-Pleistocene, approximately 80 000 years ago. It may perhaps be reasonably assumed that the other islands of the archipelago have a similar history and were colonized by angiosperms after their emergence. It follows that the successful establishment of the giant tortoise could only have taken place after the vegetation had been sufficiently well established to ensure its successful regeneration as well as withstanding the depredations of the tortoise for food and shade.

We have no knowledge of the constituents of this original flora from its initial development from strand species and the later development of an interior scrub or woodland as more and more land became exposed with the lowering of the sea level. The increased land exposure and distance from the sea would have permitted the development of freshwater resources, which in turn would have permitted the establishment of an inland flora consisting of species that are relatively intolerant of saline conditions (Whitehead & Jones 1969). At present we know very little about the salt tolerance capabilities of this inland flora on Aldabra.

It is estimated that during the period of maximum exposure (400 km²) the native flora would, according to the species-area formula of MacArthur & Wilson (1967), have consisted of between 210 and 250 taxa, as compared with the 175 present today on 155 km². This period of maximum exposure was followed by a rise in sea level, culminating some 4000–5000 years ago in the breaching of the land rim to form the present lagoon, thus reducing the then available land area by nearly 60 %. The establishment of the mangrove vegetation is believed to post-date this event. It is tempting to suggest that those birds that nest exclusively in the mangrove trees, such as the frigate birds (*Fregata minor* and *F. ariel*), red-footed booby (*Sula sula*) and the white tern (*Gygis alba*), were not resident on the island until the formation of the lagoon and its mangrove fringe.

The close association of the fig-wasp and the fig raises the problem of their joint dispersal. The fig-wasp is essential for the pollination of the fig, with a specific wasp being generally associated with a single species of *Ficus* (Corner 1940). The fig-wasps on Aldabra have been investigated by Wiebes (1975). Does the same wasp–fig relation exist throughout the distribution of the fig on the various islands? The fruits of the fig are known to be eaten by birds and apparently dispersed from island to island. How are the wasps dispersed?

It is hoped that at least some of the problems raised by these speculations on seed dispersal will encourage other workers, including those from disciplines other than botany, to carry out further field work in an attempt to find the solutions.

8. Conclusions

The period during which the present flora evolved is a measure of the success of the combined processes of transport and establishment. It is evident that man with his cultivated plants and weeds has been extremely successful. Wind transport has been the least effective. Considering the large number of viable propagules that are washed up annually but are not present in the flora, sea dispersal is extremely efficient, although the changes of establishment are relatively poor. The largest proportion of the native flora is believed to have been carried by birds, mainly internally. This has been a slow but efficient process, the apparent shortage of suitable vectors being the limiting factor. It is perhaps interesting to note that the apparent carrying capacity of the vegetation in terms of abundance of seeds and fruit seems to be far in excess of the requirements of the present bird population.

The writer has been helped by a number of people who have either assisted by critically reading the text or by supplying answers to my many queries. I should especially like to thank the following: C. W. Benson, W. R. P. Bourne, J. P. M. Brenan, W. D. Clayton, M. J. Coe, C. B. Frith, P. S. Green, S. H. Hnatiuk, R. M. Melville, R. K. Murton, S. A. Renvoize, A. J. Scott, D. R. Stoddart and S. R. J. Woodell.

References (Wickens)

Alexander, H. G. L. 1979 A preliminary assessment of the rôle of the terrestrial decapod crustaceans in the Aldabran ecosystem. *Phil. Trans. R. Soc. Lond.* B **286**, 241–246 (this volume).

Alston, A. H. G. 1925 Revision of the genus *Cassipourea*. *Bull. misc. Inf. R. bot. Gdns, Kew* **1925**, 241–276.

Bailon, M. H. 1850 *Étude génerale du groupe des Euphoriacées*. Paris: Libraire de Victor Masson.

Baker, J. G. 1875 Revision of the genera and species of *Asparagaceae*. *J. Linn. Soc.* **14**, 508–632.

Baker, J. G. 1877 *Flora of Mauritius and the Seychelles*. Ashford: L. Reeve & Co.

Baker, J. G. 1883 Contributions to the flora of Madagascar. *J. Linn. Soc.* **20**, 87–304.

Baker, J. G. 1894 Flora of the Aldabra Islands. *Bull. misc. Inf. R. bot. Gdns Kew* **1894**, 146–151.

Bannerman, D. A. 1930–51 *The birds of tropical West Africa*, vols 1–8. London: Crown Agents.

Baty, S. C. E. 1896 A report on Aldabra and Cosmoledo groups of islands. Seychelles: unpublished report (in Library, Royal Botanic Gardens, Kew).

Bayne, C. J., Cogan, B. H., Diamond, A. W., Frazier, J., Grubb, P., Hutson, A., Poore, M. E. D., Stoddart, D. R. & Taylor, J. D. 1970 Geography and ecology of Cosmoledo Atoll. *Atoll Res. Bull.* **136**, 37–56.

Benson, C. W. 1970*a* Land (including shore) birds of Cosmoledo. *Atoll Res. Bull.* **136**, 67–81.

Benson, C. W. 1970*b* Land (including shore) birds of Astove. *Atoll Res. Bull.* **136**, 115–120.

Benson, C. W. & Penny, M. J. 1971 The land birds of Aldabra. *Phil. Trans. R. Soc. Lond.* B **260**, 417–427.

Bor, N. L. 1960 *The grasses of Burma, Ceylon, India and Pakistan (excluding Bambuseae)*. London: Pergamon Press.

Bosser, J. 1976 Le genre *Hederorkis* Thou. (Orchidaceae) aux Mascareignes et aux Seychelles. *Adansonia: N.S.* **16**, 225–228.

Boucher, K. 1975 *Global climate*. London: English University Press.

Braithwaite, C. J. R., Taylor, J. D. & Kennedy, W. J. 1973 The evolution of an atoll: the depositional and erosional history of Aldabra. *Phil. Trans. R. Soc. Lond.* B **266**, 307–340.

Candolle, A. P. de 1862 *Prodromus systematis naturalis regni vegetabilis*, vol. 15. Paris: Treuttel & Würtz.

Carlquist, S. 1965 *Island life*. New York: The Natural History Press.

Carlquist, S. 1974 *Island biology*. Columbia: Columbia University Press.

Collinge, W. E. 1924–7 *The food of some British wild birds*. York: Collinge.

Corner, E. J. H. 1940 *Wayside trees of Malaya*. Singapore: Government Printer.

Diamond, A. W. 1971 The ecology of the sea birds of Aldabra. *Phil. Trans. R. Soc. Lond.* B **260**, 561–571.

Drive Publications Ltd 1969 *Book of British birds*. London: Readers Digest Association Ltd.

Dupont, R. P. 1907 *Report on a visit of investigation to St. Pierre, Astove, Cosmoledo, Assumption and the Aldabra group*. Victoria, Mahé: Government Printer.

Falla, R. A. 1960 Oceanic birds as dispersal agents. *Proc. R. Soc. Lond.* B **152**, 655–659.

Findlater, J. 1974 The low-level cross-equatorial air current of the western Indian Ocean during the northern summer. *Weather, Lond.* **29**, 411–415.

Fosberg, F. R. 1974 Miscellaneous notes on the flora of Aldabra and neighbouring islands: III. *Kew Bull.* **29**, 253–266.

Fosberg, F. R. 1977*a* Miscellaneous notes on the flora of Aldabra and neighbouring islands: IV. *Kew Bull.* **31**, 829–835.

Fosberg, F. R. 1977*b* Miscellaneous notes on the flora of Aldabra and neighbouring islands: VI. *Kew Bull.* **32**, 253–258.

Fosberg, F. R. 1978*a* Miscellaneous notes on the flora of Aldabra and neighbouring islands: VII–XI. *Kew Bull.* **33**, 133–144 and 181–190.

Fosberg, F. R. 1978*b* Studies in the genus *Boerhavia* L. (Nyctaginaceae), 1–5. *Smithson. Contrib. Bot.* **39**, 1–20.

Frith, C. B. 1974 New observations of migrants and vagrants for Aldabra, Farquhar and Astove Atolls, Indian Ocean. *Bull. Br. orn. Club.* **94**, 12–19.

Frith C. B. 1976 A twelve-month field study of the Aldabra Fody, *Foudia eminentissima aldabrana*. *Ibis* **118**, 155–178.

Gaymer, R. 1967 Observations on the birds of Aldabra in 1964 and 1965. *Atoll Res. Bull.* **118**, 113–125.

Gentilli, J. 1958 *A geography of climate.* Perth: University of W. Australia Press.

Gillett, J. B., Polhill, R. M. & Verdcourt, B. 1971 *Flora of Tropical East Africa: Leguminosae subfamily Papilionoideae* (2 vols). London: Crown Agents.

Gunn, C. R. & Dennis, J. V. 1976 *World guide to tropical drift seeds and fruits.* New York: Quadrangle/The New York Times Book Co.

Guppy, H. P. 1890 The dispersal of plants as illustrated by the flora of the Keeling or Cocos Islands. *J. Trans. Vict. Inst.* **24**, 267–306.

Guppy, H. P. 1906 *Observations of a naturalist in the Pacific between 1896 and 1899.* Vol. 2, Plant dispersal. London: Macmillan & Co.

Guppy, H. P. 1917 *Plants, seeds and currents in the West Indies and Azores. The results of investigations carried out in those regions between 1906 and 1914.* London: Williams & Norgate.

Harrison, C. J. O. & Walker, C. A. 1978 Pleistocene bird remains from Aldabra Atoll, Indian Ocean. *J. nat. Hist.* **12**, 7–14.

Hemsley, J. H. 1966 Notes on African Sapotaceae IV–VIII. *Kew Bull.* **20**, 461–510.

Hemsley, W. B. 1916 Flora of Seychelles and Aldabra. *J. Bot., Lond.* **54**, 361–363 and suppl. 2, 1–24.

Hemsley, W. B. *et al.* 1919 Flora of Aldabra with notes on the flora of the neighbouring islands. *Bull. misc. Inf. R. bot. Gnds. Kew* **1919**, 108–153.

Hill, J. E. 1971 The bats of Aldabra Atoll, western Indian Ocean. *Phil. Trans R. Soc. Lond.* B **260**, 573–576.

Hnatiuk, R. J. & Merton, L. F. H. 1976 A vegetation study of Aldabra. (Mimeo.)

Horsburgh, J. 1841 *The Indian Directory, or, Directions for sailing to and from the East Indies, China, Australia, . . ., resulting from the experiences of twenty-one years in the navigation of these seas,* edn 5, 2 vols. London: W. H. Allen.

Leenhouts, P. W. 1967 A conspectus of the genus *Allophylus* (Sapindaceae). The problem of the complex species. *Blumea* **15**, 301–358.

MacArthur, R. H. & Wilson, E. O. 1967 *The theory of island biogeography.* Princeton: Princeton University Press.

Macnae, W. 1971 Mangroves on Aldabra. *Phil. Trans. R. Soc. Lond.* B **260**, 237–247.

Marais, W. 1971 The extra-Madagascan species of *Lomatophyllum* (Liliaceae). *Kew Bull.* **29**, 721–723.

McAtee, W. L. 1947 Distribution of seeds by birds. *Am. Midl. Nat.* **38**, 214–223.

Melville, R. 1973 Continental drift and the distribution of the island floras of the Indian Ocean. *J. Mar. biol. Ass. India* **15**, 236–241.

Moreau, R. E. 1938 Bird migration over the north-western part of the Indian Ocean, Red Sea, and the Mediterranean. *Proc. zool. Soc. Lond.* A **108**, 1–26.

Moresby, F. 1822 Memoir on the isles in the Indian Ocean. Manuscript, London: India Office Records Dept.

Muir, J. 1937 The seed-drift of South Africa and some influences of ocean currents on strand vegetation. *Mem. bot. Surv. S. Afr.* no. 16.

Page, J. S. & Jeffrey, C. 1975 A palyno-taxonomic study of African *Peponium* (Cucurbitaceae). *Kew Bull.* **30**, 495–502.

Passmore, W. M. 1971 *South Indian Ocean pilot,* edn 8. London: Ministry of Defence, Hydrographic Dept.

Peake, J. F. 1971 The evolution of the terrestrial fauna in the western Indian Ocean. *Phil. Trans. R. Soc. Lond.* B **260**, 581–610.

Penny, M. J. 1971 Migrant waders at Aldabra, September 1967–March 1968. *Phil. Trans. R. Soc. Lond.* B **260**, 549–559.

Penny, M. J. & Diamond, A. W. 1971 The White-throated Rail *Dryolimnas cuvieri* on Aldabra. *Phil. Trans. R. Soc. Lond.* B **260**, 529–548.

Porter, D. M. 1976 Geography and dispersal of Galapagos Islands vascular plants. *Nature Lond.* **264**, 745–746.

Renvoize, S. A. 1971*a* The origin and distribution of the flora of Aldabra. *Phil. Trans R. Soc. Lond.* B **260**, 227–236.

Renvoize, S. A. 1971*b* Miscellaneous notes on the flora of Aldabra and neighbouring islands: I. *Kew Bull.* **25**, 417–422.

Renvoize, S. A. 1972 Miscellaneous notes on the flora of Aldabra and neighbouring islands: II. *Kew Bull.* **26**, 433–438.

Renvoize, S. A. 1975 A floristic analysis of the western Indian Ocean coral islands. *Kew Bull.* **30**, 133–152.

Ridley, H. N. 1930 *The dispersal of plants throughout the world.* Ashford: L. Reeve & Co.

St John, H. 1951 The distribution of *Pisonia grandis* (Nyctaginaceae). *Webbia* **8**, 225–228.

St John, H. 1974 Revision of the genus *Pandanus* Stickman: part 37. *Pandanus* on Aldabra Island, Indian Ocean. *Pac. Sci.* **28**, 83–100.

Sauer, J. D. 1961 Coastal plant geography of Mauritius. *La St. Univ. Stud., Coastal Studies Series,* no. 5.

Sauer, J. D. 1967 *Plants and man on the Seychelles coast. A study in historical biogeography.* Madison: University of Wisconsin Press.

Sauer, J. D. 1972 Revision of *Stenotaphrum* (Gramineae: Paniceae) with attention to its historical geography. *Brittonia* **24**, 202–222.

Schinz, H. 1897 Zur Kenntnis der Flora der Aldabra-Inseln. *Abh. Senckenb. naturforsch. Ges.* **21**, 77–91.

Simberloff, D. S. 1974 Equilibrium theory of island biogeography and ecology. *A. Rev. Ecol. Syst.* **5**, 161–182.

Spurs, T. J. 1892 (Report on Aldabra to T. Risely Griffiths, Esq., Administrator of Seychelles Islands, Port Victoria, Seychelles, July 19, 1891) Colonial Reports – Annual, no. 40. Mauritius (Seychelles and Rodriguez). Annual Reports for 1889 and 1890, with a report on the island of Aldabra (50 pages). London: H.M.S.O. Aldabra report, pp. 46–50; letters of transmittal by T. R. Griffiths, pp. 44–45.

Stirling, W. 1843 *Narrative of the wreck of the ship 'Tiger' of Liverpool . . ., on the desert island of Astova, . . .* Exeter: Stirling private publication.

Stoddart, D. R., Benson, C. W. & Peake, J. F. 1970 Ecological changes and effects of phosphate mining on Assumption Island. *Atoll Res. Bull.* **136**, 121–145.

Taylor, G. 1930 Notes from the British Museum Herbarium. *Nesogenes africanum* Taylor. *J. Bot., Lond.* **68**, 84.

Turrill, W. B. *et al.* 1918 Diagnoses Africanae: LXXI. *Bull. Misc. Inf. R. bot. Gdns. Kew* **1918**, 202–207.

van der Pijl, L. 1957 The dispersal of plants by bats (Chiropterochory). *Acta bot. neerl.* **6**, 291–315.

van der Pijl, L. 1972 *Principles of dispersal in higher plants*, edn 2. Berlin: Springer–Verlag.

Verdcourt, B. 1975 Studies in the *Rubiaceae–Rubioideae* for the 'Flora of Tropical East Africa': I. *Kew Bull.* **30**, 247–326.

Whitehead, D. R. & Jones, C. E. 1969 Small islands and the equilibrium theory of insular biogeography. *Evolution* **23**, 171–179.

Wickens, G. E. 1976 Speculations on long-distance dispersal and the flora of Jebel Marra, Sudan Republic. *Kew Bull.* **31**, 105–150.

Wiebes, J. T. 1975 Fig insects from Aldabra (Hymenoptera, Chalcidoidea). *Zoöl. Meded., Leiden* **49**, 225–236.

MICROFICHE

The relevant frames of the microfiche included with this publication contain the following tables referred to in the text of this paper.

TABLE 1. CHECK LIST OF THE TERRESTRIAL FLORA:
ITS DISTRIBUTION, MODE OF DISPERSAL AND STATUS

TABLE 2. ENDEMIC TAXA OF THE INDIAN OCEAN ISLANDS PRESENT IN THE ALDABRA ARCHIPELAGO AND THEIR AFFINITIES

Phil. Trans. R. Soc. Lond. B. **286**, 99–108 (1979) [99]
Printed in Great Britain

The rôle of unspecialized pollinators in the reproductive success of Aldabran plants

By S. R. J. WOODELL

Botany School, University of Oxford, Oxford, U.K.

Plants dispersed to remote islands may leave their usual pollinators behind. They are faced with extinction, inbreeding, or acceptance of other pollen vectors, possibly of the 'generalist' type. There are few specialized pollinator–plant relations on Aldabra. Two species, the sunbird *Nectarinia sovimanga* and the cetoniid beetle *Mausoleopsis aldabrensis*, visit many plant species. The latter was observed visiting flowers of 58 % of those species observed in flower on Aldabra in early 1974. It was apparently indifferent to distributional origin of the species, flower colour, flower morphology or whether the plants were native or introduced. It exhibited a high degree of constancy to a plant species in a foraging flight. The parallels between this beetle and the carpenter bee *Xylocopa darwinii* on the Galápagos Islands are pointed out. The importance of such a generalist pollinator to the chances of establishment of new immigrants to islands, and to the breeding systems of island plants in general, are discussed.

1. INTRODUCTION

Plant species dispersed over a long distance and becoming established far from their existing ranges may be beyond the range of their normal pollinators. For plants pollinated by generalists, such as some flies and beetles, or by wind, this might not matter. Other species may be at a disadvantage. Those which have evolved adaptations to a particular type of pollinating animal, or which have a very close relationship with a highly specific pollinator, are especially likely to have pollination problems.

The breeding system of the plant is also relevant here. Autogamic, and especially self-pollinating species will be at less of a disadvantage than self-incompatible, outcrossing species. Baker (1955, 1967) and Carlquist (1966, 1974) disagree over the relative likelihood of establishment on islands by inbreeding and outbreeding plants, and the importance of outbreeding in the island context. Obviously this problem is related to that of pollination and the two must be considered together.

The chance of the 'normal' pollinator being dispersed to an oceanic island along with the plant's propagules is likely to be remote. What happens under these circumstances? Are wind-pollinated species favoured? Do plants fail to become established as a result of lack of pollinators? Are pollinators accepted from among the existing fauna? Do new plant–pollinator relations evolve? Are 'generalist' pollinators important? This paper is an account of a preliminary broad survey carried out in a period of 7 weeks from late January to mid-March 1974. The limited time available did not permit a detailed investigation of plant–pollinator relations.

Aldabra has advantages for such a study. Its flora is numerically small, so a large proportion of the species can be observed in a short time. The fauna is also depauperate. The relatively recent last emergence of the island (up to 80 000 years ago) may make it unlikely that many new pollinator–plant special relations will have evolved. The flora and its origins are well known and the accessibility of some of the floras from which that of Aldabra has been drawn may facilitate a follow-up programme of work to compare plant–pollinator interactions elsewhere with that on Aldabra.

2. METHODS

As many plant species as possible were observed and pollinator visits were recorded. Though most observations were made on Ile Picard, several different areas on the atoll were visited. Observations were recorded on a cassette tape recorder. My observations were supplemented by those of other workers on the atoll and by notes and comments from previous visitors. Not all plant species were given equal attention; some were very abundant, others were very local and only seen on brief visits to other parts of the atoll. Each species observed in flower was observed for an absolute minimum of 1 h, most for more than this, and some for much longer. These observations were made during periods of high and low insect activity. Plants which might be visited by bats or nocturnal insects were observed during the hours of darkness. Further evidence, such as bat-inflicted damage indicating that visits had occurred, was also collected.

3. RESULTS

(a) Special pollinator–plant relations

Few of these were observed. Several fig-wasps have been identified from my collections of the three species of fig on Aldabra (*Ficus nautarum, F. avi-avi, F. reflexa*) (Wiebes 1975). The presence on the atoll of species which exhibit complex obligate pollinator–plant relations poses distributional problems that go beyond the scope of this paper. *Tournefortia argentea* is closely associated with the moth *Utetheisa aldabrensis*, a day-flying species which goes through its whole life-cycle on this plant. Close relatives of this moth are associated with *Tournefortia* on other islands (B. Cogan, personal communication). *Guettarda speciosa* was seen to be visited in large numbers by the beetle *Oxythyrea aldabrensis* by Dawn Frith (pers. comm.). This may have been a fleeting relation; I did not see this beetle on the plant, but large numbers of another, as yet unidentified, beetle were once seen swarming on *Tournefortia* at Cinq Cases. *Lomatophyllum aldabrense* was frequently visited by a small bee (*Megachile seychellensis*) that can enter the tubular flowers easily, and which was not observed on any other species. Signs of possible bat visits were observed on some flowers of *Capparis cartilaginea* and *Sonneratia alba*. No doubt other close pollinator–plant relationships exist that would be revealed by more detailed observations. Dawn Frith (pers. comm.) has suggested that some hawkmoths are associated especially with *Convolvulus* species. Such close relationships are apparently rare in the Aldabran flora.

(b) Non-specific and infrequently observed pollinators

Ants are numerous all over the atoll, as elsewhere in the tropics, and they were frequently seen running from flower to flower on the same plant. They are likely to be responsible for at least occasional pollinations, and they merit further study. It seems unlikely that ants alone are responsible for sufficient pollination to maintain a population of any species; they appear to be essentially casual pollinators on Aldabra. Some of the tiny 'tortoise turf' species may be ant pollinated, as they are easily visited by walking insects (Hickman 1974). Many small flies, bugs, weevils, beetles and occasional individuals of other insect groups were seen on flowers, but none was observed to move systematically from flower to flower. Butterflies were quite abundant though rarely seen to visit flowers. Some hunting wasps (*Sphex torridus*) were seen, especially on *Colubrina asiatica*, and they occasionally alighted on flowers during their searches for cater-pillars. A species of *Xylocopa* (*X. calens*) was the only large bee seen; it was found on *Thespesia populnea* and *Cordia subcordata*, both capacious flowers, but it was uncommon. Hermit crabs have been observed on flowers of *Pemphis acidula* (H. G. L. Alexander, pers. comm.). There is certainly no apparent shortage of casual pollinators of various kinds, but none of them is likely to play a regular rôle in the successful fertilization of many Aldabran plants.

TABLE 1. SPECIES SEEN TO BE VISITED BY *NECTARINIA SOVIMANGA* (ALDABRA SUNBIRD)

native	introduced
Abutilon angulatum	*Gossypium hirsutum*
Suriana maritima	*Moringa oleifera*
Allophyllus aldabricus	*Caesalpinia bonduc*
Sophora tomentosa	*Delonix regia*
Ceriops tagal	*Passiflora suberosa*
Pemphis acidula	*Catharanthus roseus*
Tricalysia sonderana	*Lantana camara*
Polysphaeria multiflora	*Stachytarpheta jamaicensis*
Guettarda speciosa	*Leonotis nepetifolia*
Scaevola taccada	*Cocos nucifera*
Pleurostelma cernuum	
Cordia subcordata	
Euphorbia pyrifolia	
Lomatophyllum aldabrense	

(c) Birds

The Aldabran fody (*Foudia eminentissima aldabrana*) has been observed by Frith (1976, 1979) visiting four species for nectar (*Cocos nucifera, Pemphis acidula, Polysphaeria multiflora, Vernonia grandis*). The whiteye (*Zosterops maderaspatana*) has also been recorded visiting *Abutilon angulatum, Abrus precatorius, Pemphis acidula* and *Polyphaeria multiflora* for nectar. The bird most frequently seen feeding on flowers is the Aldabra sunbird (*Nectarinia sovimanga*) and I have records of it visiting 27 species (table 1). It may be a very important pollinator, but it is not easy to deter-mine whether pollination actually occurs as a result of sunbird visits, or indeed whether the visits are always for nectar or for insects. The data presented by Frith (1979, this volume) indicate that the sunbird consumes large quantities of nectar on occasions. There are few species on Aldabra which appear to be adapted for pollination by birds. Two, *Lomatophyllum aldabrense* and *Leonotis nepetifolia* (Gill & Wolfe 1975), are visited by sunbirds on Aldabra and produce abundant nectar.

(d) Beetles

Though beetles are numerous and frequent flower visitors (Müller 1883) they are regarded as of relatively little importance in flower pollination (Proctor & Yeo 1973) and they are primitive pollinators of the 'mess and soil' type (Faegri & van der Pijl 1972). Some feed destructively on flowers. Grant (1950) has suggested that beetles are much more important as pollinators in semi-desert areas than in moister regions. In Britain I have observed numerous individuals of Staphylinidae in *Primula* flowers and I have recorded very frequently numerous beetles of the genus *Meligethes* on *Primula* and *Armeria*, in Britain and Denmark (Woodell, Mattsson & Philipp 1977). These little beetles feed on pollen and move actively between flowers. On Aldabra, a number of small beetles were observed on flowers, but none of them was abundant during my visit. Among larger beetles, one cetoniid, *Mausoleopsis aldabrensis*, was extremely abundant. It is about 1 cm long, with well developed mouthparts. It has a striking black and white pattern which has a disruptive effect despite its conspicuousness. Its extreme abundance on flowers of all kinds made it a very obvious candidate as a 'generalist' pollinator, and it was soon evident that it was visiting a large diversity of plant species.

Initially every observation of a visit to a flower by *Mausoleopsis* was recorded and its behaviour noted. It fed both on nectar and pollen. It could often be seen chewing vigorously on the anthers, sometimes completely destroying them, and pollen was found in the gut of some dissected individuals. When feeding on nectar it was motionless, lapping at the nectar. Some species, e.g. *Gouania scandens*, *Cocos nucifera* and *Pandanus tectorius*, were favoured for nectar, and individuals spent a long time on each flower or inflorescence, whereas those eating pollen moved around more quickly. Individuals feeding on nectar became sluggish, and when a flower or inflorescence was shaken they fell to the ground, apparently intoxicated. Proctor & Yeo (1973) point out that though flower-visiting beetles are more active than others, they tend to depend on their horny exterior and repellent secretions, rather than flight, for protection. Apart from lingering on the nectar-producing flowers, *Mausoleopsis* was very active and readily took flight. It flew very strongly, hovered around flowers often for some time, walked rapidly from flower to flower on the same inflorescence, and frequently flew between inflorescences. At times so many individuals were flying at once that the sound was like that around a beehive. Copulation on inflorescences was frequent. Some individuals were timed in their movements, and they showed that (1) individual foraging flights could include up to 22 flower visits, (2) individuals spent about three times as long on flowers as they did flying, and (3) the time spent on flowers varied from a mean of 18s on *Allophyllus aldabricus* (9 visits) through a mean of 31s on *Maytenus sene-galensis* (43 visits) to one of 97s on *Gouania scandens* (19 visits). The rapidity of flight and number of flowers visited, together with the large amounts of pollen found on bodies and legs of the beetles, indicate that they are likely to be efficient pollen transfer agents.

Flower constancy is a phenomenon encountered among several groups of pollinators, especially bees, bumble bees and solitary bees, butterflies and birds. I can find no records of flower constancy in beetles, though M. Rothschild (pers. comm.) has reported some species of *Anthicoma* in Israel which show behaviour during breeding which probably involves short-term constancy to *Papaver*. Though the advantages of flower constancy to both plants and insects are obvious, for an unspecialized pollinator which feeds apparently haphazardly on nectar and pollen, constancy would appear to have little advantage. *Mausoleopsis aldabrensis* exhibited surprising constancy. Numerous observations were made on individual beetles while large numbers were active, and with two exceptions they were constant to one species. To test whether beetles were visiting only plants that gave sufficient reward, beetles were watched visiting groups of shrubs where several species grew in close proximity. Several species of shrub were visited simultaneously, each individual beetle remaining constant to the species on which it was first seen. Whether this is a permanent feature of the behaviour of *Mausoleopsis* is not known, but even in the short term it must enhance the pollination efficiency of the beetle.

Mausoleopsis aldabrensis was extremely abundant during the rainy season of early 1974. Its abundance in earlier years has been remarked upon by other visitors (B. Cogan & D. Frith, pers. comm.). It could be found everywhere on Aldabra, even on some of the small lagoon islands. It is a strong flier and the distances involved are probably no barrier to its movements around Aldabra. It was very active from 2 h after sunrise until around noon, at which time activity decreased rapidly. Those individuals still visible were often sluggish, remaining motionless and falling to the ground when vegetation was shaken. During the afternoon few could be found visiting flowers.

TABLE 2. FLOWERING PLANT SPECIES SEEN TO BE VISITED BY *MAUSOLEOPSIS ALDABRENSIS*

family	species	flower colour	blossom type	level of activity
Capparidaceae	Cleome strigosa	pink/mauve	flag	low
	Capparis cartilaginea	white	flag	low
Flacourtiaceae	Flacourtia ramontchii	purple	brush	low
Guttiferae	Calophyllum inophyllum	white	dish	low to moderate
Malvaceae	Thespesia populnea	yellow	bell	low
	T. populneoides	yellow	bell	low
Simaroubaceae	Suriana maritima	yellow	dish	moderate
Ochnaceae	Ochna ciliata	yellow	bowl	moderate
Icacinaceae	Apodytes dimidiata	white	brush/dish	high
Celastraceae	Maytenus senegalensis	cream	brush/dish	intense
	Mystroxylon aethiopicum	yellow	brush/dish	moderate
Rhamnaceae	Colubrina asiatica	green	dish	moderate
	Gouania scandens	cream	brush/dish	intense
Sapindaceae	Allophyllum aldabricus	cream	brush/dish	intense
Moringaceae	Moringa oleifera	white	brush/dish	low
Leguminoseae	Caesalpinia bonduc	green/yellow	tube/flag	moderate
	Delonix regia	red	tube/flag	low
	Dicrostachys microcephala	lilac	brush	low
Lythraceae	Pemphis acidula	white	dish	low/moderate
Caricaceae	Carica papaya	white	bowl	low
Rubiaceae	Guettarda speciosa	white	tube	low
	Polysphaeria multiflora	white	brush/dish	moderate
	Tricalysia sonderana	white	dish	low
Compositae	Vernonia grandis	mauve/white	dish	low
Goodeniaceae	Scaevola taccada	white	tube/flag	moderate
Oleaceae	Jasminum elegans	white	tube	low (robbing)
Apocynaceae	Catharanthus roseus	magenta or white	tube	low (robbing)
Asclepiadaceae	Sarcostemma viminale	white	dish	moderate
	Pleurostelma cernuum	cream	dish	low
	Secamone fryeri	white to yellow	brush/dish	high
Boraginaceae	Tournefortia argentea	white	dish	moderate
	Cordia subcordata	orange	funnel	moderate
Convolvulaceae	Ipomoea macrantha	white	funnel	low
Solanaceae	Datura metel	white	funnel	low
Verbenaceae	Lantana camara	mauve	dish	moderate
Labiateae	Leonotis nepetifolia	orange	gullet	low (robbing)
Liliaceae	Lomatophyllum aldabrense	red	tube	moderate
Pandanaceae	Pandanus tectorius	yellow	dish	intense
Palmae	Cocos nucifera	yellow	dish	intense

'Low' activity, rare to occasional visits; moderate, beetles seen frequently on species; high, individuals seen on almost every flowering plant; intense, insects swarming around the flowers in large numbers.

I observed 73 flowering plant species and saw *Mausoleopsis* visiting 39, or 53 % of them (table 2); 28 flowering plant families and a variety of flower colour and blossom types were represented.

The Aldabran flora can be split on the basis of several criteria. In order to see whether *Mausoleopsis* shows any kind of discrimination in the types of plant it visits, the flora has been classified in several ways (tables 3–6). (Figs, wind pollinated plants, and aquatic species have been omitted from these analyses.)

TABLE 3. SPECIES OBSERVED IN FLOWER AND VISITED BY *M. ALDABRENSIS*, ARRANGED BY DISTRIBUTION CLASSES

distribution class	no. of spp. seen in flower	no. visited by *Mausoleopsis*	percentage
pantropical	30	12	40
palaeotropical	20	12	60
Indian Ocean	2	1	50
Africa, Madagascar, Aldabra, Low Islands	6	5	83
Madagascar, Mascarenes, Seychelles, Aldabra, Low Islands	8	6	75
Aldabra Group	7	3	43
total	**73**	**39**	**53**

TABLE 4. SPECIES IN THE ALDABRA FLORA OBSERVED IN FLOWER AND VISITED BY *M. ALDABRENSIS*, CLASSIFIED INTO NATIVE AND INTRODUCED GROUPS

native or introduced	Aldabra flora	seen in flower	visited by *Mausoleopsis*	percentage
native	117	54	36	57
introduced:				
weeds	14	8	2	25
cultivated	6	5	2	40
other	20	7	6	86
total	**157**	**73**	**39**	**53**

TABLE 5. THE ALDABRA FLORA AND NUMBERS VISITED BY *M. ALDABRENSIS*, CLASSIFIED ACCORDING TO FLOWER COLOUR

flower colour	Aldabra flora	no. visited	percentage
white	50	17	34
yellow	38	8	21
cream	9	3	33
orange	6	2	33
red	4	2	50
green	20	2	10
purple/mauve	18	5	27
blue/lilac/brown/magenta/ pink	8	—	—

TABLE 6. THE ALDABRA FLORA: NUMBER VISITED BY *M. ALDABRENSIS*, CLASSIFIED ON 'BLOSSOM TYPE'

blossom type	Aldabra flora	no. visited	percentage
dish	51	12	24
brush/dish	40	8	20
bowl	7	2	29
bell/funnel	18	5	28
brush/head	9	2	22
flag/tube	26	9	35
gullet	4	1	25

Classification on the basis of world distribution (table 3) indicates that *Mausoleopsis* visits every group; the only under-represented group is endemics (Renvoize 1975). *Mausoleopsis* is also seen to be indifferent to whether the plants are native or introduced (Wickens 1979, this volume) with weeds being the least well represented group (table 4).

Flower colour and structure influence pollinators (Faegri & van der Pijl 1972). Though by no means absolute, discrimination for these attributes occurs. Some insect groups are highly selective; beetles are less so. They do tend to favour large flat flowers or inflorescences providing a firm platform, and they prefer pale coloured flowers and those with strong scents. Table 5 indicates that *Mausoleopsis* does not discriminate on the basis of colour; the only colours un-visited were those rare on the atoll. Blossom type is also apparently unimportant, about a quarter of the species in each blossom type were visited by *Mausoleopsis* (table 6). (The category 'brush/dish' not used by Faegri & van der Pijl, was created to distinguish the many Aldabran plants which have large brush-like inflorescences providing a large landing platform consisting of many dish-like flowers.)

Mausoleopsis is unlikely to pollinate species like *Catharanthus roseus*, *Leonotis nepetifolia* or *Lomatophyllum aldabrense*, though it may possibly effect self-pollination. On each of these species beetles were seen that had bitten through the base of the corolla tube and were 'robbing' nectar, a habit characteristic of *Bombus* spp. For most plants visited it is clear that pollen transfer can and does take place as a result of the visits of *Mausoleopsis*.

4. Discussion

(a) Pollination

My observations indicate that on Aldabra two pollinating species are widespread and common, and visit many species of flowering plant.

The sunbird visits many flowers and the gut contents analysed by Frith (1979, this volume) showed that it consumes quantities of nectar and many insects. Frith's analysis was carried out on birds from a limited area of Ile Picard and there are no data available on the frequency with which different flowers were visited. A record in table 1 may represent anything from one to many observations. My own observations indicated that the sunbird favours certain species, such as *Cocos nucifera*, but is also seen often moving from species to species and frequently can be seen taking insects from flowers. Current ecological theory suggests that species on islands, where competition may be less severe than in mainland habitats, may occupy wider niches. If so, sunbirds might be expected to visit a wide range of flowers, including some not normally bird-pollinated. The data in table 1 support this view. The pollination effectiveness of the sun-bird on Aldabra requires more research but it may be potentially important in enabling plants to become established.

The species that stands out as an important 'generalist' is the beetle *Mausoleopsis aldabrensis*. It visits an impressive variety of flowering plants, however one classifies the Aldabran flora: on distribution type, whether native or introduced, on flower colour or on blossom type. *Mauso-leopsis* cuts across the categories, and visits plants of all types. A large herbivorous beetle of this nature, in possibly less competitive conditions than on the mainland, may well respond in the same way as the sunbird, broadening its niche to include a wide variety of plants in its diet. In this context the conclusions of Becker (1975) are very relevant. In an analysis of the beetle faunas of a number of island groups he demonstrated that carnivores are relatively better represented than herbivores on islands. Becker suggested that this might be because carnivores are trophic generalists, whereas most herbivores are monophagous or oligophagous, very few being polyphagous, and thus herbivores have difficulty in becoming established on islands. If so a generalist herbivore on an island may be at a considerable advantage. Such a phenomenon could account for the success of *Mausoleopsis aldabrensis* in its rôle as a wide ranging pollinator. A study of its close relatives on the African mainland would be revealing.

Mausoleopsis avoids annuals, and since many introduced weeds and endemics to Aldabra are annuals, they are the groups least frequented by the beetle. Another generalist pollinator on the Galápagos Islands, the carpenter bee *Xylocopa darwinii*, was observed by Linsley, Rick & Stephens (1966) during a 5 week visit to six islands. The bee was recorded on 60 flowering plant species from 28 families. The Galápagos flora is much richer than that of Aldabra, with many more endemics.

Xylocopa collects both nectar and pollen. On occasions when it was seen visiting *Boerhavia scandens* and *Bacopa monnieri*, and showing some constancy to both species, the most abundant species in the vicinity, *Portulaca oleracea*, was avoided on Galápagos. *P. oleracea*, which is also common at some localities on Aldabra, was never seen to be visited by *Mausoleopsis aldabrensis*, nor was any other prostrate herb visited there.

Eisikowitch & Woodell (1975) noted that *Bombus* spp. visiting *Armeria maritima* in a British saltmarsh, avoided slender stemmed saltmarsh plants and suggested that the process of being deposited on wet ground when visiting a flower might be a 'negative experience' (Wickler 1968) which deters the insects from visiting such flowers. D. Eisikowitch (pers. comm.) has noted that in Israel *Xylocopa* spp. appear to avoid flowers that are close to the ground and as they drop before flying they may have difficulty in taking off from such flowers. This might account for *Xylocopa darwinii*'s avoiding *Portulaca oleracea* on Galápagos. Further, *Mausoleopsis aldabrensis* was often seen to drop vertically from flowers on Aldabra before actually flying, and thus may be similarly deterred from visiting flowers near to the ground.

Linsley, Rick & Stephens noted that the species visited by *X. darwinii* differed from place to place and time to time. On Aldabra, *Mausoleopsis* turned its attention sequentially to different species in any one place over the few weeks during which it was observed. The parallels between the carpenter bee on the Galápagos Islands and the beetle on Aldabra are striking. In each place there is a large insect acting as a generalist pollinator; each is polyphagous, abundant, shows some constancy, visits a wide variety of flower types, and avoids flowers near the ground.

Linsley, Rick & Stephens suggest that *Xylocopa darwinii* is a relatively recent immigrant to the Galápagos, and they base this view partly on the fact that endemics are under-represented among the plants it visits, whereas the abundance of weeds and adventives on the island suggests that they have become established with ease, their attractiveness to the bees indicating that the latter may have helped in establishment. *Xylocopa*'s avoidance of endemics may suggest that they became established without the bees' help.

Such arguments are not easy to apply to *Mausoleopsis* on Aldabra. Aldabra is a much more recent island than the Galápagos, and there is no indication that *Mausoleopsis* has difficulty in getting around. The species has been recorded on other islands in the area: Cosmoledo, Assumption, Astove, St Pierre and Wasin I. and some of the varieties of *Mausoleopsis amabilis* (its closest relative, found all over the African mainland) are more different from each other than from *aldabrensis* (B. Cogan & M. Bacchus, pers. comm.). These beetles are strong fliers and I see no reason to believe that the species is a recent arrival on Aldabra. Why a beetle, rather than the *Xylocopa* species that occurs on Aldabra, has filled the generalist pollinator niche here is a problem that merits further research.

(b) Breeding systems

The relative frequency of outbreeding mechanisms, especially dioecism, among island floras (Carlquist 1974) has been adduced as evidence for intense selection for outbreeding among isolated island populations. The exact proportion of outbreeding species on Aldabra is far from easy to ascertain, but there are several dioecious species, e.g. *Euphorbia pyrifolia* and *Flacourtia ramontchii*, many heterostyle species, e.g. Rubiaceae and *Pemphis acidula*, and my own observations on living and herbarium material, and the unpublished notes of D. Wood, suggest that several Aldabran species are unstable in respect to their breeding system. Some exhibit a degree of male sterility, for example *Apodytes dimidiata*, *Allophylus aldabricus*, *Clerodendrum glabrum* and *Acalypha claoxyloides*. Perhaps some are evolving toward a higher degree of outbreeding. Though I believe that it is not difficult for dioecious species to be dispersed over long distances, because propagules are often carried in large numbers together, the fact that some species appear to be incipient outbreeders on Aldabra provides some support for Baker's (1955) views on dispersal and breeding systems. The adoption of outbreeding by an island species can overcome the disadvantage of inbreeding in an isolated population. The advantages of dioecism or heterostyly must be considerable, as the former mechanism has arisen in many families of flowering plants. An additional advantage of dioecism on an island may lie in the successful resolution of a competitive struggle for pollinators in short supply. Any species which can increase its number of flowers, hence increasing its attractiveness to pollinators, may gain in such competition. Similarly, spreading the flowering peak period over a longer time, by staggering peaks of male and female (or long-styles and short-styles in heterostyle plants), may give a species a competitive advantage. Such staggering of peaks of flowering occurs in the British *Primula vulgaris*, a heterostyle species which flowers when few pollinators are active (Woodell, unpublished). The presence of an abundant non-discriminatory generalist pollinator like *Mausoleopsis aldabrensis* must be an important factor favouring the chances of new immigrant species becoming successfully established on the atoll.

5. CONCLUSIONS

For immigrants to islands the presence of 'universal pollinators' like *Mausoleopsis aldabrensis* on Aldabra and *Xylocopa darwinii* on Galápagos may well be vital in the train of events leading to successful establishment of new immigrant plants. Even a relatively inefficient pollen vector like a beetle may be crucial in such circumstances. Other island floras should be investigated to see whether this is a frequent phenomenon on islands, and a study should be made of the close relatives of *Mausoleopsis aldabrensis* in Africa. If this beetle has adopted its present behaviour patterns since it arrived on Aldabra, we would have good evidence of a species broadening its niche in an island habitat. Even if it was already a generalist, then its arrival on Aldabra was an event with possibly great significance for the Aldabran flora.

My visit to Aldabra was made possible by a grant from the Royal Society, for which I am very grateful. Dr R. Hnatiuk and Mr F. Topliffe have both been very helpful on the atoll. I

108S. R. J. WOODELL

have had invaluable help from Mr B. Cogan at the British Museum (Natural History) in identifying insects. Others who have helped in many ways are Mr M. Bacchus, Mr C. Frith, Dr D. Frith, Dr D. Eisikowitch, Dr S. Hnatiuk, Mr S. A. Renvoize and Mr R. Wilson.

REFERENCES (Woodell)

Baker, H. G. 1955 Self-compatibility and establishment after long-distance dispersal. *Evolution* **9**, 347–349.

Baker, H. G. 1967 Support for Baker's Law – as a rule. *Evolution* **21**, 853–856.

Becker, P. 1975 Island colonization by carnivorous and herbivorous Coleoptera. *J. anim. Ecol.* **44**, 893–906.

Carlquist, S. 1966 The biota of long-distance dispersal. IV. Genetic systems in the floras of oceanic islands. *Evolution* **20**, 433–455.

Carlquist, S. 1974 *Island biology.* New York and London: Columbia University Press.

Eisikowitch, D. & Woodell, S. R. J. 1975 Some aspects of pollination ecology of *Armeria maritima* (Mill.) Willd. in Britain. *New Phytol.* **74**, 307–322.

Faegri, K. & van der Pijl, L. 1971 *The principles of pollination ecology*, 2nd edn. Oxford: Pergamon Press.

Frith, C. B. 1976 A twelve-month field study of the Aldabra Fody *Foudia eminentissima aldabrana*. *Ibis* **118**, 155–178.

Frith, C. B. 1979 Feeding ecology of land birds on West Island, Aldabra Atoll, Indian Ocean: a preliminary survey. *Phil. Trans. R. Soc. Lond.* B **286**, 195–210 (this volume).

Gill, F. B. & Wolf, L. L. 1975 Economics of feeding territoriality in the Golden-winged Sunbird. *Ecology* **56**, 333–345.

Grant, V. 1950 The protection of the ovules in flowering plants. *Evolution* **4**, 179–201.

Hickman, J. C. 1974 Pollination by ants: a low-energy system. *Science, N.Y.* **184**, 1290–1292.

Linsley, E. G., Rick, C. M. & Stephens, S. G. 1966 Observations on the floral relationships of the Galapagos Carpenter Bee. *Pan-Pacif. Ent.* **42**, 1–18.

Müller, H. 1883 *The fertilization of flowers.* London: MacMillan.

Proctor, M. C. F. & Yeo, P. 1973 *The pollination of flowers.* London: Collins.

Renvoize, S. A. 1975 A floristic analysis of the western Indian Ocean coral islands. *Kew Bull.* **30**, 133–162.

Wickens, G. E. 1979 Speculations on seed dispersal and the flora of the Aldabra archipelago. *Phil. Trans. R. Soc. Lond.* B **286**, 85–97 (this volume).

Wickler, W. 1968 *Mimicry in plants and animals.* London: World University Library.

Wiebes, J. T. 1975 Fig insects from Aldabra (Hymenoptera, Chalcidoidea). *Zoöl. Meded., Leiden* **49**, 225–236.

Woodell, S. R. J., Mattsson, O. & Philipp, M. 1977 A study in the seasonal reproductive and morphological variation in five Danish populations of *Armeria maritima*. *Bot. Tidsskr.* **72**, 15–30.

Phil. Trans. R. Soc. Lond. B. **286**, 109–117 (1979)   [109]

Printed in Great Britain

Distribution of soil and litter arthropods on Aldabra Atoll

BY V. W. SPAULL

*South African Sugar Association Experiment Station, P.O. Mount Edgecombe, 4300, Natal,
Republic of South Africa;
formerly at the Royal Society Aldabra Research Station*

Data from a general survey of the soil and litter arthropods of Aldabra have been
analysed in an attempt to reveal patterns in the distribution of the species. Analysis
by means of a similarity index suggests that their distribution within 14 sites that were
sampled quantitatively is to a large extent independent of vegetation type. This is
supported by the results of a correspondence analysis of the faunal content of a total
of 70 sites representing a variety of vegetation types from several localities around the
atoll. It is suggested that this apparent lack of any clear association between vegetation
type and fauna may be due to niche expansion by the immigrant species.

INTRODUCTION

There have been a number of publications dealing with the soil and litter invertebrates of
Aldabra. Most of these have been taxonomic studies or records of occurrence (see Westoll &
Stoddart (orgs) 1971 for references), but Spaull (1976) described certain aspects of the
biology of a millipede on Aldabra, and Peake (1971) discussed the species–area curve of terrestrial
Mollusca on the atoll compared with other islands in the western Indian Ocean. None have
described the overall distribution of the soil and litter fauna on Aldabra. By using data collected
over a period of 18 months, an attempt was made to correlate the distribution of selected
groups of arthropods with the litter associated with different species of plants. The results are
described in this paper.

The vegetation on Aldabra forms a complex of evergreen and semideciduous scrub and scrub
forest together with a variety of grasses, sedges and ephemeral herbs. Apart from areas dominated by a single species it is difficult to recognize distinct habitat types, as delimited by the
presence of recurring constant associations of plant species. Consequently, for the present
study, the litter below one particular plant species was considered to be one type of habitat.
An exception to this was the 'mixed scrub' litter. Here the plant species were often growing so
close together that the litter below one species frequently included that produced by neighbouring, different species. In selecting the sample sites an effort was made to include examples
of all the more common litter habitats on Aldabra.

SAMPLE SITES AND EXTRACTION OF THE ARTHROPODS

Replicated quantitative samples of soil and litter were taken from the following habitats, the
primary sample sites. (The location of place names used in this paper can be found in Stoddart
1971.) (1) *Casuarina equisetifolia* woodland near the old settlement, Ile Picard and (2) at Anse
Cèdres, Ile Grand Terre; (3) *Calophyllum inophyllum* woodland, Takamaka Grove, Ile Grande
Terre; (4) *Pandanus tectorius* scrub near Pointe Hodoul, Ile Grande Terre; (5) mixed scrub near

Croix Blanc, Ile Grande Terre – plant species included *Ochna ciliata, Polysphaeria multiflora* and *Ficus nautarum*; (6) mixed scrub near the Royal Society's research station, Ile Picard – plant species included *Acalypha claoxyloides, Azima tetracantha, C. equisetifolia, Dracaena reflexa, Clerodendrum glabrum, Erythroxylon acranthum, Euphorbia pyrifolia, Gouania scandens, Ipomoea macrantha, Maytenus senegalensis, O. ciliata* and *Tarenna supra-axillaris*; (7) *Pemphis acidula* scrub near Middle Camp, Ile Malabar, (8) at Anse Porche, Ile Malabar, (9) northeast of Anse Polymnie, Ile Polymnie and (10) north of Dune d'Messe, Ile Grande Terre; (11) *Fimbristylis* cf. *cymosa* turf growing beneath *C. equisetifolia* near Middle Camp, Ile Malabar; (12) *Cyperus niveus* turf amongst coconut trees (*Cocos nucifera*); (13) *Cyperus ligularis* turf at Anse Malabar, Ile Malabar; (14) *Sporobolus virginicus* turf inland of Dune Patates, Ile Grande Terre.

The arthopods were extracted from the samples over a 9 day period using Tullgren funnels similar to those described by Macfadyen (1961, fig. 2) except that there was no air conditioning. Species counts were made within the Isopoda, Diplopoda, Pseudoscorpiones, Chilopoda, Coleoptera, Diplura, Symphyla, Pauropoda, Embioptera, Psocoptera, Dictyoptera, Thysanoptera, Hemiptera, and Thysanura. Only a few of the species have been identified to a binomial but the others were recognized as distinct taxa. Representatives of all the species collected on Aldabra have been deposited at the British Museum (Natural History). In addition to the quantitative samples from the 14 primary sites, other samples of soil and litter were collected by hand from 56 secondary sites representing a variety of different vegetation types around the atoll. A list of these sample sites and their location on Aldabra are given in appendix 1. The soil and litter from these secondary sites were sorted by hand and a record kept of the species present.

CORRELATION OF THE ARTHROPOD FAUNA WITH DIFFERENT VEGETATION TYPES

In order to reveal patterns in the distribution of the arthropod fauna and to characterize the different vegetation types, three methods were used to analyse the data from the sample sites: (*a*) the similarity method of Renkonen (1938); (*b*) the reciprocal averaging method of Hill (1973, 1974); (*c*) the rarefaction technique of Sanders (1968).

(*a*) Renkonen's index of similarity

The fauna of the 14 primary sites were compared by using the similarity method of Renkonen (1938). The degree of similarity is calculated for any pair of sites by selecting and summing the lower relative abundance value for each of the species present in both sites. Species absent from one site are ignored. This calculation was made for all the possible pairs of sites and the hierarchial relation of the sites, based on their degree of similarity, was then determined by using the method of Mountford (1962) (figure 1). It is clear from the figure that in several instances different vegetation types possess a more comparable fauna than similar vegetation types (compare the four *Pemphis* sites, the two *Casuarina* sites and the two mixed scrub sites). This was unexpected since it was assumed at the outset that major differences in the vegetation would result in marked differences in the type of habitat within the litter and that the fauna would be a reflexion of these differences.

(*b*) Reciprocal averaging

Data from both the primary sample sites and the non-quantitative secondary sample sites were analysed by means of a type of correspondence analysis known as reciprocal averaging

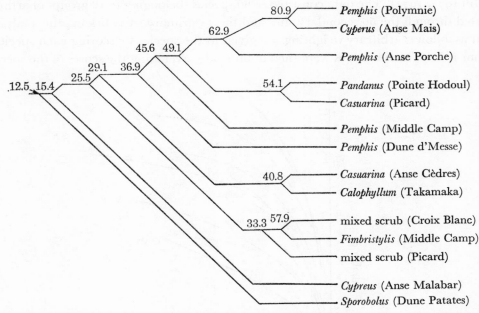

FIGURE 1. Hierarchial relation of the primary sample sites based on their degree of similarity. Derived from the Renkonen numbers of the sites by using 49 species of the selected arthropod groups.

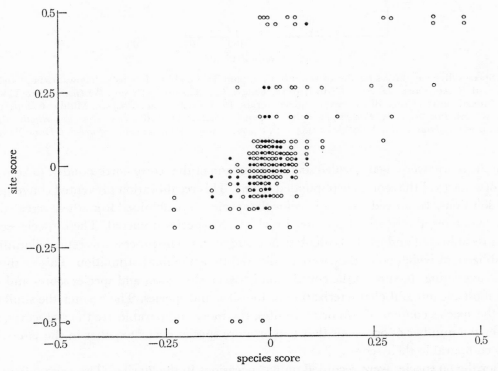

FIGURE 2. Computer print-out of the reciprocal averaging scores of arthropod species plotted against the scores of the sample sites in which they occur. See appendices 1 and 2 for a list of the scores of sites and species. Full circles represent multiple points.

(Hill 1973, 1974). The data consisted of 60 species (belonging to 12 groups of arthropods) distributed through the 56 secondary sites and the 14 primary sites. Briefly, the analysis was carried out as follows: arbitrary weighting was given to the species by scoring each species in sequence from 1–60. The site scores were then obtained by averaging the scores of the species within the

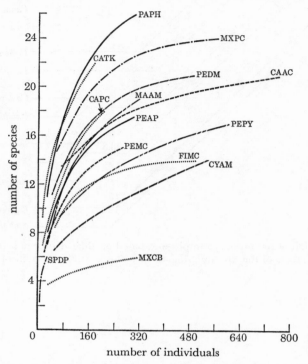

FIGURE 3. Species diversity curves for the 14 primary sites. Sample site abbreviations as follows: CAPC, *Casuarina*, Ile Picard; CAAC, *Casuarina*, Anse Cèdres; CATK, *Calophyllum*, Takamaka; PAPH, *Pandanus*, Pointe Hodoul; MXCB, mixed scrub, Croix Blanc; MXPC, mixed scrub, Ile Picard; PEMC, *Pemphis*, Middle Camp; PEAP, Pemphis, Anse Porche; PEPY, *Pemphis*, Ile Polymnie; PEDM, *Pemphis*, Dune d'Messe; FIMC, *Fimbristylis*, Middle Camp; CYAM, *Cyperus niveus*, Anse Mais; MAAM, *C. ligularis*, Anse Malabar; SPDP, *Sporobolus*, Dune Patates.

sites. The site scores were then rescaled such that the sum of the scores corresponded to zero and the sum of squares of the scores corresponded to one. This recalibration prevented convergence to trivial solutions. Improved calibrations for the species were obtained from these rescaled site scores by averaging the scores of the sites in which the species occurred. These species scores were then recalibrated and used to calculate new site scores. The process was repeated until the scores stablized, at which point they were considered to be the final ordination. This method of reciprocal averaging maximizes the correlation between site scores and species scores and thus gives the most meaningful characterization of the sites and species. The greater the similarity between the species content of two or more sites, the more comparable are the site scores, and the greater the number of occasions that two or more species occur together in the same sites, the more comparable their scores.

Together the 60 species were recorded on 687 occasions in the 70 sites. The scores of each of the sites and species are given in appendixes 1 and 2 respectively. Figure 2 shows the species scores plotted against the scores of the sites in which the species occur. Most of the site and species scores are concentrated around the zero point. In fact the scores of 62 of the 70 sites and

50 of the 60 species fall within the range −0.1 to +0.1. This indicates that the species composition of most of the sites is broadly similar. It therefore appears that, for the most part, vegetation type does not limit the distribution of soil and litter arthropods on Aldabra.

(c) Rarefaction

There is further evidence that, based on faunal composition, different vegetation types on Aldabra cannot be separated into distinct groups. Applying the rarefaction technique developed by Sanders (1968) and modified by Simberloff (1972) to the (selected) species composition of the 14 primary sample sites the relative species diversity of the sites can be illustrated as shown in figure 3. Rarefaction is a method whereby, from an analysis of the relative frequency of specimens within species, an estimate can be made of the number of species that would have been present had the sample size been smaller (the size of the sample here being the number of specimens extracted from the litter). Thus it is possible to compare estimated diversities at a constant sample size. It should be noted that such comparisons can only be made if the curves do not cross. It is clear from figure 3 that the species diversity curves for the primary sample sites form a series of increasing diversity but that there is no clear separation of dissimilar sites or grouping of similar sites. By definition, habitats of similar complexity have broadly similar species diversities and diversity reflects the number of available niches within one habitat, or at least the number of occupied niches. Thus it is concluded from the diversity curves that the number of niches available or occupied in the primary sample sites is not sufficiently different to allow distinct habitat groups to be recognized.

DISCUSSION

During the present survey, samples were taken from the soil and litter below 12 species of broad leafed scrub plants belonging to ten families, 1 species of narrow leafed tree, 2 species of two families of broad leafed trees, 4 species of sedges, 1 species of grass, 1 species of orchid as well as from beach debris. Such a variety of sample sites might be expected to include a number of contrasting invertebrate habitats each containing a recognizably distinct fauna. For example, the litter below *Calophyllum* (broad leaves, constant shade, relatively moist conditions and overlying a deep organic soil) appears to be very different from that below *Pemphis* (small leaves, never completely shaded, relatively dry and overlying a shallow organic soil), and both contrast with the litter below *Casuarina* (needle-like minutely leaved twigs, partly shaded and overlying a deep sandy soil). However, analysis by the Renkonen method and reciprocal averaging indicates that, with a few exceptions, the distribution of the selected soil and litter arthropods on Aldabra is largely independent of vegetation type.

This apparent lack of any clear association between vegetation type and fauna may, possibly, be due to niche expansion by the immigrant species. Such ecological expansion is a common feature of island faunas and is explained by the ability of colonizing species to occupy a more diverse niche if competitors are absent (see MacArthur 1972; MacArthur & Wilson 1967). On Aldabra, competition is likely to be small since the species:family and species:genus ratios of the soil and litter arthropods, for which data are available, are very low (table 1, see also Cogan, Hutson & Schaffer 1971).

Data given by Stoddart & Walsh (1979, this volume) indicate that there have probably been long term fluctuations in rainfall on Aldabra, ranging from periods of drought to periods of relatively high rainfall in successive years. Such a climate might be expected to select those species that can survive arid conditions and cause the extinction of less tolerant species. It would thereby reduce the number of potential competitors and thus compound the ecological expansion of the successful species. This expansion may also be increased by the short-term or localized fluctuations in rainfall that have been recorded on Aldabra (Hnatiuk 1979, this volume). Relating birthrate, death rate and maximum population size attainable on an island with the probability of survival of propagules and the average duration of populations, MacArthur & Wilson (1967) showed that populations that cannot exceed some very small size are likely to become extinct much faster than those that can reach a very large size. Thus recent immigrants that can not multiply rapidly due to an unfavourable climate are likely to become extinct before they can compete with older more successful colonists. If the fluctuations in rainfall, both temporal and local, are sufficient to cause repeated extinctions of the fauna then at any one time opportunist species that have a high dispersal and reproductive potential and can tolerate new conditions, but are not necessarily good competitors, are likely to form a large proportion of the fauna on Aldabra. Conversely, more specialized species which are better competitors but which have a slower rate of colonization are likely to form a small proportion of the fauna.

TABLE 1. NUMBERS OF FAMILIES, GENERA AND SPECIES OF SELECTED GROUPS OF SOIL AND LITTER INVERTEBRATES ON ALDABRA

group	no. of families	no. of genera	no. of species	species/ family	species/ genus
Coleoptera	16	22†	27	1.7	1.2‡
Hemiptera	8	8†	9	1.1	1.1‡
Hymenoptera	1	6	7	7.0	1.2
Embioptera	1	1	1	1.0	1.0
Dermaptera	1	1	1	1.0	1.0
Dictyoptera	1	2	2	2.0	1.0
Collembola	4	9	10	2.5	1.1
Diplura	2	2	2	1.0	1.0
Isopoda	5	7†	8	1.6	1.1‡
Pseudoscorpiones	5	6	6	1.2	1.0
Scorpiones	1	1	1	1.0	1.0
Schizopeltida	1	1	1	1.0	1.0
Diplopoda	4	4	4	1.0	1.0
Chilopoda	3	3†	6	2.0	2.0‡
Symphyla	1	1	1	1.0	1.0
Pauropoda	1	1	1	1.0	1.0

† Minimum number.   ‡ Maximum ratio.

As a result of reciprocal averaging, the exceptional site scores reflect the restricted distribution of some of the species within the sites. Such a distribution may be due to the special habitat requirements of these species. For example the pseudoscorpion *Anagarypus oceanus-indicus* (score +0.3889) and the isopod *Tylos minor* (score +0.4613) are both restricted to similar coastal habitats, namely beneath driftwood and other dry vegetation cast up onto the beach crest. *A. oceanus-indicus* was also found among the basal shoots of *Cyperus ligularis* growing a short distance inland from the beach crest. It should be noted, however, that neither the isopod nor the pseudoscorpion were present in a sample taken from *C. ligularis* growing in a similar situation near Dune Jean-Louis. This is reflected in the less extreme site score of −0.004. Other species with a limited distribution appear to be restricted to a particular locality rather than to a particular habitat. For example, the tenebrionid beetle. *Opatrinus attenvatus* (score -0.2271) was only found in four apparently dissimilar sites in the Cinq Cases–Bassin Flamant area at the southeastern corner of the atoll, namely litter below *Mystroxylon, Pandanus, Thespesia* and *Lumnitzera*. In the same way an unidentified ptiliid beetle (score -0.0932) was only recorded at the eastern end of Ile Grande Terre. Here it occurred in samples taken from ten sites of seven different vegetation types. Of several samples taken from three of these vegetation types from other parts of the atoll, none were found to contain this beetle.

Thanks are due to several members of staff of the British Museum (Natural History), particularly Dr B. H. Cogan, Mr P. N. Lawrence and Mr D. Macfarlane, for their help in identifying specimens collected on Aldabra; to Dr M. Beier, Naturhistorisches Museum, Vienna, for identifying the pseudoscorpions; to Miss K. Shaw and Dr M. Hill for their advice and assistance in selecting and computing the program for the reciprocal averaging analysis; and to Mrs C. N. Taylor who wrote the computer program for the species diversity curves. I am indebted to Mr J. F. Peake for much valuable discussion during the preparation of this manuscript, to the personnel on Aldabra from October 1973 to May 1975 for their help and to the Royal Society for making my trip to Aldabra possible.

REFERENCES (Spaull)

Cogan, B. H., Hutson, A. M. & Shaffer, J. C. 1971 Preliminary observations on the affinities and composition of the insect fauna of Aldabra. *Phil. Trans. R. Soc. Lond.* B **260**, 315–325.

Hill, M. O. 1973 Reciprocal averaging: an eigenvector method of ordination. *J. Ecol.* **61**, 237–249.

Hill, M. O. 1974 Correspondence analysis: a neglected multivariate method. *Appl. Statist.* **23**, 340–354.

Hnatiuk, R. J. 1979 Temporal and spatial variations in precipitation on Aldabra. *Phil. Trans. R. Soc. Lond.* B **286**, 25–36 (this volume).

MacArthur, R. H. 1972 *Geographical ecology*. New York: Harper & Row.

MacArthur, R. H. & Wilson, E. O. 1967 *The theory of island biogeography*. Princeton, New Jersey: Princeton University Press.

Macfadyen, A. 1961 Improved funnel-type extractors for soil arthropods. *J. Anim. Ecol.* **30**, 171–184.

Mountford, M. D. 1962 An index of similarity and its application to classification problems. In *Progress in soil zoology* (ed. P. W. Murphy), pp. 43–50. London: Butterworth.

Peake, J. F. 1971 The evolution of terrestrial faunas in the western Indian Ocean. *Phil. Trans. R. Soc. Lond.* B **260**, 581–610.

Renkonen, O. 1938 Statistisch-ökologische untersuchungen über die terrestrische kaferwelt der finnischen bruchmoore. *Soumal. elain-ja Kasvit Seur van Julk* **6**, 1–226.

Sanders, H. L. 1968 Marine benthic diversity: a comparative study. *Am. Nat.* **102**, 243–282.

Simberloff, D. S. 1972 Properties of the rarefaction diversity measurement. *Am. Nat.* **106**, 414–418.

Spaull, V. W. 1976 The life history and post-embryonic development of 'Spirobolus' bivirgatus (Diplopoda: Spirobolida) on Aldabra, western Indian Ocean. *J. Zool., Lond.* **180**, 391–405.

Stoddart, D. R. 1971 Place names of Aldabra. *Phil. Trans. R. Soc. Lond.* B **260**, 631–632.

Stoddart, D. R. & Walsh, R. P. D. 1979 Long-term climatic change in the western Indian Ocean. *Phil. Trans. R. Soc. Lond.* B **286**, 11–23 (this volume).

Westoll, T. S. & Stoddart, D. R. (organizers) 1971 A discussion on the results of the Royal Society Expeditions to Aldabra 1967–68. *Phil. Trans. R. Soc. Lond.* B **260**, 1–654.

APPENDIX 1. RECIPROCAL AVERAGING SCORES AND LOCATION OF THE SAMPLE SITES ON ALDABRA

$+0.4860$, Beach debris between Dune Jean-Louis and Anse Du Bois, Jan. 75; $+0.4685$, beach debris between Dune d'Messe and Anse Imagination, Jan. 75; $+0.2525$, *Mariscus ligularis* inland of beach crest, Cinq Cases, Mar. 74; $+0.1680$, *Cyperus niveus* below *Ochna ciliata*, west of Dune d'Messe, Jan 75; $+0.0888$, *C. ligularis*, Dune Au Pic, Jun. 74; $+0.0770$, *Casuarina equisetifolia* with *Suriana maritima*, Ile Esprit, Jul. 74; +0.0730†, *C. ligularis*, Anse Malabar, Feb. 75; +0.0637†, *Fimbristylis* cf. *cymosa* below *Casuarina*, east end of Ile Malabar, Jun. 74; +0.0575†, *Pemphis acidula*, north coast of Ile Polymnie, Dec. 74; +0.0573, *C. equisetifolia* and *Cocos nucifera*, Ile Esprit, Dec. 74; +0,0572†, *Sporobolus virginicus*, Dune Patates, Jan. 75; +0.0472†, *P. acidula*, east end of Ile Malabar, Nov. 74; +0.0470, *Sideroxylon inerme* among *Pemphis*, Anse Porche, Dec. 74; +0.0456, *Maytenus senegalensis* between Cinq Cases and Bassin Flamant, Mar. 74; +0.0437†, *C. equisetifolia*, northwest coast of Ile Picard, Dec. 74; +0.0393†, *P. acidula*, north of Dune d'Messe, Jan. 75; +0.0337, *Calophyllum inophyllum*, Takamaka, Dec. 73; +0.0306†, *P. acidula*, Anse Porche, Dec. 74; +0.0283, *Mystroxylon aethiopicum* and *Tarenna supra-axillaris*, Ile Esprit, Dec. 74; +0.0261†, *C. inophyllum*, Takamaka, Jan. 75; +0.0266, *M. aethiopicum*, near Anse Coco, Dec. 74; +0.0235, *S. inerme*, Dune d'Messe, Jan. 75; +0.0189, mixed scrub, south end of Ile Picard, Nov. 74; +0.0182†, *Pandanus tectorius*, southwest of Pointe Hodoul, Mar. 74; +0.0158, *C. equisetifolia*, south end of Ile Picard, Dec. 74; +0.0121†, *C. niveus* among *C. nucifera*, Anse Mais, Oct. 74; +0.0112, *Dracaena reflexa*, northwest of Anse Polymnie, Nov. 73; +0.0094, *S. inerme* between Anse Coco and Anse Porche, Dec. 74; +0.0061†, mixed scrub, south end of Ile Picard, Feb. 75; +0.0049, fallen *C. nucifera*, west coast of Ile Picard, Oct. 74; +0.0030, *S. inerme* between Cinq Cases and Bassin Flamant, Mar. 74; +0.0026, *M. senegalensis*, south end of Ile Picard, Oct. 73; −0.0043, *C. ligularis*, inland of beach crest, Dune Jean-Louis, Jan. 75; −0.0098, mixed scrub, Anse Tambalico, Oct. 74; −0.0117, mixed scrub, south end of Ile Picard, Dec. 74; −0.0120†, mixed scrub, Croix Blanc, Nov. 74; −0.0142†, *C. equisetifolia*, Anse Cèdres, Feb. 75; −0.0143, *C. ligularis*, just south of Pointe Hodoul, Mar. 74; −0.0203, *C. ligularis*, among low scrub, Dune Jean-Louis, Jun. 74; −0.0213, *S. inerme*, between Cinq Cases and Bassin Flamant, Mar. 74; −0.0225, *D. reflexa*, between Anse Coco and Anse Porche, Dec. 74; −0.0229, *S. inerme*, among *Pemphis*, Au Parc, Feb. 75; −0.0314, *Tricalysia sonderana*, west end of Ile Polymnie, Nov. 73; −0.0351, *S. inerme*, near Cinq Cases, Nov. 73; −0.0352, *M. aethiopicum* and *D. reflexa*, Anse Coco, Dec. 74; −0.0353, *M. senegalensis*, between Cinq Cases and Bassin Flamant, Mar. 74; −0.0362, 'three-leaf plant', west end of Ile Polymnie, Nov. 73; −0.0363, *C. ligularis* beneath *Ochna*, Dune Jean-Louis, Jan. 75; −0.0377, *S. inerme*, between Cinq Cases and Bassin Flamant, Mar. 74; −0.0378, *C. ligularis*, Anse Cèdres, Feb. 75; −0.0395, Gramineae sp. beneath *Casuarina*, Anse Coco, Dec. 74; −0.0429, *P. acidula*, southwest of Pointe Hodoul, Mar. 74; −0.0431, *S. inerme*, Anse Cèdres, Feb. 75; −0.0472, *S. inerme*, between Cinq Cases and Bassin Flamant, Mar. 74; −0.0474, *Guettarda speciosa*, Dune d'Messe, Jan. 75; −0.0494, *S. inerme*, Ile Michel, Mar. 75; −0.0498, *S. inerme*, between Cinq Cases and Bassin Flamant, Mar. 74; −0.0526, *M. senegalensis*, between Cinq Cases and Bassin Flamant, Mar. 74; −0.0530, *O. ciliata*, Bassin Flamant, Mar. 74; −0.0644, mixed scrub, south end of Ile Picard, Jul. 74; −0.0688, *C. equisetifolia*, Ile Michel, Mar. 75; −0.0754, *Fimbristylis ferruginea*, between Cinq Cases and Bassin Flamant, Mar. 74; −0.0856, *F.* cf. *cymosa* below *Casuarina*, east end of Ile Malabar, Jun. 74; −0.0970, *Acampe rigida*, lagoon islet near Bras des Cèdres, Feb. 74; −0.0975, *S. inerme*, just inland of Cinq Cases, Mar. 74; −0.0985, *P. tectorius*, just inland of Cinq Cases. Mar. 74; −0.1047, *S. maritima*, south of Pointe Hodoul, Mar. 74; −0.1359, *M. aethiopicum* just inland of Cinq Cases, Mar. 74; −0.2098, *Thespesia* sp., west of Cinq Cases, Nov. 74; −0.4965, *Lumnitzera racemosa* between Cinq Cases and Bassin Flamant, Mar. 74.

† Primary sample sites.

APPENDIX 2. RECIPROCAL AVERAGING SCORES OF ARTHROPOD SPECIES COLLECTED FROM THE
SAMPLE SITES

+0.4613, *Tylos minor* Dollfus, Isopoda; +0.3889, *Anagarypus oceanus-indicus* Chamberlin,
Pseudoscorpiones; +0.2921, Nitidulidae sp. 1, Coleoptera; +0.2701, *Phaleria* sp., Coleoptera;
+0.2441, unidentified arthropod sp. 1; +0.1624, Staphylinidae sp. 1, Coleoptera; +0.1302,
Astenus sp., Coleoptera; +0.0952, unidentified Coleoptera sp. 1; +0.0933, Elateridae sp. 1,
Coleoptera; +0.0666, Porcellionidae sp., Isopoda; +0.0518, Curculionidae sp. 1, Coleoptera;
+0.0444, *Scolopendra amazonica* (Bucherl), Chilopoda; +0.0422, unidentified arthropod sp. 2;
+0.0422, Curculionidae sp. 2, Coleoptera; +0.0338, Elateridae sp. 2; Coleoptera; +0.0311,
unidentified Symphyla sp.; +0.0294, Staphylinidae sp. 2, Coleoptera; +0.0278, Nitidulidae
sp. 2, Coleoptera; +0.0265, unidentified Pauropoda sp.; +0.0266, Pselaphidae sp., Coleoptera;
+0.0255, *Plesioderes* sp., Coleoptera; +0.0252, Dytiscidae sp., Coleoptera; +0.0226, unidentified Coleoptera sp. 2; +0.0225, Geophilomorpha sp. 1, Chilopoda; +0.0214, Cossonidae sp.,
Coleoptera; +0.0195, *Carpelinus* sp., Coleoptera; +0.0177, Polyxenidae sp., Diplopoda;
+0.0170, *Oligotoma saundersii* Westwood, Embioptera; +0.0139, *Tyrannochthonius contractus*
(Tullgren), Pseudoscorpiones; +0.0123, Scarabaeidae sp., Coleoptera; +0.0121, Japygidae sp.,
Diplura; +0.0026, *Spirobolus bivirgatus* Karsch, Diplopoda; −0.0005, *Allowithius congicus* Beier,
Pseudoscorpiones; −0.0008, *Geogarypus impressus* Tullgren, Pseudoscorpiones; −0.0019, Geo-
philomorpha sp. 2, Chilopoda; −0.0028, *Xenolpium madagascarienses* (Beier), Pseudoscorpiones;
−0.0040, *Pseudochiridium africanum* (Beier), Pseudoscorpiones; −0.0082, Armadillidae sp. 1,
Isopoda; −0.0105, *Alphitobius crenatus* Klub. Coleoptera; −0.0121, Armidillidae sp. 2, Isopoda;
−0.0142, Scolopendromorpha sp. 1, Chilopoda; −0.0152, Hydrophilidae sp., Coleoptera;
−0.0191, Oniscidae sp. 1, Isopoda; −0.0227, Chrysomelidae sp., Coleoptera; −0.0248,
Temnopteryx dimidiatipes Bolivar, Dictyoptera; −0.0291, Lygaeidae sp., Hemiptera; −0.0320,
Lithobiomorpha sp., Chilopoda; −0.0339, Gelastocoridae sp., Hemiptera; −0.0360, *Stenus* sp.,
Coleoptera; −0.0402, Anthocoridae sp., Hemiptera; −0.0418, Carabidae sp. 1, Coleoptera;
−0.0434, *Margattea* sp., Dictyoptera; −0.0458, unidentified arthropod sp. 3; −0.0464, *Tachys*
sp., Coleoptera; −0.0615, Geophilomorpha sp. 3, Chilopoda; −0.0772, *Euborellia plebeja*
(Dohrn), Dermaptera; −0.0932, Ptiliidae sp., Coleoptera; −0.1373, Oniscidae sp. 2, Isopoda;
−0.2271, *Opatrinus attenuatus* Klug., Coleoptera; −0.4799, unidentified Coleoptera sp. 3.

Phil. Trans. R. Soc. Lond. B. **286**, 119–126 (1979) [119]
Printed in Great Britain

A twelve month study of insect abundance and composition at various localities on Aldabra Atoll

By Dawn W. Frith†

Royal Society Aldabra Research Station, Seychelles

Insect populations were sampled at regular intervals, by using Heath light traps, throughout a 12 month period at various localities about Aldabra Atoll. Abundance and fluctuations in numbers throughout the year of the predominant orders, families and species of insects are given for localities on West, South and Middle Islands, and Ile Michel. Differences between the composition, diversity and density of insect populations at selected localities are discussed in relation to ecological factors such as vegetation, rainfall and the presence or absence of higher animals, in particular giant tortoises, *Geochelone gigantea*, and/or colonial breeding birds.

1. Introduction

The majority of earlier publications concerning Aldabran insects were based on collections made by Abbott in 1892, Voeltzkow in 1895, Dupont in 1906 and 1910, Thomasset in 1907 and Fryer in 1908–9. The collections by Fryer were made during the Percy Sladen Trust Expeditions to the Western Indian Ocean and, incorporated with the collections of Dr Hugh Scott from the Seychelles, form the basis of a series of comprehensive papers covering a wide range of insect taxa (see Scott 1933). For detailed accounts of these earlier studies and a bibliography of pertinent literature see Stoddart (1967a, b, 1971). Stoddart & Wright (1967) briefly reviewed the status of Aldabran insect faunas in the light of current knowledge, and Cogan, Hutson & Shaffer (1971) discussed the Aldabran insect faunas in general terms based on their own collecting during a Royal Society Expedition to Aldabra in 1967–8 and on the findings of previous investigations.

More recently, intensive studies on selected taxa of Aldabran insects have been made by Blackman & Pinhey (1967) on Odonata, by Viette (1958), Berio (1962), Herbulot (1962), Diakonoff (1969) and Legrand (1965, 1971) on Lepidoptera, by Webb (1975) on Fulgoroidea (Hemiptera-Homoptera), and by Wiebes (1975) on Chalcidoidea (Hymenoptera). Apart from a study by Woodell (1977) on a number of insect pollinators on Aldabra, and a preliminary account of insect abundance on West Island by myself (Frith 1975, 1979) no other ecological data are available on Aldabran insects. Data presented here provide information concerning composition, diversity and density of insect populations about the atoll which are considered in view of ecological factors such as vegetation and the presence or absence of higher animals, in particular giant tortoises, *Geochelone gigantea*, and colonial breeding birds. Furthermore, abundance and seasonal fluctuations of insect taxa predominant at various localities about the atoll are discussed.

Families listed in the tables are arranged according to the systematic lists in the book *The insects of Australia* (C.S.I.R.O. 1970) and species within each family are listed alphabetically.

† Present address: 'Prionodura', Paluma, via Townsville, Queensland, Australia 4810.

2. Trap localities, vegetation and trapping periods

Heath light traps were placed at the following localities (listed from west to east) about Aldabra:

Research Station, West Island. Trap 1; about 70 m inland from the west coast and behind the research station; on champignon in *Pemphis* thicket (see appendix 1†). Monthly samples (2–8 nights a sample) were taken from September 1971 to August 1972. Trap 2; about 60 m inland from the west coast and just north of the research station; on champignon in diverse mixed scrub (see appendix 1). Monthly samples (2–10 nights a sample) were taken from September 1971 to August 1972.

Anse Mais, South Island. About 150 m inland from the west coast; in coastal palm grove surrounded by diverse mixed scrub (see appendix 1). Monthly samples (2–4 nights a sample) were taken from September 1971 to August 1972.

Gionnet, Middle Island. About 10 m inland from the north coast; on champignon in poor mixed scrub (see appendix 1). Monthly samples (1–2 nights a sample) were taken from September 1971 to August 1972.

Middle Camp, East Channel, Middle Island. About 10 m inland from East Channel; on champignon in poor mixed scrub (see appendix 1). Samples were taken about every 6 weeks (1–3 nights a sample) from November 1971 to August 1972.

Ile Michel. About 10 m inland of the east coast: in palm grove surrounded by mixed scrub and mangrove (see appendix 1). Samples were taken about every 6 weeks (1 night a sample) from November 1971 to August 1972.

Takamaka (old camp), South Island. About 30 m south of the old camp; on platin in diverse mixed scrub (see appendix 1). Samples were taken about every 6 weeks (1 or 2 nights a sample) from December 1971 to August 1972.

Cinq Cases (lagoon side), South Island. At extreme landward end of tidal mangrove creek on champignon. Samples were taken about every 6 weeks (1 night a sample) from December 1971 to August 1972.

The number of catch samples is small for some localities owing to their relatively poor accessibility, particularly for those samples taken at the extreme east end of the atoll. Results from these localities are presented, however, as they provide important evidence of particularly interesting and undescribed situations of taxonomic diversity of insect populations with respect to the apparent presence or absence of ecological factors such as vegetation and/or higher animal communities.

3. Results

Details of mean nightly catch of insect taxa predominant in Heath light trap catches are given for all localities in tables 1–8. Relative proportions of each predominant insect order, expressed as a precentage of the total catch, is included in these tables. It should be noted that insects rarely caught in Heath light traps are referred to by the subheading 'others' in these tables and, apart from West Island catches (for species details see Frith 1975, 1979), remain unsorted. Figures for monthly rainfall on West Island during the present study period are given in table 1.

† Appendix 1 and tables 1–8 appear on the microfiche included with this publication; see note at end of this paper for details.

(a) Composition of catches about the atoll

Insect catches were similar in general composition at all coastal localities (West Island, Anse Mais, Gionnet and Middle Camp) being dominated by Lepidoptera and to a lesser extent by Hemiptera, Coleoptera, Diptera and Hymenoptera (tables 1–5). It is noteworthy that Lepidoptera represented a much higher proportion of the catch at Middle Camp than at any other coastal trap locality (table 5). At lagoon localities (Ile Michel, Takamaka and Cinq Cases), Coleoptera and Diptera were as well represented in the catches as Lepidoptera (tables 6–8). In addition, insect orders Odonata, Isoptera, Dictyoptera, Embioptera, Orthoptera and Neuroptera were present in catches at some localities about the atoll (tables 1–8) but owing to their relative sparsity in samples they are not discussed further as only insect taxa predominant in catches will be examined here. The numbers of those predominant insect taxa caught in Heath light traps at all localities are summarized in tables 1–8 and these data represent the quantitative results of this study.

(b) Variations in diversity and density of catches about the atoll

Most insects caught in the two Heath light traps on West Island were identified to species (Frith 1975, 1979). Of the 261 identified species in West Island catches, 201 (77 %) occurred in trap 1 catches (*Pemphis* thicket) and 251 (96 %) in trap 2 catches (mixed scrub); 193 (74 %) were common in both catches. Results thus indicated a greater diversity of insects in the mixed scrub habitat, as is to be expected in view of the greater floral diversity found there than in *Pemphis* thicket (see §4). An analysis of these West Island catches showed, however, that species diversity of the predominant orders differed considerably in the two habitats (tables 1 and 2). In total 107 lepidopteran, 31 hemipteran, 44 coleopteran, 48 dipteran and 18 hymenopteran species occurred in West Island catches. Of these species totals, 75 and 106 species of Lepidoptera, 27 and 28 species of Hemiptera, 36 and 42 species of Coleoptera, 37 and 47 species of Diptera, and 17 and 16 species of Hymenoptera occurred in trap 1 and 2 catches respectively. Thus species diversity of Lepidoptera and, to a lesser extent, Coleoptera and Diptera was greater in mixed scrub than in *Pemphis* thicket. As catches for localities other than West Island are only sorted to predominant insect taxa no data indicative of relative diversity are, as yet, available for them. At a preliminary examination of material from these localities, however, it would appear that species diversity was relatively lower in the mangrove habitat at Cinq Cases than in other habitats from which samples were taken (see §4).

As shown in tables 1 and 2, the average number of species in families of the predominant orders Lepidoptera, Hemiptera, Coleoptera and Diptera was relatively low (8.9, 2.4, 2.4 and 2.4 respectively), but that the average number of families in each of these orders was relatively high.

Insect density was in general greater at the east end than at west end of the atoll localities, but this may have been due, to some extent, to the smaller number of samples taken from the former localities. It is noteworthy that results showed, however, a markedly higher density of insects in the mangrove habitat at Cinq Cases and a markedly lower density of insects in *Pemphis* thicket on West Island (tables 1 and 8). In palm grove habitats at Anse Mais and Ile Michel the insect densities were similar to each other (tables 3 and 6), and of the mixed scrub habitats insect density was greater at Takamaka than at West Island, Gionnet or Middle Camp (tables

2, 4, 5 and 7). Relative densities of insect taxa predominant in traps are summarized in tables 1–8 for all localities and these are discussed below (see §4).

(c) Seasonal fluctuations in insect numbers

At all localities, insects were most abundant during the wetter months from November 1971 to April 1972, particularly during December–January and March–April. Monthly fluctuations in insect numbers on West Island followed very closely the monthly patterns of relative rainfall (tables 1 and 2). Insects on West Island were particularly abundant during December and March when there was a sudden marked increase in precipitation (tables 1 and 2). Catch size decreased, however, during January and April despite the fact that rainfall remained relatively high. Monthly fluctuations of insect numbers on West Island do not correspond with those from Anse Mais or Gionnet (tables 3 and 4). At Anse Mais the marked increase in catch size was during November and March and to a lesser extent during June and August, and at Gionnet during January and April, these results probably reflecting local variations in rainfall about the atoll (see §4). Unfortunately rainfall data were not available for localities other than West Island during the present survey. It is noteworthy that the two smaller peaks of higher rainfall in June and August on West Island did not apparently affect catch size during those months (tables 1 and 2). While figures of insect abundance for the east end of the atoll are not available for all months, results do show that there was a marked increase in relative abundance during December–January (tables 5–8).

Various aspects of seasonal fluctuations of numbers of predominant insect taxa at all collecting localities are comprehensively summarized in tables 1–8. It is noteworthy that as Lepidoptera, particularly Tortricidae, Tineidae and Pyralidae (Phycitinae), were extremely abundant in monthly catches at all localities, relative peaks of the total monthly insect abundance therefore reflect relative abundance of these predominant taxa. Furthermore monthly fluctuations in numbers of Coleoptera and Diptera at lagoon localities, in addition to the above mentioned Lepidoptera, greatly affected the total monthly catch size at those localities.

4. DISCUSSION

Most insects caught in the light traps were phytophagous and, therefore, differences found in the taxonomic composition of insect populations at localities about the atoll probably reflect, first and foremost, floral differences in these areas. Insufficient life-history knowledge of the vast majority of the Aldabran phytophagous insect taxa does not however, permit, any significant understanding of variations in their distribution and/or relative abundance indicated by the results of the present study (tables 1–8). It is nevertheless hoped that variations such as the greater abundance of the moths *Rhodogastria aldabrensis* and *Eilema aldabrensis* (Lepidoptera, Arctiidae), and the bug *Lethaeus stellatus* (Hemiptera, Lygaeidae) on West Island; of the bug *Chaetormenis madagascariensis* (Hemiptera, Flatidae) at Anse Mais; of the beetle *Ananca aldabrana* (Coleoptera, Oedemeridae) at Ile Michel and Anse Mais; and the notable absence of the weevil *Cratopus viridisparsus* (Coleoptera, Curculionidae) in the mangrove habitat at Cinq Cases, found during the present survey will provide suitable subjects for more intensive studies.

A comparison between insect populations of *Pemphis* thicket and mixed scrub habitats on West Island (see §3*b*) clearly indicated that the florally less diverse *Pemphis* thicket supported fewer insect species. A preliminary analysis of insect populations in the mangrove habitat at

Cinq Cases, the other uniform habitat investigated during the present study, indicated that species diversity there was also lower than that of florally more diverse habitats. It is noteworthy in this respect that both *Pemphis* and mangrove habitats have been found to support far less insectivorous bird feeding activity than any of the other habitats on Aldabra (C. B. Frith 1979, this volume).

The notable differences in the composition of catches of Coleoptera and Diptera at coastal and lagoon localities were apparently related to factors other than vegetation in many cases. Unique to the eastern end of the atoll, particularly the areas of Takamaka and Cinq Cases, are a number of temporary and permanent fresh and brackish water pools. These provide significant ecological niches to insects unavailable elsewhere on the atoll. It was not surprising, therefore, that collections from trap localities at Takamaka and Cinq Cases contained a larger number of aquatic and/or semi-aquatic insects, in particular members of families Dytiscidae and Hydrophilidae (Coleoptera) and Tipulidae, Culicidae and Ceratopogonidae (Diptera), than was found in collections taken elsewhere about the atoll. Moreover, the greater abundance of Culicidae and Ceratopogonidae (mosquitoes and biting midges) in the mangrove habitat at Cinq Cases than in mixed scrub at Takamaka was probably due to the fact that the saline conditions of mangrove waters provide more favourable breeding grounds for many species of these families (Macnae 1968). It is noteworthy that Cogan *et al.* (1971) pointed out that the wide range of aquatic habitats on Aldabra, from truly marine to freshwater, in relatively close proximity to Madagascar 'must be responsible for the very rich aquatic insect fauna in comparison with other island groups' within the western Indian Ocean. Doubtless future intensive studies of the aquatic insects of these eastern areas will show that a number of insect taxa are found there and nowhere else on the atoll.

The very large populations (about 150 000) of the endemic giant tortoise, *Geochelone gigantea*, on South Island, in particular about Takamaka and Cinq Cases (Coe, Bourn & Swingland 1979, this volume), constitute a most significant factor of the terrestrial ecology of the Aldabran fauna. It is not surprising, therefore, that the presence or absence of these animals was found to apparently affect insect populations and their densities about the atoll markedly. While this finding was to be expected, results of the present study provide the first evidence of a relation between the giant tortoise and insect populations on Aldabra and suggest important and rewarding future lines of investigation. In addition to the tortoises themseves providing a food source for blood-sucking insects, their decaying corpses provide a temporary rich feeding and breeding ground for many insect groups that presumably could not exist on Aldabra without the presence of these larger terrestrial vertebrates. In addition, tortoise dung provides a widespread and continuously abundant and available food source and breeding ground for many insect species. Thus the presence of the large numbers of giant tortoises about trap localities at Takamaka and, in particular, at Cinq Cases probably accounts for the abundance of such insects as some Hydrophilidae and Staphylinidae (Coleoptera), and Tipulidae and Tethinidae (Diptera) which are known to feed on or associate with dung and decaying animal matter as well as members of the families Culicidae and Ceratopogonidae (Diptera) that feed on blood. The relative sparsity of these particular insect groups at localities investigated elsewhere about the atoll, where tortoises are few or absent, supports this conclusion. These findings are noteworthy in that Cogan *et al.* (1971) considered the number of insects associated with animal waste products on Aldabra to be very low, and while the results of this present preliminary survey support their findings, they also indicate that the few species concerned are apparently very abundant, especially in mangroves. It would be of particular interest to establish to what degree, or dependence, certain insects have adapted to the utilization of tortoise dung on Aldabra. Moreover, the presence of large seabird colonies (*Fregata* spp. and *Sula* spp.) (Diamond 1971, 1975) would not only provide an additional food source for such insects as the blood-sucking mosquitoes and biting midges, but the bird's nests might also provide suitable microhabitats for insects such as staphylinid beetles (Britton 1970) and thus contribute to the larger numbers of these insect taxa found in mangroves at Cinq Cases than in mixed scrub at Takamaka. It is also noteworthy that the humid conditions of the mangrove forest environment and the associated slow-decaying plant detritus (providing an important food source) probably accounts for the larger numbers of certain insect species found in this habitat.

While the Coleoptera and Diptera were well represented in catches at Ile Michel, an analysis of them showed that in composition they differed somewhat from Takamaka and Cinq Cases catches. Diptera were represented predominantly by mosquitoes which is surprising in view of the sparsity of tortoises (only one or two during the study period) and dense seabird populations at this locality. It is possible, however, that the large population of feeding and roosting bat colonies in the coconut palms at Ile Michel (observed during the present study) supported this large mosquito population. Coleoptera at Ile Michel consisted mainly of terrestrial rather than aquatic species, as is to be expected in view of the sparsity of non-marine aquatic habitats at this locality. It is noteworthy that the beetle *Ananca aldabrana* (Coleoptera, Oedemeridae) was abundant at this locality (see above).

Seasonal fluctuations in the relative monthly abundance of insects on West Island was greatly affected by rainfall (Frith 1975; C. B. Frith 1976). Insect numbers suddenly increased with periods of sudden higher rainfall, as is typical of insect populations in tropical areas of marked seasonal precipitation. This is worthy of particular note with regard to the insect fauna of Aldabra, however, as fluctuations in relative insect numbers varied considerably about the atoll, which is suggestive of rainfall variations from one locality to another. That rainfall does in fact vary in distribution and relative monthly production about the atoll has been established during the last few years, and apparently these variations are inconsistent in character (i.e. from year to year) (R. J. Hnatiuk, personal communication). C. B. Frith (1976, 1977) has shown that certain endemic, and predominantly insectivorous, birds on West Island begin breeding with the marked increase in insect abundance at the onset of the rainy season. It seems possible, therefore, that as monthly variations in insect abundance are governed by relative rainfall, these insect fluctuations might in turn be responsible for small variations in breeding seasons within the year about the atoll in the more insectivorous bird species. This is, however, speculative and requires further studies involving the simultaneous observations of bird and insect populations at various localities about the atoll.

5. Conclusions

(1) The vast majority of insects on Aldabra are phytophagous feeders and thus the distribution, diversity and/or density of the taxa concerned presumably relates closely to the presence or absence of food plant species.

(2) A number of extremely important environmental or ecological factors to insect populations are restricted in their distribution on Aldabra Atoll. It is not possible to account for the presence, absence and/or relative abundance of certain insect populations without due

consideration to factors such as (*a*) the presence of mangroves along the lagoon shore of Aldabra, which provide a major vegetation type unavailable elsewhere about the atoll; (*b*) fresh and brackish water pools at the east end of the atoll, predominantly at Takamaka and Cinq Cases, which provide significant ecological niches unavailable elsewhere; (*c*) the giant tortoises which apparently provide a vast and important biomass which is utilized by insects in various ways, and (*d*) additional populations of larger vertebrates, notably colonial seabird breeding populations, and bat roosts and feeding aggregations, provide important foods and microhabitats restricted in their geographical availability on Aldabra.

(3) Relative abundance of insect populations on West Island was controlled by rainfall. Peaks of relative monthly abundance, however, differed about the atoll and these differences therefore almost certainly reflect differences in local rainfall.

I thank all staff at the Royal Society of London and the British Museum (Natural History) concerned with Aldabra for making my visit possible and all those present with me on Aldabra for their help and encouragement in various ways. I am indebted to Professor T. R. E. Southwood for supervising the research programme and to the National Environmental Research Council for providing funds. I am grateful to Mr J. F. Peake, Dr P. Freeman and the trustees of the British Museum (Natural History) for providing me with working space and use of facilities at the Museum for 1 year. I thank staff of the Entomological Department, in particular Mr Brian H. Cogan, for time and help with identifications and Dr P. Viette, Museum of Natural History, Paris, for allowing me access to Legrand's collection and for help with identification of some Lepidoptera. I acknowledge the help of Dr D. Wood in identifying plants on West Island and Dr S. Renvoize, Kew Gardens, for kindness in providing me with a list of plants predominantly surrounding traps at localities other than on West Island. I also thank Dr R. Hnatiuk for helpful correspondence concerning climate. Lastly I thank my husband for discussions on various aspects of this paper and for reading and providing useful criticisms of earlier drafts of this paper.

REFERENCES (Frith)

Berio, E. 1962 Diagnosi di alcune *Noctuidae* delle isole Seicelle e Aldabra. *Annali Mus. civ. Stor. nat. Giacomo Doria* 73, 172–180.
Blackman, R. A. A. & Pinhey, E. C. G. 1967 Odonata of the Seychelles and other Indian Ocean island groups, based primarily on the Bristol University Expedition of 1964–1965. *Arnoldia* 3 (12), 1–38.
Britton, E. B. 1970 Coleoptera. In *The insects of Australia*, pp. 495–622. C.S.I.R.O., Melbourne: Melbourne University Press.
Coe, M. J., Bourn, D. & Swingland, I. R. 1979 The biomass, production and carrying capacity of giant tortoises on Aldabra. *Phil. Trans. R. Soc. Lond.* B 286, 163–176 (this volume).
Cogan, B. H., Hutson, A. M. & Shaffer, J. C. 1971 Preliminary observations on the affinities and composition of the insect fauna of Aldabra. *Phil. Trans. R. Soc. Lond.* B 260, 315–325.
C.S.I.R.O. 1970 *The insects of Australia*. Melbourne: Melbourne University Press.
Diakonoff, A. 1969 Tortricidae from the Seychelles and Aldabra (Lepidoptera). *Tijdschr. Ent.* 112, 81–100.
Diamond, A. M. 1971 The seabirds of Aldabra. *Phil. Trans. R. Soc. Lond.* B 260, 561–571.
Diamond, A. W. 1975 Biology and behaviour of frigate birds, *Fregata* spp., on Aldabra Atoll. *Ibis* 117, 302–323.
Frith, C. B. 1976 A twelve-month field study of the Aldabran Fody, *Foudia eminentissima aldabrana. Ibis* 118, 155–178.
Frith, C. B. 1977 Life history notes on some Aldabran land birds. *Atoll Res. Bull.* 201, 1–15.
Frith, C. B. 1979 Feeding ecology of land birds on West Island, Aldabra Atoll, Indian Ocean: a preliminary survey. *Phil. Trans. R. Soc. Lond.* B 286, 195–210 (this volume).
Frith, D. W. 1975 A preliminary study of insect abundance on West Island, Aldabra Atoll, Indian Ocean. *Trans. R. ent. Soc. Lond.* 127, 209–226.

Frith, D. W. 1979 A list of insects caught in light traps on West Island, Aldabra Atoll, Indian Ocean. *Atoll Res. Bull.* **225**, 1–11.

Herbulot, C. 1962 Nouveaux Geometridae d'Aldabra. *Revue. fr. Ent.* **29**, 235–237.

Legrand, H. 1965 Lepidoptères des Iles Seychelles et d'Aldabra. *Mém. Mus. natn. Hist. nat., Paris* **37**, 1–210.

Legrand, H. 1971 Notes sur les Geometridae des Seychelles et d'Aldabra. *Bull. Soc. ent. Fr.* **76**, 81–82.

Macnae, W. 1968 A general account of the flora and fauna of mangrove swamps in the Indo-West Pacific region. *Adv. mar. Biol.* **6**, 73–720.

Scott, H. 1933 General conclusions regarding the insect fauna of the Seychelles and adjacent islands. *Trans. Linn. Soc. Lond.* **19**, 307–391.

Stoddart, D. R. 1967a Scientific studies on Aldabra. *Atoll Res. Bull.* **118**, 1–10.

Stoddart, D. R. 1967b Bibliography of Aldabra. *Atoll Res. Bull.* **118**, 127–141.

Stoddart, D. R. 1971 Scientific studies at Aldabra and neighbouring islands. *Phil. Trans. R. Soc. Lond.* B **260**, 5–29.

Stoddart, D. R. & Wright, C. A. 1967 Geography and ecology of Aldabra Atoll. *Atoll Res. Bull.* **118**, 11–52.

Webb, M. D. 1975 Fulgoroidea from Aldabra, Astove and Cosmoledo Atolls collected by the Royal Society Expedition 1967–68 (Hemiptera–Homoptera). *Atoll. Res. Bull.* **177**, 1–10.

Wiebes, J. T. 1975 Fig insects from Aldabra (Hymenoptera, Chalcidoidea). *Zool. Med.* **49**, 225–236.

Woodell, S. R. J. 1979 The rôle of unspecialized pollinators in the reproductive success of Aldabran plants *Phil. Trans. R. Soc. Lond.* B **286**, 99–108 (this volume).

Viette, P. 1958 Note sur des petites collections des lepidoptères recoltés aux Iles Comores et en Aldabra. *Lambillionea* **58**, 60–65.

Microfiche

The relevant frames of the microfiche included with this publication contain the following material referred to in the text of this paper.

APPENDIX 1. A LIST OF PLANT SPECIES (ARRANGED ALPHABETICALLY) SURROUNDING HEATH LIGHT TRAPS AT LOCALITIES ON ALDABRA ATOLL

TABLE 1. MEAN CATCH PER NIGHT OF PREDOMINANT INSECT TAXA CAUGHT IN A HEATH LIGHT TRAP (1) ON WEST ISLAND ALDABRA ATOLL

TABLE 2. MEAN CATCH PER NIGHT OF PREDOMINANT INSECT TAXA CAUGHT IN A HEATH LIGHT TRAP (2) ON WEST ISLAND ALDABRA ATOLL

TABLE 3. MEAN CATCH PER NIGHT OF PREDOMINANT INSECT TAXA CAUGHT IN A HEATH LIGHT TRAP AT ANSE MAIS, SOUTH ISLAND, ALDABRA ATOLL

TABLE 4. MEAN CATCH PER NIGHT OF PREDOMINANT INSECT TAXA CAUGHT IN A HEATH LIGHT TRAP AT GIONNET, MIDDLE ISLAND, ALDABRA ATOLL

TABLE 5. MEAN CATCH PER NIGHT OF PREDOMINANT INSECT TAXA CAUGHT IN A HEATH LIGHT TRAP AT MIDDLE CAMP, MIDDLE ISLAND, ALDABRA ATOLL

TABLE 6. MEAN CATCH PER NIGHT OF PREDOMINANT INSECT TAXA CAUGHT IN A HEATH LIGHT TRAP AT ILE MICHEL, ALDABRA ATOLL

TABLE 7. MEAN CATCH PER NIGHT OF PREDOMINANT INSECT TAXA CAUGHT IN A HEATH LIGHT TRAP AT TAKAMAKA, SOUTH ISLAND, ALDABRA ATOLL

TABLE 8. MEAN CATCH PER NIGHT OF PREDOMINANT INSECT TAXA CAUGHT IN A HEATH LIGHT TRAP AT CINQ CASES, SOUTH ISLAND, ALDABRA ATOLL

Phil. Trans. R. Soc. Lond. B. **286**, 127–145 (1979)   [127]

Printed in Great Britain

Indian Ocean giant tortoises: their systematics and island adaptations

By E. N. Arnold

Department of Zoology, British Museum (Natural History),
Cromwell Road, London SW7 5BD, U.K.

Although wild populations are now confined to Aldabra, giant tortoises were originally present on many other Indian Ocean islands. All belong to the genus *Geochelone* but are referable to two distinct subgenera, *Cylindraspis* in the Mascarene islands and *Aldabrachelys* on Madagascar, Aldabra, the Seychelles and neighbouring islands. These are distinguishable by skull and nasal structure, degree of shell ankylosis and structure of the plastron. Neither group has obvious close relatives in other areas. Mascarene tortoises, which are completely extinct, comprised several species: *G. vosmaeri* and the smaller *G. peltastes* on Rodrigues, *G. inepta* and *G. triserrata* on Mauritius, and what should probably be called *G. indica* on Réunion. All the tortoises of Aldabra, the Seychelles and neighbouring islands seem to be referable to one species, *G. gigantea* which appears to have shown some geographical variation. Madagascar probably had two species, *G. grandidieri* and another usually named *G. abrupta* which may well be conspecific with *G. gigantea* and was possibly the source of the Aldabra populations.

Many of the distinctive features of Indian Ocean and Galápagos giant tortoises are interpretable as adaptations to the peculiar environment of ocean islands, particularly their lack of big predators and competing herbivores.

1. Introduction

When Europeans reached the various small islands of the west Indian Ocean, they encountered giant tortoises on many of them (Stoddart & Peake 1979, this volume). All of these populations, except that on Aldabra, became extinct in the wild by the early nineteenth century, largely as a result of human exploitation for food, but introduced mammals, such as dogs, rats and pigs, may also have played a part in at least some cases, particularly by destroying nests and young animals. Giant tortoises also existed on Madagascar but had apparently disappeared by the time Europeans arrived. Their remains are quite abundant, often looking very fresh, and radiocarbon dates suggest that some of them are only about two millenia old (see §5b). So it is not impossible that the species they represent overlapped with the first human colonists of Madagascar, who may have occupied the island not much more than 1100 years ago (Mahé & Sourdat 1973), and were exterminated by them.

Comprehensive systematic studies of the Indian Ocean giant tortoises were largely initiated by Albert Günther whose investigations culminated in the appearance of his monograph, *Gigantic tortoises (living and extinct) in the collection of the British Museum*, published just over a century ago. This stimulated a great deal of work over the next 30 or 40 years (see, for example, Boulenger 1889, 1891, 1894; Gadow 1894; Günther 1898; Rothschild 1906, 1915; Sauzier 1892, 1893; Vaillant 1885, 1893, 1898, 1899, 1900, 1903) but since then there has been relatively little interest in the relationship of these animals. It is therefore, perhaps appropriate to review their systematics here and at the same time speculate about their adaptations to island life.

In the following account, *tortoise* is used for members of the family Testudinidae, *carapace* refers to the usually domed upper part of the shell of a tortoise, *plastron* to its lower section and *bridge* to the regions joining the two. Unless otherwise stated, shell lengths given are maximum straight-line lengths of carapaces. The following abbreviations are also used: B.M.(P), British Museum (Natural History), Department of Palaeontology; B.M.(Z), British Museum (Natural History), Department of Zoology; C.A.S. California Academy of Sciences, San Francisco; M.H.N.P.(P), Muséum Nationale d'Histoire Naturelle, Paris, Institut de Palaeontologie; M.H.N.P.(R), Muséum Nationale d'Histoire Naturelle, Paris, Reptiles et Poissons; U.M.C., University Museum of Zoology, Cambridge; unreg., unregistered.

2. Main groups of Indian Ocean giant tortoises

All of the Indian Ocean giant tortoises belong to a single genus, *Geochelone* Fitzinger 1835, which, until some 20 years ago was regarded as part of *Testudo* Linnaeus 1758, but appears to have had a long independent history (Loveridge & Williams 1957). *Geochelone* also includes the Galápagos giant tortoise, *G. elephantopus* (Harlan 1827), and about 13 smaller species found in the warmer parts of South America, Africa, Madagascar and southern Asia. It has a fossil record extending back to the Eocene (Auffenberg 1974) and its members are quite varied, being grouped into a number of subgenera, three of which are now restricted to the Indian Ocean. One, *Asterochelys* Gray 1873, is confined to Madagascar and contains relatively small tortoises, *G. radiata* (Shaw 1802) and the possibly conspecific *G. ynophora* (Vaillant 1885), while the others are made up of giant species. Of these *Cylindraspis* Fitzinger 1835 contains all the Mascarene forms and *Aldabrachelys* Loveridge & Williams 1957 those of Madagascar and the islands lying north of it. The moderately large tortoises of Africa, *G. pardalis* (Bell 1828) and *G. sulcata* (Miller 1779) belong to yet another subgenus, *Geochelone sensu stricto*. *Cylindraspis* and *Aldabrachelys* show several clear points of difference which are summarized below.

(a) Skull and nasal passages

The skull of *Cylindraspis* is essentially similar to those of other relatively large members of the genus *Geochelone*. It is not particularly elevated, the external nasal opening is about as high as wide and the supraoccipital crest is relatively long, laterally compressed and blade-like (figure 1). In *Aldabrachelys* the skull is high, especially in front, the external nasal opening vertically elongated and the supraoccipital crest quite short, and not usually compressed. This combination of specialized cranial structures is not known in any other recent tortoise and the elevated anterior region is correlated with a peculiar arrangement of nasal passages, at least in *G. (Aldabrachelys) gigantea*. No material exists of *Cylindraspis* in which the structure of the nasal chambers and their adnexae can be investigated but, from the formation of the anterior part of the skull, it is likely that it did not differ significantly from the basic arrangement found in nearly all modern species of *Geochelone*. In these, the passage from the nostril to the nasal chamber is short and not very inclined, the chamber itself is rounded in outline and its olfactory section is broadly open anteriorly (figure 2). In *G. gigantea*, on the other hand, the passage from the nostril is broad and long and ascends quite steeply. It is also singular in having a posteriorly directed diverticulum arising from its ventral wall. The olfactory part of the nasal chamber is elongate, extending further backwards than in other *Geochelone*, and anteriorly there is a flap-like ridge that contains cavernous tissue projecting from the medial wall. This may be capable of closing off the olfactory area in life.

It is not easy to envisage what selective pressures might have been responsible for the development of the specialized head structure found in *Aldabrachelys*. The deepening of the skull and shortening of the supraoccipital crest produce some alteration in the arrangement of the big adductor muscles running to the jaw but the functional consequences of this are not known. Observations by I. R. Swingland (personal communication) do, however, suggest a possible reason for some aspects of the peculiar nasal structure. He found that *G. gigantea* sometimes drinks by drawing water in through the nostrils instead of through the mouth. This ability would be beneficial to a tortoise living in arid habitats since water could be extracted from shallow puddles and cavities far too small to allow the mouth to be submerged below the surface for conventional drinking. The rather pointed snout of *G. gigantea* would also be advantageous in reaching the bottom of such hollows. In this context, the configuration of the olfactory section of the nasal chamber and the development of a possibly valvular structure

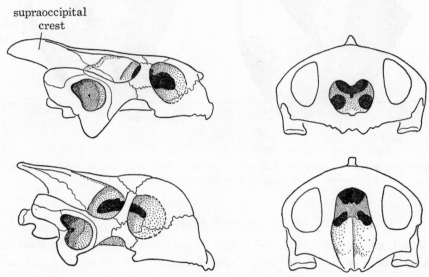

FIGURE 1. Skulls of Indian Ocean giant tortoises, lateral and anterior views. top, *G. (Cylindraspis) inepta* from Mauritius; bottom, *G. (Aldabrachelys) gigantea* from Aldabra.

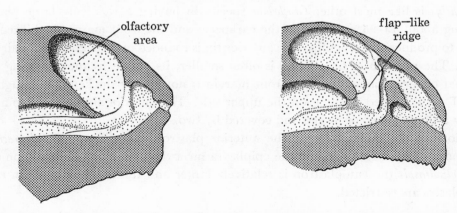

FIGURE 2. Right nasal passages of tortoises, lateral views: left, usual arrangement in *Geochelone* (based on *G. pardalis*, B.M.(Z) 1931.7.20.411); right, arrangement in *G. (Aldabrachelys) gigantea* based on B.M.(Z) 1978.772.

at its entrance could be interpreted as devices that prevent its flooding, something that might be expected to happen in tortoises with more usual nasal structure (figure 3).

(b) Shell thickness and ankylosis

The species of *Aldabrachelys* have shells that are typically either moderately or very thick and, as in most other tortoises, the component bones usually remain separate although in a few (usually large and apparently old) animals there is at least some fusion. In *Cylindraspis*, shells are much thinner and in some cases even large shells may be only 1 or 2 mm thick in places. Also, nearly all of the available shells exhibit considerable ankylosis.

FIGURE 3. Hypothetical results of drinking water through nose: left, typical *Geochelone*, olfactory section partly flooded; right, *G. gigantea*, olfactory section free of water.

(c) Size of front opening of shell

In shells where it can be measured, the height of the front opening of the shell divided by its width gives about 0.28–0.43 for *Aldabrachelys* and about 0.45–0.9 for *Cylindraspis*.

(d) Structure of the plastron

Aldabrachelys is like most other *Geochelone* species in having a relatively large plastron, its length being about 73–95 % of that of the carapace, and the front margin is thickened on its upper side to produce a distinct lip. The anterior tip is rounded and covered by a pair of scales, the gulars. The plastron of *Cylindraspis* is often smaller, its length frequently being only 66–77 % of that of the carapace and the front margin is not clearly thickened although there is usually a T or + shaped swelling on the upper side. The anterior tip is either rounded and covered by a single gular, or forked and covered by two.

Proportions of the bones forming the anterior plastron also differ. In *Aldabrachelys*, the entoplastron is of moderate size and the epiplastra meet the hypoplastra broadly on each side of it. In *Cylindraspis* the entoplastron is relatively larger and the contacts between epiplastra and hypoplastra are restricted.

3. Relationships and origins

Aldabrachelys and *Cylindraspis* each possess characters that are specialized (apomorphic in the terminology of Hennig (1966)) compared with equivalent conditions in the other and in *Geochelone* as a whole. *Aldabrachelys* has its peculiar skull and nasal structure and *Cylindraspis* is singular in the frequent ankylosis of its shell and in some features of its plastron. Given the marked nature of their differences, it seems likely that the two groups have had substantial separate histories and neither in its present form can be regarded as very close to the stock that gave rise to the other. Little can be said about the affinities of these subgenera to other tortoises. Mascarene examples with forked plastral tips, usually named *Geochelone gadowi* (Van Denburgh 1914) are often thought to be related to the Pleistocene *Geochelone* (*Megalochelys*) *atlas* (Falconer & Cautley 1837) of the Siwalik hills, north India, since it too shows this feature (Rothschild 1915). But some degree of plastral forking occurs in members of a number of disparate tortoise groups, so it is quite likely to have arisen independently, a hypothesis strengthened in the present case by the fact that, apart from their forked tips, the anterior plastra of *G. gadowi* and *G. atlas* are very different. In fact there may be a better case for associating *G. atlas* with *Aldabrachelys*, for a poorly preserved skull that may be attributable to this species (Lydekker 1885) appears to have a vertically elongated external nasal opening, approaching the specialized condition found in the Aldabran tortoises and their relatives. However, a great deal more would need to be known about *G. atlas* and allied forms before such a connection could be accepted. The Indian Ocean giant tortoises differ in the uncertainty of their origin from those of the Galápagos which have clear affinities to extant species in South America and are referred to the same subgenus, *Chelonoidis* Fitzinger 1835.

All three groups of insular tortoise seem likely to have reached their present ranges by transmarine migration. This is certainly true for Aldabra which has probably been submerged twice during quite recent times (Braithwaite, Taylor & Kennedy 1973) so that postulations about earlier land connections could not be used to explain the presence of tortoises. Floating or rafting seem feasible means of dispersal, for giant tortoises appear to tolerate contact with salt water quite well. The Galápagos *G. elephantopus* is known to float without injury for at least several days (Van Denburgh 1914) and Townsend (1936) records two that survived apparent transport across the sea by a hurricane for over 32 km (20 miles). *G. gigantea* is reputed to have made rather similar journeys (Vaillant 1899) and Grubb (1971) notes that it can swim reasonably well, unlike the Galápagos tortoise (Van Denburgh 1914), and has been seen floating well offshore. As it frequently forages on beaches, the chances of its being washed out to sea must be quite high.

4. Giant tortoises of the Mascarenes (subgenus *Cylindraspis*)

The tortoises of the Mascarenes are reviewed elsewhere (Arnold 1981), so only a brief account of them will be given here. They abounded on all three large islands but were exterminated by about the end of the eighteenth century. Because they disappeared so early, very few specimens were collected from living populations and knowledge of the group is based largely on fossils, in all samples of which the main elements of the skeleton are dissociated.

(a) Rodrigues

Shells from Rodrigues show great variation in shape and, because of this, have been assigned to more than one species, Vaillant (1898) and Rothschild (1915) recognizing three and Auffenberg (1974) two. Examination of available material shows that shells and shell fragments certainly fall into two distinct classes. One, to which the name *G. peltastes* is given, consists of relatively small shells up to only 42 cm in length which are smooth, domed in outline and with unreflexed margins (figure 4*a*). The other, on which *G. vosmaeri* is based, contains shells reaching a maximum length of 85 cm with lumpy surfaces, strongly raised fronts and reflexed margins (figure 4*b*, *c*). Although some populations of the Galápagos tortoise (*G. elephantopus*) show ontogenetic change from rounded juveniles to adults with high-fronted shells (figure 4*d–f*), a single-species interpretation based on growth changes cannot be applied to the

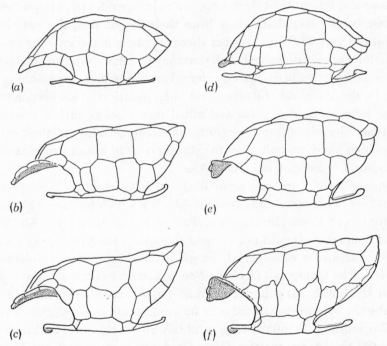

FIGURE 4. Tortoise shells from Rodrigues (left) and some Galápagos islands (right). (*a*) *G. peltastes*, male (40 cm); (*b, c*) *G. vosmaeri*, males (56 cm, 85 cm); (*d*) *G. elephantopus*, young animal (32 cm); (*e*) female from Pinzón (52 cm); (*f*) male from Fernandina (86 cm) ((*b*) based on Vaillant (1893); (*e*) and (*f*) on Van Denburgh (1914)).

Rodrigues tortoises, for, while known *peltastes* and *vosmaeri* shells almost overlap in size, there are no specimens that could be regarded as intermediate in morphology. Furthermore, all the larger *peltastes* shells have their constituent bones completely fused together, a situation that would have made further growth impossible. Nor can the two shell types be regarded as sexual variants. The degree of dimorphism in size and form that would be involved is far greater than in any known tortoise species and there are strong indications that they both included animals of two sexes. Each contains some individuals with deeply concave plastra and others with relatively flat ones, in living tortoise populations typically characteristic of males and females respectively. It seems very probable therefore that there were two species of tortoise on Rodrigues. The third form described by Vaillant (1898) as *Testudo commersoni* is apparently synonymous with *G. vosmaeri*.

One problem with this interpretation is that no young *G. vosmaeri* shells are known but this may well be an artefact. Unlike similarly sized adult *G. peltastes*, their bony shells would not have been fused together, and being thin would have been very liable to fall apart after death. As the nineteenth century excavators who collected much of the known Rodrigues material consistently ignored small fragments, it is not surprising that no certain material of young *G. vosmaeri* is represented.

The two species of tortoise apparently present on Rodrigues must have been closely related for, although the shells are distinct, it does not seem possible to separate the other skeletal elements into two classes, except for the humeri. Such a degree of similarity is known in other sympatric tortoise species, for instance the Mediterranean members of *Testudo*, and *Geochelone denticulata* and *G. carbonaria* in South America. The two Rodrigues species seem to have been synchronous as shells of both are known in which the external keratinous scutes are present, suggesting recent origin, and both types appear to occur in the same cave deposits. The presence of two species of relatively large tortoise on such a small island is extraordinary. However, although Rodrigues is only about 118 km² now, it is very likely that it was considerably larger in the past (see, for example, Montaggioni 1970) and the two forms may even have speciated *in situ*.

The differences in adult size and shell shape in the two Rodrigues tortoise species may be functionally correlated with reducing direct competition by utilization of different food resources. Some support for this hypothesis is available from still surviving Galápagos tortoises. Here, where there were originally 14 separate tortoise populations, forms with high fronted ('saddle-backed') shells are largely associated with dry islands supporting only sparse vegetation and more rounded shells with lusher habitats. Mascarene tortoises show some tendency to follow this pattern, Rodrigues, the driest island, having the most saddle-backed animals. It is argued (Snow 1964; White & Epler 1972) that shell shape is related to differences in browsing opportunities. In rich habitats there is an abundance of food near the ground which can be reached easily and a smooth, rounded shell allows easy progress through dense vegetation. On dry islands where food is less easily available there is a premium on being able to browse over a more extensive vertical range, and a long neck is therefore advantageous. Its length may be as much as three-quarters that of the shell in some Galápagos saddle-backed males and *G. vosmaeri* must have at least approached this. The high shell front allows greater extension of the neck and raises its base, increasing the maximum upward reach; it also provides the necessary increased storage space when the head is withdrawn (the proximal part of the necks of tortoises forms a relatively rigid vertical arc when contracted that cannot be compressed easily). In the sparsely vegetated habitats usually occupied by saddle-backed tortoises, the unstreamlined shell is not a great disadvantage in locomotion. The sexual dimorphism in shell form and neck length found in saddle-backed Galápagos populations may increase the efficiency of exploiting the total feeding niche, but no observations on this point seem to have been reported.

The Galápagos situation suggests that on Rodrigues the large, high-fronted *G. vosmaeri* may have occupied more open habitats than *G. peltastes* and browsed higher. As might be expected where two species instead of one occupy roughly the same ecological space, the two Rodrigues forms show restricted variability in features that probably correlate with resource exploitation.

Thus there appears to be less variation in shell shape than is encountered in some Galápagos populations and there is no indication of marked sexual dimorphism.

(b) Mauritius

At least nine names have been applied to the Mauritian tortoises. Most of these are synonyms, but it seems that, as on Rodrigues, two well defined species were present which should be called *Geochelone inepta* Günther 1873 and *G. triserrata* Günther 1873. The skulls of *G. inepta* have two ridges on each side of the palate, like nearly all other tortoises. These support the horny,

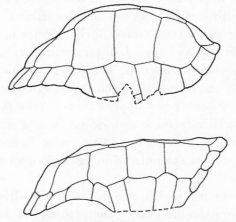

FIGURE 5. Top, domed shell from Mauritius, possibly of *Geochelone inepta* (based on U.M.C. R. 3846); bottom, carapace thought to be from Réunion (M.H.N.P.(R) 452), similar to high fronted Mauritius shells which may be attributable to *G. triserrata* (based on Vaillant 1900).

blade-like structures with which food is bitten. *G. triserrata*, on the other hand, is unique in having three ridges on each side. This difference correlates with others, such as the relative width of the partition between the internal nasal openings and degree of bone fusion, and it is therefore impossible to regard it as attributable to variation within a single species. Two kinds of shell were found associated with the skulls, one of which (upper shell, figure 5) is essentially domed with a rounded plastral tip covered by a single gular scale and all the bones are completely ankylosed. The other, represented only by fragments, has a roughly horizontal anterior dorsal profile (rather like the lower shell in figure 5), a forked plastral tip covered by two gular scales (on which the name *G. gadowi* is based), and the bones of the shell are incompletely fused. It is not certain to which species they should be assigned but the degree of ankylosis suggests that domed shells may be *G. inepta*. The two forms were almost certainly synchronous for their remains appear to have been found promiscuously mixed at two sites (the marsh called Mare aux Songes in the southeast of the island and in caves near La Pouce in the northwest). They are less alike than the two Rodrigues tortoises but, as on that island, anatomical features suggest that they may have reduced direct competition by exploiting different ranges of resources. The palatal structure indicates that there could have been dietary specialization and shell shapes might be interpreted as adaptations to different habitats and different browsing ranges.

No evidence exists as to how the two species came to inhabit Mauritius. One possibility is that it resulted from a double invasion. The skull and presumed shell of *G. inepta* are quite similar to ones found on Rodrigues in several features and it may be that the ancestors of this species reached Mauritius from that island after *G. triserrata* was established. The direction of predominant currents and winds are appropriate for this. It might be thought that colonists landing on an island occupied by a similar species would be excluded but, while this may usually be so in stable conditions, it need not apply in periods of climatic change such as have frequently occurred in the Quaternary. For instance, in a period of increased aridity, the success of *G. triserrata* on Mauritius might have been reduced, perhaps resulting in its exclusion from some dry coastal areas. This could have allowed a more dry-adapted invader to survive the critical period of early colonization. Once coexistence had been established on the basis of differences in tolerance of aridity, other niche differences and their anatomical concommitants could have evolved.

(c) Réunion

Réunion tortoises are very poorly known, the only available material that certainly originated there being some bone fragments collected recently by G. S. Cowles. They show only that at least some animals had the ankylosis of shell bones frequent on the other Mascarene islands. Apart from these, there is a carapace without data in Paris (M.H.N.P.(R) 452; figure 5) that is the type of *Testudo indica* Schneider 1783 and may have come from Réunion. It is rather similar to the high-fronted shell type from Mauritius, possibly referable to *G. triserrata*, but differs in the shape of its anterior margin and greater thickness. If the supposition about its locality is correct, then the name *Geochelone indica* would apply to at least some Réunion tortoises. Petit (1737) investigated what he believed to be a Réunion tortoise and illustrated its palate which is very like that of *Geochelone triserrata*, but given the inaccuracy of many eighteenth century localities it is difficult to know what credence to give this report; the tortoise might after all have come from Mauritius. Taken at its face value, the little evidence available suggests that a tortoise similar to *G. triserrata* may have occurred on Réunion, which would not be entirely unexpected as this island is close to Mauritius and the two have some other reptile types in common. Whether Réunion was like Mauritius in having two species of tortoise is unknown.

5. Giant tortoises of Aldabra, the Seychelles and Madagascar (subgenus *Aldabrachelys*)

(a) Aldabra, the Seychelles and nearby islands

With the exception of Aldabra, wild tortoises disappeared from these islands by the early nineteenth century. Some continued to exist in captivity and semi-feral conditions but had often been transported from their natural localities to other places. With the rise in interest in giant tortoises, many of these animals found their way to museums and private collections to join the few earlier ones already there, but, as with these, any locality data attached to them were almost always suspect. It was on such material that a total of seven species was described between 1812 and 1906 (see §5c). Examination of the descriptions, and in most cases the types, of these forms, as well as of over 80 other specimens now in the British and Paris Museums, strongly suggests that all of them are assignable to a single species for which the applicable name is (fortunately) *Geochelone gigantea*. The total variation encountered is considerably less than that found in the Galápagos tortoises, which are all generally acknowledged to be assignable to one species. There is no evidence that more than one kind of tortoise existed at any locality and it does not seem possible to divide the available material into discrete groups on the basis of the differences encountered within it. Furthermore, as a proportion of the specimens have been in captivity, some of the variation present may be attributable to this, for tortoises are notorious for their tendency to develop odd shell shapes when subjected to unnatural conditions (see, for example, Schweizer 1965). Considerable emphasis has been placed on the presence or absence of the nuchal scale in classifying these animals and one supposed species, *G. sumeirei* was separated partly because the type lacks this scale. However, the condition may vary within an island population. This is true for the Aldabran tortoises where, although most have a nuchal, it is absent in a small minority (Gaymer 1968).

While only one species appears to have been present, this would be expected to have shown some geographical variation, since it extended over at least 1200 km of ocean, a far bigger range than any other insular tortoise. But the lack of specimens with good locality data, apart from Aldabra animals, makes it difficult to check this adequately and impossible to describe the pattern of regional variation formally in terms of subspecies. All that can be done is to compare known Aldabran material with the sample lacking reliable data, on the assumption that, although the latter certainly contains some tortoises from Aldabra, other populations will be represented. This seems likely, for some of the individuals included appear to have histories extending back to a time when the Seychelles still had tortoises and Aldabra was not often visited. When such a comparison is made, a clear difference in incidence of the nuchal scute is found. Of 236 Aldabran animals, the nuchal is absent in only three (most data from Gaymer 1968) but in the sample with poor data it is absent in 8 out of 77 (statistically significant: $p < 0.01$, χ^2 test). Shell shape is difficult to quantify but Aldabran adults more frequently have the anterior marginal scutes of the shell clearly reflexed upwards and the hind margin flared than those with poor data. It could be argued that the different pattern of variation in the sample with doubtful localities results from bias in its selection, managers of taxonomic collections tending to place a higher premium on specimens showing minority conditions. This factor undoubtedly exists but is probably insufficient to explain wholly the differences between the two samples. It might be minimized if Aldabra tortoises could be compared with the long established herds of *G. gigantea* on Mauritius which have probably not been subjected to such selection.

Although the sample with poor data suggests that non-Aldabran tortoises may in general have had less reflexion of the anterior edge of the shell, there was almost certainly considerable inter-populational variation in this and other features. In the British Museum, there are two recent fossil bony carapaces and some fragments (B.M.(P) R.4682, R.9373) which were received from the Cambridge Museum in 1919 and are attributable to *G. gigantea*. Unfortunately they lack firm data but correspondence related to their transfer suggests they may well have been collected by the Percy Sladen Trust Expedition to the Indian Ocean on one of the Seychelles or neighbouring islands (Gadow 1918, letter, British Museum, Palaeontology Department archives). In this material both the anterior and latero-posterior margins of the carapace are strongly reflexed and there is a distinct tendency for the fronts of the carapaces to be raised. So the latter modification has arisen independently in all three recent groups of insular giant tortoises (see §6b).

(b) Madagascar

Remains of giant tortoises are especially common in marshy areas in the west and southwest of Madagascar (Mahé 1972) but also occur in caves (Boulenger 1894). Much material is fragmentary and not many substantially whole shells are available for examination. The nine located and investigated in this study fall into two groups. Seven†, to which the name *Geochelone grandidieri* (Vaillant 1885) is applicable, are distinctly flattened and the carapace is very robust, sometimes being over 40 mm thick at the margins and from 18 to 30 mm in the thinner areas of the posterior dorsolateral region. It is usually very rugose and lumpy although smoother towards the periphery and the sutures marking the contiguous borders of the horny pleural and marginal suites are sinuous. The anterior and posterior margins of the carapace are often flared and a nuchal scute is usually present. A skull associated with B.M.(P) R. 1972 is clearly of the *Aldabrachelys* type but differs from that of *G. gigantea* in its flatter frontal region and more robust post-orbital bar; Mahé (1965 a) describes a similar skull from Beloha, SW Madagascar. Boulenger (1894) provides good illustrations of this form, which attained a carapace length of at least 122 cm. Auffenberg (1966) suggests that the manus of *G. grandidieri* may differ from those of other *Geochelone* in having many elements fused, but I have not been able to confirm this.

The other two shells examined‡ include the type of *Geochelone abrupta* (Vaillant 1885) and differ from the *G. grandidieri* material in having a less flattened carapace with less bulging flanks which is also relatively thin, being 20–25 mm at the edges and 8–10 mm in the less robust parts of the posterior dorsolateral area. Also, the sutures between the costals and marginals tend to be straighter. In both specimens, the posterior margin of the carapace is slightly flared and in B.M.(P) R 5890 this is also true of the front edge, which lacks a nuchal scute, but this region is missing in the Paris individual. No skull has yet been firmly associated with *abrupta*-type shells (Mahé, personal communication) which attained a carapace length of at least 115 cm.

It is likely, in view of the degree of difference between their shells, that *G. grandidieri* and *G. abrupta* are not conspecific, although they appear to be closely related, but more material is needed to confirm this. On present evidence, *G. grandidieri* seems to be a good species but, so far as can be checked, *G. abrupta* is very similar to *G. gigantea* and may be referrable to the synonymy of this form. The two kinds of giant tortoise in Madagascar both seem to have occurred quite widely, at least in the west of the country and may well have been synchronous. The radiocarbon dates cited by Mahé & Sourdat (1973) as being based on tortoise bones were determined with shell fragments of *G. grandidieri* (Mahé 1977, personal communication). These are: Bemafandry, 2060 ± 150 B.P.; Behavoha, 2160 ± 110 B.P. and Taolambiby, 2290 ± 90 B.P. Ages of specifically identified fragments of *G. abrupta* are not available but Mahé & Sourdat do give dates for two sites from which remains of this form have been extracted: Amparihingidro, 2850 ± 200 B.P. and Ampoza, 1910 ± 120 B.P. These figures suggest that the two types of Madagascan tortoise overlapped in time, a conclusion supported by the fact that at Ampasambasimba shell fragments apparently attributable to both forms occur in the same deposit (Mahé 1977, personal communication). Although there is no indication of differences in browsing ranges or of food specialization in the known anatomy of the two tortoise types, dietary differences may have existed, as might differences in habitat.

† M.H.N.P.(P) unreg.; Etséré (= Etsara), SW Madagascar; ♂ (holotype of *G. grandidieri*). M.H.N.P.(P) unreg., carapace only; Etséré; (paratype of *G. grandidieri*). B.M.(Z) 94.6.5.1; Ambatumifuku, 110 km (70 miles) north of Nossi Bé; ♂. B.M.(Z) 1978. 773, carapace only; near Nossi Bé. B.M.(P) R.1972; SW Madagascar; ♀. B.M.(P) R.1975; SW Madagascar; ♂. C.A.S. 39606; near Nossi Bé.

‡ M.H.N.P.(P) 1884-30; Amboulitsate (= Ambolisatra), SW Madagascar; ♂ (type of *Geochelone abrupta*). B.M.(P) R.5890; Ampoza, SW Madagascar; ♂.

Remains assigned to *G. abrupta* occur near the northwest seaboard of Madagascar at Ampari-hingidro (Mahé 1965*b*) and, although known *abrupta* do not have the anterior margin of the shell so clearly reflexed upwards or the hind margin so flared as in typical Aldabran animals, such populations may perhaps have been the source of the tortoises of the atoll for the prevailing currents run towards it from this coast. Most of the extinct Pleistocene lizards of Aldabra have very close relatives in Madagascar and seem likely to have arrived from there by transmarine migration (Arnold 1976), so it is not improbable that the tortoises did likewise. Possibly the Seychelles also received their tortoises from this source.

(c) Synonymy of Geochelone gigantea (Schweigger)

Testudo gigantea Schweigger, 1812: 327. Type locality: 'Brasilien'.

Testudo indica (part): Gray, 1831: 9.

Testudo elephantina Duméril & Bibron, 1835: 110. Type locality: Islands in Mozambique Channel (Anjouan, Aldabra, Comores) where frequently taken to Bourbon (Réunion) and Maurice (Mauritius). Types from Bourbon, Anjouan and Île de France (Mauritius). Types: M.H.N.P.

Testudo daudinii Duméril & Bibron, 1835: 123. Type locality: 'Indes orientales'. Type M.H.N.P.

? *Testudo abrupta* Milne-Edwards, 1868: 1161 (*nomen nudum*).

Megalochelys indica: Gray, 1873: 724.

Testudo ponderosa Günther, 1877: 35. Type locality: unknown. Type: B.M.(Z) 64.12.20.27 (skeleton and shell with scutes).

Testudo hololissa Günther, 1877: 39. Type locality: Aldabra. Type: B.M.(Z) 88.3.20.1. (stuffed).

? *Testudo abrupta* Vaillant, 1885: 874. Type locality: Amboulitsate (= Ambolisatra, SW Madagascar). Types: M.H.N.P.(P) 1884–30 (a partial shell, shell fragments, pectoral girdles and vertebrae).

Testudo sumeirei Sauzier, 1892: 395. Type locality: 'Mauritius'. Type: B.M.(Z) 1929.12.27.1/ 1947.3.4.1.(stuffed).

Testudo gouffei Rothschild, 1906: 753. Type locality: Thérèse Island, Seychelles. Type: B.M.(Z) 1949.1.4.66.(skeleton and shell; scutes and skin mounted separately).

6. ISLAND ADAPTATIONS

(a) Adaptive pressures in small island environments

Three quite discrete groups of tortoises have reached isolated oceanic islands and survived there until historic times and it is of some interest to consider to what extent their distinctive common characters are results of adaptation to these environments. *A priori*, substantial modification of colonizing species would be expected since ecological conditions on small distant islands are very different from those of the continental or large-island areas where they presumably originated. Among the more obvious features of small islands inhabited by giant tortoises that seem relevant in this context are the following: (i) absence of large predators; (ii) absence of large competing herbivores; (iii) relative simplicity of community structure, (iv) climatic variability: all the tortoise islands show marked seasonal fluctuation in rainfall, and both the Indian Ocean (Stoddart & Walsh 1979, this volume) and the Galápagos area

(Palmer & Pile 1966) are prone to longer term changes. A probable result of these factors would be a tendency for tortoise biomass to vary, possibly cyclically. Lack of predators and competitors might allow rapid increase of a colonizer to levels where vegetation resources were damaged, after which decline in density could result in recovery of the vegetation and possible repetition of the sequence. The relative simplicity of the ecosystem might reduce any possible buffering of this cycle and long-term weather changes would also be likely to change carrying capacity. No clear evidence of natural change in biomass is available for the Galápagos or the Mascarenes but Aldabra has shown a huge population increase in the last 70 years that appears to be having an adverse effect on the vegetation (see, for example Hnatiuk, Woodell & Bourn 1976).

The features of small-island environments outlined above might be expected to produce the following changes in continentally derived tortoises. (i) Loss or modification of antipredator devices. (ii) Increase in width of food niche exploited: continental tortoises are grazers and low browsers, being partly restricted to this spatial range by competition from mammalian herbivores and, in the absence of these, modifications to utilize a broader spectrum of food resources are likely. (iii) Increase in intensity of direct intraspecific competition especially for food as a result of at least intermittently severe conditions and high densities. (iv) An increased tendency to store resources in response to fluctuation in food supply.

Many aspects of the morphology of giant tortoises can be interpreted in terms of these factors, particularly reduction in antipredator devices which is important in allowing development of features related to the others.

(b) Reduction of anti-predator mechanisms and its advantages

In order to discuss the modifications to anti-predator devices that have taken place in island tortoises, it is first necessary to describe the protective strategy typical of continental species. These are potential prey for a wide range of medium sized and large carnivores and for some omnivores, as is apparent in the Galápagos where anti-predator mechanisms are poorly developed and introduced dogs and pigs kill many tortoises up to curved carapace lengths of at least 55 and 40 cm respectively (MacFarland, Villa & Toro 1974). Young tortoises are of course preyed on by a much wider variety of animals. Having little agility or speed and not being aggressive, tortoises are almost entirely dependent on their shell for protection and many of the distinctive features of this group, when compared with the primitive emydine terrapins (Emydidae) that are almost certainly ancestral to them, seem to be adaptations to increase its efficiency. While not always impenetrable, the shell makes feeding on mature tortoises expensive in terms of effort and, although continental species are attacked by a variety of animals, this is probably only when more easily processed prey is unavailable; no specialist tortoise predator seems to exist. Among the more obvious features increasing shell protection is the pronounced doming of the carapace. This reduces the range of predators that can take a tortoise of given volume in their jaws, and also ensures that others will have to open them very widely, a position where their crushing efficiency is relatively low. As well as this, doming produces a very strong configuration for resisting external pressures. Its development in land tortoises was presumably permitted by the lack of hydrodynamic constraints that act on aquatic chelonians and it is also important in providing additional space within the shell for housing the longer gut characteristic of these vegetarian animals. Shell strength is further enhanced by stout buttresses running from the carapace to the plastron on each side of the anterior and posterior openings which increase the rigidity of the bridge regions. The bones of the shell are thick and there is very extensive interdigitation at their sutures. The costal bones forming the dorsolateral areas are wedge-shaped, the members of the series becoming alternately broader and narrower ventrally (fig. 3 in Auffenberg 1974), an arrangement that reduces possible distortion.

Anterior and posterior openings are small so that easy access is prevented, the carapace arching downwards from above and the plastron being very large, often flexed upwards in front and terminating posteriorly in two points, each of which extends between the opening for the tail and that for one of the hind legs. Bridge regions tend to be long and a secondary effect of this is that the humerus is bowed anteriorly so that its distal section can project more easily outwards in front of the bridge. In times of danger, the shell openings are blocked by the limbs which fit them very closely and have heavily armoured exposed surfaces.

The shell pattern outlined above occurs in the vast majority of present continental tortoises, the only exception being the soft shelled *Malacochersus* which takes refuge in rock crevices, but all the insular species deviate from it to varying extents. This is most marked in the Mascarene forms. In these, the domed profile of the carapace may be extensively modified and the buttresses become very slender. The bones of the shell are often very thin (in Rodrigues tortoises, bony shells 50–60 cm in length may be only 1 mm thick in places). In such shells the efficacy of interdigitation in producing strong and rigid joints between the constituent bones is greatly reduced and it may be that the ankylosis frequent in Mascarene tortoises is a substitute means of strengthening the shell, which has important skeletal functions apart from protective ones. If this is so, it is at first sight curious that more tortoises elsewhere do not show ankylosis since some added strength against crushing might be obtained with little increase in mass. Such fusion does of course prevent further growth but many tortoises do not increase much in size over a substantial period of their adult lives, so this is not necessarily a drawback. However, lack of sutures may well have disadvantages, at least in some circumstances. An ankylosed tortoise shell is rather like a bird's egg. Here, external pressures are transmitted widely through the shell when intact keeping unit stress low, but if pierced (for instance by the teeth of a predator), stresses concentrate at the edges of the resultant small holes, leading to swift and extensive spread of cracks (Gans 1951). Such far-reaching fractures are sometimes visible in Mascarene shells although usually appearing to be *post mortem* in origin. In a typical continental tortoise, the deeply interdigitating nature of the sutures produces enough rigidity for the shell to transmit external pressures widely but the structural discontinuity between the constituent bones of the shell means that cracks are unlikely to spread beyond the one in which they were initiated. Only in extreme circumstances, such as where shells are very thin, and small puncture wounds rare, would the advantages of ankylosis in giving added general strength outweigh the risks of extensive failure if penetrated.

The free edges of the carapace are somewhat thickened in Mascarene tortoises (probably because these areas would be liable to damage by bumping against hard objects) but this is not so marked as in continental animals and the plastron has extremely thin margins. Posterior and especially anterior openings of the shell are very large (figure 6). The front of the carapace does not extend so far ventrally and its dorsal profile may be horizontal or even inclined upwards, and the plastron is reduced (figure 7) with small anterior and posterior lobes. Bridges tend to be rather short and the humerus consequently straighter. The shell openings are too large to have been blocked completely by the limbs, which, at least in *G. vosmaeri*, had very little armour.

Many of the features typical of Mascarene shells contribute to making them lighter. Estimates suggest that Rodrigues shells of about 40 cm length would only have been about one-third the mass of that of an equivalent-sized African *Geochelone pardalis*. Such lightening may be beneficial in a number of ways. It would reduce the cost of building, maintaining and carrying the shell and allow its development in conditions where calcium was in short supply, which may be true of some of the volcanic areas of the Mascarenes. Reduction in mass should also increase

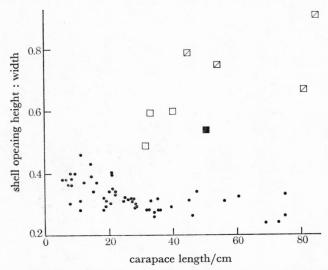

FIGURE 6. Proportions of anterior shell opening. □, Rodrigues shells, *G. peltastes*; ▨, Rodrigues shells, *G. vosmaeri*; ■, Mauritian shell, possibly of *G. inepta*; •, 12 species of continental and Madagascan *Geochelone*, namely *G. carbonaria*, *G. chilensis*, *G. denticulata*, *G. elegans*, *G. elongata*, *G. emys*, *G. forsteni*, *G. impressa*, *G. pardalis*, *G. platynota*, *G. radiata* and *G. sulcata*.

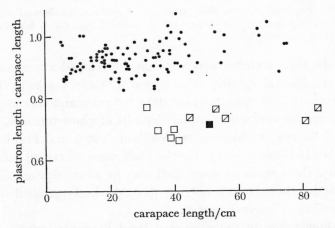

FIGURE 7. Relative length of plastron. □, Rodrigues shells, *G. peltastes*; ▨, Rodrigues shells, *G. vosmaeri*; ■, Mauritian shell, possibly of *G. inepta*; •, 12 species of continental and Madagascan *Geochelone* (see figure 6 for details).

agility, an advantage in exploiting a wider spatial range of food resources than continental tortoises, and in conditions of strong intraspecific competition. Enlargement of the front orifice of the shell also has clear benefits in increasing upper limit of browsing (§4a). The large shell openings and reduction of the plastron are important in permitting more extensive limb movements, again contributing to agility. Observations on living *G. elephantopus* and *G. gigantea* suggest that movement of the humerus in particular is considerably freer than in continental species and this, coupled with the relatively longer legs typical of the island forms, enables them to adopt a gait better adapted for coping with difficult terrain. In walking, the lower limbs appear to be held more vertically than in other tortoises, so that the shell is kept well clear of the ground and, although the humerus follows the edge of the plastron during the power stroke, it may be raised when returning forwards, so that the foot is more able to clear any irregularities in the substrate.

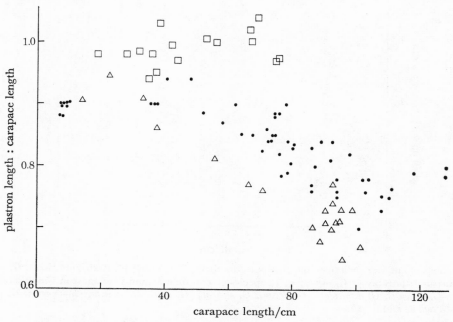

FIGURE 8. Change in relative length of plastron with growth. □, ·G. *sulcata*, continental Africa; •, *G. gigantea*, islands to the north of Madagascar; △, *G. elephantopus microphys*, Tagus Cove, Isabela island, Galápagos (data partly from Van Denburgh 1914).

As suggested previously, these tortoises may well have developed a tendency to store more resources than many continental species, in response to their markedly fluctuating food supply. This is difficult to confirm since relevant data for mainland species are lacking, but many authors comment on the very extensive fat deposits of giant tortoises, particularly the females, where it is used for egg production (see Vaillant (1893) and Froidevaux (1899) for the Mascarenes; and Van Denburgh (1914) for the Galápagos where an industry was based on collecting tortoise oil). Here again an open shell may be advantageous, for stored fat can easily be accommodated by the tortoise's bulging through the large shell orifices, avoiding displacement or compression of internal organs.

Galápagos tortoises show many of the presumed insular adaptations seen in Mascarene species but some are considerably less marked. Development is greatest in dry-island populations but even these are not so extreme in their general shell thinness, tendency to ankylosis, reduction of plastral lobes and thinness of plastral margins. Tortoises from moister, better vegetated habitats deviate even more but still show differences from continental tortoises in their often thinner shells and reduced plastra, bigger shell openings and relatively long necks and legs. Most Indian Ocean island *G. gigantea* are rather similar to these. They show comparatively little difference from their possible ancestral populations in Madagascar but this is not really unexpected, as here too predator pressure was probably not nearly as great as on the continental mainland.

At least some Galápagos and Indian Ocean populations show a tendency not discernible in available Mascarene material. This is for the plastron to decrease in relative size with growth (figure 8), which may be connected with the natural patterns of predation on these islands. In the Galápagos (MacFarland *et al.* 1974) and on Aldabra (Bourn & Coe 1979, this volume) large tortoises are immune to endemic predators but juveniles are not. In these circumstances, reduction of the plastron with growth means that young animals are well protected but adults gain the advantages of a less restricting shell. In all of the island tortoise species, there is an analogous trend in size of the anterior shell opening which increases with age. This is most obvious in saddleback populations but also occurs in the others.

Pigmentation may also have been modified in response to lack of predators. Nearly all continental species of tortoise appear to be cryptically coloured, and in many cases have disruptive markings, especially when young, but most island giants are almost entirely uniformly blackish which makes them conspicuous in some environments. Occasional *G. gigantea* (such as the type of *Testudo gouffei*) are paler and some of the few Mascarene shells with scutes are brownish but in the latter instance this is probably due to change *post mortem* in very old material. Sombre colouring may be important for thermal reasons since a dark surface will absorb a greater amount of solar radiation than a lighter one. This could be advantageous in cool conditions in allowing tortoises to approximate more closely to their optimum body temperature. But any such benefit would have to outweigh the increased risk of overheating at high temperatures, a common cause of death on Aldabra in areas where shade is unavailable (Bourn 1976).

If, as suggested here, development of many features typical of island tortoises was possible only in the absence of large predators and competing herbivores, it would be expected that exposure to these would be more harmful to the most strongly modified tortoise populations. A variety of mammals have been introduced to many islands but interpretation of any decline in tortoises is not easy as human exploitation has often apparently overshadowed the effects of other predators. However, it may be significant that the highly modified tortoises of the Mascarenes have disappeared completely with no survival in captivity even though the introduced *G. gigantea*, which shows less reduction in anti-predator mechanisms, has been kept on Mauritius for many years and breeds successfully there. Similarly in the Galápagos, figures quoted by MacFarland *et al.* (1974) suggest that on the whole the saddle-backed races have suffered more than those approaching closer to the continental type.

(c) *Large size*

Nearly all recent populations of oceanic island tortoise are characterized by large size. Usual maximum carapace lengths in historic times of the various populations range from about 75 to 130 cm, so that the largest are about 1.75 times the length of the smallest. This compares with a range of about 10–130 cm in all modern tortoises (largest 13 times length of smallest) and, if fossil forms such as *Geochelone atlas* are included, the maximum is extended to more than 180 cm (largest over 18 times length of smallest). So there may well be factors acting to restrict size in the island forms to a fairly limited range. Relatively large dimensions may be beneficial in increasing the vertical limit of browsing possible and big animals may be likely to survive longer in adverse conditions, an undoubted advantage on small islands. The only exception to large size in these insular tortoises is *G. peltastes* of Rodrigues which is only known to have reached a carapace length of 42 cm. However, this may be because the much bigger *G. vosmaeri* had pre-empted the niche-space where large size was an advantage.

Although the island tortoises are nearly all large compared with present continental species, it is not certain that any of them evolved great size in direct response to small-island conditions. In the past, very big tortoises were found in continental areas and on large islands and these forms may have been the source of some of the recent oceanic populations, as already suggested for Aldabra. This seems quite probable, for large tortoises are more likely to survive long spells of drifting than small ones since their dimensions and apparently greater buoyancy would enable them to keep their heads clear of the water and decrease the risk of drowning. Their survival time without food or fresh water would also probably be much greater. In the case of the Aldabran tortoises, the only instance where it is possible to make a relatively precise suggestion of the origin of an island population, there is no evidence of size increase. The supposed parent form in Madagascar, *G. 'abrupta'*, reached a carapace length of at least 115 cm (though admittedly the few remains are of a later date than that likely for the last colonization of the atoll by tortoises), whereas Grubb's (1971) biggest Aldabran specimen was 105 or 106 cm and the large fossil humerus mentioned by this author probably came from an animal with a carapace length of around 110–115 cm.

I should like to thank the following for letting me examine material in their care: Dr R. Roux-Estève and Dr F. de Broin (Paris), Mr C. A. Walker and Mr G. S. Cowles (British Museum), D. Ball (Zoological Society of London), Mr J. Hull (Oxford), Dr K. Joysey and Mr R. D. Norman (Cambridge). These, together with Dr W. Auffenberg, Professor A. d'A. Bellairs, Mr A. S. Cheke, Miss C. Fisher, Dr T. H. Fritts, Mr H. Gruchet, Dr M. S. Hoogmoed, Dr A. E. Leviton, Dr J. Mahé, Miss E. McCartney, Mr C. Michel, Dr H. Wermuth and Professor E. E. Williams, provided much information and useful comment.

References (Arnold)

Arnold, E. N. 1976 Fossil reptiles from Aldabra atoll, Indian Ocean. *Bull. Br. Mus. nat. Hist.* (Zool.) **29**, 85–116

Arnold, E. N. 1981 The extinct tortoises of the Mascarene islands. (In the press.)

Auffenberg, W. 1966 The carpus of land tortoises (Testudininae). *Bull. Fla St. Mus. biol. Sci.* **10**, 159–191.

Auffenberg, W. 1974 Check list of fossil land tortoises (Testudinidae). *Bull. Fla St. Mus. biol. Sci.* **18**, 121–251.

Boulenger, G. A. 1889 *Catalogue of the chelonians, rhynchocephalians and crocodiles in the British Museum (Natural History)*, 2nd edn. London: Trustees of the British Museum (Natural History).

Boulenger, G. A. 1891 On the skull of an extinct land-tortoise from Mauritius indicating a new species (*Testudo microtympanum*). *Proc. zool. Soc. Lond.* **1891**, 4–5.

Boulenger, G. A. 1894 On the remains of an extinct gigantic tortoise from Madagascar (*Testudo grandidieri*, Vaillant). *Trans. zool. Soc. Lond.* **13**, 305–311.

Bourn, D. M. 1976 The giant tortoise population on Aldabra (Cryptodira: Testudinidae), part 1: Preliminary results. *Zool. afr.* **11**, 275–284.

Bourn, D. & Coe, M. J. 1979 Features of tortoise mortality and decomposition on Aldabra. *Phil. Trans. R. Soc. Lond.* B **286**, 189–193 (this volume).

Braithwaite, C. J. R., Taylor, J. D. & Kennedy, W. J. 1973 The evolution of an atoll: the depositional and erosional history of Aldabra. *Phil. Trans. R. Soc. Lond.* B **266**, 307–340.

Duméril, A. M. C. & Bibron, G. 1835 *Erpétologie générale ou histoire naturelle complète des reptiles*, vol. 2. Paris: Librairie Roret.

Froidevaux, H. 1899 Textes historiques inédits ou peu connus relatifs aux tortues de terre de l'Île Bourbon. *Bull Mus. Hist. nat. Paris* **5**, 214–218.

Gadow, H. 1894 On the remains of some gigantic land-tortoises, and of an extinct lizard, recently discovered in Mauritius. *Trans. zool. Soc. Lond.* **13**, 313–324.

Gans, C. 1951 The functional morphology of the egg-eating adaptations in the snake genus *Dasypeltis*. *Zoologica, N.Y.* **37**, 209–244.

Gaymer, R. 1968 The Indian Ocean giant tortoise *Testudo gigantea* on Aldabra. *J. Zool. Lond.* **154**, 341–363.

Gray, J. E. 1831 *Synopsis reptilium....* Part 1. *Cataphracta*. London: Treuttel, Wurtz.

Gray, J. E. 1873 On the skulls and alveolar surfaces of land-tortoises (*Testudinata*). *Proc. zool. Soc. Lond.* **1873**, 722–728.

Grubb, P. 1971 The growth, ecology and population structure of giant tortoises on Aldabra. *Phil. Trans. R. Soc. Lond.* B **260**, 327–372.

Günther, A. C. L. G. 1877 *The gigantic land-tortoises (living and extinct) in the collection of the British Museum*. London: Trustees of the British Museum.

Günther, A. C. L. G. 1898 *Address delivered at the anniversary meeting of the Linnean Society of London on 24th of May, 1898*. London: Linnean Society.

Hennig, W. 1966 *Phylogenetic systematics*. Urbana: University of Illinois.

Hnatiuk, R. J., Woodell, S. R. J. & Bourn, D. M. 1976 Giant tortoise and vegetation interactions on Aldabra atoll. Part 2. Coastal. *Biol. Conserv.* **9**, 305–316.

Loveridge, A. & Williams, E. E. 1957 Revision of the African tortoises and turtles of the suborder Cryptodira. *Bull. Mus. comp. Zool. Harv.* **115**, 161–557.

Lydekker, R. 1885 Siwalik and Narbada Chelonia. *Mem. geol. Surv. India Palaeont. indica* (10) **3**, 155–208.

MacFarland, C. G., Villa, J. & Toro, B. 1974 The Galápagos giant tortoises (*Geochelone elephantopus*). Part 1. Status of the surviving populations. *Biol. Conserv.* **6**, 118–133.

Mahé, J. 1965a Le crâne de *Testudo grandidieri* Vaillant 1885. *Bull. Soc. géol. Fr.* (7) **7**, 124–128.

Mahé, J. 1965b Une gisement nouveau de subfossile à Madagascar. *C.r. somm. Séanc. Soc. géol. Fr.* **1965**, 66.

Mahé, J. 1972 The Malagasy subfossils. In *Biogeography and ecology in Madagascar* (eds R. Battistini & G. Richard-Vindard), pp. 339–365. The Hague: W. Junk.

Mahé, J. & Sourdat, M. 1973 Sur l'extinction des vertébrés subfossiles et l'aridification du climat dans le Sud-Ouest de Madagascar. *Bull Soc. géol. Fr.* (7) **14**, 295–309.

Milne Edwards, M. 1868 Sur les découvertes zoologiques faites récemment à Madagascar par M. Alfred Grandidier. *C.r. hebd. Séanc. Acad. Sci., Paris* **67**, 1165–1167.

Montaggioni, L. 1970 Essai de reconstitution palaeographique de l'Île Rodrigue (Archipel des Mascareignes, Océan Indien) *C.r. hebd. Séanc. Acad. Sci., Paris* D **271**, 1741–1744.

Palmer, C. E. & Pyle, R. L. 1966 The climatological setting of the Galápagos. In *The Galápagos* (ed. R. I. Bowman), ch. 12. Berkeley and Los Angeles: University of California.

Petit, M. 1737 Description anatomique des yeux de la grenouille et de la tortue. *Hist. Acad. Sci. Paris* **1737**, 142–169.

Rothschild, W. 1906 A new species of giant tortoise. *Novit. zool.* **13**, 753–754.

Rothschild, W. 1915 On the gigantic land tortoises of the Seychelles and Aldabra–Madagascar group with some notes on certain forms of the Mascarene group. *Novit. zool.* **22**, 418–442.

Sauzier, T. 1892 Tortue de terre gigantesque. *Nature, Paris* **1892**, 395–398.

Sauzier, T. 1893 *Les tortues de terre gigantesques des Mascareignes et des certaines autres iles de la Mer des Indes*. Paris: G. Masson.

Schweigger, A. F. 1812 *Konigsb. Arch. Naturg. Math.* **1**, 327.

Schweizer, H. 1965 Ei-Zeitigung, Aufzucht und Entwicklung einer Strahlenschildkrote (*Testudo radiata* Shaw). *Salamandra* **1**, 67–73.

Snow, D. W. 1964 The giant tortoises of the Galapagos Islands. Their present status and future chances. *Oryx* **7**, 277–290.

Stoddart, D. R. & Peake, J. F. 1979 Historical records of Indian Ocean giant tortoise populations. *Phil. Trans. R. Soc. Lond.* B **286**, 147–161 (this volume).

Stoddart, D. R. & Walsh, R. P. D. 1979 Long-term climatic change in the western Indian Ocean. *Phil. Trans. R. Soc. Lond.* B **286**, 11–23 (this volume).

Townsend, C. H. 1936 Two giant tortoises were swept twenty miles by hurricane. *Bull. N.Y. zool. Soc.* **39**, 119–120.

Vaillant, L. 1885 Remarques complémentaires sur les tortues gigantesques de Madagascar. *C.r. hebd. Seanc. Acad. Sci., Paris* **100**, 874–877.

Vaillant, L. 1893 Les tortues éteintes de l'île Rodrigues d'après les pièces conservées dans les galeries du Muséum. In *Centenaire de la fondation du Muséum d'Histoire Naturelle, volume commémoratif*, pp. 253–288. Paris: Muséum d'Histoire naturelle.

Vaillant, L. 1898 Dessins inédits de cheloniens tirés des manuscrits de Commerson. *Bull. Mus. Hist. nat. Paris* **4**, 133–139.

Vaillant, L. 1899 Nouveaux documents historiques sur les tortues terrestres des Mascareignes et des Seychelles. *Bull. Mus. Hist. nat. Paris* **5**, 19–23.

Vaillant, L. 1900 La tortue de Perrault (*Testudo indica*, Schneider). *Nouv. Archs Mus. Hist. nat. Paris* (4) **2**, 25–48.

Vaillant, L. 1903 Les tortues de terre gigantesques. *Revue scient. Paris* (4) **19**, 705–715.

Van Denburgh, J. 1914 The gigantic land tortoises of the Galápagos archipelago. *Proc. Calif. Acad. Sci.* **2**, 203–374.

White, A. & Epler, B. 1972 *Galapagos guide*.

Phil. Trans. R. Soc. Lond. B. **286**, 147–161 (1979)   [147]
Printed in Great Britain

Historical records of Indian Ocean giant tortoise populations

By D. R. Stoddart† and J. F. Peake‡

† *Department of Geography, University of Cambridge, Downing Place, Cambridge, U.K.*
‡ *Department of Zoology, British Museum (Natural History), Cromwell Road, London SW*7 5*BD, U.K.*

with appendixes by
C. Gordon and R. Burleigh

Historical records from the seventeenth to the nineteenth centuries indicate that giant tortoises became extinct on many western Indian Ocean islands during this period, and that by 1900 the surviving population on Aldabra was very small. These data are reviewed, the causes of decline and extinction discussed, and the implications for the history of the Aldabra population are considered.

Introduction

The main sources of historical information on the giant tortoises of the western Indian Ocean are the papers by Günther (1877, 1898), Sauzier (1895) and Rothschild (1915). Rothschild gives the most comprehensive geographical summary, including records from the following localities: Madagascar, Aldabra, Farquhar, Astove, Providence, Iles Africaines, Alphonse, 'Amirante', Agalega, Cosmoledo, Iles Glorieuses, Assumption, 'Chagos', the Comores, Mauritius, Réunion and Rodrigues, and in the Seychelles, Mahé, St Anne, Moyenne, Ile aux Cerfs, Conception, Silhouette, Ile du Nord, Ile aux Récifs, Ile aux Frégates, Praslin, Aride, Félicité, Marianne, La Digue, Les Soeurs, and Ile aux Vaches marines. These distributions were summarized by Stoddart (1971, pp. 619–622). During the last 10 years the literature search for tortoise references has been extended, especially by the Aldabra Data Unit at the British Museum (Natural History), and it has also been possible to examine archives in Seychelles, Mauritius, Bombay, London and Paris.

In summarizing present knowledge, four sources of confusion need to be kept in mind. First, some early travellers' accounts may be fictional in part or in whole. Leguat's *New voyage to the East Indies* (1708), which gives the most detailed early account of tortoises on Réunion, has been argued by Atkinson (1921, 1922) to be wholly imaginary, though Dehérain (1926), using archival evidence, considers that the voyage probably took place, and zoologists have generally accepted that the descriptions of tortoises and birds are based on observation. Secondly, many early accounts are at least partly based on plagiarism, both in circumstantial biological detail and in illustrations. Examples relating to marine mammals in the western Indian Ocean are given by Stoddart (1972). Thirdly, there is long-standing confusion between land tortoises and marine turtles, which in many cases is now impossible to resolve; it is certainly true that some of the islands listed as tortoise localities by Rothschild have no other supporting records but are well known as breeding areas for green turtle (e.g. Agalega, Coetivy, Diego Garcia). Fourthly, there is much confusion in seventeenth and eighteenth century accounts over the identity and even existence of islands, especially the smaller coral islands: thus Farquhar is often called Juan de Nova even though there is another island with the latter name in the Mozambique Channel.

In this paper we review present knowledge of giant tortoise distribution and history in these islands, revising some of Rothschild's judgements, and making particular use of 'Papers on tortoises of Mauritius, Seychelles and Aldabra, and of the Galapagos' collected by Albert Günther and now in the British Museum (Natural History) (Günther Collection, 72).

THE MASCARENE ISLANDS

Mauritius

Mauritius was discovered in 1511 but was not settled for many decades. The first Dutch expedition in 1598 was followed by the establishment of a Dutch settlement in 1638 which lasted until 1710; the French colonized the island in 1715, and thereafter occupation was continuous. In 1630 Herbert (1634, pp. 213–214) described 'land Tortyses, (so great that they will creepe with two mens burthen, and serve more for sport, then service or solemne Banquet) ... The Ile has no humane inhabitants. These creatures that possesse it, have it on condition, to pay tribute (without exception) to such ships, as famine, or foule weather force to anchor there.' Herbert himself (1638, p. 349) thought tortoises 'odious food' and 'better meat for Hogs' than man. Other early reports of large tortoises in great numbers are those of Morisot (1651, p. 8), Flacourt (1658, p. 169) and Mandelslo (1669, pp. 199–200). As early as 1671, however, they had become rare on the main island, though still numerous on nearby islets such as Ile aux Cerfs (Pitot 1905, p. 126). Hubert Hugo in 1673 described the taking of tortoises for salted meat, the making of fat (400–500 animals yielding about 100 l), and the destruction of eggs and young tortoises by pigs, as a result of which the animals had almost disappeared (Pitot 1905, p. 163). In May 1674 Hugo was still able to take 320 tortoises from Ile Plate (Pitot 1905, p. 164). The date of their final extinction on the main island is not known: Grant (1801, p. 194) reported that they were still abundant in 1741, which seems unlikely, but by 1778 they were rare (Sauzier 1895, p. 17).

Réunion

Réunion was discovered in 1512 but the first account of the tortoises is dated 1650 (Leguat 1708, p. 40). According to Du Quesne,

'The Land Turtles are also some of the Riches of the Island. There are vast Numbers of them: Their Flesh is very delicate; the Fat better than Butter or the best Oil, for all sorts of Sawces. Some of the Sea Turtles weigh above 500 Pound weight. The Land Turtles are not so big; but the great ones carry a Man with more ease than a Man can carry them. This Oil of Turtle, for 'tis a sort of Fat, which do's not congeal as other Fat do's, is an excellent Remedy in several Distempers.'

In 1665 Rennefort found tortoises everywhere, though with the young and eggs much disturbed by pigs (Grant 1801, p. 149), and in 1671 it was reported that one could not go six steps without finding one (Froidevaux 1899, p. 216). One of the fullest accounts of the Réunion tortoises came from Dubois (1897, pp. 79–80):

'All the Island is filled with land-tortoises, which is one of the good gifts of the place. They have the neck long, the head made like the tortoises of Europe, a large tail, and four feet. They are from two or three feet in length and one foot and a half broad, or thereabouts, and more than a foot in thickness. One of the Tortoises carries a man easily on its back, and tis as much as a man can do to carry one of them. The flesh of this Tortoise is like that of ox, and their tripe has the same taste. The liver of these Tortoises is very large; tis one of the most delicate morsels which man can eat; who had any of the same in France would make good cheer on fast days. There's enough to feed four persons in one of these livers. At the side of the flanks of these Tortoises there are *pannes* which they take for melting, from which they make oil which never congeals. This is as good for all things as good butter – tis the butter of this land. These *pannes* yield ordinarily two pots of oil, more or less, if the season allows of finding these tortoises fat. They are not always so. This oil is marvellous for rubbing afflicted limbs.' (Original French version in Vaillant 1899*a*, p. 20.)

By 1688 the tortoise had become the ordinary food of the people on Réunion (P. Bernardin, in Froidevaux 1899, p. 217).

Numbers not surprisingly fell rapidly over the next half-century. An anonymous writer described them as 'entièrement détruites' in 1732 (Froidevaux 1899, p. 217), though two small ones could still be found to be sent to the Académie Royale des Sciences in Paris in 1737 (Vaillant 1899*b*). They were described as rare in 1754 (Vaillant 1899*a*, p. 22). It is not clear when they finally became extinct, though Bory de St Vincent (1804, vol. 1, p. 248) mentions animals up to about 230 kg, perhaps domesticated.

Rodrigues

Rodrigues was the last of the Mascarenes to be discovered (in 1638). Francois Leguat (1708, pp. 64–65) gave the first detailed description of the tortoises in 1691, if indeed his account can be accepted as factual and not imaginary as has been alleged:

'We saw no four-footed Creatures, but Rats, Lizards and Land-Turtles, of which there are different sorts. I have seen one that weigh'd one hundred pound, and had Flesh enough about it, to feed a good number of Men. This flesh is very wholsom, and tastes something like Mutton. The Fat is extremely white, and never Congeals nor rises in your Stomach, eat as much as you will of it. We all unanimously agreed, 'twas better than the best Butter in Europe. To anoint one's self with this Oil, is an excellent Remedy for Surfeits, Colds, Cramps, and several other Distempers. The Liver of this Animal is extraordinarily delicate, 'tis so Delicious that one may say of it, it always carries its own Sauce with it, dress it how you will.

The Bones of the Turtles are Massy, I mean they have no Marrow in them. Every one knows, that these Animals in general are hatch'd of Eggs. The Land-Turtles lay theirs in the Sand, and cover them, that they may be hatch'd: The Scale of it, or rather the Shell, is soft, and the Substance within good to eat. There are such plenty of Land-Turtles in this Isle, that sometimes you see two or three thousand of them in a Flock; so that one may go above a hundred Paces on their Backs; or, to speak more properly on their Carapaces, without setting foot to the Ground. They meet together in the Evening in shady Places, and lie so close, that one wou'd think those Places were pav'd with them. There's one thing very odd among them; they always place Sentinels at some Distance from their Troop, at the four corners of their Camp, to which the Sentinels turn their Backs, and look with the Eyes, as if they were on the Watch. This we have always observ'd of them; and this Mystery seems the more difficult to be comprehended, for that these Creatures are uncapable to defend themselves, or to fly.'

An anonymous author in 1725 found them very abundant, reaching 0.9–1.1 m in length (Milne-Edwards 1875). Herbert & Nichelson (1750, pp. 274–276) refer to a settlement formed to collect tortoises for export to Mauritius. At the time of the Transit of Venus Expedition in 1761, the Abbé Pingré found 12–15 negroes so occupied at the settlement, and the Abbé himself ate nothing else while at Rodrigues: 'soupe de tortue, tortue en fricassée, tortues en daube, tortues en godiveau, oeufs de tortue, foie de tortue, tels étaient presque nos uniques ragouts' (Dupon 1969, pp. 24–27). The trade was extremely wasteful. Milne-Edwards (1875) gives details of six voyages during 1759–61 in which nearly 21000 animals (presumably mostly small) were removed from the island: two of these voyages each carried 5000 animals, but of these only 1350 and 3800 survived the journey.

Within a few years numbers had collapsed. D'Après de Mannevillette in 1775 reported this decrease and ascribed it to the depredations of rats and wild cats as well as to the export trade and local consumption for food (Dupon 1969, pp. 38–40). According to Pierre Poivre, the export reached 4000–5000 animals per year in the period 1750–70, each animal with an average mass of 9 kg (Froberville 1848). By 1795 they had been virtually exterminated; Marragon saw two in a remote area (Dupon 1969, pp. 27–31). By 1800 the Rodrigues tortoises could be considered extinct.

THE GRANITIC SEYCHELLES

The granitic Seychelles were first discovered in 1609, when John Jourdain arrived at North Island, near Silhouette. A boat sent ashore 'brought soe many land tortells as they could well carrie. . .The tortells were good meate, as good as freshe beefe, but after two or three meales our men would not eate them, because they did look soe uglie before they weare boyled; and soe greate that eight of them did almost lade our skiffe' (Foster 1905, p. 47). Jourdain then went on to Mahé, finding 'much fishe and fowle and tortells (but our men would not eate any of them, but the tortells wee could kill with staves at our pleasure)' (Foster 1905, p. 49). On the same voyage, William Revett also noted 'lande turtles of so huge a bignes which men will think incredible; of which our company had small luste to eat of, being such huge defourmed creatures and footed with five claws lyke a beare' (Foster 1905, p. 350).

Thereafter the Seychelles were not revisited until an expedition arrived from Mauritius in 1742, though settlement was not attempted until after 1768. Tortoises rapidly became the chief export of the islands, and remained so until the end of the century. Toussaint (1965) has documented the scale of the trade from Mauritius customs records. He lists 25 ships entering Mauritius from Seychelles and carrying tortoises between 1773 and 1810. With an average ship load of 200–250, and assuming that those landed in Mauritius represented about half those removed from Seychelles, the total export was about 10000, or less than 300 each year. These records undoubtedly substantially underrepresent the scale of the trade. Malavois, who became commandant in 1786, wrote a 'Mémoire sur la tortue de terre', dated 25 March 1787, in which he estimated the total remaining population as 6000–8000. The decline had resulted not only from the export trade to Mauritius and local consumption for food, but also from predation by cats and rats. A tradition had also arisen whereby naval vessels in the harbour had the right to be supplied with tortoises for food, and this had accounted for 3000 in 1784–6; it is also recorded that between 25 August 1782 and 30 June 1784 the then commandant had supplied nine ships with 1103 animals. Malavois saw that some measure of control was needed if the tortoises were not to become extinct. He proposed that they should be concentrated in two reserves, one of 3000 on St Anne and one of 3000–4000 on Ile aux Cerfs (Fauvel 1909, p. 278).

By November 1803 the administrator reported that there were no more tortoises to be had, though the alternative sources then mentioned (Agalega, Coetivy, Diego Garcia) suggest that he could have meant marine turtles rather than land tortoises. As late as 1826 two cargoes of 2400 tortoises were landed in Mauritius from Seychelles, but their precise provenance is not recorded (Sauzier 1895, p. 27). By 1839, tortoises were being imported to Mahé from Aldabra (Harrison 1839, p. 443). Froberville (1848, p. 92) noted that they had become rare, though still a delicacy at Seychellois feasts.

The later history of tortoises in the granitic Seychelles is one of domesticated animals in small numbers. Gordon wrote in 1874 to Joseph Hooker telling of scores of tortoises kept in small enclosures before being killed and eaten when 4 years old (Günther Papers, 72). In 1881 Gordon wrote a hitherto unpublished memorandum (appendix 1) entitled 'Gigantic land tortoises of Seychelles', in which he named 13 families with domestic herds on five islands, seven of them on Mahé; he also included much interesting biological information. The largest of the animals was 1.7 m long and weighed 230 kg. In March 1882 Coppinger (1883, p. 215) saw two large animals at Government House, a male of 181 kg and a female of 227 kg, and commented that 'of late years [tortoises have] been introduced into many of the neighbouring islands'. From 1902 to 1922 a herd was maintained at Government House, and detailed records (now lost) were kept of breeding performance (Davidson 1911; *Seychelles Bulletin*, 2, 3 and 5 June 1976). A colony was also established on Curieuse, numbering 42 in 1895 (Administrator, Seychelles, to Secretary of State, 13 March 1896: Gunther Papers, 72; Gunther 1898, p. 26). Nothing is known of the future of this colony, and almost nothing is known of tortoises on other granitic islands, although according to Froberville (1848, p. 98) the tortoises were more numerous and larger on Silhouette than on Mahé. There is an urgent need to catalogue and record existing domestic tortoises on islands such as Frégate, and to establish their history from their owners.

Western Indian Ocean coral islands

The historical evidence concerning tortoises on the smaller coral islands of the western Indian Ocean is much more fragmentary than that for the Mascarenes or granitic Seychelles. It is briefly summarized for each island or group of islands, other than Aldabra itself, below.

African Banks

Rothschild (1915, p. 423) includes African Banks (Ilots Africaines) in his list of tortoise localities, presumably on the basis of a reference by Froberville (1849, p. 111). The Banks comprise two small sand cays with low scrub which could not support a tortoise population (Stoddart & Poore 1970b, p. 188). C. Shackleton's *Plan of the African Islands* (Dalrymple 1805) mentions 'turtle in abundance'. African Banks should be deleted from the list of Indian Ocean tortoise localities.

Agalega

This is also listed by Rothschild (1915, p. 423). D'Unienville (1838, vol. 3, pp. 193–194) states that the island has no land quadrupeds, though Froberville (1848, p. 83) refers to the existence of a few land tortoises there in 1785. These were probably landed from a passing ship. The two islands of Agalega are large, and if tortoises had naturally existed there they would probably have formed a considerable population. Agalega should also be deleted as a tortoise locality.

Alphonse

Alphonse is listed by Rothschild (1915, p. 423), presumably on the basis of Foberville's (1848, p. 111) reference to very abundant land tortoise. D'Unienville (1838, vol. 3, p. 212), however, specifically states that the island has sea turtles only. We have seen no other reference to tortoises on Alphonse, and it should accordingly be deleted from the list of known localities.

Amirantes

Froberville (1848, p. 111) mentions many land tortoises on islands in the Amirantes, without specific locality, and Rothschild (1915, p. 423) includes the group in his locality list. As with Alphonse, however, D'Unienville (1838, vol. 3, p. 212) refers only to sea turtles. Günther (1898, pp. 15–16) describes fossil tortoise eggs embedded in conglomerate from the Amirantes, but these specimens cannot now be found in the British Museum (Natural History) and their precise provenance is not known. Without further confirmation the presence of tortoises on any of the Amirantes must be considered doubtful.

Assumption

Froberville (1848, p. 114) mentioned 'tortues', without qualification, and Rothschild (1915, p. 423) includes Assumption in his tortoise distribution list. No other historical records have been found, though Fryer (1908; 1911, pp. 421–423) found fossil tortoise bones and Honegger (1966) fossil tortoise eggs (cf. Stoddart et al. 1970, p. 132). Further tortoise bones and a possible egg were collected by S. Blackmore and M. Walker in 1977. The fossil material requires further investigation: there is no evidence of the existence of tortoises at the time of discovery or settlement, and the remains may be Pleistocene rather than Recent in age.

Astove

Tortoises have undoubtedly existed on Astove. Froberville (1848, p. 114) refers to 'quantités de grosses tortues' on the northern plain during the visit of the *Charles* and *Elisabeth* in October 1742, and the island is listed by Rothschild (1915, p. 423). But there were no tortoises there in 1836 (Stirling 1843), and we have found no earlier reference. Fryer (1911, p. 428) gives a second-hand report of large bones, probably of tortoises, found in the limestone, and this would repay further investigation. As on Assumption, the Astove tortoises may have been Pleistocene rather than Recent. In 1968 there were several recently released Aldabran tortoises on the island (Bayne *et al.* 1970).

Bird

This island is not listed by Rothschild (1915) and Froberville (1848, p. 99) mentions only turtles there. We have found no indication of tortoises having existed on it.

Cargados Carajos

These small remote sand cays originally had considerable populations of green turtles on them (Staub & Guého 1968) but there is no evidence that tortoises ever existed there; they are not listed by Rothschild (1915).

Chagos Archipelago

Rothschild (1915, p. 423) lists 'Chagos' without precise identification of islands. D'Unienville (1838, vol. 3, pp. 187–190) mentions 'tortues' on Three Brothers and Peros Banhos, but these references are almost certainly to turtles. A famous large tortoise, said to be 150 years old, lived on Egmont in the last century, but it was a domesticated animal, reputedly from Aldabra and said to have been the largest living land tortoise (Rothschild 1897, p. 407; Günther 1898, p. 25). It seems unlikely that wild tortoises ever existed in the Chagos Archipelago, but the swamps on Peros Banhos and other islands should be searched for their remains.

Coetivy

No tortoises were reported here by Captain Laurent of *Le Foudroyant* in 1781 (Froberville 1848, p. 88) but turtles were reported by D'Unienville (1838) and Froberville (1848, p. 88). There is no evidence of tortoises ever having existed here, and the island is not listed by Rothschild (1915).

Cosmoledo

Cosmoledo is listed as a tortoise island by Rothschild (1915, p. 423) but we have found no historical references to it at all. Moresby (1842) visited Cosmoledo in 1822 but does not mention tortoises, nor did Rivers (Seychelles Archives, MS) in 1878. Fryer (1911, pp. 420–421 and 428), however, found fossil eggs on West Northeast Island. Whether tortoises have existed on Cosmoledo in historic times thus remains uncertain.

Denis

Denis is not listed as a tortoise island by Rothschild (1915). When it was discovered in August 1773 by Denis de Trobriand, however, it was described as 'généralement couverte de tortües de terre et de mer' (Fauvel 1909, p. 47). We have found no further mention of tortoises here, and the date of their extinction is not known. James Hornell collected fossil tortoise eggs on Denis in 1927, presumably from phosphorites. A radiocarbon age of 1308 ± 85 a B.P. has been obtained for this by R. Burleigh (appendix 2): this date is particularly significant since it pre-dates the discovery of the Seychelles by Europeans and hence lessens the possibility of artificial introduction.

Europa

Europa is not listed by Rothschild (1915) and we have found no reference to tortoises existing there.

Farquhar

Rothschild (1915, p. 423) includes Farquhar in his list of tortoise islands, presumably on the basis of a description by J. Grossin in 1742. Grossin described 'quantité de Tortue de terre dont les plus petite sont plus grosse que les plus grosse de l'isle Rodrigues' (Fauvel 1900). He named the island as Juan de Nova, and Fauvel identified it with Farquhar. This identification needs re-examination, since it does not appear to accord with Grossin's course relative to Agalega; Grossin's latitude also does not seem appropriate for Farquhar. It may be significant that the comment quoted above is the same as that given for Aldabra by Dalrymple in his chart of 1784. Margaro charted what is unmistakeably the modern Farquhar in 1776 (Dalrymple 1784), and specifically stated that 'There is no fresh water, nor any quadruped'. D'Unienville (1838, vol. 3, p. 214) noted only sea turtles. There is substantial doubt, therefore, over the presence of wild tortoises on this island. In 1968 there were two semi-domesticated ones, recently imported (Stoddart & Poore 1970a).

Gloriosa

There are no historical records of tortoises on the Iles Glorieuses, nor are they included in Rothchild's (1915) list. Battistini & Cremers (1972, p. 2), however, have found fossil tortoise bones in raised reef limestones on Grande Glorieuse. Whether tortoises have existed there in historic times is not known.

Platte

There are no historic records or other indications of tortoises on Platte. 'Several' domestic ones were placed there from Mahé in 1883 (Gunther 1898, p. 26). The island is not listed by Rothschild (1915).

Providence

The former status of tortoises on this island is highly uncertain. Froberville (1848, pp. 111–112) mentions 'grande quantité de tortues de mer et de terre', but D'Unienville (1838, vol. 3, p. 213) mentions only sea turtle. Sauzier (1895, p. 27) refers to a cargo of 800 'tortoises' from Providence landed at Mauritius in 1826, but it is possible that these were turtle. In 1882 Coppinger (1883, p. 234) found seven animals imported from Aldabra. Providence is listed as a tortoise island by Rothschild (1915, p. 423), but this must be regarded as doubtful in the absence of less ambiguous evidence.

St Pierre

There are no historic references to tortoises on St Pierre, nor is the island in Rothschild's list (1915). Moresby (1842) went there in 1822 but does not mention tortoises. The only indication of their former existence is that Fryer (1911, p. 434) reported seeing a fossil tortoise egg, said to have come from St Pierre, when he was in Seychelles. The possible existence of fossil material needs investigation.

Tromelin

There are no records of tortoises on Tromelin, either historic or fossil, and the island is not listed by Rothschild (1915).

ALDABRA

Accounts of tortoises on Aldabra in historic times are more complete than for any other western Indian Ocean coral island. The first visit from which records are available was that by the *Charles* and *Elisabeth* in 1744: Dalrymple (1784) records 'a great many land-turtle much larger than those at Rodrigue' in an annotation to the 1744 chart. Early in the nineteenth century the island was said to 'abound with land turtle' (Horsburgh 1809, p. 125). In 1822, when Moresby (1842, pp. 676 and 741) went there, tortoises were very abundant; there was an annual export to Mahé and Mauritius, where they were sold for 1–3 Spanish dollars each. Richard Owen, H.M.S. *Leven*, made a new chart in 1824 and inscribed Ile Malabar with the words 'abundance of land tortoise'.

It is likely that serious cropping only began at about this time. Toussaint's catalogue of Mauritius ship movements (1967, pp. 470–475) mentions only four vessels, all of 30–50 tons, arriving at Mauritius from Aldabra in 36 years (one in 1796, two in 1798, one in 1803). But whalers started operating in Seychelles waters after 1823, and by 1839 there was a regular export of Aldabra tortoises to Mahé, where local supplies had become extinct (Harrison 1839, p. 443). Stone enclosures were built on the atoll in the early nineteenth century to serve as pens for captured animals (Sauzier 1895; Voeltzkow 1897, p. 52; Stoddart 1971; McKenzie 1971).

Kersten (1871, p. 119) records that in 1842 two ships from Hamburg with 100 men collected 1200 tortoises, some weighing 360–410 kg, and this gives some indication of the scope of a considerable if episodic trade.

The effects of this cropping on the population are uncertain. There was concern in scientific circles in England about the possible extinction of the Aldabra tortoise, following reports that the atoll was to be leased for wood-cutting, and in April 1874 a Memorial was sent to the Governor of Mauritius, signed by Hooker, Owen, Darwin, Newton, Günther and others, asking for conservation measures (Günther 1877, pp. 20–22). That numbers had probably considerably declined was indicated by Wharton's experience in H.M.S. *Fawn* in 1878, when a party of sailors took 3 days to find one animal (Wharton 1883, p. 77). Rivers, who visited the atoll in December 1878, thought there were plenty of tortoises but saw none. He reported that they were concentrated at Cinq Cases, and only appeared during the rains. He did see large footprints, nine inches in diameter (Chief Civil Commissioner to Governor, 21 January 1879, Günther Papers, 72; in a similar report in the Seychelles Archives the footsteps have become faeces with the same dimension: Chief Civil Commissioner to Governor, Letter Book Outward 1878–80, Seychelles Archives B37). Rivers also noted the absence of dead carapaces, now a common sight, and he also recorded that the population had been damaged by pigs introduced some years before, but which had themselves died out. The Seychelles Government was already alarmed at the status of the Aldabra tortoises: the Chief Civil Commissioner, Mahé, noted that 'many vessels call at Aldabra for the sake of capturing land tortoises. The only way to protect these animals, in fact the only way to save them from eventual annihilation, is to have a Govt. Guardian on the Island and to strictly preserve the forest' (Chief Commissioner to Governor of Seychelles, 21 January 1879: Seychelles Archives).

Aldabra was first settled by a small fishing party at the end of 1889, and the first land lease was granted to James Spurs on 15 July 1891. This and subsequent leases included specific prohibitions on the killing of tortoises. When G. Cayley visited Picard in 1890 he found 15 Seychellois who in 2 months had seen only a single tortoise, though numbers were said to exist on Malabar (Seychelles Archives C/55/73).

Spurs, the new lessee, thought the tortoises generally to be 'still numerous', though extinct on Picard. He reintroduced 11 to that island from other parts of the atoll (Spurs 1892, p. 48); Rothschild (1915, p. 433) says that tortoises were reintroduced to Aldabra from Seychelles, but this may result from a misreading of Spurs. In 1892 Griffith reported that the tortoises were 'apparently prolific', and he recorded Spur's belief that there were not less than 1000 on the atoll (Griffith to Administrator, 13 June 1892: Seychelles Archives). He also felt that rats were an important element in limiting numbers (Griffith to Lt. Governor, Mauritius, 1893: Seychelles Archives). In 1895 Abbott 'met with but few' in a visit of 3 months and thought the population had been 'greatly diminished' by whalers and fishermen: he considered (as did Nicoll 11 years later (1908, p. 130) that there were more domesticated tortoises in the Seychelles proper than wild ones on Aldabra (Abbott 1893, p. 761), and that Spur's estimate of 1000 was 'very considerably overestimated' (Griffith to Lt. Governor, Mauritius, 4 April 1893: Gunther Papers).

Siebert Baty in 1893 saw 'traces' near Anse Var of tortoises turned loose on Picard by Spurs; his map of the Settlement includes a tortoise pen. Voeltzkow (1897, pp. 52–56) in the same year, while thinking there were 'still a great many', saw no skeletons and found few living animals: he saw two on his first day of search, none on the second, one on the third, and later six on the south coast, all in areas where they are now prolific. He was also the first to record the existence of tortoise enclosures at Takamaka. Bergne (1900) does not mention tortoises at all. Nicoll, who visited both Picard and Takamaka in 1906, almost incredibly saw none either (Nicoll 1908, p. 130). There thus seems little doubt that from about 1880 until the first years of this century tortoise numbers were very low.

Thereafter there is some indication in the records of increasing numbers. On 29 July 1900 the Governor of Seychelles reported to the Secretary of State for the Colonies (Seychelles Archives C/55/73) that there were 'large numbers' on Picard (he saw five in 30 minutes) and 'great abundance' on Malabar. In 1906 Dupont (1907, p. 22) found that tortoises were 'still to be found in great number' in many parts of the atoll; he did not see them on Malabar but spent little time there. Fryer (1908), however, hardly mentions tortoises at all. He reports them plentiful at the east end of Grande Terre, on Malabar, and on Picard. Some indication of the population levels may be obtained from the fact that he saw a maximum of 17 in 1 day on Grande Terre (J. S. Gardiner to Under-Secretary of State for the Colonies, 12 July 1901: Günther Archives). Though he cut a trace right across Malabar near Anse Malabar he found only two young tortoises there (Fryer 1911, p. 420). 'It would be possible to live for years on Aldabra', he reported (1910, p. 258), 'and never see a specimen'. The Governor of Seychelles took a gloomy view of their survival. 'In a wild state at Aldabra practically all the young are destroyed by florentins (cranes), rats, and wild cats. . . No plan will effectively prevent the final extinction of these curoius survivals in a wild state in their natural habitats' (Davidson 1911, pp. 623–624).

Not until 1916 do we find estimates of really substantial numbers. In that year Dupont estimated that there were 'many thousands' at Cinq Cases, and that tortoises were present in other parts of the atoll also, though in smaller numbers. In August 1929 he 'saw a great many land tortoise all over the place in their natural surroundings and they all looked very healthy' (Dupont 1929, p. 17).

During this time, Aldabran tortoises were also being exported from the Seychelles. Thirteen animals were exported between 1890 and 1900 (Treasurer to Administrator, Seychelles Archives C/55/73). There are no records for the period 1900–27, but after 1927 there are annual statements of export in Seychelles *Blue books* (1922–39) and *Trade reports* (1932 to date). Almost all of these animals must have derived directly from Aldabra. During 1927–76 a total of 1117 tortoises left Seychelles (some years are missing), an average of 22 per annum; for some years the annual quota has been 50. The destination of most is given as Kenya though the ultimate destination of these is not known. The trade records do not, of course, include animals taken from Aldabra and consumed, killed or relocated within the Seychelles.

CONCLUSION

This analysis can be summarized briefly. Tortoises were widespread on the volcanic and granitic islands of the western Indian Ocean, on Aldabra, and possibly on some coral islands at the time of discovery and early settlement (up to the late eighteenth century). They were already rare by 1670 on Mauritius and by 1790 on the granitic Seychelles; and they were extinct on all the high islands by about 1800. Apart from Aldabra, historical evidence is scarce for the limestone islands, and it is at least possible that the tortoise remains on most of these islands are of Pleistocene rather than Recent age. At Aldabra itself, the population came close to extinction because of predation by man at the end of the nineteenth century, and the present very high population levels are a recent phenomenon. The evidence of the existence of tortoises on the sand cays and limestone islands are summarized in table 1.

TABLE 1.

	sand cays	limestone islands
no evidence	6	1
suggested in the secondary literature but no direct evidence; record therefore doubtful	5	0
historical records	0	1
fossil materials	2	5
existing wild population	0	1

We thank Mrs S. Lomas, Aldabra Data Unit, for her work on a bibliography of western Indian Ocean tortoises.

REFERENCES (Stoddart & Peake)

Abbott, W. L. 1893 Notes on the natural history of Aldabra, Assumption and Glorioso Islands, Indian Ocean. *Proc. U.S. natn. Mus.* **16**, 759–764.

Atkinson, G. 1921 A French desert island novel of 1708. *Publs mod. Lang. Ass. Am.* **36**, 509–528.

Atkinson, G. 1922 *The extraordinary voyage in French literature from 1700 to 1720.* (147 pages.) Paris: Librairie Ancienne Honoré Champion.

Battistini, R. & Cremers, G. 1972 Geomorphology and vegetation of Iles Glorieuses. *Atoll Res. Bull.* **159**, 1–10.

Baty, S. C. E. 1896 *A report on the Aldabra and Cosmoledo groups of islands.* Victoria: Government Printer.

Bayne, C. J., Cogan, B. H., Diamond, A. W., Frazier, J., Grubb, P., Hutson, A., Poore, M. E. D., Stoddart, D. R. & Taylor, J. D. 1970 Geography and ecology of Astove. *Atoll Res. Bull.* **136**, 83–99.

Bergne, H. A'C. 1900 Fair record of islands in the Indian Ocean. Manuscript.

Bory de St-Vincent, J. B. G. M 1804 *Voyage dans les quatres principales iles des mers d'Afriques.* (3 vols: 412, 431 and 473 pages.) Paris: F. Buisson.

Coppinger, R. W. 1883 *Cruise of the 'Alert': four years in Patagonian, Polynesian, and Mascarene waters (1878–82).* (256 pages.) London: W. Swan Sonnenschein.

Dalrymple, A. 1784 *Plan of the Islands John de Nova by M. Margaro 1776.* London: published by the author.

Dalrymple, A. 1805 *Plan of the African Islands.* London: published by the author.

Davidson, W. E. 1911 Land tortoises in the Seychelles. *Proc. zool. Soc. Lond.* **1911**, 622–624.

Dehérain, H. 1926 Le voyage de Francois Leguat dans l'Océan Indien (1690–1698) est-il imaginaire? *Bull. Sect. Géogr. Com. Trav. hist. scient.* **41**, 159–177.

Dubois, Sieur 1897 *The voyages made by the Sieur D.B. to the islands Dauphine or Madagascar and Bourbon or Mascarenne in the years 1669, 70, 71 and 72.* London: D. Nutt.

Dupon, J. F. 1969 *Recueil de documents pour servir à l'histoire de Rodrigues.* (121 pages.) Port Louis: R. Coquet, Imprimerie Commerciale.

Dupont, R. P. 1907 *Report on a visit of investigation to St Pierre, Astove, Cosmoledo, Assumption, and the Aldabra Group.* (51 pages.) Victoria: Government Printer.

Dupont, R. P. 1929 *Report on a visit of investigation to the principal outlying islands of the Seychelles Archipelago.* (20 pages.) Mahé: Department of Agriculture, typescript.

Fauvel, A. A. 1900 Textes inédits concernant les tortues de terre gigantesques de l'ile Juan de Nove (I. Farquhar) (Océan Indien). *Bull. Mus. Hist. nat. Paris* **6**, 170–174.

Fauvel, A. A. 1909 Unpublished documents on the history of the Seychelles Islands before 1880. Mahé: Public Library.

Flacourt, E. de 1658 *Histoire de la Grande Isle Madagascar.* (384 pages.) Paris.

Foster, W. (ed.) 1905 *The Journal of John Jourdain 1608–1617, describing his experience in Arabia, India, and the Malay Archipelago.* (394 pages.) Cambridge: Hakluyt Society.

Froberville, E. de 1848 Rodrigues, Galéga, Les Séchelles, Les Almirantes, etc. In *Iles de l'Afrique*, (ed. M. A. P. d'Avezac), part 3 (Iles Africaines de la Mer des Indes), vol. 2. Paris: Firmin Didot Frères.

Froidevaux, H. 1899 Textes historiques inédits ou peu connus relatifs aux tortues de terre de l'ile Bourbon. *Bull. Mus. Hist. nat. Paris* **5**, 214–218.

Fryer, J. C. F. 1809 Diary. Manuscript.

Fryer, J. C. F. 1910 The south-west Indian Ocean (being an account of Aldabra and certain neighbouring islands, which were not explored by Prof. J. Stanley Gardiner in H.M.S. 'Sealark'). *Geogrl J.* **37**, 249–268; discussion 268–271.

Fryer, J. C. F. 1911 The structure and formation of Aldabra and neighbouring islands – with notes on their flora and fauna. *Trans. Linn. Soc. Lond.* (2) *Zool.* **14**, 397–442.

Grant, C., Baron de Vaux 1801 *The history of Mauritius, or the Isle of France, and the neighbouring islands.* (571 pages.) London: W. Bulmer.

Günther, A. C. L. G. 1877 *The gigantic land-tortoises (living and extinct) in the collection of the British Museum.* (96 pages.) London: Taylor & Francis.

Günther, A. C. L. G. 1898 The president's anniversary address. *Proc. Linn. Soc. Lond.* **1897–98**, 14–29.

Harrison, G. 1839 The Seychelles. *Naut. Mag.* **8**, 443–446.

Herbert, T. 1634 *A relation of some years travaile, begunne anno 1626. Into Afrique and the greater Asia, especially the Territories of the Persian Monarchie: and some parts of the Orientall Indies, and Iles adiacent.* (225 pages.) London: W. Stansby & J. Bloome.

Herbert, W. & Nichelson, W. 1780 *A new Directory for the East-Indies.* 5th edn. (554 pages.) London: Henry Gregory.

Honegger, R. 1966 Beobachtungen an der Herpetofauna der Seychellen. *Salamandra* **1–2**, 20–36.

Horsburgh, J. 1809 *Directions for sailing to and from the East Indies, China, New Holland, Cape of Good Hope, and the interjacent ports.* Part 1. (397 pages.) London: Black, Parry & Kingsbury.

Kersten, O. 1871 *Baron Claus von den Decken's Reisen in Ost-Afrika in den Jahren 1862–65.* (2 volumes.) Leipzig and Heidelberg: Winter.

Leguat, F. 1708 *A new voyage to the East Indies by Francis Leguat and his two companions, containing their adventures in two desart islands.* (248 pages.) London: R. Bonwicke.

Mandelslo, J. A. de 1669 *The voyages and travels of J. Albert de Mandelslo.* 2nd edn London.

McKenzie, K. G. 1971 Note on evidence of human interference on South Island, Aldabra. *Phil. Trans. R. Soc. Lond.* B **260**, 629–630.

Milne Edwards, A. 1874 Recherches sur la faune éteinte des iles Mascareignes. *Ann. Sci. nat. (Zool.),* (5) **19**, iii, 1–31.

Moresby, F. 1842 On the Seychelle Islands. *Naut. Mag.* **11**, 585–590, 676–682 and 739–746.

Morisot, C. B. 1651 *Relations véritables et curieuses de l'Isle de Madagascar, et du Brésil.* (3 vols: 307, 212 and 158 pages.) Paris: Augustin Courbe.

Nicoll, M. J. 1908 *Three voyages of a naturalist, being an account of many little-known islands in three oceans visited by the 'Valhalla' R. Y.S.* (246 pages.) London: Witherby.

Pitot, A. 1905 *T'Eylandt Mauritius: esquisses historiques (1598–1710).* (372 pages.) Port Louis: Coignet Frères.

Rothschild, W. 1897 Further notes on gigantic land tortoises. *Novit. Zool.* **4**, 407–408.

Rothschild, W. 1915 On the gigantic land-tortoises of the Seychelles and Aldabra-Madagascar group, with some notes on certain forms of the Mascarene group. *Novit. Zool.* **22**, 418–442.

Sauzier, T. 1895 *Les tortues de terre gigantesques des Mascareignes et de certaines autres iles de la Mer des Indies.* (32 pages.) Paris: G. Masson.

Spurs, T. J. 1892 Report on Aldabra. *Colonial Reports Annual;* (Mauritius (Seychelles and Rodrigues), Ann. Rept 1889 and 1890) pp. 46–50.

Staub, F. & Guého, J. 1968 The Cargados Carajos or St Brandon: resources, avifauna and vegetation. *Proc. R. Soc. Arts Sci. Mauritius* **3**, 7–46.

Stirling, W. 1843 *Narrative of the wreck of the Ship Tiger, of Liverpool ...on the desert island of Astova.* (154 pages.) Exeter: W. Roberts.

Stoddart, D. R. 1971 Settlement, development and conservation of Aldabra. *Phil. Trans. R. Soc. Lond.* B **260**, 611–628.

Stoddart, D. R. 1972 Pinnipeds or sirenians at western Indian Ocean islands? *J. Zool., Lond.* **167**, 207–217.

Stoddart, D. R., Benson, C. W. & Peake, J. F. 1970 Ecological change and effects of phosphate mining on Assumption Island. *Atoll Res. Bull.* **136**, 121–145.

Stoddart, D. R. & Poore, M. E. D. 1970a Geography and ecology of Farquhar Atoll. *Atoll Res. Bull.* **136**, 7–26.

Stoddart, D. R. & Poore, M. E. D. 1970b Geography and ecology of African Banks. *Atoll Res. Bull.* **136**, 187–191.

Toussaint, A. 1965 Le trafic commercial des Seychelles de 1773 à 1810. *J. Seychelles Soc.* **4**, 20–61.

Toussaint, A. 1967 La route des Iles: contribution à l'histoire maritime des Mascareignes. *Ecole pratique des Hautes Etudes, 6th Sect., Centre de Recherches Historiques, Ports-Routes-Trafics,* **22**, 1–540.

d'Unienville, M. C. A. M. 1838 *Statistigue de l'Ile Maurice et ses Dépendances, suivie d'une Notice historique sur cette Colonie et d'une Essai sur l'Ile de Madagascar.* (3 vols: 387, 333 and 340 pages.) Paris: Gustave Barba.

Vaillant, L. 1899a Nouveaux documents historiques sur les tortues terrestres des Mascareignes et des Seychelles. *Bull. Mus. Hist. nat.,* Paris, **5**, 19–23.

Vaillant, L. 1899b Documents relatifs à la tortue gigantesque de la Réunion. *Bull. Mus. Hist. nat.,* Paris, **5**, 354–356.

Voeltzkow, A. 1897 Einleitung: Madagaskar, Juan de Nova, Aldabra. *Abh. senckenb. naturf. Ges.* **21**, 1–76.

Wharton, W. J. H. 1879 [Letter on Aldabra]. *Ann. Mag. nat. Hist.* (5) **3**, 165–166.

Appendix 1. Gigantic land tortoises of Seychelles†

By C. Gordon

In 1691 Leguat writes that these tortoises were so numerous that you could go for 100 yards on their backs, they were in herds of hundreds, they are only found now in their natural state on the isle Aldabra in the Amirantes Group.

They carry a supply of about 2 gallons [9.1 l] of water in a bag at the root of the neck, they have no hearing. The Male has a long tail, the female a short one, but they are usually coiled up, the male exceeds the female in size, the temperature of their blood remains at 62° [F; 26°C] vide Work on Gigantic tortoises by A. Gunther 1877, which contains the petition of Sir J. Hooker and others to the Government requesting that they should be preserved.

The following families of Seychelles possess the best specimens of these tortoises.

At Mahé: R. Gonthier, Mrs Savy, Mr Duchenne, Mr Serret, Mr E. Nageon, Mr C. Button, Mr C. Dupuy.

At Praslin: Mr Laprude.

At Ladigue: Mr A. Nageon, Mr F. Payette, Mr B. Payette.

At Ile Cerf: Mr D. Calais.

At Deux Soeurs: Mr J. Berlories.

If kept in a large space, they increase rapidly in size, and they increase slowly, if confined.

The males couple with the female in February and March: the females scoop out a hole some 7″ [18 cm] in diameter and 1′ 6″ [46 cm] deep, and entering it, lays her eggs, urines over them, and making a paste with the mud, covers them over, heaping in the mud, and then standing over it, on the tips of her toes, flops down with all her weight on the heap, making the roof of her nest very hard and level with the ground around, this ground is so hard that when eggs come forth, the small tortoises are obliged to burrow under and come out at the edge of this roof, the eggs which are round 2½″ [6 cm] diameter with hard shell are laid in batches of 15–18 and come out in 6 months after being laid, generally they are laid in April and come out in September or October. In 1877–8–9 no eggs were laid by any of the tortoises of this colony. The female lays two batches of eggs with an interval of 18 days between them, and she goes with the male in this interval, after this the male notices not the female.

The male mounts on the back of the female, and remains coupled for an hour uttering loud grunts, the under plate of the male is concave, in order to fasten over convexity on the back of the female, the under plate of the female is flat in order that she may ram down the earth of her nest as described.

(N.B. The turtle couples with the male for 12 h at a time in the water, generally at night, when he can be approached without shifting his seat. The turtle eggs are covered with membrane, the male has two hooks with which he holds on to the female, the under plate of the turtle male is flat.)

The female commences to lay her eggs at age of 15 years, she searches a dry suitable place, she opens a ditch of hole 10″ [25 cm] deep with her front feet, she then enters this ditch, and,

† Günther Papers; British Museum (Natural History).

with her hind feet opens a hole 6″ to 8″ [15–20 cm] deep quite round, it takes her 10–12 hours to do this, she removes about a table spoonful each time with her nails, and waits 3 or 4 minutes between each scoop.

This information comes from a very intelligent gentleman Mr Charles Button of Providence Mahé.

The tortoises never quarrel among themselves. Some of these tortoises weigh 500 lbs [277 kg], and are 5′ 6″ long, 4′ 6″ wide and 3 ft thick [168 cm long, 137 cm wide and 91 cm thick].

Appendix 2. Radiocarbon dating of eggshell of giant tortoise from Denis Island, Seychelles

By R. Burleigh

Research Laboratory, The British Museum, London WC1B 3DG, U.K.

A radiocarbon date has been obtained at the British Museum Research Laboratory for an eggshell of the giant tortoise (*Geochelone gigantea*) from Denis Island on the northern rim of the Seychelles Bank (3° 47′ S, 55° 39′ E). The eggshell came from the collection of the British Museum (Natural History), Reg. no. 1927. 5.14.18, and was submitted for dating by Dr E. N. Arnold and Dr J. D. Taylor of the Department of Zoology, B.M.(N.H.). It was originally collected in 1927 by J. Hornell from a deposit which recent analysis has indicated was probably a calcareous beach sand incorporated in a soil. Although the eggshell was incomplete it could be identified with certainty as that of a giant tortoise. The purpose of the radiocarbon measurement was to indicate whether tortoises were present on Denis Island before people arrived there in historic times and, indirectly, to provide a minimum age for the deposits in which the eggshell was found.

A preliminary computer search of the 40 000 or so radiocarbon dates that have been published revealed no other instance in which the eggshells of reptiles had been dated. The nearest comparisons that could be found were with ostrich eggshell for which about 30 dates have been reported in *Radiocarbon*, and with three dates for eggshells of the extinct giant bird *Aepyornis maximus* from Madagascar. Although there was no direct information regarding the suitability for radiocarbon dating of the eggshell of the giant tortoise its isotope chemistry might reasonably be expected to be similar to that of these other apparently reliable materials.

Examination by X-ray diffraction showed that the eggshell was composed of unaltered aragonite. From the absence of any recrystallization to calcite it was inferred that no post-depositional exchange of carbon isotopes had taken place and no appreciable error in the apparent radiocarbon age of the eggshell was to be expected from this cause. The sample used for dating was a single fragment weighing approximately 15 g and comprising about two-thirds of a complete eggshell, presumably broken by the emergence of a hatchling. As it was otherwise well preserved and uncontaminated no special pretreatment was required and the entire sample was dissolved in dilute hydrochloric acid yielding about 3 l of carbon dioxide. All of this in turn was converted via acetylene to benzene for measurement of ^{14}C activity by liquid scintillation counting, the standard method in use for radiocarbon dating at the British Museum laboratory. The date obtained (BM–1331) was 1308 ± 85 radiocarbon years before A.D. 1950 (bp) on the basis of the conventional 5570 year half-life for ^{14}C; the error quoted with this date was derived purely from counting statistics and is equivalent to ± 1 standard deviation. The stable carbon isotope ratio ($\delta^{13}C$) measured for this sample was -2.22 ± 0.18 parts per mille (‰) relative to the international P.D.B. standard (a Cretaceous belemnite), a value within the range in which some inorganic carbonates lie. The ^{14}C activity measured was age corrected for the difference between the $\delta^{13}C$ value of -2.22‰ obtained for the eggshell and the accepted average value for plant material (wood) of -25.00‰ to which all dates are normally referred. There is no *prima facie* reason to doubt the correctness of this procedure in this instance since, although giant tortoises do occasionally eat carrion, for example, and forage on the sea-shore, their diet is predominantly vegetarian and most of the carbon they assimilate must be derived directly from living plants. Therefore, any intake of older carbon is most probably negligible. Independently, if normalization against some $\delta^{13}C$ value more positive than that of plant material is actually more appropriate for the eggshell of giant tortoise because of fractionation during metabolism, then the effect would be to shift the date somewhat nearer the present, perhaps by up to 200 years. In principle this uncertainty could be resolved empirically by measuring the apparent radiocarbon age of the eggshell of a modern giant tortoise. Unfortunately any such measurement would be equivocal because of the dilution resulting from large scale combustion of fossil fuel since about A.D. 1850 and overcompensation of this by artificial ^{14}C derived from nuclear weapon testing.

Assuming that the date of 1308 ± 85 bp obtained from the eggshell is not seriously in error it is nevertheless strictly a 'radiocarbon age'. For greater absolute accuracy this must be corrected to allow for past variations in the level of natural ^{14}C and for the more accurate 5730 year half-life (although for convenience dates are still reported in *Radiocarbon* on the basis of the orginal 5570 year half-life). In practice these corrections have little effect on relatively recent dates. By using one of the more comprehensive and accessible of the published tables for correction of raw radiocarbon dates (*Antiquity* **49**, 251–266 (1975)), a calendar date of 1270 years before 1950 or A.D. 680 would be obtained. This date probably has an inherent error of about ± 100 years.

From this date it would appear that Denis Island was occupied by giant tortoises well before the arrival of European voyagers in the seventeenth century. The result also provides a reasonable minimum age for the deposit in which the eggshell was found, which analysis suggested was fairly recent. It would be of considerable interest to follow up this result by dating the remains of giant tortoises from other isolated islands or island groups in the western Indian Ocean where there appear to be early records, such as the Amirante Islands. Some other problems relating to the former distribution and the contemporaneity or otherwise of the different species of giant tortoise may also be amenable to radiocarbon dating.

Phil. Trans. R. Soc. Lond. B. **286**, 163–176 (1979)   [163]

Printed in Great Britain

The biomass, production and carrying capacity of giant tortoises on Aldabra

By M. J. Coe, D. Bourn and I. R. Swingland

*Animal Ecology Research Group, Department of Zoology, University of Oxford, South Parks Road,
Oxford OX1 3PS, U.K.*

The giant tortoise (*Geochelone gigantea* (Schweigger)) population of Aldabra has varied greatly in numbers since the beginning of the present century. Recent estimates have shown that the population is composed of 150 466 ± s.e. 16 441 animals. Of this total, 60 % are located in an area of 33.6 km² at the eastern end of Grande Terre.

Animals composing the small population of 2000 tortoises on Malabar grow continuously, while those on Grande Terre only grow seasonally and are much smaller than their less numerous counterparts on Malabar. It is suggested that shade factors limit the time available for feeding in Grande Terre.

Records of movement show that while some animals do move large distances 56 % of the population are not relocated more than 500 m from their initial marking point.

A mean annual rainfall of 941 mm would be expected to yield 1887 g m^{-2} a^{-1} (dry mass) of primary production, with a range of from 2337 to 4037 g m^{-2} a^{-1}. Tortoises of average mass (20–30 kg) consume 79 kg a^{-1}. Estimates of total consumption for areas with differing tortoise densities suggest that they would consume 11.3 % at the eastern end of Grande Terre and 0.7 % in the *Pemphis* scrub.

Defecation records suggest that the gross assimilation efficiency of giant tortoises is about 50 %.

The mean mass of tortoises on Aldabra are 21.7 kg on Grande Terre, 49.9 kg on Malabar and 51.3 kg on Picard. Standing crop biomasses derived from these weights are 35 387 kg km^{-2} on Grande Terre, 35 084 kg km^{-2} on Malabar and 25 342 kg km^{-2} on Picard. These biomass data are significantly higher than those achieved by large herbivores on mainland African wildlife ecosystems.

By using data available on biomass mortality, P/B ratios (turnover times) of 0.042 for Grande Terre and 0.034 for Malabar are obtained. Annual production calculated from these ratios are 1486 kg km^{-2} a^{-1} for Grande Terre and 1193 kg km^{-2} a^{-1} for Malabar.

The production efficiency of the giant tortoise population is about 2.1 % which is in close agreement with figures obtained for other long-lived poikilotherms.

Potential production for Grande Terre predicted from the mean rainfall only differs by 2.6 % from that estimated. The eastern end of Grande Terre, however, exceeds this predicted figure by 61 % and it is suggested that this is due to increased primary production induced by water available from the freshwater lens raised by spring tides. This phenomenon is similar to mainland African wildlife ecosystems fed by abundant ground water.

1. Introduction

Fossil evidence suggests that Aldabra has been inundated and subsequently recolonized by Giant tortoises three or four times in the last 170 000 years (Braithwaite, Taylor & Kennedy 1973; Taylor, Braithwaite, Peake & Arnold 1979, this volume). These discoveries illustrate the fact that these large cold-blooded vertebrates must be able to stand long periods floating in sea water without access to either food or fresh water. Indeed it was their ability to stand long periods without food that made them a prime target for early seafaring people who visited Aldabra and other Islands in the Indian Ocean and who removed large numbers of tortoises as a food source which could provide fresh meat on extended sea voyages. To a large degree it must be presumed that man is largely, if not wholly, responsible for the extinction of tortoises on all of the islands that they previously occupied in the Indian Ocean. The difficult terrain of Aldabra and its comparative isolation have probably been prime factors in their survival on this their last remaining stronghold.

A number of authors (Grubb 1971; Stoddart & Peake 1979, this volume) have drawn attention to the fact that the numbers of tortoises on Aldabra have varied greatly during the present century from an apparent increase at its beginning, falling to very low numbers in the late 1930s and then rising again to their very high numbers at the present time.

Evidence of actual numbers of tortoises present on Aldabra is lacking in these earlier anecdotal accounts of casual visitors, the first contemporary estimate being that of Palombelli (1954) who concluded that the population size was about 80000 animals. In 1964 Gaymer (1968) visited Aldabra as a member of the Bristol University Seychelles Expedition and marked animals with red and yellow cellulose paint marks on the carapace. He revisited Aldabra (Gaymer 1968, 1973) and provided tortoises with permanent marks with the use of numbered titanium disks. These operations were carried out at several points on Grande Terre and in the vicinity of Passe Houareau on Malabar. These disks were embedded in a shallow hole drilled in the third vertebral scute with a hand drill and secured with Devcon resin. From the ratio of marked to unmarked animals in the areas he censused he concluded that the tortoise population of Aldabra was about 33000 animals.

Grubb (1971), working with the early phases of the Royal Society Expedition to Aldabra (Phases I–III) in 1967–8, carried out a detailed study of the tortoise population in the southeast of Grande Terre and concluded that an area of 10.6 km² contained up to 40830 tortoises. He further extrapolated this data to the whole of the Platin area of Grande Terre (30.7 km²) and suggested that the total population was 98240 animals.

Frazier (1971) studying the thermoregulation and behaviour of the Aldabran giant tortoise estimated the total population of the atoll as 120000 animals, but his calculations were based on restricted census data although it does agree with later estimates.

Since Aldabra probably represents the only terrestrial environment in the world where a cold blooded vertebrate is the only significant primary consumer, the Aldabra Research Committee encouraged Coe to devise and coordinate a more detailed study of the tortoise's ecology. This programme was designed to be conducted in three phases. The first of these was conducted by Bourne who studied animal numbers, their distribution and population structure (1973–4), while the second, recently completed by Swingland, studied reproduction and recruitment (1975–6). The last phase, yet to be initiated, will investigate feeding in relation to tortoise production and vegetation–tortoise interactions.

The marking technique used by Gaymer (1973) was improved by Bourn (1976) who used an electric drill and a specially designed counter-sinking bit. Numbered titanium disks were embedded in the fourth central scute with Devcon resin. During this first phase of the population study, 6014 animals were given permanent marks on Grande Terre, and 168 on Malabar. Including those animals marked by Gaymer, a total of 6882 tortoises have been provided with permanent marks on the atoll. As a result of these operations and subsequent transect censuses, preliminary analysis indicated a total population of 140019 animals (Bourn 1976) but more detailed study (Bourn & Coe 1978) has raised this estimate to 150466 (95% confidence limits 134020–166907) animals. A study of marked–release–recapture data for the main census area (Morgan 1976; Morgan & Bourn 1978) has confirmed that these estimates are acceptable.

In the light of this information, which has revealed especially high densities on Grande Terre, the object of the present paper is to examine these data in relation to biomass and secondary production of the giant tortoise population and to compare this information with data available for large herbivore dominated communities on the African mainland.

THE TORTOISE POPULATION

(a) Animal numbers and their distribution

The most recent estimate of tortoise numbers on Aldabra (Bourn & Coe 1978) has demonstrated that 97.7% of the total population of 150466 animals occurs on Grande Terre, with 60.2% occupying an area of 33.6 km² in the eastern census area and 20.5% along the south coast. Thus of a total land area of 138 km² 80.7% of the total population occupy little more than 37% of this area. This striking feature of the tortoises' distribution is in large part related to the geology of Aldabra, where large areas of broken and fissured 'champignon' limestone render the *Pemphis* scrub carried virtually unavailable to tortoises.

In addition to the large number of animals occupying Grande Terre (146912) 2250 are located in an area of 3.2 km² on Malabar (out of a total land area of 29.56 km²), 1235 animals live on Picard and up to 70 live on the small lagoon islands.

The phenomena of ultra high densities and biomass are therefore only of real importance on Grande Terre. Since, however, it has been shown that recruitment to Malabar and Grande Terre populations is regulated by density (Swingland & Coe 1979, this volume), it is important to examine whether biomass and production data may be used to assess their respective relations to the potential carrying capacities of the two main islands.

While densities on Grande Terre vary between 27.0 ($\pm$1.8) in the eastern census area and 1.6 ($\pm$0.6) in the *Pemphis* scrub, such figures do not take into account patterns of micro-distribution within the area censused. Areas with local densities as high as 70 animals per hectare in the southeast of Grande Terre are characterized by scattered trees and abundant *Sporobolus* grassland, in coastal areas and 'tortoise turf', a complex mixture of apparently genetically dwarfed species (Merton, Bourn & Hnatiuk 1976) inland. Gibson (1977, personal communication has recently pointed out that these high densities are to a large degree concentrated on these preferred vegetation types even when they only compose a small percentage of the total area examined.

Bourn & Coe (1978) have analysed the distribution of tortoise density in relation to their habitat type and have demonstrated that the highest numbers occur in association with low vegetation and a percentage tree cover (available shade) of 10%. Clearly these two factors demonstrate the importance of a vegetation layer that is all potentially available as tortoise food on the one hand and strict thermoregulatory requirements on the other.

The transect data obtained by Swingland have yet to be analysed but preliminary studies (Bourn & Coe 1978) have failed to show a significant association between areas of differing tortoise density and factors related to geomorphology, freshwater pools, rain, time of day or season. We are, however, well aware of the importance of local seasonal migrations between inland scrub area and coastal grassland.

If we examine the available data on tortoise distribution (Grubb 1971; Bourn & Coe 1978), we note that the animals may be potentially limited by the nature of the terrain, food availability, shade and water. Tortoises are virtually excluded from areas of deeply dissected and fissured limestone. Additionally, however, we are also aware that large areas of open grassland which provide abundant potential food are also not visited by tortoises due to the absence of adequate shade. This fact is well illustrated by the differences in the standing crop biomass of grazed and ungrazed *Sporobolus* grassland measured on the south coast between Cinq Cases and Takamaka which differed by a factor of 7.5 (230 and 1725 g dry mass m^{-2} respectively) despite the fact that the two sites measured were only a few metres apart. A distinct graze line is evident at a point where the tortoise's movement is limited by its distance from shade. Swingland (1976) has demonstrated that this grazing cut-off distance occurs at about 300 m from the nearest shade.

On Malabar where tortoises are limited to a small area of suitable terrain and their numbers are low there is abundant tree cover but the tortoises are able to feed for much longer periods of the day than they can on Grande Terre without needing to seek shade. Additionally, studies of growth (Swingland 1976) have demonstrated that tortoises on Malabar grow virtually continuously while their abundant counterparts on Grande Terre only grow seasonally. Indeed these differences are exemplified by the fact that tortoises of the same age are much heavier on Malabar than their neighbours on Grande Terre. Thus through problems associated with the effect of limited shade on feeding time the Grande Terre population would seem to be food limited.

While tortoises do require access to water, the Grande Terre animals have abundant semi-permanent pools and temporary pools associated with fresh water lenses that are made available at high spring tides when they are elevated to the surface. By contrast, the animals of Malabar have little permanent fresh water available to them although evaporative losses are less due to the increased shade. The water that they may obtain from a predominantly browse dominated vegetation may well be a factor that renders the Malabar animals less dependent on free standing water.

(b) Movement

Frazier (1970) reported tortoises moving up to 47 km from the point at which they were marked. Recent analysis of recapture data (Bourn & Coe 1978) has indicated that such long-distance movement is exceptional and that 56 % of the animals recaptured during transect censuses on Grande Terre had moved less than 500 m from the hectare in which they were initially marked. Of the remainder only 8 % had moved more than 2 km and of these ten marked individuals had moved between 5.7 and 25.5 km (straight line distance). Clearly, therefore, in terms of studying density and biomass density, these long distance movements are unimportant although they do clearly illustrate that the whole population of Grande Terre may be considered as one population both from an ecological and a genetic standpoint.

(c) Tortoise numbers and food supply

Walter (1954) and Whittaker (1970) have demonstrated that over a wide geographical area rainfall may be used to predict primary production. Rosenzweig (1968) has established a similar log–linear relation between actual evapotranspiration (E_A) and net above-ground primary production (p_{nap}) in grams dry mass per square metre per year.

Rainfall data for Aldabra (Stoddart & Mole 1977) indicate that between 1958 and 1974 the mean annual rainfall was 940.6 mm with wide year to year variation from 547 mm (1968) to 1473 mm (1974). More recently, Stoddart & Walsh (1979, this volume) have examined data from other areas in the Indian Ocean and have suggested that by using 10 and 20 year running means it is possible to detect a cycle of high and low rainfall with a periodicity of about 35 years. This information is of considerable interest, for it closely coincides with the periodicity proposed by Phillipson (1975) and Cobb (1977) who have studied rainfall records for the Tsavo National Park in eastern Kenya. It is therefore possible that the short-term mean (1070 mm) derived from the Royal Society weather station on Picard indicates that we are at present in or entering a period of higher rainfall. In terms of considering the influence of rainfall on the food supply of tortoises the long-term mean (941 mm) has been used.

TABLE 1. FOOD CONSUMPTION

season	number of observations	average dry mass/(g d^{-1})	observer
wet season (Jan.)	5	380 ± 64.8	Swingland
dry season (June)	4	160 ± 116.7	Swingland
late dry season (Sept.)	2	110 ± 77.9	Bourne & Coe

mean food intake = 217 g dry mass d^{-1}.

In order to apply the formulation of Rosenzweig (1968) it is necessary to know the potential evapotranspiration, but in semi-arid environments where potential evapotranspiration is greater than actual precipitation (P_A), $E_A = P_A$. Coe, Cumming & Phillipson (1976) have considered them to be equal up to 700 mm. In the absence of suitable evaporation data for Aldabra the long-term mean rainfall of 194 mm is not likely to deviate far from this presumed relation.

Thus we may calculate p_{nap} for Aldabra by using Rosenzweig's predictive equation:

$$\log_{10} p_{nap} = \log_{10} E_A (1.66 \pm 0.27) - (1.66 \pm 0.07),$$

from which we observe that p_{nap} is 1887 g m^{-2} a^{-1} (dry mass). We should, however, note here that on the same basis the calculated p_{nap} for the short-term mean (1070 mm) would be 2337 g m^{-2} a^{-1} and a range from 768 g m^{-2} a^{-1} in 1968 to 4037 g m^{-2} a^{-1} in 1974. Clearly these differences in available food could have a profound effect on year to year recruitment (Swingland & Coe 1979, this volume), on short-term food shortage and nutritive stress, or even be responsible for catastrophic mortality of adults as Phillipson (1975) has postulated for elephants in the Tsavo National Park (Kenya).

Detailed studies of food consumption by tortoises on Aldabra have yet to be carried out but preliminary measurements give a first approximation (table 1). It will be noted that by using animals of average size on Grande Terre, the amount of food consumed varies from 380 g d^{-1} (dry mass) in the wet season to 110 g d^{-1} at the height of the dry season in September. If we assume that the three rates of feeding described are each representative of consumption for 4 months of the year, we may estimate that these animals will eat 217 g d^{-1} or 79 kg a^{-1}. The most striking feature of these measurements is the very small amount of food being eaten by these cold-blooded herbivores in relation to their mass (20–30 kg) and also the great annual variation which must to a large degree be related to the restricted time available for feeding during the dry months of the year. This reduction in feeding time would certainly account for the absence of any sign of active growth for animals on Grande Terre over much of the year, and from which we might predict that the production efficiency of these creatures would be very low.

During the course of culling operations, animals were fed coloured paper markers 1–3 days before being killed and dissected as part of the reproductive study. These investigations yielded data on the amount consumed and the throughput times for animals in the medium size range. Throughput times obtained during this study are shown in table 2. It will be noted that there is again considerable seasonal variation in this parameter. With this preliminary sample it is not possible to establish a relation between the size of the animal and either food consumed or the throughput time. The mean throughput time for an animal in the 20–30 kg size class is 27 days.

TABLE 2. FOOD PASSAGE THROUGH GUT

season	number of observations	average throughput time (+s.e.)/d	observer
wet season (Jan.)	5	6 ± 2.8	Swingland
dry season (June)	4	30 ± 10.7	Swingland
late dry season (Sept.)	2	49.4 ± 38.5	Bourn & Coe
not specified	8	23.5 ± 11.9	Frazier (1971)

Mean throughput time = 27.2 days.

Using the mean tortoise densities for the four census localities on Grande Terre (Bourn & Coe 1978) and the estimated p_{nap} calculated for the mean annual rainfall (P_A), we may estimate the percentage of the primary production consumed. These figures (table 3) vary from 11.3 % in the eastern census area to 0.7 % in the *Pemphis* scrub. The mean figure of 7.2 % represents considerable pressure on the available food resource, bearing in mind that much of the browse is unavailable until leaves, flowers or fruits fall, when they are also eaten by tortoises. Indeed, virtually all litter produced in the areas of high tortoise density comprise an important item of diet for this broad-spectrum opportunistic herbivore.

TABLE 3. RELATIONSHIP OF FOOD CONSUMED TO ESTIMATED p_{nap}

Grande Terre	tortoise density ha^{-1}	vegetation consumed (C) g m^{-2} a^{-1}	estimated p_{nap} g m^{-2} a^{-1}	$100\,C/p_{nap}$
E census area	26.95	212.47	1887.3	11.3
S coast census area	20.17	159.02	1887.3	8.4
other suitable areas	20.00	157.68	1887.3	8.4
other *Pemphis* areas	1.64	12.93	1887.3	0.7
mean	17.19	135.53	1887.3	7.2

Daily defecation rates were measured for tortoises in the Cinq Cases area of Grande Terre in the late dry season of 1974. Ten animals in the 20–30 kg size class were followed from 05h 30–08h 00. The mean mass of dung produced per individual was 34.8 g dry mass d^{-1} (s.e. ± 17.03). Since Frazier (1971) has shown that 68 % of all defecations occur in the early morning the total amount of dung produced per animal would be 51.2 g dry mass d^{-1}. Observations on defecation and food consumption were carried out on animals of the same size range in 1974 so we may calculate that the gross assimilation efficiency for the giant tortoise in the late dry season would be about 50 %. It should be noted that this figure approximates that of wild ruminants which perhaps suggests that more detailed studies on the giant tortoise may show that this figure is too high. The virtually intact leaves recovered from dung boli suggest that the assimilation efficiency is more likely to approximate that of the non-ruminant African elephant (*Loxodonta africana* Blumenbach) which has recently been measured as 22% (Rees 1977).

(d) Biomass

The very high densities recorded on Grande Terre represent animals of a wide size range and tell us little about the actual standing crop of animals present or more realistically the proportion of that standing crop that can be attributed to annual production. If we calculate mean masses for the large sample of animals measured on Aldabra we obtain figures of 21.65 ± 0.15 kg for Grande Terre, 49.9 ± 4.2 kg for Malabar, and 51.3 ± 6.9 kg for Picard. It is immediately apparent that the mean mass for the less dense populations of Malabar and Picard are respectively 130 and 137% greater than animals on Grande Terre, a difference which cannot be solely accounted for in terms of the age structure of the different populations.

TABLE 4. TORTOISE DENSITY AND BIOMASS

	area/(km²)	tortoise density km⁻²	total no. of tortoises	biomass kg km⁻²	production kg km⁻² a⁻¹
Grande Terre (mean mass $21.65 + 0.15$ kg)					
E census area	33.60	2695.2	90 560	58 352	2450.8
S coast census area	18.40	1678.9	30 891	36 347	1526.6
other suitable areas	9.60	2000.0	19 200	43 300	1818.6
other *Pemphis* areas	38.17	163.9	6 260	3 548	149.0
		$\bar{x} = 1634.5$		$\bar{x} = 35\,387$	1486.3
Malabar (mean mass 49.9 ± 4.2 kg)					
census area	3.20	703.1	2 250	35 084	1192.8
whole area	27.96	80.5	2 250	4 017	136.6
Picard (West Island) (mean mass 51.3 ± 6.9 kg)					
non-*Pemphis*	2.47	494.0	1 235	25 342	861.6
whole area	7.47	163.3	1 235	8 480	288.3
other islands	0.11	636.0	70	—	—

Production = biomass × (0.034) kg km⁻² a⁻¹ (Malabar);
= biomass × (0.042) kg km⁻² s⁻¹ (Grande Terre).

The standing crop biomass derived for the three main island populations (table 4) range from 58352 to 3548 kg km⁻² on Grande Terre (mean **35387 kg km⁻²**), 35084 on Malabar and 25342 kg km⁻² on Picard. The biomass data for Grande Terre are calculated for the whole land area since even though they occur at low density (164 km⁻²), in *Pemphis* scrub it is difficult to assess accurately the area from which they are totally excluded. The figures for Malabar and Picard, however, refer to the area over which the tortoises are known to range. If we express the biomass for the whole area of Malabar and Picard that is potentially, if not actually, available we see that the biomasses are reduced to 4017 and 8480 kg km⁻² respectively.

The mean biomass of Grande Terre (**35387 kg km⁻²**) is higher than any wildlife area of the African mainland dominated by large herbivorous mammals. The closest figures to these Aldabra biomasses are those recorded for the Rwindi Plain, Zaire (17448 kg km⁻²), Bunyoro North, Uganda (13261), Rwenzori National Park, Uganda (19928) and Manyara National Park, Tanzania (19189) (Coe *et al.* 1976). It is of interest, however, to note that the mean annual rainfall of all these four areas (863–1150 mm) closely approximates that of Aldabra.

Very few comparable figures are available for reptile biomasses recorded elsewhere in the world, and more particularly where they comprise a dominant element in the fauna. Lizard biomasses range from 26.7 kg km for Texas (Tinkle 1967) to 376 kg km^{-2} for Kansas (Fitch 1967). Harris (1964) has recorded a biomass of 240 kg km^{-2} for the *Agama* lizard (*Agama agama*) in Nigeria, and Western (1974) a mean biomass of 102 kg km^{-2} for several species of lizard in South Turkana, Kenya. It must, however, be remembered that all these measurements refer to ecosystems in which reptiles compose a very small part of a very complex community. Graham (1968) studying the Nile crocodile (*Crocodylus niloticus*) in Lake Rudolf, Kenya, has recorded biomasses ranging from 3475 to 13 900 kg km^{-2}, but these figures do not take into account the fact that a large part of the material required to sustain this biomass is derived from a very much larger area than that used to estimate these biomass densities. Ruibal & Philibosian (1974) have reported a biomass of between 1300 and 2300 kg km^{-2} for an arboreal new world lizard (*Anolis acutus*).

TABLE 5. COMPARATIVE TISSUE COMPOSITION OF AFRICAN ELEPHANT AND ALDABRAN TORTOISE

(Results expressed as a percentage of total mass.)

component	*Loxodonta africana* (Coe 1977)	*Geochelone gigantea*
bone	18.6	42.9
skin	11.6	—
soft tissues ⎫	51.5	⎰ 21.8
intestines and organs ⎭		⎱ 16.7
gut contents	16.3	12.0
liquid	2.0	6.6

Measurements of biomass provide a good indication of the standing crop supported by an ecosystem but they do not take into account such important factors as the turnover time (expressed as the ratio production:biomass) which will largely be determined by the generation time of the dominant species composing that community. The giant tortoises of Aldabra represent an almost single-species herbivore community whose generation time approximates that of the African elephant.

In addition to living for up to 65 years, the giant tortoise's body contains relatively little soft tissue. Dissections conducted by Swingland during the study of reproduction on Aldabra have indicated that 43 % of the tortoise's body mass is composed of bone while only 38 % is represented by soft tissue. If we compare these figures with those of the African elephant (Coe 1978) we note that only 18.6 % (or 30 % including the skin) is bone while 51.5 % makes up the contribution of soft tissues (table 5). Thus we might expect that the amount of annual production going into soft tissue and bone replacement would be much less in the tortoise than it is in the equally long-lived elephant, apart from obvious differences in their metabolism.

(e) Production

Coe *et al.* (1976) have examined the relation between rainfall and biomass, energy expenditure and secondary production for 24 wildlife ecosystems in Africa. Using production and biomass data in the literature, they have shown that the production:biomass ratio (P/B) for herbivores grouped into large (over 800 kg), intermediate (110–750 kg), and small (5–90 kg) size categories were respectively 0.05, 0.20, and 0.35. When data for the large herbivore biomasses were converted to production by using the above ratios they established that a linear relation existed between this parameter and rainfall (regression coefficient = 0.832; probability = <0.001).

Calculation of a P/B ratio for the Aldabra tortoise requires that annual production can be measured directly, or estimated indirectly. By using accurate data available on the age distribution of the Malabar and Grande Terre populations it is possible to calculate a mean survival time and from this to estimate the percentage of the population that can be presumed to be turned over or replaced each year. Age distributions given by Grubb (1971) and Bourn & Coe (1978) yield P/B ratios of 0.074 (7.4% a^{-1}) for Grande Terre and 0.064 (6.4% a^{-1}) for Malabar. Since, however, the age distribution data available only refer to those animals up to 30 years old which can be aged directly from scute rings, these P/B ratios do not take into account those animals in the population that are older than 30 years. It is therefore to be expected that the actual rate of turnover will be 1–2% below the 6.4–7.4% estimated above.

An alternative approach is to estimate the animal biomass lost by mortality and assuming that the population is relatively stable (Bourn & Coe 1978; Swingland & Coe 1979, this volume) at present, this figure can be taken to be equivalent to the amount of material being added each year in secondary production.

Bourn & Coe (1978) have calculated that the annual mortality rates for the Malabar and Grande Terre population are respectively 2.7 and 2.9% for animals over 60 cm curved length. We may therefore estimate that on Malabar 19 animals per square kilometre die each year compared with 44 on Grande Terre. The mortality of animals on Grande Terre has been estimated by 5 year age classes from 15–65 years (Bourn & Coe 1978). If the mean individual tortoise mass is calculated for each of these age classes it is possible to derive the biomass lost each year to the population owing to mortality. Thus for the Grande Terre animals we may obtain a P/B ratio of 0.04. Since, however, this figure does not take into account those animals lost each year from the 0.15 year age classes, a correction has been calculated based on the percentage of animals which falls in these three 5 year age classes, from which we obtain a corrected P/B ratio of 0.042.

The low population size on Malabar presents difficulties in estimating mortality in individual age classes. If, however, the mean mass per 5 year age class is calculated and a figure of 2.71% mortality per annum is used in the same proportions that animals are observed to die on Grande Terre we obtain a P/B ratio of 0.033 for the 15–65 year age classes and 0.034 for the whole age range of 0–65 years.

Table 4 shows the estimated annual tortoise production in relation to biomass and density from the above ratios. It is immediately apparent that in spite of the high densities and biomasses recorded on Grande Terre the annual production ranges from only 149 kg km^{-2} a^{-1} in the *Pemphis* areas to 2450.8 in the densely populated areas of the southeast, the mean production for the whole land area being 1486 kg km^{-2} a^{-1}. Similarly for Malabar the annual secondary production for the census area occupied by tortoises is 1193 and 137 kg km^{-2} a^{-1} for the whole island. By using the same P/B ratio as Malabar for Picard in the absence of adequate mortality data to calculate the ratio separately, annual productions of 862 km kg^{-2} a^{-2} are obtained for the tortoise area and 288 for the whole island.

The production figures for Malabar are close (-26%) to that of Grande Terre indicating that although the population of the former is so much less dense, the larger body size ($+130\%$) of these animals allows them to achieve similar production, suggesting that we are observing two strategies for operating within the available food resources. Swingland (1976) has suggested that the greater shade cover on Malabar allows these animals to achieve greater size by spending longer periods feeding.

We have calculated that the tortoises of Grande Terre eat 0.136 kg m^{-2} a^{-1} or 136 000 kg km^{-2} a^{-1}. If we therefore use a gross assimilation efficiency of 50 %, the population should assimilate 72 050 kg km^{-2} a^{-1}. The population has, however, only been calculated to produce 1486 kg km^{-2} a^{-1} in secondary production, which only represents 2.1 % of the material assimilated.

McNeill & Lawton (1970) have examined the relation between annual production and respiration and have demonstrated that they can distinguish regressions for homeotherms and poikilotherms. Additionally, though, they have also shown that they can distinguish data for long-lived poikilotherms (animals in which a proportion of the population exceeds 2 years of age) from short-lived poikilotherms (animals in which all individuals live less than 2 years). Although they do not include data for reptiles they have presented data for five species of fish which are comparatively long lived. The percentage of energy going to production is here expressed as a percentage of that being available from assimilation (production + respiration). These figures vary from 7.7 % for the roach (*Rutilus rutilus* L.) to 6.0 % for the dace (*Leuciscus leuciscus* L.), which are very low compared with those obtained for short-lived poikilotherms which may achieve production efficiencies as high as 62 %. McNeill & Lawton (1970) explain the low production efficiencies of long-lived poikilotherms in terms of the high respiratory cost, and extended non-productive periods experienced by animals that live for more than 2 years. Clearly, for an animal like the giant tortoise of Aldabra, we not only know that these creatures are very long lived but also that they experience long dry periods when their production must be virtually nil. Thus in terms of the tentative production efficiency calculated above (2.1 %) this figure would appear to be of the right order of magnitude. In the event, however, that further work on feeding may well reveal a lower gross assimilation efficiency (*ca.* 30 %), the production efficiency will still only be raised to 3.6 %. Heatwole (1976) has presented data for the Australian Scincid Lizard (*Egernia cunninghami*) taken from Shine (1971) where the production efficiency for growth is less than 1 %.

3. DISCUSSION

We have shown that the high biomass of giant tortoises on Aldabra tells us very little about the manner in which the resources of this Indian Ocean island can sustain such a large herbivore standing crop. When, however, we calculated the P/B ratio for this long-lived reptile we found that the secondary production represents only 3–4 % of the standing crop biomass. It is now necessary for us to examine the relations of the annual production data to factors which may potentially limit production and through it the standing crop biomass. Clearly, shade is an important factor which may drastically limit the time available for feeding in a cold-blooded vertebrate, which may account for the difference in mean mass between animals on Grande Terre and Malabar. Here it is argued that the availability of food both in terms of quantity and quality is liable to influence animal size, their numbers and recruitment.

Coe *et al.* (1976) have produced a predictive equation by which production and biomass may be calculated from the mean annual rainfall. This relation is valid up to 700 mm and is not expected to deviate significantly up to the mean rainfall for Aldabra (941 mm a^{-1}). These expressions may therefore be used to predict the herbivore production and biomass for comparison with that estimated for Aldabra. Table 6 compares the relation between the estimated production with that predicted from the expression

$$(1.649 \pm 0.486) \, x - (1.720 \pm 1.357) \quad [x = 2.973].$$

It will be observed that while estimated production for the whole atoll deviates by up to 60 % from that of predicted production (1525 kg km^{-2} a^{-1}), that for the area occupied by tortoises only differs by 23 %. Additionally, and most notably, there is the fact that the production estimated for Grande Terre (where 98 % of the tortoise population is located) only differs by 2.6 % from that predicted from the mean rainfall. This would suggest that if we accept that the level of primary production is dependent on available precipitation, the present tortoise population of Grande Terre closely approximates the 'carrying capacity'.

TABLE 6. ESTIMATED AND PREDICTED PRODUCTION

	mean biomass kg km^{-2}	estimated production† kg km^{-2}	predicted production‡ kg km^{-2}	% difference between estimated and predicted productions
Grande Terre	35 387	1486	1525	−2.6
Malabar				
whole area	4 017	137	1525	−91.0
tortoise area	35 084	1193	1525	−21.8
Picard				
whole area	8 480	288	1525	−81.1
tortoise area	25 342	862	1525	−43.5
mean				
whole area	15 961	637	1525	−58.2
tortoise area	31 937	1180	1525	−22.6

† Estimated production for Grande Terre = biomass (0.042) kg km^{-2} a^{-1}; estimated production for Malabar and Picard = biomass (0.034) kg km^{-2} a^{-1}.

‡ Predicted production = $(1.649 \pm 0.486) \, 2.973 - (1.720 \pm 1.357)$ (formula after Coe et al. 1976).

Semi-arid environments on the African mainland are characterized by large annual variations in rainfall, so that while the mean rainfall may indicate the general level of primary production available to herbivores it does not take into account short-term and perhaps periodic fluctuations in climate. If we assume that there are periodic climate fluctuations, we can predict that the potential 'carrying capacity' of Aldabra in terms of available food resources may vary with the same period. Although the mean annual precipitation on Aldabra is 941 mm, measurements during the operation of the Royal Society meteorological station suggest that since 1968 the mean rainfall has been 1070 mm, which would sustain an annual tortoise production of 1886 kg km^{-2}. The highest and lowest rainfalls recorded by the station have been 547 mm (1968) and 1487 mm (1974) which would sustain annual productions of respectively 624 and 3245 kg km^{-2} a^{-1}. Thus it would appear that the present observed biomass on Grande Terre is closely related to the mean annual rainfall in terms of the annual production achieved by the tortoise population.

On the African mainland, large herbivores with relatively long generation times are incapable of taking advantage of short-term variation in rainfall. Indeed Phillipson (1975) has shown that low rainfall and concomitant low primary production can be related to catastrophic death in the elephant populations of the Tsabo National Park, Keyna. In contrast with this situation, the tortoises of Aldabra simply stop growing during drought and provided these periods are comparatively short they can maintain a high biomass but reduce their annual production. The manner in which the tortoises can respond to sudden increases in rainfall and food is exemplified by the study of their reproduction (Swingland & Coe 1978), which has shown that during a period of increased and unseasonal rain in 1975 the animals of Grande Terre increased the number of eggs per nest and mean egg mass in an almost immediate response to increased food availability. Hence although the tortoises of Aldabra have a similar generation time and P/B ratio to that of the African elephant (0.05) their response to temporal variations in climate and food supply is more reminiscent of that of insects, small mammals and birds which may respond immediately to sudden rain and produce large numbers of young.

The production data we have examined above refer only to the mean recorded on the whole of Grande Terre and do not take into account the high densities and biomass observed in the southeast of this island. Here a biomass of 58 352 kg km^{-2} would be estimated to sustain an annual production of 2451 kg km^{-2} a^{-1} which is 61% higher than that predicted from its rainfall.

TABLE 7. COMPARATIVE BIOMASS AND PRODUCTION DATA FOR AFRICAN WILDLIFE ECOSYSTEMS AND ALDABRA

locality	rainfall	estimated production kg km^{-2}	biomass kg km^{-2}	predicted biomass[†] kg km^{-2}	predicted production[†] kg km^{-2}	% difference between estimated and predicted production
Amboseli (Kenya)	350	934	4848	1555	299	+68
Rwidindi (Zaire)	863	1936	17448	7115	1323	+31
Manyara (Tanzania)	915	2405	19189	7852	1457	+39
Rwenzori (Uganda)	1010	2554	19928	9274	1714	+33
Aldabra (SE Grande Terre)	941	2450	58352	8231	1525	+61

[†] Predicted biomass $= (1.685 \pm 0.238)x - (1.095 \pm 0.661)$; predicted production $= (1.649 \pm 0.486)x - (1.720 \pm 1.357)$, where $x =$ mean annual precipitation. (Both after Coe *et al.* 1976).

Coe *et al.* (1976) noted that of the 24 wildlife systems examined for the African mainland, four of them exceeded the potential large herbivore 'carrying capacity'. On examining the data for these four areas, they concluded that four of them were supplied with abundant ground water while the fourth was located on a fertile volcanic soil. Under these circumstances we might expect that the available primary production might exceed that predicted from measures of mean rainfall. Table 7 compares the biomass and production data for these four areas and demonstrates that their estimated production exceeds that estimated from standing crop biomass by between 30 and 68%. The large production observed in Amboseli being in large part accounted for by the presence of a large swamp area fed by abundant spring water from Kilimanjaro. Southeast Grande Terre on Aldabra seems to fall into the same category as Amboseli, for its estimated production exceeds that predicted from rainfall by 61%. While there are clearly few direct similarities between these two areas the availability of ground water may well be a significant factor. In most arid regions of the world, rainwater is rapidly lost by percolation and runoff, but in the east and southeast of Grande Terre a large lens of fresh water is raised close to the surface by high spring tides which would make much of the precipitation potentially available for plant growth even in the absence of appreciable rain. Additionally but of probably minor significance, is the presence of guano-based soils (Piggott 1968) in this area. It is perhaps no coincidence that the genetically dwarfed 'tortoise turf' (Merton *et al.* 1976) which is so abundant on Grande Terre and of great importance as tortoise food may also be related to the availability of this periodically abundant ground water and perhaps also to the pockets of fertile soil on which it occurs.

The authors would like to thank the Royal Society who provided logistical support for this work on Aldabra. During the preparation of this manuscript we have had the benefit of discussions with Professor George Dunnett and Dr John Phillipson. The population dynamics and reproductive phases of the tortoise programme have been supported by generous grants from the Natural Environment Research Council. Last but by no means least we would like to thank the Seychellois of Aldabra without whose technical help and field skills this work would never have been completed.

REFERENCES (Coe *et al.*)

Bourn, D. 1976 The giant tortoise population of Aldabra (Cryptodira: Testudinidae). Part 1. Preliminary results. *Zool. afr.* **11**, 275–284.

Bourn, D. & Coe, M. 1978 The size, structure and distribution of the giant tortoise population of Aldabra. *Phil. Trans. R. Soc. Lond.* B **282**, 139–175.

Braithwaite, C. J. R., Taylor, J. D. & Kennedy, W. J. 1973 The evolution of an atoll: the depositional and erosional history of Aldabra. *Phil. Trans. R. Soc. Lond.* B **266**, 307–340.

Cobb, S. 1977 The distribution and abundance of the large herbivore community of Tsavo National Park, Kenya. D.Phil. thesis, University of Oxford.

Coe, M. J., Cumming, D. H. & Phillipson, J. 1976 Biomass and production of large African herbivores in relation to rainfall and primary production. *Oecologia* **22**, 341–354.

Coe, M. J. 1977 The decomposition of elephant carcases in the Tsavo (East) National Park, Kenya. *J. arid. Envir.* **1**, 71–86.

Fitch, H. S. 1967 Ecological studies of lizards on the University of Kansas Natural History Reservation. In *Lizard ecology: a symposium.* Columbia: University of Missouri Press.

Frazier, J. G. 1971 Behavioural and ecological observations on Giant tortoises on Aldabra Atoll. D.Phil. thesis, Oxford University.

Gaymer, R. 1968 The Indian Ocean Giant tortoise *Testudo gigantea* on Aldabra. *J. Zool., Lond.* **154**, 341–363.

Gaymer, R. 1973 A marking method for giant tortoises and field trials on Aldabra. *J. Zool., Lond.* **169**, 393–401.

Graham, A. 1968 The Lake Rudolf crocodile (*Crocodylus niloticus* Laurentis) population. M.Sc. thesis, University of Nairobi.

Grubb, P. 1971 The growth, ecology and population structure of giant tortoises on Aldabra. *Phil. Trans. R. Soc. Lond.* B. **260**, 327–372.

Harris, V. A. 1964 *The life of the rainbow lizard.* London: Hutchinson.

Heatwole, H. 1976 *Reptile ecology.* Brisbane: University of Queensland Press.

McNeill, S. & Lawton, J. H. 1970 Animal production and respiration in animal populations. *Nature, Lond.* **255**, 472–474.

Merton, L. F. H., Bourn, D. M. & Hnatiuk, R. J. 1976 Giant tortoise and vegetation interactions on Aldabra Atoll. Part 1: inland. *Biol. Conserv.* **9**, 292–304.

Morgan, D. D. V. 1976 A statistical study of data on Giant tortoises on Aldabra. M.Sc. thesis, University of Oxford.

Morgan, D. D. V. & Bourn, D. M. 1978 A comparison of two methods of estimating the size of a population of giant tortoise on Aldabra. Manuscript.

Palombelli, F. 1954 L'isola della tartorughe. *Epoca* **7**, March issue.

Phillipson. J. 1975 Rainfall, primary production and 'carrying capacity' of Tsavo National Park (East), Kenya. *E. Afr. Wildl. J.* **13**, 171–201.

Piggott, C. J. 1968 *Soil survey of Seychelles. Tech. Bull.* no. **2**, Ministry of Overseas Development, Directorate of Overseas Surveys, London.

Rees, P. A. 1977 Some aspects of the feeding ecology of the African elephant (*Loxodonta africana africana* Blumenbach 1797) in captivity. Honours thesis, University of Liverpool.

Rosenzweig, M. L. 1968 Net primary productivity of terrestrial communities: production from climatological data. *Am. Nat.* **102**, 67–74.

Ruibal, R. & Philibosian, R. 1974 The population ecology of the lizard *Anolis acutus. Ecology* **55**, 525–37.

Shine, R. 1971 The ecological energetics of the scincid lizard *Egernia cunninghami* (Gray 1832). Unpublished Hons. thesis, Australian National University, Canberra.

Stoddart, D. R. & Mole, L. V. 1977 Climate of Aldabra. *Atoll Res. Bull.* **202**, 1–21.

Stoddart, D. R. & Peake, J. F. 1979 Historical records of Indian Ocean giant tortoise populations. *Phil. Trans. R. Soc. Lond.* B **286**, 147–161 (this volume).

Stoddart, D. R. & Walsh, R. P. D. 1979 Long-term climatic change in the western Indian Ocean. *Phil. Trans. R. Soc. Lond.* B, **286**, 11–23 (this volume).

Swingland, I. R. 1976 Ecological studies of the giant land tortoise *Geochelone gigantea* on Aldabra Island. Report to Aldabra Research Committee, April 1976, pp. 1–14.

Swingland, I. R. & Coe, M. J. 1979 The natural regulation of giant tortoise populations on Aldabra Atoll: recruitment. *Phil. Trans. R. Soc. Lond.* B **286**, 177–188 (this volume).

Taylor, J. D., Braithwaite, C. J. R., Peake, J. F. & Arnold, E. N. 1979 Terrestrial faunas and habitats of Aldabra during the late Pleistocene. *Phil. Trans. R. Soc. Lond.* B **286**, 47–66 (this volume).

Tinkle, D. W. 1967 Home range, density, dynamics and structure of a Texas population of the lizard *Uta stansburiana*. In *Lizard ecology: a symposium.* Columbia: University of Missouri Press.

Walter, H. 1954 Le facteur eau dans les régions arides et sa signification pour l'organisation de la végétation dans les contrées sub-tropicales. In *Les divisions ecologiques du monde.* Paris: C.N.R.S.

Western, D. 1974 The distribution, density and biomass density of lizards in a semi-arid environment in Northern Kenya. *E. Afr. Wildl. J.* **12**, 49–62.

Whittaker, R. H. 1970 *Communities and ecosystems.* London: Collier-Macmillan.

Phil. Trans. R. Soc. Lond. B. **286**, 177-188 (1979)   [177]

Printed in Great Britain

The natural regulation of giant tortoise populations on Aldabra Atoll: recruitment

By I. R. Swingland and M. J. Coe

Animal Ecology Research Group, Department of Zoology, University of Oxford,
South Parks Road, Oxford OX1 3PS, U.K.

The reproductive ecology of the giant tortoise (*Geochelone gigantea* Schweigger) in three isolated populations was studied for 2 years on Aldabra Atoll.

Density-dependent recruitment was demonstrated. Nest destruction in the low density area was dependent on the density of mature females providing a mechanism for regulating population size. Increases in annual rainfall and the resultant increase in food availability induced an increase in mean egg mass in the low density area (and thereby total hatchling production), whereas in the high density population mean clutch size, mean egg mass, total number of nests and total hatchling production all increased significantly. Large eggs produced large hatchlings which survived better during the first year than hatchlings from small eggs.

Hatchling mortality was 94 and 81 % in the first year in the high and low density populations respectively. Recruitment into the 5 year age class (after which predation is considered negligible) had almost ceased in the high density population compared with 0.44 per 100 breeding females per year in the low density population.

Introduction

Aldabra Atoll (in the western Indian Ocean) has the largest population (150 000) of giant land tortoises known. Because the Atoll is split by lagoon passes into a number of discrete land masses, the tortoise populations on three of these masses (Picard, Malabar and Grande Terre), which have different population densities, are isolated from one another.

The Aldabran giant tortoise (*Geochelone gigantea* Schweigger) is a tractable subject for ecological research because (i) it is long lived; (ii) it retains a record of growth and ageing by deposition of rings on the scutes; (iii) it is a seasonal breeder facilitating monitoring of the nests and hatchlings; (iv) it is the principal herbivore; and (v) the adults are not affected by predation, most deaths being caused by thermal stress. The uniqueness of this situation gives an unusual opportunity to make a comparative study of natural regulation in a terrestrial vertebrate population.

By using information on the Aldabran giant tortoise, an attempt has been made to answer four main questions: (i) what are the limiting factors determining the mean level of a population; (ii) is regulation taking place; (iii) if so, what is the mechanism; and (iv) is the primary or ultimate cause of regulation resource limitation, predation or disease? This paper on recruitment is the third of a number concerning the natural regulation of tortoise populations on Aldabra Atoll (Swingland 1977; Swingland & Coe 1978).

Several theories on the natural regulation of animal numbers (Chitty 1960; Christian 1961; Wynne-Edwards 1962) require that variations in reproductive success act as a negative feedback regulator within the population. To investigate this, measurements of the reproductive rate over a period of time within two isolated populations are needed. That variations occur between populations of reptiles is well known (Tinkle 1961; Gibbons & Tinkle 1969; Ernst 1971; Christiansen & Moll 1973) but none have been shown to be density-dependent.

A further problem concerns whether or not nutrition influences reproductive rate. The changes in recruitment are described in two isolated populations of the Aldabran giant tortoise over a period of 2 years (1975 and 1976). Some information on individual growth, mortality, nest destruction, predation and ovarian characteristics is also presented. These data are discussed in relation to variations in rainfall, population density and food supply.

THE STUDY AREAS

Two principal study areas were used in this work, southeast Grande Terre and eastern Malabar. The Grande Terre study area was 11 km² while that of Malabar was 2 km².

The highest tortoise densities occur in southeast Grande Terre where there is low vegetation or bare ground and where there is little, but at least some, shade (Bourn & Coe 1978). Tortoises, although browsers as well as grazers, are primarily grazers, feeding largely on grasses, herbs and sedges, e.g. 'tortoise turf' (Grubb 1971; Merton et al. 1976) and Sporobolus virginicus L. (Hnatiuk et al. 1976), which are the two major components of low vegetation. In areas composed mainly of bare ground there are large expanses of exposed rock, but there are also small soil pockets in which a variety of plant species commonly eaten by tortoises occur. High tortoise concentrations occur in habitats where favoured food plants are more plentiful. 'Tortoise turf' is a complex of at least 21 plant species whose growth form has been suggested by Grubb (1971) and Merton et al. (1976) to be the result of selection through intense tortoise grazing pressure. Moreover, the effects of heavy browsing are conspicuous with browse lines on most tree species, particularly on those woody plant species which are palatable (Grubb 1971; Frazier 1972; Merton et al. 1976). Tortoises, through their activities by shading, are responsible for considerable soil erosion and the death of many trees and shrubs with the resultant reduction in the amount of shade cover (Merton et al. 1976). Indeed a significant relation exists between tortoise density and the density of dead trees (I.R.S.).

The Malabar population is restricted to the comparatively open mixed scrub of a relatively narrow coastal belt on the ocean side of the island. This vegetation type is coincident with and probably dependent on, the underlying rock structure of Aldabra Limestone (Braithwaite et al. 1973), which has some accumulations of soil in which various grasses, sedges and herbs commonly eaten by tortoises (Grubb 1971; Frazier 1972) are found. Very dense scrub, dominated by Pemphis acidula Forst., is further inland and grows on Takamaka Limestone. It is at a slightly lower elevation, much more deeply pitted and eroded, has very little soil and few forms of low vegetation. This scrub is not inhabited by tortoises.

Unlike southeast Grande Terre, Malabar has (i) no residual pools of freshwater during the dry season, (ii) abundant shade, (iii) no evidence of overbrowsing or overgrazing, (iv) few areas suitable for nesting, and (v) a much less dense population (7 per hectare compared with 27). Moreover, the tortoises on Malabar continue to grow almost throughout the year in contrast to Grande Terre (I.R.S.) and are larger for their age (Bourn & Coe 1978).

In order to collect comparative information on tortoise densities and clutch size, two additional study areas were investigated in 1976. The first area, Picard, has a tortoise density of 5 per hectare and in most other respects is similar to Malabar. The second lies just outside the main Malabar study area and consists of two adjacent nesting sites, both approximately 20 m².

Methods

Data on the location of nests, clutch size, egg mass, fertility, the number of eggs that successfully hatched and the number of hatchlings that left the nest were obtained from the 431 nests examined, 206 from southeast Grande Terre, 213 from Malabar, and 12 from Picard. In the first year (1975) intensive nest searches were carried out each month during the laying season beginning in June. Once a nest had been located and opened for examination it was closed and left undisturbed until November by which time those eggs which would hatch had done so. In the second year (1976) the same procedure was adopted, although special attention was paid to searching the same nest areas used in the previous year.

After the nest had been located and opened the eggs were removed, individually marked with a pencil, weighed, measured and replaced in the nest in the same order. Care was taken to ensure that the orientation of the egg remained the same at all times to avoid tearing or damaging the embryo inside. The nest was marked.

By examining the eggs and interfering with the nests it was possible that the successful development of the eggs may have been impeded or that the chance of a predator locating and destroying the eggs was increased. To test this, several nests were left unopened in each nest site and their success compared with neighbouring opened nests. No significant differences were found between opened and unopened nests in terms of the proportion of successfully hatched eggs ($t = 1.6$, $n = 40$, $p > 0.10$) or in increasing the incidence of predation ($t = 2.3$, $n = 40, p > 0.01$).

For the purposes of this paper, recruitment is defined as the number of hatchlings per 100 adult females. Once they have left the nest they lead a secretive existence for up to 2–3 years. Hatchlings were marked and intensive searches carried out up to 1 year after emergence (from the nest) in an attempt to estimate mortality.

The method of determining age was the same as in Bourn & Coe (1978) or by counting annual rings on the scutes. Rainfall data were collected using standardized plastic rain gauges (Hnatiuk 1979, this volume).

The variables in the following analyses were normally distributed, and Student two-tailed t and z-score tests were used to compare mean values.

Results

Seasonality of breeding

On both Malabar and Grande Terre the first nests were found in late June (slightly earlier on Grande Terre in 1976) and nesting continued until late September, the peak being in July and August. Moreover, hatching occurred from early October and mid-December. The data show that incubation periods varied from 98 to 148 days and that the earlier a nest is laid during the nesting season, the longer the incubation period. Additionally once the yolk sac is absorbed the hatchling emerges from the nest from mid-October to December. This is before and at the start of the single rainy season.

Maturity and age-specific fertility

Information from post-mortem examinations (Swingland & Coe 1978) indicates that female tortoises reach sexual maturity on Grande Terre at 23 ± 1.7 years and 17 ± 0.8 years on Malabar (age determination from a modification of the method used by Bourn & Coe (1978)), the criterion of sexual maturity in females being the presence of pre-ovulatory follicles or corpora lutea. Maturity in males was somewhat less clearly defined and was determined by a seasonal increase in size of the testes during the copulation season (January–June). Males on Malabar reach sexual maturity at 20 ± 2.3 years and on Grande Terre at 26 ± 5.8 years. The mean age of copulating males was 29 ± 2.8 years on Grande Terre but 21 ± 4.3 years on Malabar. Grande Terre males appear to mature before they are of sufficient size to mount females successfully.

No cases of reproductive senescence were observed and there was no detectable relation between age and the numbers of non-atretic pre-ovulatory follicles at the beginning of the nesting season (i.e. potential clutch size) in either study area (Swingland & Coe 1978). The information from examinations *post mortem* indicates that most sexually mature females in both study areas had follicles of pre-ovulatory size (> 3.5 cm) during March and April, a month or two before nesting (Swingland & Coe 1978).

The incidence of infertility in eggs is difficult to determine. Where an egg had been cracked or broken during laying the whole clutch would generally become infected regardless of fertility. Moreover, as infertility could only be determined by the absence of embryonic development, eggs which had become infected at an early stage, although perhaps fertile, would appear infertile. Nevertheless, a crude estimate of infertility from nests which did not contain mechanically damaged eggs nor any evidence of having produced live young varied between 10 and 20 % with no difference between Malabar and Grande Terre.

TABLE 1. POPULATION DENSITY, CLUTCH SIZE, EGG MASS AND REPRODUCTIVE
SUCCESS IN TWO ISOLATED POPULATIONS (1975–6)

	Grande Terre	Malabar
mean tortoise density per hectare (± s.e.)	27.0 ± 1.8 ($n = 168$)	7.0 ± 0.7 ($n = 32$)
mean clutch size (± s.e.)	4.9 ± 0.1 ($n = 206$)	13.7 ± 0.5 ($n = 213$)
mean egg mass (± s.e.)	78.5 ± 0.6 g ($n = 1008$)	87.1 ± 0.9 g ($n = 2913$)
mean live hatchlings per clutch (± s.e.)	3.8 ± 0.5 ($n = 206$)	8.1 ± 0.3 ($n = 213$)

All figures within rows are significantly different at $p < 0.01$.

MEAN POPULATION REPRODUCTIVE SUCCESS

The mean population density in southeast Grande Terre was nearly four times higher than on Malabar (Bourn & Coe 1978). Moreover, the mean clutch size on Grande Terre was almost three times smaller than on Malabar, the eggs were smaller, and fewer hatchlings emerged successfully from a nest (table 1). Nevertheless, nearly 80 % of Grande Terre eggs produced hatchlings whereas only 60 % of Malabar eggs were successful.

As has already been mentioned, Malabar, in contrast to Grande Terre, has few nesting areas, which resulted in high levels of nest destruction by nesting females. No records of nest destruction were recorded from Grande Terre. The mean annual density of mature females is correlated to the proportion of nests destroyed (figure 1).

The trend of increasing clutch size with decreasing population density is corroborated when the figures from Picard are included (table 2). Nevertheless, this trend is not followed by mean egg mass which, although larger at Malabar than Grande Terre, is actually smaller on Picard.

However, if one considers the individual reproductive output ((mean egg mass) × (mean clutch size)) the effect of increasing density on suppressing reproduction can be seen (1450:1260: 432 for Picard:Malabar:Grande Terre).

The study areas are considered to be representative of the two populations and their habitats. On Grande Terre, the study area covered most of the southeastern portion; moreover, three nests found at Dune Blanc, where the population density is 20 ± 2.3 tortoises per hectare, had four, five and six eggs, the mean of which is similar to the study area mean clutch size of five. Likewise the study areas on Malabar and Picard did not circumscribe the whole of the two islands. The figures of clutch size and egg mass from Picard were collected on two successive occasions in 1976 and no significant differences were found between samples ($t = 1.4–1.7$, $p > 0.05$). Those figures from the Malabar study area (table 3), when compared with those from another neighbouring area, also show no significant differences.

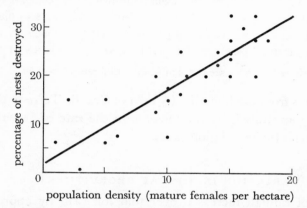

FIGURE 1. The relation between the proportion of nests destroyed and the density of mature females on Malabar. Regression coefficient = 0.78; probability < 0.01.

TABLE 2 COMPARISON OF CLUTCH SIZE, EGG MASS, POPULATION DENSITY AND 'REPRODUCTIVE OUTPUT' IN THREE ISOLATED POPULATIONS (1976)

	Grande Terre	Malabar	Picard
mean tortoise density per hectare ($\pm$ s.e.)	27.0 ± 1.8 ($n = 168$)	7.0 ± 0.7 ($n = 32$)	5.0†
mean clutch size ($\pm$ s.e.)	5.3 ± 0.2 ($n = 129$)	14.0 ± 1.1 ($n = 84$)	19.2 ± 0.7 ($n = 12$)
mean egg mass ($\pm$ s.e.)	81.6 ± 0.7 g ($n = 684$)	90.0 ± 1.3 g ($n = 1176$)	75.5 ± 0.4 g ($n = 230$)
individual reproductive output‡	432	1260	1450

All figures within rows are significantly different at $p < 0.01$.
† Extensive search estimate.
‡ (Mean egg mass) × (mean clutch size).

The production of more than one set of eggs in a single breeding season is common in reptiles, particularly chelonians, but is often undetected. It is practically impossible to observe the same female tortoise in successive natural layings. Most of our evidence for multiple clutches is inferential and based on examination of the ovaries of 115 females. The ovaries of mature females from Grande Terre showed no evidence of both old and fresh sets of corpora lutea and since these structures regress and disappear within a few weeks of ovulation there is little chance that a set from one breeding season would persist to the next. However, on Malabar all mature ovaries showed evidence of different sets of corpora lutea during the nesting season indicating they would have laid from two to four clutches (mean 2.2 ± 0.9 clutches per year). The presence of sets of corpora lutea of differing sizes together with non-atretic pre-ovulatory follicles were commonly found in females from Malabar but not in females from Grande Terre.

Although the importance of follicular atresia or regression in chelonian ovarian cycles is not clearly understood, an experiment carried out during 1976 (Swingland & Coe 1978) suggests that a reduced (or an inadequate) diet induces atresia in pre-ovulatory follicles. The contention that food may be limiting on Grande Terre is also supported by the retarded/suppressed growth, and the delay in maturity, of individuals in this high density population compared with Malabar.

TABLE 3. COMPARISON OF CLUTCH SIZE, EGG MASS, AND REPRODUCTIVE
SUCCESS IN TWO AREAS ON MALABAR (1976)

	main study area	comparative study area
mean clutch size ($\pm$ s.e.)	14.0 ± 1.1 ($n = 84$)	14.7 ± 0.9 ($n = 45$)
mean egg mass ($\pm$ s.e.)	90.0 ± 1.3 g ($n = 1176$)	90.8 ± 1.4 g ($n = 662$)
mean live hatchlings per clutch ($\pm$ s.e.)	9.2 ± 0.7 ($n = 84$)	8.8 ± 1.4 ($n = 45$)

Figures within rows are not significantly different ($p > 0.50$).

Translocation of tortoises from the high density area of Grande Terre to the very low density area of Picard clearly demonstrated, by the increase in the rate of growth (over 80%), the food limitations under which the population exists.

VARIATION IN ANNUAL RECRUITMENT

In 1976 the amount of rainfall increased over that for 1975 by approximately 40% by raining significantly more in January and March and by continuing to rain longer (through June, July and August) into the dry season (i.e. nesting season). Because of this unusually extended wet season, tortoises continued to feed actively, particularly on Grande Terre where various shrubs atypically flowered and fruited (also R. P. Prŷs-Jones 1976, personal communication). Additionally the white growth rings around scute margins, indicative of growth, persisted for longer than usual in Grande Terre animals.

On Malabar this increase in rainfall did not affect the numbers of nests present nor did it significantly increase the clutch size (see table 4). However, egg mass did increase by 10% and total hatchling production increased by 35%. In contrast on Grande Terre there was no significant change in the number of hatchlings produced from each nest; therefore the principal reason for the increase in total hatchling production (55%) was due to the increase in the number of nests (67%) (table 5). This increase in nests was caused either by breeding females' producing multiple clutches or a greater proportion of the mature females' breeding. Nevertheless, no evidence of multiple clutches was seen during post-mortem examination.

SEX RATIO OF HATCHLINGS

The sex ratio of the hatchlings was determined by dissection. On Grande Terre, of 43 hatchlings examined, 21 were males and 22 females; from Malabar, of 37 hatchlings, 18 were males and 19 were females. Combining the figures, a total of 39 males and 41 females have been recorded, indicating an equal sex ratio at birth.

TABLE 4. RAINFALL-INDUCED MODIFICATIONS OF REPRODUCTIVE RATE
AND SUCCESS ON MALABAR (1975–6)

	1975	1976	percentage change
corrected total rainfall, October–September	878 mm	1205 mm	+37†
mean clutch size (± s.e.)	12.8 ± 0.7 (n = 84)	14.0 ± 1.1 (n = 84)	+9
mean egg mass (± s.e.)	81.8 ± 0.7 g (n = 1075)	90.0 ± 1.3 g (n = 1176)	+10†
mean egg mass per clutch	1047 g (n = 84)	1260 g (n = 84)	+20†
total number of nests	84	84	—
mean live hatchlings per clutch (± s.e.)	6.8 ± 0.6 (n = 84)	9.2 ± 0.7 (n = 84)	+35†
total live hatchling production	571	773	+35†

† Significant at $p < 0.01$.

TABLE 5. RAINFALL-INDUCED MODIFICATIONS OF REPRODUCTIVE RATE
AND SUCCESS ON GRANDE TERRE (1975–6)

	1975	1976	percentage change
corrected total rainfall, October–September	923 mm	1315 mm	+43†
mean clutch size (± s.e.)	4.3 ± 0.2 (n = 77)	5.3 ± 0.2 (n = 129)	+23†
mean egg mass (± s.e.)	70.5 ± 1.4 g (n = 332)	81.6 ± 0.7 g (n = 685)	+16†
mean egg mass per clutch	303 g (n = 77)	432 g (n = 129)	+42†
total number of nests	77	129	+67†
mean live hatchlings per clutch (± s.e.)	4.0 ± 0.7 (n = 77)	3.7 ± 0.2 (n = 129)	−8
total live hatchling production	308	477	+55†

† Significant at $p < 0.01$.

NEST AND HATCHLING PREDATION

The incidence of predation is higher on eggs and hatchlings than any other stage in the life cycle. On Malabar the major nest predator is the coconut crab (*Birgus latro* L.). Moreover, the density of *Birgus* increases as the density of nests increases (figure 2), which is not so on Grande Terre where the principal nest predator is the land crab (*Cardisoma carnifex* Latr.). The incidence of nest predation here is lower (7 compared with 17 %) and occurs at any time throughout the period of incubation whereas on Malabar nest predation is highest during the period when the hatchlings are erupting from the nest (October and November). *Birgus*, *Cardisoma*, the white-throated rail (*Dryolimnas cuvieri* Pucheran) and the rat (*Rattus rattus* L.) are the main predators of hatchlings. The rail is not found on Grande Terre.

Immediate post-emergence recruitment figures, where Grande Terre females are taken to lay one clutch per year (an overestimate, as not all adult females will breed annually) and Malabar females an average of 2.2 clutches per year, is 3–5 times higher per 100 mature females on Malabar than on Grande Terre (Malabar 924 in 1975, 1251 in 1976; Grande Terre 379 in 1975, 370 in 1976). However, in reviewing these figures it must be borne in mind that, although hatchling recruitment per 100 adult females did not increase on Grande Terre because of the greater proportion of adult females that laid in 1976, the total hatchling production did increase (table 5).

RECRUITMENT AND HATCHLING MORTALITY

Of 100 marked hatchlings released by hand from nests on Malabar (once their yolk sacs were absorbed) in 1975, 19 were found after an exhaustive search 1 year later. An equal number of marked hatchlings were released on Grande Terre and a year later only 6 could be found.

Assuming all those alive were found this represents a maximum mortality rate during the first year of 94 % on Grande Terre and 81 % on Malabar. The denser vegetation and heavily dissected champignon (rock substrate type) of Malabar compared with the more open habitat of SE Grande Terre and the predominance of the flat pavé and platin substrates made it more difficult to find young tortoises on Malabar than on Grande Terre.

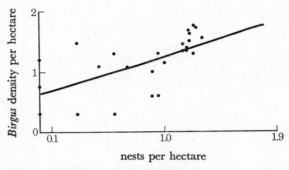

FIGURE 2. The relation between the density of the coconut crab (*Birgus latro* L.), the principal nest predator, and the density of nests on Malabar. Regression coefficient = 0.62; probability < 0.01.

TABLE 6. COMPARISON OF EGG MASS, HATCHLING MASS AND RELATIVE SURVIVAL
OF 100 HATCHLINGS RELEASED IN 1975 IN EACH STUDY AREA

	mean egg mass (± s.e.)	mean hatching mass (± s.e.)	minimum number surviving to one year
	g	g	
Malabar			
heaviest 50 eggs	86.7 ± 3.1	60 ± 4	13
lightest 50 eggs	78.3 ± 1.9	48 ± 5	6
Grande Terre			
heaviest 50 eggs	76.0 ± 2.3	42 ± 4	6
lightest 50 eggs	63.2 ± 5.6	32 ± 3	0

Figures within columns for each separate study area are significantly different at $p < 0.01$.

If one also assumes a steady mortality rate (although mortality rate would probably decrease) with increasing age until 5 years old, after which mortality by predation is assumed to be low and relatively constant, then the proportion in the population was an index of the minimum proportion that would reach sexual maturity. By 5 years old only 0.00008 of the original 100 would be alive on Grande Terre and 0.025 on Malabar; this represents 0.00030 five year olds per 100 breeding females per year on Grande Terre and 0.44 five year olds per 100 breeding females per year on Malabar. As there were 40 % fewer nests (table 5) on Grande Terre in 1975 than 1976, and assuming that this reflects a difference in the proportion of adult females breeding, then only 0.0002 five year olds per 100 breeding females per year would be recruited.

From the release of the 200 marked hatchlings it is suggested that larger eggs produce larger hatchlings which survive better than hatchlings from small eggs (table 6). The heaviest 50 eggs in each study area produced heavier hatchlings which survived better than hatchlings from the lightest 50 eggs.

Moreover, the change in mass over 1 year was greater in Grande Terre hatchlings (141 ± 22 g) than in Malabar hatchlings (106 ± 10 g).

DISCUSSION

The major density-dependent effects discussed in this paper are on age at sexual maturity, clutch size, egg mass, hatchling production and growth rate. The study of three isolated populations (Malabar, Grande Terre and Picard) of different densities from 5 to 27 per hectare emphasizes the extent of the reproductive adjustments and suggests that in the study areas these regulatory processes begin to operate at densities as low as 7 tortoises per hectare. On Picard (5 tortoises per hectare) clutch size was larger than on Malabar (7 tortoises per hectare). However, the Picard population was able to produce higher clutch sizes only at the expense of a reduction in egg masses. It has been suggested that large eggs produce large hatchlings which survive better than those from small eggs (also seen in birds; Skogland *et al.* 1952; Parsons 1970; Schifferli 1973). The high egg masses of the Malabar clutches (table 2) may be interpreted in terms of natural selection, implying that hatchlings in this area have greater problems in obtaining adequate food for the critical first few months than in either of the other two areas (Picard and Grande Terre). However, although few data exist on the differential growth rates of hatchlings in the three areas to support this suggestion, casual observations of the abundance of plants on Malabar, which are favoured by hatchlings, tend to confirm that there are far fewer than on Grande Terre or Picard. Additionally, Malabar hatchlings do not appear to increase in mass during the first year to the same extent as Grande Terre hatchlings.

The wide range of these reproductive adjustments (sexual maturity, clutch size, egg mass and hatchling production) implies a very considerable regulatory effect on recruitment; from the data it is evident that recruitment is influenced by population density and modified by rainfall. Such regulatory effects have been noticed in the African elephant (*Loxodonta africana* Blumenbach) by Laws (1969) and Hanks & McIntosh (1973).

Moreover, the changes in clutch size, egg mass and hatchling production clearly illustrate a very rapid response to climate changes for such a long-lived animal. The changes were most marked in the high-density population of Grande Terre where there is strong evidence to indicate that a large proportion of the mature females do not breed every year (Swingland & Coe 1978). The increase in rainfall during the second year was coincident with changes in reproductive rate not only on Grande Terre but to a lesser degree on Malabar. The fact that total hatchling production (tables 4 and 5) increased in parallel in the two populations suggests that the same external factor (rainfall) was the cause. Pianka (1970) noted latitudinal intra-specific differences in lizard populations where both clutch size and population density appeared to be positively correlated with rainfall.

The Malabar giant tortoise population is multiple-brooded with large clutches and early maturity while the Grande Terre population is single-brooded with small clutches and late sexual maturity. Thus although the Malabar reproductive characteristics agree with one of the categories of Tinkle *et al.* (1970), the Grande Terre population does not, having small clutches rather than large clutches; moreover, the early-maturing Malabar individuals produce larger eggs (not smaller eggs) than the late-maturing Grande Terre tortoises. Andrews

& Rand (1974) also rejected the suggestion that clutch size in tropical species is adjusted differently from that in temperate species because high intraspecific competition in the tropics would result in selection for large eggs with enhanced survivorship rather than for large clutch size. We also contest this suggestion in that the Grande Terre females produced small eggs under conditions of high intraspecific 'competition' and not large eggs. Malabar females did produce large eggs (and large clutches) which would enhance survivorship although little intraspecific 'competition' occurs among adults, with most resources being superabundant.

On Malabar, because of the limited nesting areas, nest destruction is dependent on population density and this provides a mechanism for regulating population size. Bustard & Tognetti (1969) produced a similar model for the green turtle (*Chelonia mydas* L.). Moreover, probably as a reflexion of the density of nests on Malabar, nest predator density (i.e. coconut crab, *Birgus*) is correlated with nest density.

A number of features support the view that food is the principal limiting factor:

(1) Mean body size is bigger (> 30%) on Malabar than on Grande Terre for mature animals of the same age and sex. (Food quality has been shown to be influential in causing large body size in populations of chelonians (Gibbons 1967; Jackson *et al.* 1976).)

(2) Growth is suppressed or severely seasonal on Grande Terre but almost continuous on Malabar.

(3) There is overbrowsing and overgrazing on Grande Terre.

(4) There is a significant increase in follicular atresia, especially preovulatory follicles, under conditions of sub-optimal diet (cf. Hahn & Tinkle 1965; Inger & Greenberg 1966; Swingland & Coe 1978); and the presence of follicular atresia in females on Grande Terre but not on Malabar.

The population density on Grande Terre is extremely high and although a large proportion of mature females did not breed in 1975, reduced but successful reproduction still occurred. It is argued that the reproductive rate is near its lowest level and that any reduction in population numbers must be brought about by mortality. The density of tortoises has been rising rapidly since the beginning of this century when numbers had probably been reduced by human activity (Stoddart 1971). It is also probable that the population on Grande Terre is currently reaching a maximum density and as young tortoises can and do feed in places inaccessible to adult tortoises they will not be so susceptible to the effects of this density asymptote. Moreover, as shade is important in influencing mortality it is interesting to note that trees and large bushes are reported as having been almost absent in SE Grande Terre at the beginning of the century. Thus the increase in available shade coincided with the increase in the population, which, together with the correlation between dead trees and tortoise density, implies (i) a very considerable regulatory effect on tortoise density by shade and (ii) that as tortoise density rises, shade is increasingly destroyed (cf. Merton *et al.* 1976). It also suggests that increases and decreases in tortoise density and shade may be correlated. Young tortoises which shade under rock or in clumps of sedges, but infrequently under bushes or trees, are isolated from such perturbations. This suggestion regarding the nature of the relation between tortoise density and shade is similar to that suggested for elephants by Caughley (1976). At present, regeneration of woody species on Grande Terre is prevented by the browsing pressure of the high tortoise density, in contrast to Malabar where shrubs and trees freely increase.

CONCLUSION

If the reproductive rate were to regulate the total population of tortoises on Aldabra one would expect it to decrease as the population increased. Although this study lasted only 2 years, the differences in reproduction between the isolated populations of Grande Terre, Malabar and Picard suggest that density-dependent population regulation is occurring.

There is evidence that food quality and quantity remains high in dry tropical environments throughout the rainy season (Coe *et al.* 1976). Since the female presumably has higher food requirements during the latter stages of follicular development there are obvious advantages to ovulating just after the optimum nutritional time of year. The high incidence of follicular atresia in the high-density population compared with its absence in the low density population clearly supports the suggestion that nutrition is affecting population regulation. Various other parameters such as growth rate and age at sexual maturity differ between the study areas.

Hatchling recruitment varies from year to year on Malabar and on Grande Terre. This recruitment is related to rainfall and hence to nutrition during late follicular development. There is evidence to suggest that undernutrition in short or dry wet seasons caused a reduction in fecundity through poor food supply.

The research was supported by a grant to M.J.C. from the Natural Environment Research Council to whom we are grateful. We are also grateful to the Royal Society of London for providing facilities on the atoll and for logistic assistance; Professor A. d'A. Bellairs, Professor R. M. Cormack and Professor G. M. Dunnet for their advice and encouragement during the last 3 years, and members of the Department of Zoology, Oxford for their help. In particular, I.R.S. should like to express a debt to M. Harry Charles and M. Bernard Legae for their untiring and willing assistance, sometimes under difficult circumstances, and their enduring companionship while on the Atoll.

REFERENCES (Swingland & Coe)

Andrews, R. & Rand, A. S. 1974 Reproductive effort in anoline lizards. *Ecology* **55**, 1317–1327.

Bourn, D. & Coe, M. 1978 The size, structure and distribution of the giant tortoise population of Aldabra. *Phil. Trans. R. Soc. Lond.* B **282**, 139–175.

Braithwaite, C. J. R., Taylor, J. D. & Kennedy, W. J. 1973 The evolution of an atoll: the depositional and erosional history of Aldabra. *Phil. Trans. R. Soc. Lond.* B **266**, 307–340.

Bustard, H. R. & Tognetti, K. P. 1969 Green sea turtles; a discrete simulation of density-dependent population regulation. *Science, N.Y.,* **163**, 939–941.

Caughley, G. 1976 The elephant problem – an alternative hypothesis. *E. Afr. Wildl. J.* **14**, 265–183.

Chitty, D. 1960 Population processes in the vole and their relevance to general theory. *Can. J. Zool.* **38**, 99–113.

Christian, J. J. 1961 Phenomena associated with population density. *Proc. natn. Acad. Sci. U.S.A.* **47**, 428–449.

Christiansen, J. L. & Moll, E. O. 1973 Latitudinal reproductive variation within a single subspecies of a painted turtle *Chrysemys picta bellii*. *Herpetologica* **29**, 152–163.

Coe, M. J., Cumming, D. H. & Phillipson, J. 1976 Biomass and production of large African herbivores in relation to rainfall and primary production. *Oecologia* **22**, 341–354.

Ernst, C. H. 1971 Population dynamics and activity cycles of *Chrysemys picta* in southeastern Pennsylvania *J. Herpetol.* **5**, 151–160.

Frazier, J. G. 1972 Behavioural and ecological observations on the giant tortoise of Aldabra Atoll. D.Phil. thesis, Oxford University.

Gibbons, J. W. 1967 Variation in growth rates in three populations of the painted turtle *Chrysemys picta*. *Herpetologica* **23**, 296–303.

Gibbons, J. W. & Tinkle, D. W. 1969 Reproductive variation between turtle population in a single geographic area. *Ecology* **50**, 340–341.

188 I. R. SWINGLAND AND M. J. COE

Grubb, P. 1971 The growth, ecology and population structure of giant tortoises on Aldabra. *Phil. Trans. R. Soc. Lond.* B **260**, 327–372.

Hahn, W. E. & Tinkle, D. W. 1964 Fat body cycling and experimental evidence for its adaptive significance to ovarian follicle development in the lizard *Uta stansburiana*. *J. exp. Zool.* **158**, 79–86.

Hanks, J. & MacIntosh, J. E. A. 1973 Population dynamics of the African elephant (*Loxodonta africana*). *J. Zool., Lond.* **169**, 29–38.

Hnatiuk, R. J. 1979 Temporal and spatial variations in precipitation on Aldabra. *Phil. Trans. R. Soc. Lond.* B **286**, 25–36 (this volume).

Hnatiuk, R. J., Woodell, S. R. J. & Bourn, D. M. 1976 Giant tortoise and vegetation interactions on Aldabra Atoll. Part 2. Coastal. *Biol. Conserv.* **9**, 305–316.

Inger, R. F. & Greenberg, B. 1966 Annual reproductive patterns of lizards from a Bornean rain forest. *Ecology* **47**, 1007–1021.

Jackson, C. G., Trotter, J. A., Trotter, T. H. & Trotter, M. W. 1976 Accelerated growth rate and early maturity in *Gopherus agassizi* (Reptilia: Testudines). *Herpetologica* **32**, 139–145.

Laws, R. M. 1969 Aspects of reproduction in the African elephant *Loxodonta africana*. *J. Reprod. Fert.*, suppl. **6**, 193–217.

Merton, L. F. H., Bourn, D. M. & Hnatiuk, R. J. 1976 Giant tortoise and vegetation interactions on Aldabra Atoll. Part 1. Inland. *Biol. Conserv.* **9**, 293–304.

Parsons, J. 1970 Relationship between egg size and post-hatching chick mortality in the Herring Gull (*Larus argentatus*). *Nature, Lond.* **228**, 1221–1222.

Pianka, E. R. 1970 Comparative autecology of the lizard *Cnemidophorus tigris* in different parts of its geographic range. *Ecology* **51**, 703–720.

Schifferli, L. 1973 The effect of egg-weight on subsequent growth in nestling Great Tits *Parus major*. *Ibis* **115**, 549–558.

Sinclair, A. 1974 The natural regulation of buffalo populations in East Africa. II. Reproduction, recruitment and growth. *E. Afr. Wildl. J.* **12**, 169–183.

Skogland, W. C., Seegar, K. C. & Ringrose, A. T. 1952 Growth of broiler chicks hatched from various sized eggs when reared in competition with each other. *Poult. Sci.* **31**, 796–799.

Stoddart, D. R. 1971 Settlement, development and conservation of Aldabra. *Phil. Trans. R. Soc. Lond.* B **260**, 611–628.

Swingland, I. R. 1977 Reproductive effort and life history strategy of the Aldabra giant tortoise. *Nature, Lond.* **269**, 402–404.

Swingland, I. R. & Coe, M. 1978 The natural regulation of giant tortoise populations on Aldabra Atoll. Reproduction. *J. Zool. Lond.* **186**, 285–309.

Tinkle, D. W. 1961 Geographic variation in reproduction, size, sex ratio and maturity of *Sternothaerus odoratus* (Testudinata: Chelydridae). *Ecology* **42**, 68–76.

Tinkle, D. W., Wilbur, H. M. & Tilley, S. G. 1970 Evolutionary strategies in lizard reproduction. *Evolution* **24**, 55–74.

Wynne-Edwards, V. C. 1962 *Animal dispersion in relation to social behaviour*. Edinburgh and London: Oliver & Boyd.

Phil. Trans. R. Soc. Lond. B. **286**, 189–193 (1979)   [189]
Printed in Great Britain

Features of tortoise mortality and decomposition on Aldabra

By D. Bourn and M. J. Coe

Animal Ecology Research Group, Department of Zoology, University of Oxford, South Parks Road, Oxford OX1 3PS, U.K.

[Plate 1]

Apart from predation on tortoise eggs and young tortoises by crabs and birds, the Aldabran giant tortoise population is virtually unaffected by predators. The decomposition of a series of tortoise bodies, with known dates of death, was monitored for periods up to 18 months. The rate of carapace disintegration provides a useful means of introducing a temporal component to the analysis of mortality data.

Introduction

During a study of the population dynamics of the giant tortoise (*Geochelone gigantea* Schweigger) on Aldabra it became apparent that while a series of marked animals provided valuable data on the numbers and distribution of living animals, this information would be incomplete unless an attempt could be made to assess mortality. The remains of adult animals are a conspicuous feature of the arid Aldabra landscape and their apparent persistence for long periods indicated a possible means of obtaining a measure of mortality. In particular the presence of this skeletal material offered the opportunity of introducing a temporal component to the study of mortality provided a time series for decomposition could be established.

The persistence of tortoise remains can be attributed to the almost complete absence of predators on the atoll. At present, land crabs, birds and feral cats are probably important agents of predation on both eggs and young but adults are not affected, although all these creatures perform an important scavenging rôle on carrion. Feral dogs, once present on Aldabra, are now extinct. Thus for animals with carapaces greater than 50–60 cm (curved length) the skeletal remains are virtually unaffected by these agencies.

The tortoise carapace is composed of an outer series of keratinous scutes and an inner layer of bony plates which in adult animals are well ossified and fused together. During decomposition the outer scutes become detached from the body plates and fall off, leaving the carapace bones to become bleached by sunlight. The presence of these remains provides an excellent marker whether above ground or in holes and crevices in the broken limestone champignon. Hence during transect and hectare surveys for living animals it is also possible to record the presence of skeletal remains.

Provided a time scale can be constructed for the time taken for tortoise skeletons to break down, the comparatively long-term persistence of these remains makes it possible to assess the mortality rate for the adult tortoise population. During the course of investigations of the dynamics of the tortoise population (Bourn 1976, 1978; Bourn & Coe 1978), individuals whose date of death was known were monitored for up to 18 months. At present, I. Swingland, who is investigating tortoise reproduction and recruitment, is recording further information on mortality. This paper describes a number of time-related stages of the breakdown process and gives estimates of the time elapsed since death.

Method

Between January 1973 and September 1974, during the course of an extensive tortoise census and marking programme, most areas of the atoll were visited on a number of occasions. The remains of many dead tortoises in various stages of breakdown were located and recorded. The fresh, unbloated appearance of certain remains and the absence of putrescent odours indicated that some animals had died very recently. In such cases carcases were marked and their position recorded. In addition, various other data were recorded, including the size and sex of the individual, its location in relation to the nearest available shade, the degree of exposure, whether or not the tortoise appeared to have been trapped in holes or fissures, and the general condition of the carcase. Subsequently, as the marking programme permitted, the remains of these animals, whose date of death was known to within a few days, were revisited and notes kept on the progress of the decay process. The presence of scavengers on or near the remains was also recorded.

As part of a preliminary reproductive study a limited number of tortoise post-mortems were performed (Bourn 1978). After post-mortem examinations had been completed a number of carcases were laid out and monitored to assess the rates of breakdown and to determine quali-tatively the importance of various scavenger species. However, as these observations progressed it became apparent that post-mortem remains were not decaying at the same rate or manner as those of natural intact carcases. In order to gain access to the tortoise's internal organs during post-mortem examination the plastron had been entirely removed so that prematurely dis-membered bodies were laid out for observation. Necrophagous species therefore had relatively easy access to the fleshy remains. In addition, the removal of the plastron meant that the dorsal carapace bones were subject to somewhat different contraction and expansion stresses, than in natural mortalities with an integral plastron. Breakdown rates of these unnatural mortalities could not therefore be regarded as typical. However, it is considered that the scavenger species seen are likely to be the most important under natural conditions.

Results

(a) Carapace breakdown

The remains of 31 natural tortoise mortalities were monitored for periods of up to 18 months after death. A total of 146 visits were made to these remains. Initially detailed descriptions were made of the status of each carcase, but after a period of familiarization with the breakdown sequence it was possible to define eight recognizable stages in the process. These are described in table 1 and photographs of the various stages are shown in figures 1–8, plate 1. Of the 31 tortoises monitored, only 6 were located in shaded positions. It was not therefore possible to determine with confidence whether these broke down less rapidly than those in the open, although shaded remains usually became discoloured by algal/bacterial growth more readily than those in open positions. Presumably the shaded positions afforded less extreme micro-climatic conditions for microbial growth to take place. It must be emphasized that although every effort was made to visit tortoise remains as frequently as possible, especially in the early stages of breakdown, when the process was relatively rapid, the observations and the estimates of the duration of each stage, especially the more attenuated later stages, are inevitably rather imprecise and the ranges are wide and sometimes overlap. There is obviously a considerable degree of individual variation and in any case the phases described compose a decay continuum. Nevertheless, useful criteria may be established from these results.

Table 2 summarizes the results; the duration of each stage is given in terms of days elapsed since death, along with the number of observations that were made, given in parentheses. The early stages of breakdown (stages 1–3) were reasonably consistent regardless of the size in the range considered. During the first 48 h after death there is little or no smell, while in the subsequent 2 weeks or so the processes of putrefaction proceed; first the limbs become bloated, the skin tissue splits and foul smelling liquid oozes from orifices and sites of scavenger activity.

TABLE 1. BREAKDOWN STAGES OF TORTOISE CARCASES ARISING FROM NATURAL MORTALITY

stage   description

1   *Freshly dead*. No bloat. No smell. Limbs entire, fleshy and covered with skin. Scutes all in place and firmly attached.

2   *Putrid*. Initially bloated with oozing orifices. Subsequently skin may begin to peel. Fleshy parts drying out and blackening. Foul putrid odour throughout. Scutes firmly attached.

3   *Soft parts absent*. Fleshy remains and entrails removed or thoroughly dried out and mummified. All scutes attached although some marginals may have become detached. Little or no smell.

4   *Scutes attached*. Most or all dorsal scutes in place, although often raised off underlying carapace bones and separated from each other. Where scutes have fallen off, exposed carapace bone usually has connective tissue still visible and attached.

5   *Scutes shed*. Most dorsal scutes detached. Exposed carapace bones usually bleached white. Initially some connective tissue between scutes and carapace may be evident. Carapace bone sutures still holding.

6   *Sutures opening*. Individual carapace bones starting to separate along sutures. Depending on exposure, bones may be more or less darkened by algal/bacterial growth.

7   *Collapse*. Carapace collapsing, with individual bones collapsing inside.

8   *Disintegration*. Carapace structure lost. Complete disintegration. Remaining bones usually grey and powdery.

Gradually the remains begin to dry out, the fleshy parts are consumed by the activity of dipterous larvae, and some limb bones are removed by scavengers. The carapace scutes usually remain firmly attached. During the following 2 weeks (until approximately 1 month after death) flesh, connective tissue and keratinous skin remains that persist become thoroughly dried out and mummified. Some scutes may begin to lift off the underlying carapace bones. The durations of subsequent stages are much more variable; in part this appears to be a reflexion of the size of the individual and probably the degree of ossification and thickness of the carapace bones. Smaller tortoises with a curved length of 61–71 cm with less robust carapace structures reach the stage of disintegration in which individual carapace bones begin to collapse after a period of between 4 and 7 months, while tortoises of 71–80 cm curved length took between 7 and 15 months to reach the same stage. Unfortunately the period of observation was too short to give a clear indication of the time required for larger individuals to reach this stage of disintegration, although it would seem likely to be about 2 years, or possibly, in the largest individuals, in excess of 3 years.

(b) Predators and scavengers

As has already been pointed out, the long-term rates of breakdown of tortoise remains laid out after post-mortem examinations were thought to be accelerated. However, the records of scavengers visiting the remains are probably a fair indication of those animals playing the most significant rôle in the initial stages of decay under natural conditions. Ten carcases were monitored at 3 h intervals for 4 days and thereafter twice a day until 1 week after death.

These qualitative observations indicated that by far the most important agents of initial decomposition were various species of dipteran larvae, which were evident within the first 24 h and were active throughout the carcase within 36–48 h. Large red ants swarmed over the remains during the hours of darkness and large black ants were evident during the day. Of the Crustacea, which were regarded as scavengers of major importance, *Birgus latro* (the robber or coconut crab) was the most frequent visitor, with as many as 14 in the vicinity of the body at a time. They were almost exclusively active at night and the very early morning and could be seen tearing off the fleshy remains, dragging away limb bones and entrails and even gnawing at the carapace with their chelae. They were thought to be responsible for the complete disappearance of the remains of one small tortoise with an incompletely ossified carapace (38.5 cm curved length). *Cardisoma carnifex* was also a common visitor at night, and where they occurred *C. cavipes* were also frequently to be seen at night and during the day. *C. hilgendorfi*, *C. perlatus* and *Geograpsis grayi* were occasional visitors.

Pied crows (*Corvus albus*) were often observed feeding on the remains and sacred ibis (*Threskiornis aethiopica abbotti*) were also often present in the vicinity. The latter were observed feeding on insect larvae and pupae as well as small particles of flesh. Grey and green herons were also occasionally seen close to the remains. No flightless rails (*Dryolimnas cuvieri*) occurred in the areas where the tortoise carcases were laid out. Where present they would have almost certainly taken advantage of the abundant insect food source associated with a tortoise corpse. Swingland

TABLE 2. RELATIVE RATES OF BREAKDOWN FOR NATURAL MORTALITIES OF TORTOISES IN DIFFERENT SIZE CLASSES

curved length cm	number of remains	duration of each breakdown stage/day						
		stage 1	stage 2	stage 3	stage 4	stage 5	stage 6	stage 7
61–70	6	1–2 (6)	2 (3)	3 (0)	14–150 (6)	60–180 (2)	90–180 (2)	120–210 (3)
71–80	7	1–2 (7)	2–12 (9)	14–30 (8)	60–210 (8)	180 (1)	180–270 (2)	210–450 (2)
81–90	10	1–2 (10)	2–12 (10)	14–17 (8)	30–210 (16)	90–180 (2)	150–270 (2)	150 (1)
91 +	8	1–2 (8)	2–16 (8)	10–30 (7)	60–540 (14)	— (0)	450 (1)	— (0)

DESCRIPTION OF PLATE 1

FIGURE 1. Bloated remains of a tortoise 4 days after death (stage 2).

FIGURE 2. Mummified remains of a tortoise some 20 days after death (stage 3).

FIGURE 3. Tortoise remains approximately 3 months after death. Most scutes still in place, some lateral and marginal scutes detached, revealing discoloured carapace bones beneath (stage 4).

FIGURE 4. After about 5 months all scutes have been removed and the carapace bones have been bleached white by the sun. This example is typical of remains found in exposed positions (stage 5).

FIGURES 5 AND 6. The initial phase of carapace disintegration can be seen: transverse cracks in the carapace are developing along the sutures (stage 6). The two photographs also show varying degrees of algal/bacterial invasion and growth. The carapace in figure 6 was found in a sheltered, well shaded position.

FIGURE 7. Tortoise remains in an advanced state of carapace disintegration (stage 7).

FIGURE 8. Stages 1–7 are here illustrated for comparison.

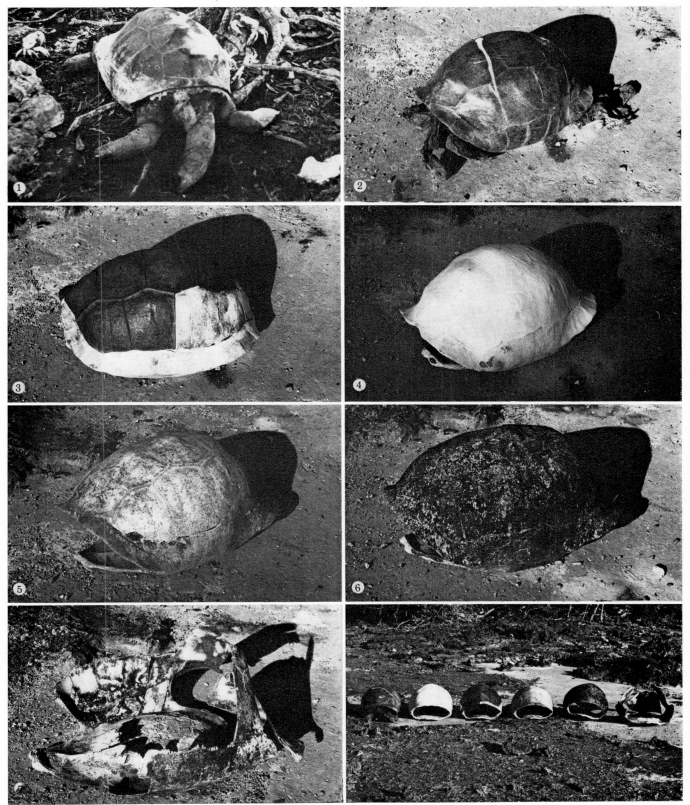

FIGURES 1–8. For description see opposite.

has demonstrated that these birds compose an important element of predation on young tortoises and hatchlings (Swingland 1976, personal communication). Finally, in the field it was not uncommon to find tortoises feeding on the putrid remains of natural tortoise mortalities.

CONCLUSIONS

There is considerable variation in the rates of breakdown of tortoise carcases on Aldabra. In part this variation is closely related to the size of the individual, larger animals having more highly ossified carapace bones which break down more slowly than those of smaller individuals. It is also likely that the degree of exposure of the remains and the general condition of the tortoise at the time of death are both important contributors to the observed variation in the rates of breakdown. In spite of the small number of carcases monitored in shade, Coe (1978) has demonstrated that the carcases of elephants dying in this position show delayed bone exfoliation compared with exposed material.

Tortoises in the size range 61–70 cm curved length took up to 7 months for their carapaces to disintegrate; those in the size range 71–80 cm curved length took up to 15 months and larger individuals had not reached this stage after 18 months when observations were terminated. It may therefore be conservatively estimated that the average persistence of the remains of adult tortoises is about 2 years. This is the figure used by Bourn & Coe (1978) in their treatment of mortality data collected during a sample census of the giant tortoise population of Aldabra. Live tortoise density was found to be 26.95/ha in the southeast of the atoll; 77 % of this population were larger than 60 cm curved length. The mortality density in the same area was 1.2/ha. If tortoise remains persist on average for about 2 years this represents a mortality of 0.6/ha/a. By proportion this is equivalent to an annual mortality rate of 29/1000 individuals. We are well aware that this procedure will underestimate the mortality rates of smaller tortoises and overestimate that of larger individuals. When, however, further data become available from the continuing monitoring programme on Aldabra we will be in the unique position of being able to determine within acceptable limits the mortality rates of a large proportion of the size ranges of tortoises present in the population.

We should like to thank the Natural Environment Research Council for funding this work on Aldabra and the Royal Society for providing facilities at the Aldabra Research Station which made life in this difficult terrain bearable and work possible. We have continuously been encouraged by members of the Animal Ecology Research Group in Oxford. Dr John Phillipson and Dr Ian Swingland have greatly assisted us both in general and specific discussions.

REFERENCES (Bourn & Coe)

Bourn, D. 1976 The giant tortoise population of Aldabra (Cryptodira: Testudinidae). Part 1. Preliminary results. *Zool. afr.* **11**, 275–284.

Bourn, D. 1978 A reproductive study of giant tortoises on Aldabra. *J. Zool. Lond.* **182**, 27–38.

Bourn, D. & Coe, M. 1978 The size, structure and distribution of the giant tortoise population of Aldabra. *Phil. Trans. R. Soc. Lond.* B **282**, 139–175.

Coe, M. 1978 The decomposition of elephant carcases in the Tsavo (East) National Park, Kenya. *J. arid. Envir.* **1**, 71–86.

Phil. Trans. R. Soc. Lond. B. **286**, 195–210 (1979)   [195]

Printed in Great Britain

Feeding ecology of land birds on West Island, Aldabra Atoll, Indian Ocean: a preliminary survey

By C. B. Frith†

Royal Society Aldabra Research Station, Seychelles

The feeding ecology of some endemic land birds on West Island, Aldabra Atoll, was examined for a complete year, involving the observation of all bird feeding activity in eight habitats for a standard period of time. Gizzard contents of a number of birds of three selected species, considered at that time ecologically close, were examined and identified to complement observational data. Results indicated that the two species previously considered to be ecologically closer than any other two species on the atoll (*Nectarinia sovimanga* and *Zosterops maderaspatana*) in fact seek predominantly different foods, by differing methods, from largely dissimilar feeding stations and habitats. Conversely, several other species share largely similar feeding stations and foods, and these are discussed with reference to possible competition and the present status of certain species. Seasonal food availability and the utilization of introduced vegetation and associated fauna and flora are discussed.

1. Introduction

Earlier studies on land birds at Aldabra are comprehensively summarized by Benson & Penny (1971); until the present study, however, quantitative data on the feeding ecology of Aldabra land birds were unavailable.

This paper outlines the feeding ecology of land birds on West Island, Aldabra, and examines proportions of food sources utilized in different habitats, and possible interspecific feeding interactions.

2. Methods

Field work was performed in time available between other projects from 1 June 1972 to 1 April 1973 and Dr Sarah Hnatiuk kindly continued field work to 1 June 1973 to complete 12 months of observation.

Quantitative data were obtained during 'fixed route walks', the walk selected including all habitats typical of West Island and within a workable distance from the research station. Four main vegetation types were easily defined on this route, each being divisible into two generally similar habitats differing in density or in influence of other floral factors as described in table 1. In each of the eight habitats a site was selected at which all bird feeding observed during a timed 10 min was recorded. The rugged and dangerous nature of substrates made it impossible to record observations on a continuous-walking basis. Walks were not taken at specific times, but when circumstance permitted (table 2). Each walk took almost exactly 2 h and each was begun at either site 1 or site 8. Feeding activity observed between sites was noted but is not included in the following analysis. A bird, or flock, seen feeding upon two distinct food types (i.e. seed and insect) constituted two records. A bird seen feeding on two types of

---

† Present address: 'Prionodura', Paluma, via Townsville, Queensland, Australia 4810.

seed, however, constituted a single record, both plants being noted as used. Unknown plants were collected for subsequent identification.

Results provide adequate data to indicate food types commonly utilized and habitats and feeding stations favoured. An obvious limitation to the method of observation was variation in degree of visibility between habitats. Figures for feeding birds may therefore reflect degrees of visibility as much as relative use in some sites to some extent. The fact that walks were made at different times of day may result in differing degrees of bird feeding activity being observed. These points have been considered and limited significance has consequently been given to some figures of relative habitat use as commented upon in species accounts (§3).

TABLE 1. VEGETATION OF FIXED ROUTE WALK SITES

vegetation type	site no.	other floral factors
mixed scrub on	1	predominantly *Pemphis*
champignon	2	predominantly mixed scrub other than *Pemphis*
Casuarina	3	mixed scrub and grasses beneath
woodland	4	very little vegetation other than grasses beneath
palm grove	5	also sparse *Casuarina* and occasional *Moringa*; cotton beneath
	6	also sparse *Casuarina*; cotton beneath
mangrove	7	low sparse mangrove woodland; tidal
	8	tall dense mangrove forest; tidal at higher tides only

TABLE 2. BIMONTHLY NUMBER (*a*) AND HOUR OF COMMENCEMENT (*b*) OF 100 FIXED ROUTE WALKS

(*a*)	June July	Aug. Sept.	Oct. Nov.	Dec. Jan.	Feb. March	April May
	10	20	18	18	17	17

(*b*)										
07h 00	08h 00	09h 00	10h 00	11h 00	12h 00	13h 00	14h 00	15h 00	16h 00
08h 00	09h 00	10h 00	11h 00	12h 00	13h 00	14h 00	15h 00	16 h00	17h 00
21	13	7	12	2	2	5	4	16	18

It will be noted that most walks were made during early morning or late afternoon, when most bird feeding activity occurs. Each walk took almost exactly 2 h to complete.

3. THE LAND BIRDS

Because of the small numbers of some species, insufficient data were obtained to describe their feeding quantitatively. Other species observed only rarely, such as ibis (*Threskiornis aethiopica*) and whimbrel (*Numenius phaeopus*), were not recorded. Pied crows (*Corvus albus*) were frequently observed in palm groves but the vast majority of their food was made available by man and the records are therefore not discussed. The nocturnal feeding Malagasy nightjar (*Caprimulgus madagascariensis*) was not observed feeding during walks but possible competitors for nocturnal flying insects might be the insectivorous bats on Aldabra (see Hill 1971).

The following list (table 3) includes those birds dealt with in this study and contains all the 'land birds proper' of Benson & Penny (1971), plus *Butorides striatus* which is included because it was frequently seen feeding inland.

Species are discussed individually, except for the Souimanga sunbird (*Nectarinia sovimanga*) and Malagasy white-eye (*Zosterops maderaspatana*), which have been considered to be ecologically close (Benson & Penny 1971) and which are therefore discussed jointly for comparative purposes. Quantitative data are followed by qualitative information. Whereas data were obtained exclusively during fixed route walks unless otherwise indicated, data concerning the Malagasy kestrel, Comoro blue pigeon, Aldabra drongo and pied crow were obtained during walks and at other times and places.

TABLE 3. STATUS AND AFFINITIES OF ALDABRAN LAND BIRDS
(AFTER BENSON & PENNY 1971)

(1) Monotypic species endemic to Aldabra:
  Nesillas aldabranus not recorded on West, South or Polymnie Islands (C, M)
  Dicrurus aldabranus (C, M)

(2) Subspecies endemic to Aldabra:
  Dryolimnas cuvieri aldabranus extinct on West and South Islands (M)
  Alectroenas sganzini minor (C)
  Caprimulgus madagascariensis aldabrensis (M)
  Hypsipetes madagascariensis rostratus (C, M)
  Nectarinia sovimanga aldabrensis (M)
  Zosterops maderaspatana aldabrensis (C, M)
  Foudia eminentissima aldabrana (C)

(3) Subspecies endemic to Aldabra and Assumption:
  Centropus toulou insularis (M)

(4) Subspecies endemic to Aldabra archipelago and Gloriosa:
  Streptopelia picturata coppingeri (C, M)

(5) Subspecies endemic to Aldabra, Assumption and the Amirantes:
  Butorides striatus crawfordi (C)

(6) Monotypic species endemic to Malagasy and Aldabra:
  Falco newtoni (M)

(7) Monotypic species in most of Africa and part of Malagasy Region:
  Corvus albus (C, M, A)

(8) Subspecies in most of Africa, Madagascar, Comoros and Aldabra:
  Tyto alba affinis extinct on Aldabra (C, M, A)

The geographical location of the systematically closest relative is indicated in parentheses: C, Comoros; M, Madagascar; A, Africa. All forms occur throughout Aldabra Atoll unless stated otherwise.

(a) Butorides striatus, *green-backed heron*

Predominantly a shore bird, but often feeding inland. During walks 38 feedings were observed, 9 in mixed scrub, 13 in *Casuarina* woodland and 16 in palm grove. All instances involved the taking of large insects except for two geckos and one skink taken from *Casuarina* woodland and one gecko from palm grove.

Feeding numbers are small and may reflect degree of visibility between habitats. It was noted, however, that geckos and skinks were less apparent in mixed scrub than in palm grove and the fewer observations in the former habitat may reflect the sparsity of this prey there, or perhaps the greater distance of mixed scrub from the intertidal zone. No preference for a particular site within a vegetation type was noted.

Rarely, single birds were flushed from low down in mangroves indicating that they saw me before I saw them and it is not surprising, therefore, that no feeding was observed in this habitat. This lack of data is unimportant to the present study as the green-backed heron lacks potential feeding competitors in mangroves among resident land birds on West Island. Elsewhere, however, it might utilize similar foods as the white-throated rail to some extent in mangroves (Penny & Diamond 1971).

(b) Falco newtoni, *Malagasy kestrel*

Kestrels are most often seen perched in dead upper tree branches from which they hunt, flying off and returning with prey caught in flight, or flying to the ground or tree trunks to pounce upon prey. Food consists mostly of larger insects, a gecko (*Phelsuma abbotti*), and a skink (*Ablepharus boutonii*). On two occasions small rats (*Rattus rattus*) were seen to be taken and the single kestrel collected by Benson & Penny (1971) contained rat remains.

(c) Alectroenas sganzini, *Comoro blue pigeon*

The Aldabran population has not been observed feeding on the ground, although Benson & Penny (1971) noted two specimens containing tiny stones in the stomach. Owing to the sparsity of birds on West Island I recorded it feeding only once on *Solanum indicum* fruits in *Casuarina* woodland (site 3). Grubb, in Benson & Penny (1971), however, lists nine other plants known to be eaten, and names six others likely to be utilized (see appendix 1).

(d) Streptopelia picturata, *Malagasy turtledove*

This bird predominantly feeds on the ground upon seeds, fruits, insects and other invertebrates. Flower buds were often taken from plants up to 4 m above ground, and flowers of *Moringa oleifera* were plucked from trees.

During walks, 38 feedings were observed, 12 in mixed scrub, 6 in *Casuarina* woodland and 20 in palm grove. All observations, except 3 of feeding upon flowers or buds in palm grove, were of birds feeding on the ground. While insects and other invertebrates are doubtless taken from the ground, I was frequently able to see seeds picked up and swallowed. No feeding in mangroves were seen, although breeding therein is recorded (Benson & Penny 1971). While most often observed feeding in palm grove, where sighting was easy, the bird probably prefers the thicker mixed scrub and *Pemphis*. Figures are few but fewer records in *Casuarina* woodland probably indicate a lack of favoured foods as the habitat provides little more than *Casuarina* seeds and invertebrates. Other than this the quiet, cryptic, nature of this bird makes observation difficult and the assessment of relative habitat utilization difficult.

(e) Centropus toulou, *Malagasy coucal*

The coucal primarily inhabits thickets and undergrowth, where observation is difficult, as indicated by the numbers of feeding observations; 3 in mixed scrub, 10 in casuarina woodland, 6 in palm grove and 1 in mangrove. Most feeding in fact very probably occurs in mixed scrub, where breeding apparently takes place exclusively (C. B. Frith 1975*b*; Woodell 1976), and secondly in *Casuarina* woodland. Within the latter, mixed scrub present in site 3 certainly made this more favourable for hunting than site 4. Palm groves were used little despite the ease of observation in them. The single mangrove record, in site 8, was of insect feeding. Arthropods and small reptiles form most of the diet and are obtained by foraging about foliage, timber and grasses, sometimes quite high up. The coucal was seen to use its heavy bill for lifting and prising tree bark, presumably in search of arthropods.

(f) Hypsipetes madagascariensis, *Malagasy bulbul*

A bird common throughout the atoll, noisy, conspicuous, and quickly attracted to disturbance. It was rarely seen feeding during walks (19 records) which must at least partly be attributable to its inquisitive nature, birds being attracted to the observer before being observed feeding. Most observed feeding occurred in mixed scrub and *Casuarina* woodland (16 records; 7 and 9 respectively). Mixed scrub is almost certainly favoured to *Casuarina* where both are locally available, as the former supports far more fruiting plants. Palm grove and mangrove are of limited use to feeding bulbuls, only 1 and 2 records being made in them respectively. A preference for mixed scrub of site 2 (6 records) over predominantly *Pemphis* scrub of site 1 (1 record) is suggested by these very small figures, which could be accounted for by the more variable flora of site 2 supporting more fruiting plants.

Insects up to large grasshoppers or mantids in size were taken and Benson & Penny (1971) record a wide range of insects utilized, most of which are foraged from foliage. Aerial feeding was not uncommonly observed. Birds were observed to snatch insects from leaves or twigs, or take fruits, in awkward fluttering flight, or hover, and were also seen to pursue and catch insects in aerial chase as also recorded by Gaymer (1967).

The fruit diet of the bulbul is as diverse as its insect diet; Benson & Penny (1971) listed 11 species of plant used, to which I add *Asparagus umbellulatus*, *Mystroxylon aethiopicum*, *Polysphaeria multiflora*, *Tricalysia sonderana* and *Ricinus communis*.

(g) Dicrurus aldabranus, *Aldabra drongo*

The Aldabra drongo has species status as a well differentiated population (Vaurie 1949, 1962; Benson 1967; Benson & Penny 1971) and is therefore of considerable interest in the Aldabran avifauna. Benson & Penny considered it to show preference for mangroves but my observations indicate that *Casuarina* is equally if not more favoured, as was inferred by Abbott (in Ridgway 1896) at least with regard to breeding. It should be noted that several small reptiles regularly eaten by drongos occur commonly in *Casuarina* and other vegetation, but not in mangroves. Feeding in mangroves was not observed, although drongos do breed in them (Benson & Penny 1971). West Island mangroves, are, however, rather dense and it is possible that drongo favours more open 'parkland-like' mangrove communities found at the east of the atoll (Macnae 1971, p. 244).

While many insects were taken in flight, equally as many were taken from the ground, tree trunks, and boughs. Hunting was often by family(?) groups of up to four, from vantage points such as dead bare twigs usually close to open ground. Birds fluttered down and snatched prey in the bill to return to the perch where it was repeatedly beaten and, particularly with reptiles, held to the perch with the feet while being ripped apart with the bill. Benson & Penny (1971) suggested that the drongo may eat smaller birds, and even an immature of its own kind.

(h) Corvus albus, *pied crow*

The pied crow is apparently much dependent upon man, being more common about human influence where it feeds upon waste. Otherwise it is a beach scavenger, taking ghost crabs (*Ocypode* spp.) and hermit crabs (*Coenobita* spp.). It prefers open ground or bare perches above the foliage, and where these situations occur near other nesting species it predates eggs and nestlings (Diamond in Benson & Penny 1971; C. B. Frith 1977).

Crows were once observed competing with white-throated rails (*Dryolimnas cuvieri*) on Middle Island for hatchling green turtles (*Chelonia mydas*) during a diurnal beach hatching (C. B. Frith 1975a).

(*i*) Nectarinia sovimanga, *Souimanga sunbird, and* Zosterops maderaspatana,
Malagasy white-eye

Total numbers for foods and vegetation types in table 4 indicate ecological isolation
between these two birds in certain respects. Conspicuous is the high proportion of flower nectar
feeding by sunbirds, 61 % of feedings, compared with only 4 % by white-eyes. Sunbirds obtain
food from both vegetations considered introduced onto Aldabra (sites 3–6) in almost equal
proportions. White-eyes, however, utilize only *Casuarina* woodland to any extent, palm groves
supporting fewer insects (also indicated by figures of insect feeding by sunbirds in table 4) and
being too open, in addition to providing no suitable flowers or fruits.

TABLE 4. *NECTARINIA SOVIMANGA* AND *ZOSTEROPS MADERASPATANA* FEEDING RECORDED
DURING 100 FIXED ROUTE WALKS

	Nectarinia sovimanga			*Zosterops maderaspatana*		
site no.†	flower	insect	total	flower	insect	total
1, 2	103	27	130	10	66	76
3, 4	29‡	65	94	1	120	121
5, 6	78	30	108	—	21	21
7, 8	2	16	18	—	81	81
total	212	138	**350** (= *N*)	11	288	**299** (= *N*)
% of *N*	61	39	—	4	96	—

† For descriptions of sites see table 1.
‡ Of this number, 22 were for site 3, reflecting greater flower abundance due to the presence of mixed scrub.

The high percentage (41) of feedings in *Casuarina* by white-eyes is noteworthy as there is
evidence of some isolation, by feeding stations, between the two species in this habitat. Height
above ground at which birds fed was estimated during the walks and recorded. In habitats
other than casuarina woodland these figures are insignificant owing to the limited zonation
of foliage (palm grove) or generally lower nature of the vegetation. In *Casuarina*, however,
foliage was consistent to a considerable height, and within this the two birds differed in their
predominant foraging levels (see §4*c*). Of **89** sunbirds feeding in *Casuarina* for which heights
were noted only 35 (39 %) occurred above 3 m whereas 83 (71 %) of 117 white-eye feedings
took place above 3 m (table 6); 3 m is used as this is the approximate maximum height of the
mixed scrub beneath the *Casuarina* woodland of site 3.

Of the annual total of 120 white-eye feedings upon insects in *Casuarina* 52 (43 %) occurred
during December–January, and as much as 86 (72 %) during December–March inclusive
(see §4*a* and table 6).

Gizzards of **19** white-eyes and 50 sunbirds were examined and material from them identified
where possible. The results appear, with percentages of frequency, in table 5. Fluid, presumably
flower nectar, was present in most, if not all, sunbirds. About one-third of the food in both
species samples consisted of unidentifiable tiny soft-bodied insect remains. Remaining identifiable material reflects differences in feeding habits of these two birds as indicated by field
observations (see §4*e*). The two instances of fruit taken by white-eyes involved the presence
of fruit stones between **2** and **3.5** mm in diameter in gizzards (table 5). Spiders were predominant in sunbird gizzards, as expected from observations of feeding birds which frequently
picked spiders, and insects, from spiders' webs in hovering flight or from a perched position.

Benson & Penny (1971) record sunbirds taking nectar from *Euphorbia pyrifolia*, *Lomatophyllum aldabrense* and *Polysphaeria multiflora* flowers, to which I add 16 plants attributed to the sunbird in appendix 1. Benson & Penny obtained no evidence of white-eyes nectar feeding but referred to Gaymer's claim (1967) that the population does so, which was confirmed during this study (table 4), although such feeding appears to be limited. White-eyes were seen taking nectar a number of times additional to fixed route walk records (table 4), mostly involving flowers of *Pemphis acidula*. Nectar was taken from *Abrus precatorius* by white-eyes, but not sunbirds or fodies (appendix 1).

TABLE 5. NUMBERS AND PERCENTAGES OF SAMPLED *NECTARINIA SOVIMANGA* AND *ZOSTEROPS MADERASPATANA* CONTAINING VARIOUS FOODS

food	*Nectarinia sovimanga* ($N = 50$)		*Zosterops maderaspatana* ($N = 19$)	
	number	% of N	number	% of N
unidentified insect mash	25	50	11	58
beetles	18	36	5	26
insect larvae	5	10	12	63
spiders	26	52	2	11
ants	2	4	—	—
cockroach oothecae	—	—	4	21
butterflies and moths	—	—	2	11
fruit stones	—	—	2	11
nectar	40+	80+	—	—

TABLE 6. HEIGHT ABOVE GROUND AND SEASONALITY OF *NECTARINIA SOVIMANGA* AND *ZOSTEROPS MADERASPATANA* FEEDING ACTIVITY IN *CASUARINA* WOODLAND

(See text, §§4*i* and 5*a*.)

feeding activity with approximate height above ground recorded	*Nectarinia sovimanga*	*Zosterops maderaspatana*
above 3 m	35 (39%)	83 (71%)
below 3 m	54 (61%)	34 (29%)
% of total recorded feeding performed during Dec.-March	34	72

TABLE 7. *FOUDIA EMINENTISSIMA* FEEDING RECORDED DURING 100 FIXED ROUTE WALKS

site no.[†]	insects	*Casuarina* seeds	other seeds	flower nectar	total
1, 2	13	—	1	3	17 (9%)
3, 4	68[‡]	21	11	—	100 (52%)
5, 6	12	36[§]	2	6	56 (29%)
7, 8	18	—	—	—	18 (10%)
total	111	57	14	9	**191** (= N)
% of N	58	30	7	5	

[†] For descriptions of sites see table 1.

[‡] Of this number 49 were for site 4, which is noteworthy in view of the more variable flora of site 3.

[§] This greater number of observed feeding may be due to denser (breeding) populations in sites 5 and 6 (see text, §4*j*).

(*j*) Foudia eminentissima, *red-headed forest fody*

This bird was found to feed predominantly in *Casuarina* habitats (52 %), upon insects (table 7). Within the study area, however, territory-holding groups of birds occurred almost exclusively in *Casuarina* woodland and palm grove (C. B. Frith 1976). Thus, during the breeding season, sites 3–6 had resident populations which doubtless raised observed feeding numbers in these areas, particularly in 5 and 6 where food is comparatively sparse throughout the year. In the latter two sites 75 % of feeding records were made during the breeding months December–March inclusive. This is to be expected as, during the height of breeding, males rarely left defended nesting areas for great lengths of time but conspicuously fed within it (Frith 1976). Figures for feeding in mixed scrub and mangroves are very small (table 7) and remained consistently so throughout the year although lower still during breeding, as expected in view of the birds' predominant presence within territories.

A list of food plants (see appendix 1) and animals found in 67 fody gizzards is given elsewhere (Frith 1976) and there is need for only brief comment here. Most insects taken proved to be larger and/or harder than the fine, soft-bodied, ones utilized by sunbirds and white-eyes, although this might to some degree be biased by deterioration of softer food parts by digestion. Particularly noteworthy is the presence of oothecae, or egg cases, of the cockroach genus *Margathea* in 46 (69 % of sample) gizzards, most individual birds containing several to many. These are obtained during bark and foliage searching (see §5c). White-eyes too take these oothecae, being present in 4 (21 %) sampled birds.

Remains of a small weevil, *Cratopus viridisparsus*, were found in 51 fody gizzards (76 % of sample), and were always present in good numbers. This insect occurs commonly in foliage of mixed scrub where it was regularly collected in large numbers by sweep-net (D. W. Frith 1979, this volume, and personal communication). Doubtless feeding in mixed scrub habitats is more common than results of fixed route walks show, but the relative difficulty of view made observation awkward. Spiders occurred only in 4 fodies (6 % of sample), but many various insect eggs were found in gizzards. Seeds of five plants other than *Casuarina* were seen to be eaten as well as flower nectar of four plants (appendix 1). Fruits are undoubtedly utilized far more than indicated by records of feeding birds, as clearly illustrated at certain times by the excretion of the unmistakable fruit stones of *Passiflora suberosa* by large numbers of mist-netted birds (C. B. Frith 1976).

Flower nectar apparently represents a small proportion of the diet, but is interesting in view of nectar feeding adaptations in other members of the genus *Foudia* (Staub 1973) and the presence of other nectar feeding birds on Aldabra (C. B. Frith 1976; and see §4c).

4. Discussion

(*a*) Seasonal food availability and use

Seasonal food fluctuations were not examined *per se* but during the study year periodical variations in relative bird feeding upon particular foods were noted which probably reflect the availability of the source concerned.

Relative monthly insect abundance followed rainfall fluctuations very closely on West Island during the study period (D. W. Frith 1975; 1979, this volume; C. B. Frith 1976). The pre-peak rise of insect numbers appears to influence the start of breeding in the fody, white-eye and, to a lesser extent, the sunbird (figure 1). The latter begins breeding just before a rise in insect numbers, possibly as a result of preceding increase in flower nectar availability (D. W. Frith 1979, this volume). The latter possibility, however, requires investigation.

The marked increase in insect feeding by white-eyes in *Casuarina* woodland during wetter months resulted in over two-thirds of the species annual insect feeding total occurring within one-third of the year (see §3*i*). Sunbirds, however, were observed taking only one-third of their

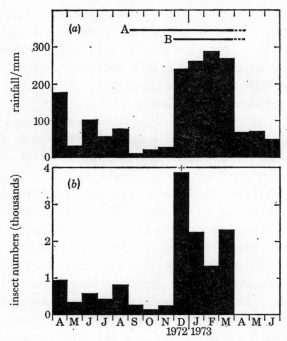

FIGURE 1. Monthly rainfall (*a*) and insect abundance (*b*) on West Island, Aldabra Atoll, April 1972 – June 1973. Insects given as total numbers caught during daylight hours by a Johnson–Taylor suction trap during 1 week of each month (by kind permission of Dawn W. Frith). Horizontal lines in upper section represent approximate point of commencement, and period, of breeding by: A, *Nectarinia sovimanga* and B, *Zosterops maderaspatana* and *Foudia eminentissima*.

annual insect catch during this period, thus showing no seasonal fluctuation in the use of insects (table 6). The fact that most of the feeding on insects by white-eyes in *Casuarina* woodland occurred during the wetter 4 months of highest insect abundance may indicate stronger competitive pressure, from the sunbird, during drier periods. Distributions of the Souimanga sunbird and Malagasy white-eye on other islands of the Aldabran group (Watson, Zusi & Storer 1963; Benson & Penny 1971) suggest that when competition between those two birds has occurred (and there is no reason to believe it has not, in view of the close proximity of these islands), sunbirds have excluded white-eyes. On Assumption only sunbirds occur (Stoddart, Benson & Peake 1970). On Cosmoledo (Benson 1970*b*) and Astove (Benson 1970*a*), each with land surface areas much smaller than Aldabra, both species occur but sunbirds are far more numerous than white-eyes (Benson & Penny 1971).

It should be noted that during breeding, the fody, white-eye and sunbird require much insect food for gonad and egg development and raising of young. At this time, therefore, all three species particularly require insects. The relative abundance of insects during this period (figure 1) might, however, be sufficient for them to share with little or no competition, particularly in view of their preference for predominantly differing insects (see table 5 and §4c).

(b) Use of introduced vegetation

Coconut palms and *Casuarina* trees are considered recently introduced onto Aldabra (Fryer 1911; Fosberg 1971) and it is thus interesting to note their utilization by endemic birds. It should be noted, however, that while there is perhaps less doubt that coconut was introduced to Aldabra, *Casuarina* occurred there before additional planting (Wickens 1979, this volume). Ridley (1930) considered it unlikely that *Casuarina* was introduced by man. Subsequently, Wickens (1979, this volume) has pointed out that the evidence is no more indicative of this tree's being an introduction than it is for its being native to Aldabra. Many endemic birds associate closely with *Casuarina* and a closer study of these relations may prove useful in establishing the status and significance of the tree on Aldabra.

The Malagasy kestrel feeds in sparse *Casuarina* woodland, whereas the Aldabra drongo feeds in denser woodland also, and frequently breeds there, (Benson & Penny 1971; C. B. Frith 1977). The two species thus utilize *Casuarina* in somewhat different ways, which is noteworthy in view of their similar diets (see §3 (Benson & Penny 1971)).

Malagasy turtledoves feed beneath *Casuarina* woodland but Comoro blue pigeons were seen only a couple of times in *Casuarina* (§3c). Coucals feed in *Casuarina*, certainly more so in woodland with mixed scrub below it, but are not known to breed in it. Malagasy bulbuls feed on insects in *Casuarina*, and on fruits of mixed scrub beneath where present. One occupied bulbul nest was found in a sapling *Casuarina* at the edge of a wood, and one of three nests found by Benson & Penny (1971) was in a *Casuarina* overgrown with creeper. Pied crows perch and nest in uppermost *Casuarina* branches, but rarely enter into denser lower woodland.

Casuarina provided sunbirds and white-eyes with the largest proportion of their insect food (table 3) and, as discussed elsewhere (§4a, c), the two birds have somewhat different feeding stations within it. In insect feeding, both birds show little preference for one or other casuarina habitats (sites 3 and 4). Owing to a very sparse flowering plant flora, pure woodland (site 3) is not favoured for feeding by sunbirds, but is much used by white-eyes.

The red-headed forest fody uses *Casuarina* extensively for food, nest building material and breeding territories. It is the favoured breeding habitat second only to sparsely available palm groves with interspersed *Casuarina* trees. *Casuarina* 'needles' are very commonly, and sometimes almost exclusively, used for nest building; 61 % of fody insect feeding occurred in *Casuarina* and most of this in the relatively pure woodland of site 4 (table 7). Thus the bird associates with *Casuarina* and insects inhabiting it.

Findings of this preliminary study, and speculative interpretations of some results concerning habitat preferences, make it difficult to imagine the coexistence of land bird forms now present on Aldabra before the appearance of *Casuarina* and, to a much smaller extent, coconut palms, without considerably more interspecific competition than exists today. If *Casuarina* is in fact a more recent naturally established species on Aldabra it is possible that fewer bird species existed there beforehand. The earliest apparent reference to *Casuarina* on Aldabra is by a Captain Laing in 1815 (Wickens 1979, this volume). *Casuarina* woodland described in 1815 was on the eastern end of Middle Island and was well established, consisting of 'very high trees, for at least a mile in extent, that may be seen 8 or 9 leagues (38–43 km) from the deck of a moderate-sized ship'. Thus *Casuarina* can be assumed to have existed on Aldabra for at least 200 years. I suspect that Wickens is correct in considering *Casuarina* to be native to Aldabra and thus to be of some antiquity there.

Coconut plantations, or groves, provide open habitats useful as feeding areas for a number of wading birds, mostly herons and sacred ibis. The Malagasy kestrel benefits greatly, using crowns of palms for nesting (Gaymer 1967; Penny 1965; C. B. Frith 1977) and trunks and bare ground beneath for hunting over. It is difficult to imagine where Aldabra kestrels would have nested in the absence of both *Casuarina* and coconut, as it has been recorded as nesting only in these two trees. Benson & Penny (1971) considered the kestrel a recent colonizer of Aldabra, 'quite possibly subsequent to any human influence'. The very limited degree of morphological differentiation in the Aldabran kestrel population (Benson & Penny 1971; Brown & Amadon 1968) supports this suggestion.

Pied crows find the open palm groves particularly favourable for scavenging and nest predation activity (C. B. Frith 1976, 1977) and also nest in the crown of palms (Benson & Penny 1971). Fodies and, to a much smaller extent, sunbirds nest in palm groves, suspending their nests from palm-leaf pinnae. Both birds nectar feed from coconut palm inflorescence, the fody being able to open the hard flowers with its heavy bill whilst these remain unavailable to the sunbird.

(c) Ecological segregation

In considering possible feeding interactions between extant land birds on West Island it is convenient to treat them in three groups: pigeons; other non-passerines and the drongo; and remaining passerines.

The Comoro blue pigeon is very predominantly found at the east of Aldabra (Benson & Penny 1971; C. B. Frith 1977) and while this might be due to past human predation it was also the situation found by Abbott (in Ridgway 1896) in 1892 and by Fryer (1911) in 1908. This disparity in distribution may be partly due to a greater abundance of *Ficus* and other fruiting plants at the east of the atoll. Birds were not seen feeding on West Island during the walks, and on the few occasions that feeding birds were seen they were in trees and not on the ground. Turtledoves feed largely on the ground upon seeds and invertebrates. Thus, the two pigeons feed in different ways and largely upon different foods (appendix 1).

While the remaining non-passerines and the drongo take similar foods they fall into two groups with regard to feeding method and, to some extent, location. Green-backed herons and Malagasy coucals hunt prey on the ground and, less frequently, in foliage to considerable heights, where food is stalked and not flown at. The heron, however, prefers open areas, doubtless taking more active insects than the slow hunting technique of the coucal permits. Larger insects and small reptiles in sites 1–6 inclusive are resources shared by these two birds, although their differences in favoured microhabitat presumably means predominantly different large insect taxa are utilized. In addition, cattle egrets, *Bubulcus ibis* (but not the more common little egret, *Egretta garzetta*), were infrequently seen feeding in sites 5 and 6 on larger insects, where they forage in a similar fashion to *Butorides*. Cattle egrets are limited on Aldabra to perhaps 'several hundred birds' (Benson & Penny 1971), which may be due to competitive pressure from *Butorides*. The five species of resident herons on Aldabra provide interesting material for an ecological study.

The Malagasy kestrel and Aldabra drongo feed a good deal in the air. The kestrel has a diet very similar to the drongo and both feed in a generally like fashion, pouncing upon prey from exposed perches and taking prey in flight. They differ, however, in that the drongo prefers denser vegetation, and is reported to show preference for mangroves (Benson & Penny 1971) and mangrove edges (Gaymer 1967). I did not, however, see drongos feeding in mangroves and I suspect that it rarely occurs in West Island mangroves. It might occur more commonly elsewhere, however (see §3*g*). In mixed scrub and palm grove, both birds take very much the same food. The drongo population is obviously a very well established one in view of its marked differentiation, but was described recently as 'not a very numerous species. The total population probably does not exceed more than a few hundred individuals' (Benson & Penny 1971). The fact that it apparently requires large breeding territory (Gaymer 1967) and is inclined to well vegetated habitats may restrict it. If, as suggested by Benson & Penny, the kestrel is a very recent colonizer it is possible that some competitive pressure between the two birds has resulted in the latter two habitats at least, an interesting situation indeed in two populations estimated to consist of no more than from one to a few hundred each. In turn, the kestrel suffers from predation upon eggs and nestling by the pied crow (C. B. Frith 1977; Penny 1965), which is considered to have reached Aldabra less than a century ago (Benson & Penny 1971). Doubtless drongos also suffer pied crow predation but evidence of this is lacking. Moreover, there can be little doubt that both species suffer from egg predation at least by rats (C. B. Frith 1977).

The Malagasy bulbul feeds upon many plant fruits (appendix 1) and takes various insects. It is noteworthy that of 16 plants known to be used by it only 8 are also used by the two pigeons, 6 being known to be taken by the Comoro blue pigeon and 5 by the Malagasy turtledove. Fruits of *Passiflora suberosa* were used by both the bulbul and the fody, but are not known to be eaten by pigeons (appendix 1). Observations of bulbuls aerial feeding (§3*f*) are particularly interesting in view of recent correspondence describing the habit as previously unknown in bulbuls (Meriwani 1973; Brooke 1973; Markus 1974).

Sunbirds and white-eyes are the most numerous birds on Aldabra, are of similar size, and have been considered ecologically closer than any other two birds (Benson & Penny 1971). In fact the two species appear to be ecologically isolated in some respects, perhaps more so than are some other endemic land birds. In order to illustrate clearly possible feeding interactions between these two birds it might be argued that it is pertinent to examine figures for feeding in the two presumed original, and currently very predominant, vegetation types, namely mixed scrub and/or *Pemphis* and mangroves. It is presumably in these that the birds would have coexisted before the (theoretical) introduction of exotics. White-eyes feed in both habitats almost equally, whereas sunbirds feed very predominantly in mixed scrub and *Pemphis* (88% of records for the two vegetation types; see table 4). Obviously mangrove lacks suitable flowers and insects for sunbirds, whereas it possibly provides slightly favoured feeding grounds (by 4% over mixed scrub and *Pemphis*) for white-eyes. These findings disagree with Benson & Penny (1971) who stated that the white-eye 'penetrates mangroves to a limited degree only'.

Sunbirds feed predominantly on nectar (61%) and, to a smaller degree, insects (39%), whereas white-eyes are almost exclusively insectivorous with the addition of some fruit and nectar (table 4). While these proportions are possibly exaggerated owing to biases inherent in the methods of study (§2), differences are so great as to indicate a fundamental difference in the diets of these birds. Sunbirds feed closer to the ground in *Casuarina* woodland than do white-eyes probably because of the greater possibility of including flower nectar and spiders (table 5) in their diet which are more abundant in mixed scrub below the woodland of site 3 (see table 6). Flowering seasonality was not examined but it is presumably possible that both of these small birds are nearly exclusively insectivorous if flowers (and fruits) are sparse or lacking. Bimonthly totals of sunbird nectar feeding indicate that April and May was the period of least suitable flower availability during the study. It should also be noted that white-eyes (*Zosterops* spp.) commonly pierce soft fruits with the bill and extract juices with a brush tongue (Moreau 1964*a*; Skead 1967, p. 288) and while I did not see this performed by Aldabran birds it doubtless occurs.

Also isolating sunbirds and white-eyes is the foraging behaviour each performs. White-eyes normally flock-feed, working the foliage thoroughly, each individual gaining some advantage from disturbance by other flock members which flush insects or draw attention to a locally abundant food such as caterpillars. Sunbirds are opportunists, usually feeding alone, or sometimes in pairs, taking insects where and when found. This may not be true of nectar feeding at all times, however, as a local abundance of flowers may permit birds to visit blooms repeatedly. An additional important consideration is the hovering ability of sunbirds. Hovering is often used to take nectar, but is also performed frequently to pick insects and spiders from spiders' webs, as was recorded 28 times during walks. These observations, and the preponderance of spiders in sampled sunbirds' gizzards (table 5) indicate that this is a significant feeding method not performed by white-eyes. Skead (1967, p. 69) draws attention to spider feeding by sunbirds and writes, 'Spiders, a favorite source of food and probably the largest in the sunbird economy, are coped with easily.' He also points out that spiders are quickly rendered unrecognizable by sunbird digestion, a fact which makes the high proportion of them in the sample of Aldabran birds the more remarkable, and suggests they are even more important than my observations and gizzard examinations indicate. R. F. Lawrence (in Skead 1967) was of the opinion that sunbirds would probably predominantly take spiders of families Argopyridae, Lycosidae, Salticidae and Thornisidae, particularly of the Argopyridae as these are spinners of large orb-webs which hang more or less in the open. In view of this an examination of relations between the sunbird and spider families important to it on Aldabra might prove particularly interesting.

White-eyes were only twice seen hovering, rather clumsily, while feeding. Infrequently, sunbirds were seen feeding on the ground, but white-eyes were never observed doing so. These differences in hunting techniques and observed feedings are generally reflected in gizzard contents of birds (table 5). The white-eye, as a result of a more methodical and social foraging, is able to exploit a more variable diet, seeking out such items as cockroach egg cases and larvae and adult Lepidoptera which are unexploited by sunbirds.

Sunbirds and white-eyes took between 40 and 50 % of their insect food in *Casuarina* woodland, but fed predominantly at different heights within it. In addition, insect feeding in *Casuarina* by white-eyes was markedly seasonal (table 6), as correlated with a peak of insect abundance on West Island. Insect feeding by sunbirds in all habitats showed no significant seasonal fluctuations.

The red-headed forest fody has a very diverse diet for a ploceid and shares with other small passerine species on Aldabra only fruit and nectar to any extent. In having a tongue adapted to nectar feeding only to a limited degree, it clearly illustrates the pressure of intergeneric competition on islands 'because the reduction in ecological diversity on islands means that even rather dissimilar species may exclude each other' (Lack 1971, p. 242). On Rodrigues the endemic fody *Foudia flavicans* has a tongue highly developed for nectar feeding (Staub 1973) which I believe it has been able to develop because of a lack of feeding competition on the island (C. B. Frith 1976). On Aldabra, however, the fody is sympatric with a sunbird and a white-eye and therefore shares nectar resources, and is thus restricted in its degree of adaptation to such feeding. In the case of the fody and perhaps the white-eye the taking of flower nectar may be seasonal, these birds utilizing this food over periods of temporary superabundance and at other times taking very predominantly their respective insect prey and, in the fody, seeds. Such diet overlap during temporary superabundance of a particular food is well known (Lack 1971) and would be particularly useful to avifaunas of small islands.

Whether or not the broad, generalized, diet and limited adaptation to nectar feeding in the fody indicates prior colonization of Aldabra by the sunbird and white-eye is an interesting question, but in view of the former's marked morphological differentiation (Moreau 1960 a, b; Benson & Penny 1971) it must currently remain a matter of conjecture.

In the taking of *Casuarina* and grass seeds direct from plants (37 % of feedings) the fody lacks significant competitors. Fruits of some plants are taken by both the fody and the bulbul (appendix 1). The fody has developed intensive and thorough hunting techniques enabling it to utilize foods unobtainable to other small species with less robust bills and feeding habits. Its foraging methods particularly make available insect eggs and crevice-dwelling insects and their larvae, as indicated by gizzard contents (C. B. Frith 1976). Insect feeding accounted for 58 % of all recorded feedings. Similar insect feeding behavioural development exists in species of the unrelated Darwin's finches (Geospizinae) of the Galapagos Islands, where it reaches a peak of specialization in the tool-using bird *Camarhynchus pallidus* (Lack 1947; Bowman & Biller 1965). It should be noted that bill and tongue morphology and associated feeding behaviour of species of the fody genus *Foudia* provide material for a rewarding study of adaptive radiation and speciation within a closely related group of island dwelling birds of little less significance as the now classic studies of the Geospizinae (Lack 1947, 1969; Bowman 1961, 1963; Hamilton & Rubinoff 1963, 1967; and numerous references therein).

I am grateful to all persons present with me on Aldabra. I particularly acknowledge assistance and kindness of Dr Sarah Hnatiuk. Thanks are due to staff of the Royal Society of London and British Museum (Natural History) concerned with Aldabra. I am grateful to Mr B. H. Cogan for identifying insects, and to Mr A. Donaldson, Dr R. J. Hnatiuk, Mr S. A. Renvoize, Dr B. A. Whitton and Dr D. Wood for identifying plants.

For valuable discussion I am indebted to Mr C. W. Benson, Mr D. Goodwin, Dr C. J. O. Harrison, Mr C. R. Huxley, Mr J. F. Peake, Dr R. Prŷs-Jones and Dr D. W. Snow. My wife, Dawn W. Frith, kindly identified and discussed Aldabran insects, read drafts of this paper, and provided useful discussion and encouragement.

REFERENCES (Frith)

Benson, C. W. 1967 The birds of Aldabra and their status. *Atoll. Res. Bull.* **118**, 63–111.
Benson, C. W. 1970 a Land (including shore) birds of Astove. *Atoll. Res. Bull.* **136**, 115–120.
Benson, C. W. 1970 b Land (including shore) birds of Cosmoledo. *Atoll Res. Bull.* **136**, 67–81.
Benson, C. W. & Penny, M. J. 1971 The land birds of Aldabra. *Phil. Trans. R. Soc. Lond.* B **260**, 417–527.
Bowman, R. I. 1961 Morphological differentiation and adaptation in the Galapagos finches. *Univ. Calif. Publs Zool.* **58**, 1–326.
Bowman, R. I. 1963 Evolutionary patterns in Darwin's finches. *Occ. Pap. Calif. Acad. Sci.* **44**, 107–140.
Bowman, R. I. & Biller, S. L. 1965 Blood-eating in a Galapagos finch. *Living Bird* **4**, 29–44.
Brooke, R. E. 1973 Aerial feeding by bulbuls. *Ibis* **115**, 606.
Brown, L. H. & Amadon, D. 1968 *Eagles, hawks and falcons of the world.* London: Country Life.

Fosberg, F. R. 1971 Preliminary survey of Aldabra vegetation. *Phil. Trans. R. Soc. Lond.* B **260**, 215–225.

Frith, C. B. 1975*a* Predation upon hatchlings and eggs of the Green Turtle, *Chelonia mydas*, on Aldabra Atoll, Indian Ocean. *Atoll Res. Bull.* **185**, 11–12.

Frith, C. B. 1975*b* Field observations on *Centropus toulou insularis* on Aldabra Atoll. *Ostrich* **46**, 251–257.

Frith, C. B. 1976 A twelve-month field study of the Aldabran Fody *Foudia esinentissima aldabrana*. *Ibis* **118**, 155–178.

Frith, C. B. 1977 Life history notes on some Aldabran birds. *Atoll Res. Bull.* **201**, 1–15.

Frith, D. W. 1975 A preliminary study of insect abundance on West Island, Aldabra Atoll, Indian Ocean. *Trans. R. ent. Soc. Lond.* (3) **127**, 209–226.

Frith, D. W. 1979 A twelve month study of insect abundance and composition at various localities on Aldabra Atoll. *Phil. Trans. R. Soc. Lond.* B **286**, 119–126 (this volume).

Fryer, J. C. F. 1911 The structure and formation of Aldabra and neighbouring islands – with notes on their flora and fauna. *Trans. Linn. Soc. Lond. Zool.* (3) **14**, 397–442.

Gaymer, R. 1967 Observations on the birds of Aldabra in 1964 and 1965. *Atoll Res. Bull.* **118**, 113–125.

Hamilton, T. H. & Rubinoff, I. 1963 Isolation, endemism and multiplication of species in the Darwin finches. *Evolution* **17**, 388–403.

Hamilton, T. H. & Rubinoff, I. 1967 On predicting insular variation in endemism and sympatry for the Darwin finches in the Galapagos Archipelago. *Am. Nat.* **101**, 161-172.

Hill, J. E. 1971 The bats of Aldabra Atoll, Western Indian Ocean. *Phil. Trans. R. Soc. Lond.* B **260**, 573-576.

Lack, D. 1947 *Darwin's finches*. Cambridge University Press.

Lack, D. 1969 Subspecies and sympatry in Darwin's finches. *Evolution* **23**, 252-263.

Lack, D. 1971 *Ecological isolation in birds*. Oxford: Blackwell.

Macnae, W. 1971 Mangroves on Aldabra. *Phil. Trans. R. Soc. Lond.* B **260**, 237-247.

Markus, M. B. 1974 Aerial feeding by bulbuls. *Ibis* **116**, 232.

Meriwani, T. N. 1973 Aerial feeding by bulbuls. *Ibis* **115**, 285.

Moreau, R. E. 1960*a* The ploceine weavers of the Indian Ocean islands. *J. Orn., Lpz.* **101**, 29–49.

Moreau, R. E. 1960*b* Conspectus and classification of the Ploceine weavers. *Ibis* **102**, 298–321 and 443–471.

Moreau, R. E. 1964*a* White-eye. In *New dictionary of birds* (ed. A. L. Thomson), pp. 1–928. London and New York: Nelson.

Penny, M. J. 1965 The birds of Aldabra. *Animals* **7**, 409–411.

Penny, M. J. & Diamond, A. W. 1971 The White-throated Rail *Dryolimnas cuvieri* on Aldabra. *Phil. Trans. R. Soc. Lond.* B **260**, 529–548.

Ridgway, R. 1896 On birds collected by Dr W. L. Abbott in the Seychelles, Amirants, Gloriosa, Assumption, Aldabra and adjacent islands, with notes on habits, etc., by the collector. *Proc. U.S. natn. Mus.* **18**, 509–546.

Ridley, R. N. 1930 *The dispersal of plants throughout the world*. Ashford: L. Reeve & Co.

Skead, C. J. 1967 *The sunbirds of southern Africa*. Cape Town: Trustees of the South African Bird Book Fund.

Staub, F. 1973 Birds of Rodrigues Island. *Proc. R. Soc. Arts. Sci. Maurit.* **4**, 17–59.

Stoddart, D. R., Benson, C. W. & Peake, J. F. 1970 Ecological change and effects of phosphate mining on Assumption Island. *Atoll Res. Bull.* **136**, 121–145.

Vaurie, C. 1949 A revision of the bird family Dicruridae. *Bull. Am. Mus. nat. Hist.* (4) **93**, 199–342.

Vaurie, C. 1962 Family Dicruridae. In *Check-list of birds of the world* (ed. E. Mayr & J. C. Greenway Jr), vol. 15, pp. 137–157. Cambridge, Mass.: Mus. Comp. Zool.

Watson, G. E., Zusi, R. L. & Storer, R. E. 1963 *Preliminary field guide to the birds of the Indian Ocean*. Washington: Smithsonian Institution.

Wickens, G. E. 1979 Speculations on seed dispersal and the flora of the Aldabra archipelago. *Phil. Trans. R. Soc. Lond.* B **286**, 85–97 (this volume).

Woodell, R. 1976 Notes on the Aldabran Coucal *Centropus toulou insularis*. *Ibis* **118**, 263–268.

APPENDIX 1. FOOD PLANT SPECIES USED BY PLANT FEEDING LAND BIRDS ON ALDABRA ATOLL, INDIAN OCEAN

food plant†	*Alectroenas sganzini*	*Streptopelia picturata*	*Hypsipetes madagascariensis*	*Nectarinia sovimanga*	*Zosterops maderaspatana*	*Foudia eminentissima*
Agave sisalana (I)‡	.	o	o	.	.	.
Lomatophyllum aldabrense (E)	?	.	.	×	.	.
Asparagus umbellulatus (E)	.	.	o	.	.	.
Cocos nucifera (N)	.	.	.	×	.	×
Cyperus niveus (N)	.	.	.	.	.	●
Dactyloctenium pilosum (N)	.	●	.	.	.	●
Lepturus repens (N)	.	.	.	.	.	●
Digitaria horizontalis (?I)	.	.	.	.	.	●
Digitaria setigera (?I)	.	.	.	.	.	●
Zea mays (I)	.	.	.	.	.	●
Flacourtia ramontchii (E)	o	●	o	.	o	.
Abutilon angulatum (I)	.	.	.	×	×	.
Gossypium hirsutum (I)	.	.	.	×	.	.
Suriana maritima (N)	.	.	.	×	.	.
Ochna ciliata (N)	?	o	.	.	.	.
Apodytes dimidiata (N)	.	●	o	.	o	.
Mystroxylon aethiopicum (N)	.	.	o	.	.	.
Scutia myrtina (N)	o	o	o	.	.	.
Allophyllus aldabricus (E)	?	o	.	×	.	.
Moringa oleifera (I)	.	o ●	.	×	.	.
Erythrina variegata (?N)	.	.	o	.	.	.
Abrus precatorius (N)	.	.	.	.	×	.
Sophora tomentosa (N)	.	.	.	×	.	.
Caesalpinia bonduc (N)	.	.	.	×	.	.
Ceriops tagal (N)	.	.	.	×	.	.
Terminalia boivinii (N)	o	.	o	.	.	.
Pemphis acidula (N)	.	.	.	×	×	×
Passiflora suberosa (I)	.	.	o	×	.	o
Guettarda speciosa (N)	?	.	.	×	.	.
Polysphaeria multiflora (N)	?	.	o	×	×	o ×
Tricalysia sonderana (N)	.	.	o	×	.	.
Triainolepis fryeri (N)	.	●	.	.	.	.
Veronia grandis (N)	.	.	.	.	.	×
Scaevola taccada (N)	o	o ●	o	×	.	.
Sideroxylon inerme (E)	o	.	.	.	.	.
Azima tetracantha (N)	.	.	.	.	×	.
Solanum indicum (E)	o	o	o	.	.	.
Clerodendrum glabrum (N)	?	.	.	.	.	.
Lantana camara (I)	.	.	o	×	.	.
Premna obtusifolia (N)	o	.	.	.	.	.
Stachytarpheta jamaicensis (I)	.	.	.	×	.	.
Leonotis nepetifolia (I)	.	.	.	×	.	.
Acalypha claoxyoides (E)	.	●	.	.	.	●
Euphorbia pyrifolia (E)	.	o	.	×	.	.
Ricinus communis (?I)	.	.	o	.	.	.
Phyllanthus casticum (N)	o	.	o	.	.	.
Ficus spp. (E, N)	o	.	.	.	o	.
Maillardia pendula (E)	o	.	.	.	.	.
Casuarina equisetifolia (N)	.	●	.	.	.	●

† Data presented are obtained from the present study and that of Benson & Penny (1971). The list of plants follows the order used in 'An annotated list of vascular plants growing on Aldabra and the neighbouring islands of Assumption, Astove and Cosmoledo' produced for limited circulation by The Royal Society of London; with a number of name changes by Wickens (1979, this volume) incorporated.

‡ E, endemic; N, native; I, introduced to Aldabra (Wickens 1979, this volume).

o, fruits, flowers or buds eaten, ●, seeds eaten; ×, nectar eaten; ?, possibly utilized (Benson & Penny 1971).

Phil. Trans. R. Soc. Lond. B. **286**, 211–224 (1978)   [211]
Printed in Great Britain

The ecology and conservation of the Aldabran brush warbler
Nesillas aldabranus

By R. P. Prŷs-Jones†

Sub-department of Ornithology, British Museum (Natural History), Tring, Herts., U.K.

The Aldabran brush warbler, *Nesillas aldabranus*, is one of the world's rarest birds. Studies conducted over the course of 2 years indicate that its distribution is probably restricted to one small area of Aldabra Atoll. Within this area it inhabits only one vegetation community, dense 'mixed scrub', and even within this it is very patchily distributed. Only five separate individuals were definitely identified during the study, but these included two pairs which held contiguous territories. Aspects of the ecology and behaviour of the species are described. The extremely rough and densely vegetated habitat in which the brush warblers live prohibits an accurate estimate of total population size, but it is probably below 25 individuals. Possible conservation measures are discussed in the light of the information collected.

Introduction

The Aldabran brush warbler, *Nesillas aldabranus*, is endemic to Aldabra Atoll, Indian Ocean, and was first described by Benson & Penny (1968) from two specimens taken in late 1967 and early 1968. Before I began my studies on the Aldabran land bird fauna in July 1974 the species was known solely from these two birds and one further individual which was mist-netted, ringed and released in April 1974. The aim of this paper is to give details of the behaviour, ecology and population size of the Aldabran brush warbler, together with a consideration of factors of probable importance to its future conservation. Five different species of brush warbler, belonging to two quite distinct genera (Diamond 1979), occur in the southwest Indian Ocean region, and information relating to the evolution and dispersal of *N. aldabranus* will be presented elsewhere in a comparative analysis incorporating all species of both genera.

Study area and methods

I was present on Aldabra for a total of 27 months (July 1974–June 1975 and November 1975–February 1977). Detailed maps, showing all places mentioned in this paper, are contained in Stoddart (1971*a*) and at the end of this volume. Extensive searches revealed that *N. aldabranus* is probably confined to one small area (Gionnet) at the west end of Middle Island (figure 1); almost all the work described below was carried out here. I visited Gionnet on 28 different occasions at roughly monthly intervals, each visit lasting on average for 3 days (table 1). Owing to the density of the scrub, human movement around this area was practicable only where narrow paths had been cleared. All my field work was conducted from on or near such paths which were marked with coded stakes set at 50 m intervals so that observations could be mapped accurately (see figure 1 for details). Before 1974 only the coast path between Anse Coco and Anse Porche (A10–A20) existed, but in April of that year another path was

† Present address: c/o Edward Grey Institute, Department of Zoology, South Parks Road, Oxford OX1 3PS.

212   R. P. PRŶS-JONES

cleared between Anse Porche and the lagoon (Z1–Z13). In December 1974 and January 1975
I extended the coast path east (to A48), and cut a further east–west path (B10–B20) which ran
roughly along the dividing line between the 'mixed scrub' and 'Pemphis scrub' vegetation communities (see below). This increased the total path length available in the area to about 3 km.

The habitat at Gionnet comprises rugged pavé and champignon rock (Stoddart, Taylor,
Fosberg & Farrow 1971) covered by extremely dense 'mixed scrub' and 'Pemphis scrub'
communities (Fosberg 1971; Hnatiuk & Merton 1979, this volume). The high diversity 'mixed
scrub' occurs on a raised ridge of pavé which runs along the north coast and extends on average
only 50–100 m inland. The rest of the area is mainly lower-lying, more rugged champignon
where 'Pemphis scrub' is the dominant vegetation. This is a low diversity community, heavily
dominated by Pemphis acidula, which is composed only of plants which can tolerate conditions of
high salinity and little soil. The two communities intergrade along their boundary, and throughout the 'Pemphis scrub' there are scattered, slightly raised places on which grow some of the
species otherwise confined to the north coast ridge.

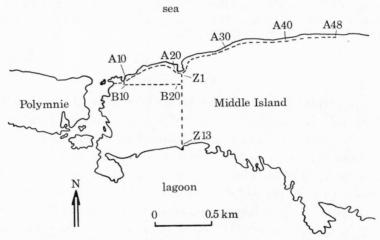

FIGURE 1. The main study area at Gionnet, with paths indicated by dotted lines. Each path was given a different
    letter ('A', 'B' and 'Z'), and had consecutively numbered stakes set at 50 m intervals along it. Distributional
    information presented in this paper and referring to this area is pinpointed to a given 50 m sector of path by
    means of these letters and numbers, e.g. an observation coded A20 would have been made between markers
    A20 and A21.

In order to permit a closer analysis of brush warbler occurrence in relation to vegetation
composition in the Gionnet area, I recorded the distribution of the different species of plant.
The data are summarized for each path in appendix 1. It was obtained by noting the identities
of all plant species growing within 2 m of different 50 m sectors of path; grasses, sedges and
small herbs were excluded as they formed only a very small percentage of the total plant biomass of the closed-canopy shrub communities which I was censusing. As the 'Z' path crossed
the main 'mixed scrub'/'Pemphis scrub' boundary at right angles, more detailed data are given
in appendix 2 for this path alone to illustrate the manner in which plant species diversity
changed along it.

Much of the study of the brush warblers themselves depended on the use of tape playback of
their vocalizations to attract them. These vocalizations were originally recorded on a Uher
4400 Stero Report IC tape recorder, and were transferred to cassette tape for playback over a
Philips 2204 recorder. This playback, supplemented by 'squeaking' (Emlen 1969) to which

brush warblers also are attracted (cf. Forbes-Watson 1969), was vital for field work because the skulking and frequently silent birds were otherwise very difficult to find in the dense vegetation. Once located, the birds showed little fear of man and could be watched from close range without apparent disturbance to them. However, the density of the scrub prohibited attempts to follow a bird far and, in conjunction with their rapid habituation to both playback and 'squeaking', this greatly restricted the amount of direct observation possible on any individual brush warbler.

RESULTS

(a) Numbers

During the entire study I definitely identified only five different individuals, one of these being the bird (W) that had been colour-ringed before my arrival on Aldabra. Of the other

TABLE 1. RECORDED DISTRIBUTION OF BRUSH WARBLERS WITHIN THE STUDY AREA
AT GIONNET, IN RELATION TO THE DATES OF MY VISITS

	brush warbler individuals (see text)					
date	W♂	UR♀	Y♂	G♀	R♂	'Unknown'†
Apr. 15–18‡ (1974)	16	—	—	—	—	—
May 10–17‡	—	—	—	—	—	—
Sept. 7–10	—	—	—	—	—	—
Oct. 13–14	—	—	—	—	10, 15–16§	—
Dec. 3–6	—	—	27–28§	27–28§	15–16	—
Dec. 17–18	—	—	27–28	27–28	—	—
Jan. 29–Feb. 2 (1975)	30	30	27–29	27–29	—	—
Feb. 16–17	30–36	30–36	28–29	28–29	—	—
Feb. 21	30–31	30–31	28–29	28–29	—	—
Mar. 10–12	30–32	30–31	28–29	28	—	—
Apr. { 9	27	27	26	—	—	—
10	—	28	28	—	—	—
11	—	27–29	27–29	—	—	—
Apr. 22–23	33	28	28	—	—	—
May 8–9	—	27–28	27–28	—	—	—
June 6–7	—	27–29	27–29	—	—	—
Nov. 26	—	—	—	—	—	—
Dec. 17–18	—	—	27–30	—	—	—
Jan. 6–7 (1976)	—	—	27–28	—	—	—
Jan. 29–31	—	—	28	—	—	—
Feb. 20–22	—	—	28–29	—	—	—
Mar. 30–Apr. 1	—	—	28	—	—	—
May 2–5	(29)‖	—	28–29	—	35	—
June 2–5	—	—	—	—	—	—
July 2–5	—	—	28	—	—	—
Aug. 2–4	—	—	—	—	14	—
Sept. 7–12	—	—	28–29	—	—	—
Nov. 5–8	—	—	—	—	—	—
Dec. 19–21	—	—	—	—	28–29	—
Jan. 23 (1977)	—	—	—	—	29	—
Jan. 29–30	—	—	29–30	—	28	16
Feb. 9–10	—	—	—	—	27–28	15–16

All sightings of brush warblers were made from the coast ('A') path, and the numbers shown refer to the marker stakes on this path (see figure 1 for details).
† Bird never seen clearly enough to check for colour rings.
‡ Data from C. Huxley and R. Wilson (personal communication).
§ Birds not yet colour-ringed so identity not certain.
‖ Very brief sighting which could not be confirmed.

four, I colour-ringed three, and could be fairly certain of the identity of the fourth during a period in which it was paired and territorial. The different individuals are referred to below by their colour-rings (R = red, Y = yellow, G = green, W = white, UR = unringed). Table 1 gives the dates and precise localities at which all sightings were made; no brush warbler was ever seen away from the coast ('A') path.

TABLE 2. BIOMETRICAL AND OTHER DATA TAKEN FROM CAPTURED BRUSH WARBLERS

authority ...	Benson & Penny (1968)	Benson & Penny (1968)	C. R. Huxley & J. R. Wilson (personal communication)	personal observation	personal observation	personal observation
date	11 Dec. 1967	29 Jan. 1968	16 Apr. 1974	5 Dec. 1974	17 Dec. 1974	17 Dec. 1974
ring colour	—	—	W	R	Y	G
sex	♀	♂	♂	♂	♂	♀
mass/g	—	19.5	18	19.7	—	19.4
wing/mm	63	70	67	68.5	69	65
tail/mm	86	91	85	—	—	—
tars./mm	24	24	26.4	—	25.5	23.7
bill length/mm						
tip to feathers	15	15	15.9	14.8	16.0	15.6
tip to skull	18	18	20.2	—	18.9	17.9
brood patch	yes	no	no	no	no	yes
remige moult	no	near start	near end	no	no	no

(b) Biometrics and sexing

Available biometrical data are summarized in table 2. The sexes are similar in appearance, but of the two pairs observed in the field one member of each was clearly larger, bolder in approaching a source of playback, more vocal, and failed to develop a brood patch in the breeding season; these individuals were assumed to be male, and the other members of the pairs taken to be female. R was never seen paired with any other individual but on both mensural characteristics and behaviour appeared to be male.

(c) Voice

The vocal repertoire of the Aldabran brush warbler consists of only two types of call which I was able to distinguish unequivocally from one another in the field, and analysis on a sound spectrograph (Kay Sonagraph 6061-B) showed that the coarse structure of even these was quite similar. Much the more common of the two was a very brief 'chak' call of wide frequency range (figure 2a). This was given by both sexes and in a wide variety of different circumstances, with differences in meaning apparently being conveyed by variation in the number and temporal spacing of calls given and by the loudness with which they were uttered. Single or short groups of soft calls were given every now and again by members of a pair to maintain contact in the dense vegetation, and were also made occasionally by unmated individuals. The male of a pair and, less frequently, unmated males would 'sing', often from a prominent perch, giving a series of loud calls as shown in figure 2(a): beginning slow, increasing in tempo, and with a few slower calls at the end. Similar call sequences were given by one or both members of a pair in response to tape playback, and the two birds sometimes 'duetted' although without relating the timing of their calls to those of their partners in any precise manner. With increasing agitation the slower initial and final calls tended to be omitted; when highly excited a bird occasionally gave what I termed in my field notes a 'machine-gun chatter', rolling the individual calls together into a long, harsh, extremely rapid stream; e.g. male W gave this response to tape playback on 23 April 1975 after he had apparently been recently dispossessed of his mate by male Y (see table 1 and below). Both the harsh 'chirr' and 'short, scolding chatter' recorded by Penny and Diamond respectively (in Benson & Penny 1968) probably refer to sequences of these 'chak' calls.

The second type of call was a loud, nasal 'chir' and was always given after one or two preliminary 'chak' calls, producing a di- or trisyllabic 'chak–chir' phrase which must correspond

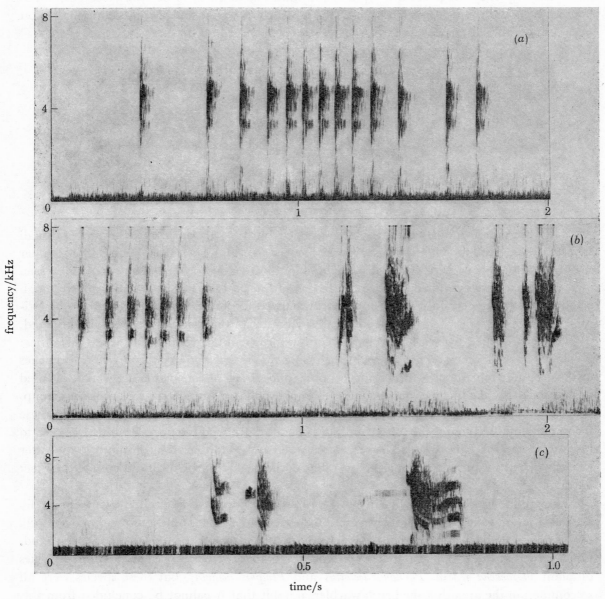

FIGURE 2. Sound spectrograms of brush warbler vocalizations. (a) Sequence of 'chak' calls. (b) 'Chak' calls followed by two 'chak–chir' phrases. (c) Details of a 'chak–chir' phrase illustrating the considerable harmonic structure which some 'chir' calls exhibited. Note that both time and frequency scales are different in (c) from those in (a) and (b).

to the 'chinkachoy' described by Penny (in Benson & Penny 1968). Figure 2(*b*) shows the end of a sequence of 'chak' calls followed by two 'chak–chir' phrases, the former of which sounded disyllabic and the latter trisyllabic. Although closely resembling the 'chak' call in coarse structure, the 'chir' is slightly more extended in duration and may show considerable harmonic structure (figure 2*c*). Both sexes used the 'chak–chir' phrase but females gave it proportionately more frequently; it was also noted that male Y used the phrase more often when unmated than when paired. However, no clear-cut distinction could be made between circumstances in which the 'chak–chir' phrase was used and those in which 'chak' calls alone were given. The brevity and wide frequency range of both types of call must enable them to be easily located (Nottebohm 1975), and the loudness with which the birds can utter the calls permits communication over considerable distances.

TABLE 3. FORAGING HEIGHT OF BRUSH WARBLERS

height/m	% of total feeding observations
above 1½	17.8
below 1½	53.3
ground	28.9

total observations: 45

(d) Feeding ecology

Field observation indicated that food consumed by *N. aldabranus* consists entirely of small invertebrates, probably largely insects and spiders (see also Benson & Penny 1968); other members of the genus *Nesillas* are also predominantly insectivorous (Benson 1960). Prey seen clearly ranged from one-third to twice the length of the birds' beaks (*ca.* 5–30 mm), although smaller items were certainly eaten but were swallowed too rapidly for their length to be estimated. Large prey were beaten violently against a branch or the ground before being consumed.

The methods used by brush warblers to capture prey can be grouped into three categories: picking, leap-snatching and probing. Picking means removal of food items from leaves, branches or the ground while the bird still has its feet on a solid surface. Leap-snatching, which was used in particular to take insects from the undersides of leaves and branches, involved a part jump, part brief flight with the prey being captured while the bird was in the air. With both these techniques loud bill snaps were often audible as the bird grabbed the prey. Probing was used to investigate clumps of live or dead leaves, rotten wood and leaf litter on the ground; in the latter case the detritus was often swept aside by a flick of the beak, but the birds did not use their feet for digging.

Although the brush warblers live in dense scrub which is about 4–5 m tall, they are essentially skulkers that move low through the vegetation and seldom fly far. Table 3 shows that over 75 % of observed foraging was carried out at heights below 1.5 m, and more than 25 % on the ground. Of all prey that I saw taken from above ground level, 75 % were captured on only three species of plant (*Dracaena reflexa*, *Pandanus tectorius* and *Pemphis acidula*), but these species were all so common in the area that the brush warblers inhabit that it cannot be concluded from this that the birds were actively selecting particular plant species in which to forage.

(e) Annual cycle

Both rainfall and insect abundance on Aldabra are highly seasonal (Stoddart & Mole 1977; Frith 1975), and most of the land bird species have regular annual cycles of breeding and moult (Prŷs-Jones 1979). Data for the brush warbler are very limited, but its breeding season probably begins in October or early November, near the onset of the wet season, and extends until late January. The female that I observed in December had a pronounced brood patch, and Benson & Penny (1968) found a female with a nest containing three eggs in this month. Rand (1936) and Benson (1960) have previously reported that other *Nesillas* species in similar seasonal environments in Madagascar and the Comoro Islands also breed at this time of year. My field observations indicated that the Aldabran brush warblers were certainly engaged in moult between the second half of February and the end of April, although the male taken by Benson & Penny (1968) had begun moulting by late January (table 2); a start this early may be unusual and may have resulted from the loss of his probable mate 6 weeks previously.

(f) Breeding success

Breeding pairs were located only during the 1974–5 breeding season (table 1), and to minimize disturbance to them I made no attempt to search for their nests. However, had any young survived I should almost certainly have been able to detect them during their post-fledging period of dependence as the paired adults were easy to locate throughout the breeding and early moult seasons. It is probable that no young were produced within the area shown in figure 1 during the entire course of the study.

(g) Territorial behaviour

The two pairs of brush warblers present in the 1974–5 breeding season held contiguous territories with the boundary separating them running inland from the north coast through marker A30 to a point about 50 m from the sea, south of which neither pair appeared to venture. By simultaneously attracting both pairs with tape playback, and thereby setting up inter-pair confrontations, I found the boundary to be closely delineated with neither pair willing to trespass across it although they would call loudly at each other while only a few metres apart. On the opposite side of their territory, Y and G were never seen to move further west than A27, and thus had a territory size of roughly ¾ ha. W and UR were found as far east as A36, indicating a territory size of over 1½ ha, but the area they commonly utilized was similar in size to the territory of Y and G (table 1).

The territorial system altered in April 1975, during the postnuptial moult, when the female G disappeared and female UR subsequently changed both its mate and its territory (table 1). G was last seen on 11 March. On the first day of my next visit to the area, 9 April, both W and UR were found foraging and calling at A27 within what had previously been the territory of Y and G. Prolonged searching revealed a very subdued Y alone at A26, i.e. about 50 m further west than his previous territorial boundary. On the following day, however, W was not present, but Y and UR were found foraging together at A28; they remained paired together in the old territory of Y and G until I left Aldabra for 5 months in June 1975. W was seen again back in his old territory at the end of April so the change of mate by female UR had certainly not been caused by his death.

From November 1975 onwards only unmated males could be found. Y had by then lost his second mate, UR, but nevertheless persisted in his territory until September 1976. No bird could be found in this territory in November, but by the following month R had taken up residence. After being ringed in December 1974 this latter bird had vanished for nearly 18 months and then made two reappearances in widely separated places during 1976 before finally taking up a territory in December between A27 and A29 where he remained until the end of the study (table 1). Y, however, was definitely still alive in 1977 as he was seen again in the vicinity of his old territory. Unmated males might thus either remain resident in one place for a long time or move around to a considerable degree, and their disappearance could not be equated with death. During periods when individuals could not be found it is uncertain whether they had moved out of the study area or whether they merely stayed silent, and therefore undetectable, within its bounds.

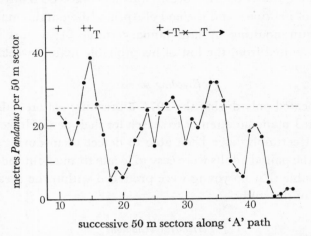

FIGURE 3. The linear abundance of *Pandanus* along the coast ('A') path, with the amount of *Pandanus* being expressed as the running mean of that in three contiguous sectors. T, sectors in which brush warblers were known to have held territories; +, other sectors in which brush warblers were seen. Above dotted line more than half the length of path in a sector was bordered by *Pandanus* on at least one side. Note that the T at A16 refers to where the pair collected by Benson & Penny (1968) had their nest.

(h) Distribution in relation to habitat

Brush warblers were never found in the low diversity '*Pemphis* scrub' (*contra* Penny 1974). Within the more diverse 'mixed scrub' the distribution of brush warbler sightings was patchy (table 1); in particular the species was found only along the coastal ('A') path although the overall composition of the vegetation bordering this path differed only in limited degree from that bordering the 'B' path (appendix 1). Of the floristic differences which did exist the most pronounced was the virtual absence of *Pandanus tectorius* from the 'B' path whereas it grew in large stands along the coast edge. Brush warblers were frequently sighted in or near these *Pandanus* stands so I investigated the possibility of a positive association between the two. For each 50 m sector along the 'A' path I measured the length which was bordered on at least one side by *Pandanus* plants. Figure 3 shows graphically the close relationship between the distribution of *Pandanus* and that of brush warblers, and statistical analysis confirmed that sectors in which brush warblers were known to have occurred were bordered by significantly greater amounts of *Pandanus* than those in which the birds were not ($\bar{x}$ for *Pandanus* in sectors where brush warblers had been sighted $= 27.7 \pm 7.2$ m, $n = 15$; $\bar{x}$ for *Pandanus* in sectors where brush warblers had not been sighted $= 10.9 \pm 4.9$ m, $n = 23$; $t = 4.08$, $p < 0.001$).

DISCUSSION

The Aldabran brush warbler is clearly an extremely uncommon species, but it is not obvious whether this has always been so or whether environmental alterations in the recent past have caused its present rarity, and may possibly also lead to its future extermination. Changes on Aldabra which may have tended to diminish the numbers of brush warblers and restrict their distribution can be summarized under four headings:

(a) '*Natural*' *alteration in vegetation distribution and abundance*. There is no direct evidence pointing to any specific alteration of this type which might have been detrimental to the brush warbler population. However, considerable change in vegetation cover has certainly occurred during the recent past on some parts of Aldabra (see, for example, Hnatiuk, Woodell & Bourn 1976; Merton, Bourn & Hnatiuk 1976), and the size and composition of the plant communities present are probably very sensitive to alterations in climate, sea level and/or the abundance of the major endemic herbivore, the giant tortoise (*Geochelone gigantea*), the population of which is known to have increased greatly since the beginning of this century (Stoddart 1971 *b*).

(b) *Introduction of goats* (Capra hircus). The history of this species on Aldabra has been described by Stoddart (1971 *b*, 1977). Goats are now common on South Island and the eastern part of Middle Island, and until recently occurred on West Island also. Their introduction has not resulted in the devastating effect on vegetation that similar introductions of goats have had on remote islands elsewhere, but their browsing activity may tend nevertheless to open up areas of dense scrub and thus make them less suitable for brush warblers.

(c) *Introduction of rats* (Rattus rattus). Most of the common small passerine species on Aldabra suffer very high nest predation (Frith 1976; Prŷs-Jones 1979), and much of this can be attributed to rats which were introduced at an unknown time in the past and are now ubiquitous on the main islands of the atoll.

(d) *Introduction of cats* (Felis catus). Cats have also been introduced to Aldabra (Stoddart 1971 *b*) but are so rare on Middle Island that it seems unlikely they could have affected the brush warbler population.

Fosberg (in Benson & Penny 1968) considered that the only apparent ecological peculiarity of the Gionnet region was the abundance of *Dracaena reflexa*, a plant not common over most of Aldabra. However, a number of different factors taken in conjunction make the north coast 'mixed scrub' habitat at Gionnet clearly distinct from any other area of the atoll. These factors are:

(1) extremely dense, closed-canopy vegetation, with a considerable leaf litter/soil layer beneath;

(2) large, dense stands of almost pure *Pandanus tectorius*;

(3) a high abundance of *Dracaena reflexa*;

(4) a total absence of both tortoises and goats.

It seems likely that some combination of the above factors is critical for the presence of brush warblers, although the relative importance of each is still speculative. The exceptionally rich 'mixed scrub', and possibly *Dracaena reflexa* in particular, may be essential for the species to forage in. It is probable that the growth form of *Pandanus* offers higher than average protection for nests from rat predation; the only active nest of a brush warbler which has been found on Aldabra was built in *Pandanus* (Benson & Penny 1968), and other land bird species very frequently select this plant to nest in in places where it is available (personal observation).

The absence of tortoises and goats from Gionnet may be of considerable importance in preventing the opening up of the 'mixed scrub' habitat and the disturbance and scattering of the leaf litter layer. Both tortoises and goats, but apparently not brush warblers, occur on Middle Island east of Anse Grande Grabeau (which is placed 2 km west of its correct position on the map in Stoddart (1971 *a*)), and here the 'mixed scrub' is much more open. However, this is not necessarily a case of cause and effect since tortoises, goats and brush warblers are all absent from rather similar open vegetation on Polymnie Island. From the east end of the Gionnet coast path (A48) to a point somewhat west of Anse Grande Grabeau there is no path of any type, and the vegetation is extremely dense; this is one of the least known areas of Aldabra. The only landing place from the sea in this region is at Opark, and my limited forays in this area revealed no signs of tortoises or goats which thus seem likely to have the westerly limits of their distribution on Middle Island between here and Anse Grande Grabeau. Tortoises tend generally to be absent from dense scrub on Middle Island (Bourn & Coe 1978), but it is more difficult to understand why goats, which elsewhere extensively utilize even dense '*Pemphis* scrub' (M. Gould, personal communication), should not have spread to the Gionnet area.

The known total world distribution of the Aldabran brush warbler is confined to a 50 m wide strip along the north coast of Middle Island running east for 2 km from Passe Gionnet. Its maximum likely distribution is bounded by the same strip extended to about 1 km west of Anse Grande Grabeau, i.e. some 9 km in length or *ca.* 0.45 km^2 in area. Extrapolation, made on the assumptions that the study area contains three potential brush warbler territories, that the unvisited but potentially suitable area contains a proportionately equivalent number of territories, and that the brush warbler occurs nowhere else on Aldabra, gives a maximum population size of about 25 birds. In fact there is no reason to believe that the population even approaches this figure as the suitability of all the included habitat is uncertain (I found no brush warblers at Opark), and there is also no evidence that even three pairs of brush warblers have ever tried to breed simultaneously within the Gionnet study area.

Aside from rat eradication, which is not now and may never be a feasible proposition, no 'active' conservation measures appear possible. 'Passive' conservation measures should include the total protection of all 'mixed scrub' lying to the west of Anse Grande Grabeau on Middle Island. In particular, no east–west paths should be cut in the intervening region between the Gionnet study site and Anse Grande Grabeau as this might permit goats and/or tortoises to infiltrate past any vegetational barriers that exist. Despite the great difficulty of coastal landings, further investigation of this region should be performed only along paths cut on a north–south axis, and these should be both very narrow (to permit rapid regeneration) and few in number. The creation of further suitable areas for brush warblers is almost certainly impracticable, but other places where it might conceivably exist undetected should be investigated further, e.g. the densely vegetated, little-known region in the southwestern corner of South Island.

The Aldabran brush warbler population is in a critical condition. This state is not directly man-induced, however, and the only feasible conservation measure at present is total protection of both it and its very restricted habitat.

Alec Forbes-Watson, Gary Hill, Chris Huxley, Oliver Prŷs-Jones and Marilyn Walker assisted me at different times in the field. Jenny Horne and Chris Huxley lent me Uher tape recorders. Tony Diamond, Gary Hill, Oliver Prŷs-Jones, David Snow and David Stoddart commented on a draft of this paper. The Royal Society provided facilities at the Aldabra

Research Station, and the Natural Environment Research Council provided financial support. To all of the above I am grateful.

REFERENCES (Prŷs-Jones)

Benson, C. W. 1960 The birds of the Comoro Islands: results of the British Ornithologists Centenary Expedition 1958. *Ibis* **103** b, 5–106.

Benson, C. W. & Penny, M. J. 1968 A new species of warbler from the Aldabra Atoll. *Bull. Br. orn. Club* **88**, 102–108.

Bourn, D. & Coe, M. 1978 The size, structure and distribution of the giant tortoise population of Aldabra. *Phil. Trans. R. Soc. Lond.* B **282**, 139–175.

Diamond, A. W. 1979 Seasonality, population structure and breeding ecology of the Seychelles Brush Warbler *Acrocephalus sechellensis*. *Ostrich, suppl.* (In the press.)

Emlen, J. T. 1969 The 'squeak lure' and predator mobbing in wild birds. *Anim. Behav.* **17**, 515–516.

Forbes-Watson, A. D. 1969 Notes on birds observed in the Comoros on behalf of the Smithsonian Institution. *Atoll Res. Bull.* **128**, 1–23.

Fosberg, F. R. 1971 Preliminary survey of Aldabra vegetation. *Phil. Trans. R. Soc. Lond.* B **260**, 215–225.

Fosberg, F. R. 1977 Miscellaneous notes on the flora of Aldabra and neighbouring islands: 5. *Pandanus tectorius* Parkinson sensu latissimo (Pandanaceae). *Kew Bull.* **31**, 837–840.

Frith, C. B. 1976 A twelve-month field study of the Aldabran Fody *Foudia eminentissima aldabrana*. *Ibis* **118**, 157–178.

Frith, D. W. 1975 A preliminary study of insect abundance on West Island, Aldabra Atoll, Indian Ocean. *Trans. R. ent. Soc. Lond.* **127**, 209–226.

Hnatiuk, R. J. & Merton, L. F. H. 1979 A perspective of the vegetation of Aldabra. *Phil. Trans. R. Soc. Lond.* B **286**, 79–84 (this volume).

Hnatiuk, R. J., Woodell, S. R. J. & Bourn, D. M. 1976 Giant tortoise and vegetation interactions on Aldabra Atoll. Part 2: coastal. *Biol. Conserv.* **9**, 305–316.

Merton, L. F. H., Bourn, D. M. & Hnatiuk, R. J. 1976 Giant tortoise and vegetation interactions on Aldabra Atoll. Part 1: inland. *Biol. Conserv.* **9**, 293–304.

Nottebohm, F. 1975 Vocal behaviour in birds. In *Avian biology* (ed. D. S. Farner & J. R. King), vol. 5, pp. 287–332.

Penny, M. J. 1974 *The birds of Seychelles and the outlying islands.* London: Collins.

Prŷs-Jones, R. P. 1979 In preparation.

Rand, A. C. 1936 The distribution and habits of Madagascar birds. *Bull. Am. Mus. nat. Hist.* **72**, 143–499.

Stoddart, D. R. 1971 a Place names of Aldabra. *Phil. Trans. R. Soc. Lond.* B **260**, 631–632.

Stoddart, D. R. 1971 b Settlement, development and conservation of Aldabra. *Phil. Trans. R. Soc. Lond.* B **260**, 611–628.

Stoddart, D. R. 1977 History of goats in the Aldabra Archipelago. Mimeographed report.

Stoddart, D. R. & Mole, L. U. 1977 Climate of Aldabra Atoll. *Atoll Res. Bull.* **202**, 1–27.

Stoddart, D. R., Taylor, J. D., Fosberg, F. R. & Farrow, G. E. 1971 Geomorphology of Aldabra Atoll. *Phil. Trans. R. Soc. Lond.* B **260**, 31–65.

APPENDIX 1. PLANT SPECIES DISTRIBUTION ALONG THE PATHS IN THE GIONNET STUDY AREA

plant species	% of 50 m sectors in which species occurred		
	'A' path	'B' path	'Z' path
Capparidaceae			
Capparis cartilaginea Decaisne	0	10	0
Maerua triphylla A. Rich.	0	0	8
Flacourtiaceae			
Flacourtia ramontchii L'Herit.	5	0	0
Malvaceae			
Abutilon angulatum (Guill. & Perr.) Mast.	32	30	0
Thespesia populnea (L.) Solander ex Correa	11	0	8
Erythroxylaceae			
Erythroxylum acranthum Hemsley	42	60	0
Simaroubaceae			
Suriana maritima L.	5	0	0
Ochnaceae			
Ochna ciliata Lam.	11	40	0
Meliaceae			
Malleastrum leroyi Fosberg	32	0	8
Icacinaceae			
Apodytes dimidiata E. Mey. ex Arn.	63	20	0
Celastraceae			
Maytenus senegalensis (Lam.) Exell	100	100	100
Mystroxylon aethiopicum (Thunb.) Loes.	100	100	58
Rhamnaceae			
Scutia myrtina (Burm. f.) Kurz	32	100	83
Sapindaceae			
Allophylus aldabricus Radlk.	79	100	25
Leguminosae			
Abrus precatorius L.	26	10	0
Caesalpinia bonduc (L.) Roxb.	5	0	0
Dicrostachys microcephala Renv.	42	70	0
Rhizophoraceae			
Rhizophora mucronata Lam.†	0	0	17
Combretaceae			
Terminalia boivinii Tul.	95	70	17
Lythraceae			
Pemphis acidula Forst.	100	100	100
Passifloraceae			
Passiflora suberosa L.	68	30	25
Rubiaceae			
Canthium bibracteatum (Bak.) Hiern	53	60	0
Polysphaeria multiflora Hiern	95	100	33
Tarenna trichantha (Baker) Bremek.	42	40	8
Tarenna supra-axillaris (Hemsley) Bremek.	95	90	33
Tricalysia sonderana Hiern‡	95	60	17
Compositae			
Vernonia grandis (DC.) Humb.	5	60	50
Goodeniaceae			
Scaevola taccada (Gaertn.) Roxb.	11	0	0
Plumbaginaceae			
Plumbago aphylla Bojer ex Boiss.	5	0	0

plant species	% of 50 m sectors in which species occurred		
	'A' path	'B' path	'Z' path
Sapotaceae			
Sideroxylon inerme L.	100	100	100
Oleaceae			
Jasminum elegans Knobl.	59	40	8
Salvadoraceae			
Azima tetracantha Lam.	68	20	0
Asclepiadaceae			
Pleurostelma cernuum (Decaisne) Bullock	100	100	58
Sarcostemma viminale (L.) R. Br.	+	40	0
Secamone fryeri Hemsley	11	0	0
Boraginaceae			
Cordia subcordata Lam.	5	0	8
Convolvulaceae			
Ipomoea macrantha Roem. & Schultes	63	10	25
Ipomoea pes-caprae (L.) R. Br.	16	0	0
Solanaceae			
Solanum indicum L. var. *aldabrense* (Wright) Fosberg	74	70	58
Verbenaceae			
Clerodendrum glabrum E. Meyer	11	10	0
Premna obtusifolia R. Br.	+	0	0
Nytaginaceae			
Pisonia grandis R. Br.	5	0	0
Amaranthaceae			
Achyranthes aspera L.	16	50	58
Deeringia polysperma (Roxb.) Moq.	11	10	0
Loranthaceae			
Bakerella clavata (Desv.) S. Balle	0	0	8
Euphorbiaceae			
Acalypha claoxyloides Hutch.	100	100	100
Euphorbia pyrifolia Lam.	100	100	25
Phyllanthus casticum Soy.-Will.	5	20	0
Margaritaria anomala (Baill.) Fosberg var. *cheloniphorbe* (Hutch.) Fosberg	11	0	0
Moraceae			
Ficus nautarum Baker	21	10	8
Ficus avi-avi Bl.	16	30	25
Ficus reflexa Thunb.	59	100	67
Liliaceae			
Lomatophyllum aldabrense Marais	100	50	17
Asparagus umbellulatus Bresler	11	0	0
Dracaena reflexa Lam.	100	100	8
Orchidaceae			
Acampe rigida Buch.-Han. ex J.E.Sn. (P. F. Hunt)	5	0	0
Pandanaceae			
Pandanus tectorius Parkinson§	95	10	0
total no. of sectors censused	19	10	12

Notes: Each sector on the 'B' and 'Z' paths was censused, but only every alternate sector on the longer 'A' path. + refers to species present along the 'A' path but not occurring within the censused sectors. Grasses, sedges and small herbs were excluded from the censuses.

† May also have included some *Bruguiera gymnorrhiza* (L.) Lam. and *Ceriops tagal* (Perr.) C. B. Robinson.

‡ May also have included some *Coptosperma nigrescens* (Hook. f.) Hiern.

§ *Sensu* Fosberg (1977).

APPENDIX 2. OCCURRENCE OF PLANT SPECIES IN SUCCESSIVE 50 m SECTORS ALONG THE 'Z' PATH AT GIONNET

plant species	| 50 m sectors (see figure 1) |											% occurrence
	1	2	3	4	5	6	7	8	9	10	11	12	
Acalypha claoxyloides	+	+	+	+	+	+	+	+	+	+	+	+	100
Maytenus senegalensis	+	+	+	+	+	+	+	+	+	+	+	+	100
Pemphis acidula	+	+	+	+	+	+	+	+	+	+	+	+	100
Sideroxylon inerme	+	+	+	+	+	+	+	+	+	+	+	+	100
Scutia myrtina	+	+	+	+	+	+	.	+	.	+	+	+	83
Ficus reflexa	+	+	+	+	.	+	.	+	.	.	+	+	67
Achyranthes aspera	+	.	.	+	.	.	+	+	+	+	+	.	58
Mystroxylon aethiopicum	+	+	+	+	+	+	+	+	.	.	.	.	58
Pleurostelma cernuum	+	+	+	+	+	+	.	.	.	.	+	.	58
Solanum indicum	+	.	.	+	.	+	+	.	.	+	+	+	58
Vernonia grandis	+	+	+	.	+	+	+	.	.	.	.	.	50
Polysphaeria multiflora	+	.	+	+	.	.	.	.	.	.	+	+	33
Tarenna supra-axillaris	+	+	.	+	.	.	.	.	.	.	+	.	33
Allophylus aldabricus	+	+	+	.	.	.	.	.	.	.	.	.	25
Euphorbia pyrifolia	+	+	+	.	.	.	.	.	.	.	.	.	25
Ficus avi-avi	.	.	+	+	.	.	.	+	.	.	+	.	25
Ipomoea macrantha	+	.	.	.	.	.	.	+	+	.	.	.	25
Passiflora suberosa	+	+	+	.	.	.	.	.	.	.	.	.	25
Lomatophyllum aldabrense	+	+	.	.	.	.	.	.	.	.	.	.	17
Rhizophora mucronata	.	.	.	.	.	.	.	.	.	.	+	+	17
Terminalia boivinii	+	.	.	.	.	.	.	.	.	.	+	.	17
Tricalysia sonderana	+	.	.	.	.	.	.	.	.	.	+	.	17
Bakerella clavata	.	.	.	+	.	.	.	.	.	.	.	.	8
Cordia subcordata	+	.	.	.	.	.	.	.	.	.	.	.	8
Dracaena reflexa	+	.	.	.	.	.	.	.	.	.	.	.	8
Ficus nautarum	.	.	.	.	.	.	.	.	+	.	.	.	8
Jasminum elegans	+	.	.	.	.	.	.	.	.	.	.	.	8
Maerua triphylla	.	.	.	.	.	.	.	.	+	.	.	.	8
Malleastrum leroyi	+	.	.	.	.	.	.	.	.	.	.	.	8
Tarenna trichantha	.	.	.	.	.	.	.	.	.	.	+	.	8
Thespesia populnea	+	.	.	.	.	.	.	.	.	.	.	.	8
number of species	25	14	14	13	7	10	8	10	8	7	16	8	

+, Present; points indicate absence. Grasses, sedges and small herbs were excluded from the census.

Phil. Trans. R. Soc. Lond. B. **286**, 225–230 (1979)   [225]
Printed in Great Britain

The tortoise and the rail

By C. R. Huxley†

Department of Zoology, British Museum (Natural History), London, U.K.

Giant tortoises (*Geochelone gigantea*) on Aldabra respond to light tactile stimulation of their soft posterior regions by adopting an immobile erect stance, previously thought to be a threat posture. It is argued that this is probably a cooperative posture assisting any potential symbiont to clean ectoparasites from the areas of soft skin thus exposed. Most Aldabran tortoises over 25 cm long respond in this way and the response appears to be unaffected by activity, sex, time of day and ectoparasite abundance. The visual stimulus of a white-throated rail *Dryolimnas cuvieri* within 1 m may also elicit this response, and rails were observed removing ectoparasites from tortoises which had adopted the cooperative posture. The distributions of the tortoise and the rail overlap only slightly and the mutualism is thought to be ecologically unimportant to both the ectoparasites and the rail. Comparisons are made with the mutualism involving Galápagos giant tortoises, *Geochelone elephantopus*, and the ground finches *Geospiza fuliginosa* and *G. fortis*, and the mockingbird, *Nesomimus parvulus*.

1. Introduction

Frazier (1972) reported that light tactile stimulation, especially of the areas of softer skin at the posterior end, usually evokes a response in the Aldabran giant tortoise, *Geochelone gigantea*, in which the neck and limbs are extended so that the body is lifted well clear of the ground (see figure 1). He called this the 'standing' posture, but was unsure of its function or cause. He had observed that it occurred during sequences of mating behaviour, and concluded that it was adopted in situations of behavioural conflict, and seemed to be a threat posture. MacFarland & MacFarland (1972) discovered a mutualistic relation between the giant tortoises of the Galápagos (*Geochelone elephantopus*) and the ground finches *Geospiza fuliginosa* and *G. fortis* in which the finches 'cleaned' the tortoise of ectoparasitic ticks. This relation was described in some detail (MacFarland & Reeder 1974) and included the adoption of a cooperative ('extended') posture by the tortoise which bore a marked resemblance to Frazier's (1972) 'standing' posture. Rodhouse *et al.* (1975) also reported this behaviour, but added the involvement of the mockingbird, *Nesomimus parvulus*. Previous descriptions of a supposed mutualistic relation involving the Aldabran giant tortoises have concerned the diurnally active gecko, *Phelsuma abbotti*, which was seen feeding on *Aedes* mosquitoes attracted to the tortoises (Honegger 1966; Stoddart & Wright 1967), but did not include the tortoise's assumption of a cooperative posture.

This paper attempts to explain the derivation of the 'standing' posture of Aldabran giant tortoises, and describes a mutualistic relation between giant tortoises and the Aldabran white-throated rail, *Dryolimnas cuvieri aldabranus*, in which the tortoise assists the rail in its cleaning rôle by assuming a cooperative posture.

† Present address: Agriculture and Fisheries Department, 393 Canton Road, Kowloon, Hong Kong.

FIGURE 1

2. METHODS AND STUDY AREAS

(a) Tactile stimulation

Tortoises were tested in December 1975 and January 1976 for response to light tactile stimulation, on Ile Malabar (mostly near Passe Houareau) and on Grande Terre at and near Dune Jean-Louis. Each tortoise was approached quitely from behind so that the observer remained apparently undetected. If the animal became aware of the observer, it would either move off rapidly or retract into its shell and was not included in the results; if it remained undisturbed the back legs were scratched lightly in the thigh region with a thin wooden stick for 30 s. The response was noted, as was the tortoise's activity before approach and stimulation, and its position relative to direct sunlight or shade. The number of ectoparasites (tabanid flies and mosquitoes, see §3 b below) present was estimated during stimulation and classified as nil, few (up to 5) or many (over 5). Finally, the tortoise was sexed (where possible) and measured (carapace straight length in centimetres). The responses were grouped into three categories; positive, in which the animal adopted the 'standing' posture, negative, in which the animal either moved off, retracted into its shell or adopted the 'protected' posture (Frazier 1972) with the rear end lowered to the ground, or no response, in which the animal apparently ignored the stimulus.

(b) Visual stimulation

Undisturbed tortoises were observed in December 1975 and January, February and March 1976 on Ile Malabar and Grande Terre (at Cinq Cases and Dune Jean-Louis), and any interactions with other animals passing within 1 m in front of the tortoise were noted. Responses were categorized as in §2 a above.

3. RESULTS

(a) The posture

It is assumed that the cooperative posture described here is identical to Frazier's (1972) 'standing' posture, and may occur as a response to certain visual stimuli, light tactile stimuli and also during sequences of attempted mating, although in this last case the stimulus is probably tactile. The four limbs are extended more or less fully so that the plastron is well clear of the ground, and the neck is stretched out nearly vertically, horizontally or in an intermediate position (figure 1). One important characteristic of this posture is that once it is adopted the tortoise remains motionless, appearing to be in an almost trance-like state, and may ignore other stimuli that would normally elicit an avoidance response. Extension of the four limbs may be either synchronous or asynchronous, but if it is asynchronous the first limbs to be extended are usually those nearest the stimulus. There was no apparent difference between the posture adopted in response to visual cues and that adopted in response to tactile stimulation, and the 'extended' posture of the Galápagos tortoises seems to be more or less identical (MacFarland & Reeder 1974; Rodhouse *et al.* 1975). Maintenance of the posture may continue for some time (up to at least 2 min) after cessation of either form of stimulation.

TABLE 1. RESPONSE OF TORTOISES TO TACTILE STIMULATION

locality	number of positive responses	number of negative responses	no response	
Ile Malabar	48 (79%)	13 (21%)	0	61
Grande Terre (Dune Jean-Louis)	69 (93%)	3 (4%)	2 (3%)	74

(b) Ectoparasites

Aldabran tortoises appear not to carry any ticks, unlike those in the Galápagos which support large numbers of *Amblyomma usingeri* and *Argas transversus*. However, mosquitoes (probably *Aedes* sp.) frequently occur in considerable numbers on and around Aldabran tortoises, and the tabanid flies *Neavella albipectus* and possibly *Aegophagamyia remota* are also commonly present. Both the mosquitoes and the flies tend to congregate around the areas of soft skin on the neck, legs and between the plastron and carapace. The tabanids are also seen on the carapace. It is not known how much the biting activity of these insects affects the tortoises' behaviour.

(c) Response to tactile stimulation

Most tortoises responded positively to tactile stimulation (table 1). The results were examined to determine whether the tortoises' activity and position affected their response, but there was no such effect. Nor was the response related to the number of mosquitoes and flies present, or the time of day. Both sexes responded more or less equally (males, 50 out of 60 = 83% positive; females, 63 out of 71 = 88% positive), and size appeared to have no effect, except that three very small tortoises (i.e. less than 25 cm straight length) tested separately all responded negatively.

In one instance a tortoise was seen to adopt the cooperative posture in response to tactile stimuli under natural conditions. The tortoise, which was feeding, was approached from the rear by a rail which was not visible to the tortoise. The rail began to peck at and around the back legs of the tortoise which immediately assumed the cooperative posture. The rail moved off after a few seconds and the tortoise lowered itself 15 s later and resumed feeding.

(d) Response to visual stimuli

Other than instances involving rails, detailed observations were made of tortoises' behaviour on 44 occasions when another animal passed in front of, and within 1 m of, an active (i.e. not sleeping) tortoise. The results are shown in table 2 from which it can be seen that tortoises normally make no response at all. On one occasion a tortoise briefly adopted the cooperative posture in response to a foraging turnstone (*Arenaria interpres*); the latter ignored the tortoise which lowered itself after a few seconds. Of the 19 instances involving rails (table 2), in only one was there no response, and in the other 18 positive responses occurred; these are described in detail in §3*e* below.

TABLE 2. RESPONSE OF NON-SLEEPING TORTOISES TO PRESENCE OF OTHER ANIMALS WITHIN
1 m AND WITHIN VISUAL RANGE

animal	area	number of positive responses	number of negative responses	no responses	total number studied
robber crab, *Birgus latro*	Ile Malabar	0	1	5	6
land crab, *Cardisoma carnifex*	Ile Malabar (5) Grande Terre (13)	0	0	18	18
sacred ibis, *Threskiornis aethiopica*	Grande Terre	0	1	4	5
turnstone, *Arenaria interpres*	Ile Malabar	1	0	3	4
turtle dove, *Streptopelia picturata*	Ile Malabar	0	0	11	11
white-throated rail, *Dryolimnas cuvieri*	Ile Malabar	18	0	1	19

(e) Tortoise/rail interactions

Tortoises responded rapidly to the sight of a rail within 1 m. Both males and females exhibited this response, and their sizes ranged from 49 to 80 cm straight length. The one animal (female) that did not respond was 64 cm straight length. In nine instances the rail apparently ignored the tortoise's assumption of the cooperative posture; on five occasions the bird showed some interest in the tortoise, but did not feed or attempt to feed on the tabanid flies and mosquitoes present, foraging instead in the disturbed area around the tortoise. However, in the remaining four instances the rail was seen to 'clean' the tortoise, searching the legs, neck and areas of exposed skin in the space between the plastron and the carapace, and in one case the bird actually pecked inside the nostrils of the tortoise, the latter seemingly unaffected by this, other than a slight retraction of the head. Rails were seen to take both tabanid flies and mosquitoes while 'cleaning' a tortoise. It should be stressed here that the presence of a human observer may have considerably affected the rails' behaviour towards the tortoises. Several of the rails observed in interactions with tortoises showed greater interest in the observer than in the tortoise.

Only adult rails were seen to be involved in cleaning behaviour, but on one occasion a 9 week old juvenile elicited the response in a tortoise and then investigated the latter's front legs, but did not attempt to take any of the tabanid flies or mosquitoes present.

4. DISCUSSION

Frazier (1972) concluded that the posture he described as 'standing' was involved in sexual behaviour, but admitted that its function and cause were not at all clear. It is suggested here that when 'standing' occurs in a sequence of mating behaviour it is out of context and that the response is elicited in these instances not by the approach of another tortoise but by light tactile stimulation. Frazier noted that 'standing' occurred in the early stages of mating behaviour and he reported that it is during these phases that the male tortoise 'noses' the partner, normally approaching from the rear. Thus it seems possible that the tortoise being 'nosed' mistakes the sexual approach of the other and adopts the cooperative posture out of context. There seems little doubt that the posture adopted in these circumstances was identical to the cooperative posture adopted when a rail approached, especially in view of the one observation of a tortoise assuming the posture in response to tactile stimulation from an unseen bird (see §3c). The evidence also points to its not being an aggressive posture since, at least in the Galápagos tortoise, this latter usually involves face to face confrontations and considerable movements of the head, neck and sometimes the legs (MacFarland & Reeder 1974). Frazier's explanation that it is a threat display elicited in a state of behavioural conflict is therefore superfluous if one accepts that it is a behaviour pattern occuring out of context in response to simple tactile stimuli. This argument is supported by the almost universal response of tortoises to experimental tactile stimulation, and the apparent lack of any factors affecting the response rate.

That this is a ritualized posture seems likely, but its origins are not clear. It may have derived from an intention movement in which the tortoise extended its limbs before locomotion, or it may have originated in the autonomic response sometimes involved in defecation (Frazier 1972) in which the hind legs only are extended, lifting the posterior clear of the ground. In either case, the exaggeration of the posture may be considered as ritualization and it is clearly functional in exposing the maximum possible area of soft skin for inspection by any mutualist. There is a third explanation for which I am indebted to H. Fricke (personal communication). He has observed a similar posture in the small Greek tortoise *Testudo graeca* and believes it to be a comfort posture; if this were the case, ritualization need not be involved, and the evolution of a mutualistic relation would be much simpler to envisage.

The Galápagos tortoises adopt the cooperative posture in response to approach either by the ground finch or the mockingbird, or to a special 'presentation' display by the ground finch (MacFarland & Reeder 1974; Rodhouse *et al.* 1975). In contrast, the Aldabran tortoises respond only to approach by a rail, and there is no apparent display by the bird. It is suggested here that the tortoise's response to the sight of a rail is learned (as is the rail's response to a tortoise in the cooperative posture), and it would be of interest to test the response of Aldabran tortoises that have never encountered a rail, such as those on Grande Terre. It is also possible that the Galápagos tortoises respond to a call given by the mockingbird (Rodhouse *et al.* 1975), but this seems less likely in view of their probably poor auditory acuity (Frazier 1972). However, O. Prŷs-Jones has recently informed me (personal communication) that he has observed Aldabran tortoises adopting the cooperative posture apparently in response to auditory stimuli only, in this case rails singing out of sight of the tortoise concerned. It would be interesting to confirm this experimentally and to determine whether the tortoises respond to the whole song or just to the low frequency notes (Huxley & Wilkinson 1977) that are within their reported range of good auditory acuity.

Penny & Diamond (1971) reported rails taking tabanid flies from tortoise carapaces on several occasions, and although they also noted one instance in which a rail pecked at the head and front legs of a tortoise, in this case the tortoise responded negatively by withdrawing into its shell. The occurrence of rails foraging in the area of disturbed litter around a tortoise was also recorded by Penny & Diamond (1971), although they did not report observing the tortoises adopting the cooperative posture and likened the relation to that occurring between the cattle egret (*Bubulcus ibis*) and ungulates.

The density of tortoises on Ile Malabar is approximately 7 per hectare in the areas of open/mixed scrub, but nil in the *Pemphis acidula* scrub which covers most of this island (Bourn 1976). Thus, although those rails living in the open and mixed scrub habitats will encounter tortoises fairly frequently (a pair of rails generally holds a territory of 1–2 ha and will thus have up to about 15 tortoises available), the great majority of rails on Ile Malabar (probably in excess of 75 % of the total population) will have little or no chance of meeting a giant tortoise. Less than 2 % of the total population of tortoises on Aldabra live in areas inhabited by rails (Bourn 1976) and it is to be concluded, therefore, that the mutualistic relation described here is unimportant to the tortoise population as a whole. The mobility and abundance of tabanid flies and mosquitoes is such that it is unlikely that even in the areas where the mutualism occurs the rails have any significant effect on their numbers. This contrasts with the situation in the Galápagos where MacFarland & Reeder (1974) found that cleaning by the finches resulted in a marked decrease in the abundance and distribution of partly to fully engorged *Amblyomma* ticks. It is not thought that the amount of food collected by rails from tortoises forms a significant part of their diet since the proportion of their time spent in this behaviour is negligible, and in this respect the relation again differs from that in the Galápagos where ticks taken from tortoises may form an important part of the finches' diet at certain times of year (MacFarland & Reeder 1974).

It appears that the relation between Aldabran tortoises and rails is a rather casual one, possibly in its evolutionary infancy, in which both species benefit, but not to any important extent. Its importance and interest lie, then, not in the ecological aspects but in the behavioural implications.

I thank the Natural Environment Research Council for financing this research, and the Royal Society of London for allowing me to visit Aldabra and for facilities provided there. I am also grateful to Dr D. W. Snow and Dr M. J. Coe for reading the manuscript of this paper and providing useful criticism.

REFERENCES (Huxley)

Bourn, D. 1976 The giant tortoise population of Aldabra (Cryptodira : Testudinae). Part 1: preliminary results. *Zool. afr.* **11**, 275–284.

Frazier, J. G. 1972 Behavioural and ecological observations on giant tortoises on Aldabra atoll. D.Phil. thesis, Oxford University.

Honegger, R. E. 1966 Beobachtungen an der Herpetofauna der Seychellen. *Salamandra* **1–2**, 20–36.

Huxley, C. R. & Wilkinson, R. 1977 Vocalizations of the Aldabra white-throated rail *Dryolimnas cuvieri aldabranus*. *Proc. R. Soc. Lond.* B. **197**, 315–331.

MacFarland, C. G. & MacFarland, J. 1972 Goliaths of the Galapagos. *Nat. geogr. Mag.* **142**, 632–649.

MacFarland, C. G. & Reeder, W. G. 1974 Cleaning symbiosis involving Galapagos tortoises and two species of Darwin's finches. *Z. Tierpsychol.* **34**, 464–483.

Penny, M. J. & Diamond, A. W. 1971 The White-throated Rail *Dryolimnas cuvieri* on Aldabra. *Phil. Trans. R. Soc. Lond.* B **260**, 529–548.

Rodhouse, P., Barling, R. W. A., Clark, W. I. C., Kinmonth, A.-L., Mark, E. M., Roberts, D., Armitage, L. E., Austin, P. R., Baldwin, S. P., Bellairs, A. d'A. & Nightingale, P. J. 1975 The feeding and ranging behaviour of Galapagos giant tortoises (*Geochelone elephantopus*) *J. Zool., Lond.* **176**, 297–310.

Stoddart, D. R. & Wright, C. A. 1967 Geography and ecology of Aldabra Atoll. *Atoll Res. Bull.* **118**, 11–52.

Phil. Trans. R. Soc. Lond. B. **286**, 231–240 (1979)   [231]

Printed in Great Britain

Dynamic ecology of Aldabran seabird communities

By A. W. Diamond

Department of Zoology, University of Nairobi, P.O. Box 30197, *Nairobi, Kenya*

The characteristics of the present seabird community of Aldabra are described, and compared briefly with others in the tropics. By comparison with Pacific Ocean communities, Aldabra is deficient especially in petrels and shearwaters, which are poorly represented in the western Indian Ocean generally and are absent probably for zoogeographic reasons. Ground-nesting species are also scarce, especially pelagic feeders that form large colonies, and this is attributed partly to their extermination by rats and partly to the proximity of Assumption, and perhaps Cosmoledo, that offer better nesting sites to these species. Inshore-feeding terns are also scarce on Aldabra, probably owing to insufficient areas of shallow water nearby. Relative population sizes are roughly in agreement with those that would be predicted, except for the fairy tern whose population may have been reduced in the past by barn owls. Almost all Aldabran seabirds nest either in mangroves or on small lagoon islets, the habitats in which birds are least vulnerable to introduced rats, which appear to have had a major effect on nesting distribution.

The seabird community is made up of two different trophic guilds, the pelagic feeders which bring in nutrients entirely from outside the ecosystem, and the inshore feeders which cycle nutrients between the intertidal and inshore parts of the system and the terrestrial part. Both result in a net input of nutrients, in the form of bird droppings, to the terrestrial ecosystem. It is estimated that about 1680 t of food are removed from the sea per year, most of the 105 t of guano resulting being channelled into the intertidal, rather than the terrestrial, parts of the ecosystem.

The seabird communities likely to have occupied Aldabra in the past are reconstructed on the basis of the known changes in the atoll's size and structure during the Pleistocene. At most times there would have been more species of seabird using Aldabra than now, and more of their guano would have passed into the terrestrial ecosystem.

Probably the most significant event in the recent history of the atoll was the arrival of rats, which exterminated probably quite considerable colonies of ground-nesting seabirds and drove the survivors into the only places where the rats could not survive – the tall mangroves and the tiny lagoon islets. In so doing, the rats destroyed a significant source of nutrient input to the terrestrial ecosystem, with major consequences for the ecology of the atoll as a whole.

1. Introduction

The object of this paper is to attempt to place the present community of seabirds on Aldabra in ecological and evolutionary perspective, and to explore its relation to the ecology and evolution of the Aldabran ecosystem as a whole. In view of the subject of this discussion, the rôle of seabirds in the terrestrial ecosystem will receive most attention. The composition of the present community is first analysed in terms of species number, population sizes and distribution, and the ecological interactions between seabirds and the rest of the ecosystem. The likely composition of former seabird communities during the evolution of the atoll is then suggested, followed by a brief comment on the future composition based on current knowledge of erosion rates. The picture presented throughout is of a constantly changing, dynamic assemblage of seabirds, responding to, and in part influencing, the changes in the physical environment around them.

2. The present community

(a) Species composition

Eleven species of seabird currently breed at Aldabra (table 2), belonging to five families: five terns (Laridae), two frigatebirds (Fregatidae), two tropicbirds (Phaethontidae), one booby (Sulidae) and one shearwater (Procellaridae). The community is thus dominated taxonomically by larids, but both numerically and in biomass terms by the three Pelecaniform families (frigatebirds, tropicbirds and boobies) which together account for 50 000 of the 55 000 breeding individuals and about 98 % of the biomass of breeding seabirds (Diamond 1971 a, b).

Comparisons with the species composition of other tropical seabird communities suggest that the species composition of Aldabra is disharmonic, chiefly in three respects, one zoogeographic and two ecological.

(i) Although comparing favourably with other Indian Ocean islands, Aldabra has six or seven fewer breeding species than would be expected on an island of similar size in the Pacific, such as Christmas Island where 18 species breed (Schreiber & Ashmole 1970). The chief group lacking on Aldabra is the petrels and shearwaters (Procellaridae); only two species breed widely in the western Indian Ocean, one of which breeds at Aldabra, compared with the five species that nest at Christmas Island. The western Pacific Ocean is the centre of distribution of tropical procellarids, which become progressively fewer westwards towards Aldabra.

(ii) Apart from procellarids, which are absent chiefly for distributional reasons, the most obvious omissions from the Aldabran seabird community are three ground-nesting species, the white and brown boobies, *Sula dactylatra* and *S. leucogaster*, and the sooty tern, *Sterna fuscata*. There is no obvious reason for any of these to be missing, other than the lack of predator-free nesting space; there is evidently sufficient food since these species frequently feed around Aldabra. All the ground-nesting species that do breed at Aldabra, do so on very small lagoon islets (Diamond 1971 a, b); probably none of these islets is large enough to support viable breeding colonies of any of these species. The absence of all ground-nesting species from the main islands of the atoll is one of the most striking features of Aldabra seabird distribution, and must be attributed to terrestrial predators, most of all the introduced rat, *Rattus rattus*, though the indigenous crab, *Birgus latro*, may also be implicated.

The sooty tern, and possibly the white booby, may be absent for a second ecological reason. Both these species are pelagic feeders, ranging for probably 160 km (100 miles) or more from the breeding colony to feed. Aldabra is thus within the feeding range of birds breeding on Assumption 27 km to the south, and even Cosmoledo 110 km east; neither species now breeds on Assumption (Stoddart, Benson & Peake 1970) but both do so at Cosmoledo (Bayne et al. 1970). Where several alternative nesting grounds are available within a common feeding area, species probably choose the most suitable breeding ground, rejecting an island that might be used if there were no better alternative nearby. Although Cosmoledo is the only island that might now draw away potential breeding seabirds from Aldabra in this fashion, Assumption carried large populations of seabirds in the past and, being so close to Aldabra, has probably played a larger part than Cosmoledo in determining past seabird community structure on Aldabra, at least until its seabird colonies were destroyed by phosphate mining.

(iii) There remain several species which are widely distributed elsewhere in the region, and for which there are apparently still suitable breeding sites on Aldabra. These are the black noddy, *Anous tenuirostris*, and the bridled and roseate terns, *Sterna anaethetus* and *S. dougalli*. All of these nest in the central Seychelles, 1000 km to the east, in considerable numbers. The most likely reason for their absence from Aldabra is a lack of suitable feeding grounds; all are inshore feeders and in Seychelles feed chiefly over the very extensive shallow waters of the Seychelles Bank; there is no comparable area of shallow water near Aldabra.

(b) Population sizes

There are two ecological models that can be used to predict the relative population sizes of species in a seabird community (Preston & Williams's log-normal model is not considered here, being a mathematical model rather than a biological one). The first is MacArthur's 'broken-stick' model (MacArthur 1957), in which species populations are treated as a random sub-set of the total number of individuals in the community. Population sizes of Aldabran seabirds do not differ statistically from those predicted by MacArthur, although one of the chief assumptions of the model, that the species' niches do not overlap, is not met (Diamond 1971 a). The second model, which is specific to tropical seabirds, predicts that species with the largest feeding ranges are the most numerous (Diamond 1978); again, the Aldabran community agrees with these predictions, but since this model was formulated partly from these Aldabra data, it cannot strictly be used to interpret them.

One species whose population size is greatly different from that which would be expected, both from the second model and from general knowledge of the natural history of the species, is the fairy or white tern, *Gygis alba*. This species usually feeds some distance from land around Aldabra, whereas in central Seychelles it feeds chiefly inshore and is very numerous. The population on Cousin Island in Seychelles, which is less than $\frac{1}{600}$ of the area of Aldabra, is about 10000 pairs (Diamond 1975 a), about 30 times the Aldabran population, whereas its larger feeding area around Aldabra, and the much greater area available for nesting, should support a very much larger population. Its rarity on Aldabra can tentatively be attributed to predation in the past by barn owls, *Tyto alba*, which used to occur on Aldabra and have greatly reduced fairy tern populations in central Seychelles since they were introduced there in the 1950s.

(c) Distribution

The distribution of nesting colonies and roosts has been described by Diamond (1971 b). Two habitats are used to the exclusion of almost all others; small lagoon islets, and mangroves on the lagoon shore. A few fairy terns and tropicbirds (*Phaethon* spp.) occasionally breed on the main land rim, and there are regular roosts of frigatebirds (*Fregata* spp.) and brown noddies (*Anous stolidus*) there, but the number of individuals that breed on the mainland rim is very small indeed. Much of it is suitable, in the sense that similar vegetation elsewhere in the tropics is often used by breeding seabirds, including species that occur on Aldabra, and its avoidance by seabirds on Aldabra can be explained only by the presence, on all the main islands of the land rim, of abundant rats (*Rattus rattus*). These are widely held to have exterminated seabird colonies elsewhere in the world, and must be presumed to have done so in the past on Aldabra. Norman (1975) concluded that the influence of rats in destroying seabird colonies has been over estimated, and that cats and man may have been at least equally culpable; this conclusion was based on the paucity of direct evidence of rat predation in seabird colonies, but such evidence is difficult to acquire, and there is still substantial circumstantial evidence implicating rats in the destruction of seabird colonies.

(d) Ecological rôles

There are two chief routes by which seabirds interact with the terrestrial ecosystem; by modification of vegetation through guano deposition at the nest or roost, and through nutrient recycling.

Vegetation modification

Vegetation may be changed radically by the guano deposited at and around the nest or roost. Trees used as roosts by frigatebirds and boobies are often leafless, and a few are apparently dead, but there has been no systematic study of the problem and it is possible that the birds choose bare trees to roost in, rather than that they cause trees in which they roost to become bare. Such effects are not common in trees used for nesting, although the leaves are often liberally splashed with droppings. The ground-nesting colonial terns, especially brown noddies and crested terns (*Sterna bergii*), undoubtedly modify vegetation; the herb *Achyranthes aspera* is particularly common and luxuriant on islets used by brown noddy colonies, and in mainland Seychelles shows a similar affinity for the ground beneath colonies of the tree-nesting black noddy (*Anous tenuirostris*). The seed of *Achyranthes* is almost certainly transported by seabirds, as is that of *Boerhavia repens* which commonly occurs on the smaller rocky islets on which noddies and black-naped terns (*Sterna sumatrana*) breed. No proper studies have been made of seabird–vegetation interactions on Aldabra but, for reasons detailed in the next section, such effects are likely to be very localized and not of major importance to the terrestrial ecology of the atoll. (Gillham's (1977) preliminary study of seabird–vegetation interactions lacks the long-term element necessary to substantiate the seabird-induced cycles proposed.)

Nutrient cycling

Seabirds obtain their food from the sea, and return to land to nest and roost. They therefore produce a net input of nutrients to the terrestrial ecosystem. However, 89% of the seabird biomass nests in trees, almost all of which are mangroves, so most of the guano will fall, or be washed by rain, into the tidal waters beneath the mangroves; thus the intertidal part of the ecosystem will be much more affected than the terrestrial part. The rich growth of corals and algae on the lagoon floor around the large frigatebird and booby colonies near East Channel may owe their existence partly to nutrient enrichment by the seabird colonies above. As marine predators, seabirds fall into two trophic guilds that play different rôles in the ecosystem as a whole:

(a) Pelagic feeders, which feed far from land, i.e. well outside the Aldabran ecosystem, returning an unknown proportion of nutrients to the terrestrial system, chiefly on lagoon islets.

(b) Inshore feeders, which catch prey in shallow waters around the atoll, again returning these nutrients to land; because much of their prey is caught either within the lagoon, or between the land and the seaward reef, they can be regarded as cycling nutrients within the atoll ecosystem although, like pelagic feeders, they produce a net input to the terrestrial ecosystem.

The total amount of nutrients that the seabirds bring in to the system can be estimated, very approximately, as follows.

(1) *Mass of food consumed.* By using the bird masses and population sizes given by Diamond

($1971\,a,b$ respectively); and assuming that a bird eats about 10 % of its body weight per day (a conservative estimate – for large birds, Hutchinson (1950) gives 17 % for the cormorant *Phalacrocorax auritus*, and Houston (1972) 8–9 % for two vultures *Gyps* spp.), the total weight of food consumed by Aldabra seabirds is approximately 1680 t per year.

(2) *Mass of guano produced*. Gamarra Dulanto (1941, quoted by Hutchinson 1950) found that 16 t of fish eaten by Peruvian seabirds resulted in 1 t of guano. Hence the 1680 t consumed by Aldabran seabirds would be equivalent to about $1680/16 = 105$ t of guano per year.

(3) *Mass of guano deposited on land*. Referring to Peruvian guano-producing species, which build nests composed chiefly of their own guano, Hutchinson (1950) estimated that very nearly all of the droppings produced by these birds would be deposited on land at the breeding colony. This is less likely to be true of the species presently breeding at Aldabra, particularly the tree-nesting species, but there are no data on which to base an estimate of the difference. Hence we can say only that a maximum of 105 t of guano is brought into the atoll ecosystem by seabirds.

(4) *Mass of major nutrients*. Again, only maxima can be given. Seychelles guano averages about 24.2 % P_2O_5 and 0.98 % N (Hutchinson 1950); 24.2 % P_2O_5 is equivalent to about 10.5 % P, so the mass of P produced by Aldabran seabirds $= 105 \times 0.105 = 11$ t p.a.; and mass $N = 105 \times 0.0098 = 1$ t p.a. As already pointed out, the great majority of this nutrient input is channelled into the intertidal, rather than the terrestrial, parts of the atoll ecosystem.

In summary, seabirds remove several hundred tonnes of nutrients from the sea and deposit a small fraction of this into the terrestrial ecosystem of Aldabra; this deposition is extremely localized and, as far as the strictly terrestrial part of the ecosystem is concerned, is limited to the small islets in the lagoon.

(e) Stability

It is 10 years since seabirds began to be studied on Aldabra; these years have presented unique opportunities for long-term work on a tropical seabird community and, in particular, for assessing its stability, in terms of both numbers and of distribution. These opportunities cannot be said to have been fully exploited, but sufficient recent observations have been made to suggest that numbers of at least two species have remained fairly stable over this time, but that the distribution of nesting colonies has changed, in some cases very substantially. These observations, which I hope will be documented fully by the observers concerned, are outlined below.

(i) *Frigatebirds*. In a recent census (1976), B. Reville (personal communication) found little change from the population sizes of *Fregata minor* and *F. ariel* that I found in 1967 (Diamond 1975 b). However, the distribution of species within colonies had changed greatly (figure 1), although the main colonies were still in approximately the same places.

(ii) *Terns*. Regular observations by S. Hnatiuk and R. Prŷs-Jones of some of the lagoon islets used by tern colonies suggest little change in the total numbers of either brown noddies, crested terns or caspian terns (*Hydroprogne caspia*), but major changes in the location of the main colonies of brown noddies and crested terns. These are listed in table 1.

Unfortunately it is difficult to be sure that these changes result from natural causes. Frigate-birds were killed for food by Seychellois fishermen before 1967, and are still very sensitive to human disturbance, particularly during their courtship period. Crested terns in 1967–9 were very prone to desert if disturbed, perhaps because their eggs were taken by the fishermen. Noddy colonies in the north and east part of the lagoon are evidently much more heavily preyed upon by pied crows (*Corvus albus*) now than they used to be (R. Prŷs-Jones, personal communication); the crows had evidently learnt the location of these colonies, and specialized in preying upon them, in the intervening period. Just how important these human factors might be is impossible to judge; in any case, the efficient way in which the birds do move colonies and yet breed successfully, suggests that such anti-predator behaviour has been selected for in the past, whether by human or other predators.

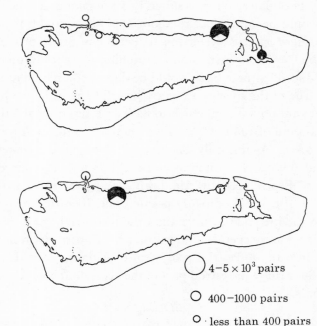

4–5 × 10³ pairs

400–1000 pairs

less than 400 pairs

FIGURE 1. Changes in size, location and composition of frigatebird colonies. Upper map: 1967 (Diamond 1975 b); lower map: 1976 (B. Reville, personal communication). *Fregata minor* shown in white, *F. ariel* in black.

The influences that have shaped the Aldabran seabird community, as we see it today, may therefore be summarized as follows.

(i) *Zoogeography.* The species making up the community are drawn from the species pool of the western Indian Ocean which, by comparison with the western Pacific, for example, is relatively poor in species, especially in petrels and shearwaters (Procellariidae).

(ii) *Proximity of alternative breeding sites.* The nearness of Assumption (in the past) and Cosmoledo may draw away pelagic feeders to breed there rather than on Aldabra. Since pelagic feeders are more numerous than inshore feeders, which will not be affected in this way (Diamond 1978), the proximity of other islands may have a major ecological effect in significantly reducing the inflow of nutrients (via seabirds) to the ecosystem.

(iii) *Undersea topography.* The steep offshore gradient of the sea floor around Aldabra allows no extensive shallow-water feeding areas for such species as bridled and roseate terns, and black noddies, which are probably at least partly dependent on such areas.

(iv) *Introduced predators.* Rats, accidentally introduced by man, have spread throughout the land rim of the atoll, and have probably exterminated past breeding colonies of seabirds that must have made significant contributions to the nutrient status of the terrestrial ecosystem. They and the barn owl (which probably reached Aldabra naturally), may also have selectively depressed the populations of species particularly sensitive to them.

(v) *Geological structure.* Different rock types on the lagoon islets offer different types of nest site, and this influences the nesting distribution of the two species of tropicbird *Phaethon* spp. (Diamond 1975*c*) and of ground-nesting terns, which breed almost exclusively on Takamaka limestone islets (Diamond 1971*a*); whether it also affects the total population sizes of these species, as well as their patterns of distribution, is not known.

TABLE 1. THE ISLETS USED BY BROWN NODDIES AND CRESTED TERNS AS NESTING COLONIES IN 1967–9 AND 1975–6

islet (grid references)	brown noddy		crested tern	
	1967–9	1975–6	1967–9	1975–6
228° E, 047° N	0	0	12	3
220° E, 044° N	0	200	26	0
302° E, 091° N	318	50	20	0
229° E, 108° N	23	0	4	0
271° E, 065° N	20	>100	20	*ca.* 18
338° E, 105° N	79	*ca.* 10	0	0
317° E, 109° N	20	<10	0	0
338° E, 105° N	14	*ca.* 10	0	0
080° E, 066° N	0	0	2	20

Figures shown are the maximum number of occupied sites. 1967–9 figures from Diamond (1971*a*), 1975–6 from R. Prŷs-Jones (personal communication).

3. THE PAST COMMUNITIES

The area and morphology of Aldabra have changed many times during the Pleistocene, and these changes have been reconstructed by Braithwaite, Taylor & Kennedy (1973). Their data (particularly as summarized in table 2) have been used to postulate the likely seabird communities that have occupied Aldabra during that time. Four principles have governed this procedure:

(1) It is assumed that past zoogeographic influences were broadly the same as now, i.e. the same pool of species was available to colonize the island. The possibility that species that now breed outside the tropics might, during glacial periods, have occupied the tropics, cannot be explored without further evidence.

(2) It is assumed that islands of a particular structure had a similar fauna then to that which they have now, i.e. a sand cay had the same avifauna 100000 years ago as a sand cay has now.

(3) The same relation between feeding strategy and population size that holds now (i.e. pelagic feeders and migrants are more abundant than inshore feeders and residents (Diamond 1978)) is assumed to have operated in the past.

(4) The possible effect, referred to above, of a nearby island in drawing away potential breeders, cannot be taken into account because too little is known of the geological histories of the nearest islands, Assumption, Cosmoledo and Astove.

Braithwaite *et al.* (1973) inferred seven periods of emergence of land before the appearance of Aldabra in its present form; of these, they were able to suggest a land area, and to describe landforms, sufficiently precisely to identify three different types of land mass for which seabird faunas can be suggested. These are shown in table 2 and described below.

(a) Sand cays

Aldabra has consisted of sand cays at least three times, all before 125000 a B.P.; the land area is unknown for the first such emergence, and was 20–25 km² on the second and third. Present sand cay islands are found in the Amirantes (e.g. African Banks) and Cargados Carajos, and their avifaunas suggest that Aldabra would then have had about 13 breeding seabird species, including large colonies of sooty tern, white booby, wedge-tailed shearwater and perhaps roseate tern. If there were sufficient trees, black noddy and fairy tern would also have bred. Species that occur now, but probably did not then through lack of suitable nest sites, include white-tailed tropicbird, Audubon's shearwater (*Puffinus l'herminieri*) and black-naped tern.

TABLE 2. SUGGESTED SEABIRD FAUNAS DURING EVOLUTION OF ALDABRA

	structure of Aldabra			
breeding species	sand cay	rocky islets	high, steep rocky island	present atoll
sooty tern, *Sterna fuscata*	×	×	×	.
red-footed booby, *Sula sula*	×	×	×	×
great frigatebird, *Fregata minor*	×	×	×	×
lesser frigatebird, *Fregata ariel*	×	×	×	×
wedge-tailed shearwater, *Puffinus pacificus*	×	.	.	.
Audubon's shearwater, *Puffinus l'herminieri*	.	×	×	×
red-tailed tropicbird, *Phaethon rubricauda*	×	×	.	×
white-tailed tropicbird, *Phaethon lepturus*	.	×	×	×
white booby, *Sula dactylatra*	×	×	×	.
brown noddy, *Anous stolidus*	×	×	×	×
fairy tern, *Gygis alba*	(×)	.	×	×
brown booby, *Sula leucogaster*	×	×	×	.
black noddy, *Anous tenuirostris*	(×)	.	.	.
roseate tern, *Sterna dougalli*	×	.	.	.
bridled tern, *Sterna anaethetus*	.	×	×	.
crested tern, *Sterna bergii*	×	×	.	×
black-naped tern, *Sterna sumatrana*	.	×	.	×
caspian tern, *Hydroprogne caspia*	.	.	.	×

Structure of Aldabra from Braithwaite *et al.* (1973). Species arranged in descending order of feeding range; species at top are pelagic feeders, those at bottom, inshore feeders. Parentheses denote cases where doubt exists as to whether there were enough trees for species to breed in.

(b) Low rocky islets

This landform was probably similar to that of Cosmoledo Atoll now, and occupied a land area of about 50 km² about 80 000 a B.P. Large colonies of sooty tern and white booby are likely to have flourished, and smaller numbers of brown booby and bridled tern may also be inferred, though the latter two species also need shallow water in which to feed. Of the present avifauna, fairy and caspian terns are likely to have been absent. Again, about 13 species probably bred.

(c) High, steep-sided, flat-topped rocky island

About 27 000 a B.P., Aldabra was larger (400 km²) and more diversified in structure and habitat than at any other time in its recent history. Its seabird community is likely to have been dominated by species nesting in the trees and shrubs that probably crowded the top of the island; the nearest comparisons at the present day are probably Christmas Island (Indian Ocean) and Monito Island in the Caribbean (C. B. Kepler, personal communication). The vegetation on top of the island would have carried large colonies of red-footed boobies (*Sula sula*) and great and lesser frigatebirds (*Fregata minor* and *F. ariel*). The more open grassy areas would afford nesting sites for sooty terns, white boobies, and smaller numbers of both species of tropicbirds and, if sufficient shallow water were nearby, bridled terns. Probably about 11 species nested, the most conspicuous losses being the shallow-water feeding terns.

Throughout its history, the avifauna has been dominated by pelagic feeders (except at any time, e.g. when the land area was least, when there were extensive areas of shallow water nearby). On the first two island types, the large colonies of pelagic feeders would have deposited large amounts of guano. The composition of the seabird fauna depends not only on the physical structure of the island, which determines to a large extent the kinds of nest site available, but also on the depth of surrounding water and, for the pelagic feeders, the proximity of alternative nesting sites on other islands.

In discussing both the present and the past seabird communities on Aldabra, I have repeatedly suggested that there have been very much larger numbers of seabirds in the past than there are now, and in particular that ground-nesting pelagic feeders, the kind that produce large amounts of guano, would have been abundant. Yet one of the most striking features of Aldabra's ecology is its lack of guano deposits; indeed this absence may be one of the chief reasons why the atoll has escaped the devastation that most of the others in the region have suffered. However, many of the superficial deposits, as well as several rock formations (e.g. the Esprit phosphorites), do contain substantial quantities of phosphate; these are not sufficiently extensive or concentrated to be of commercial value (Baker 1963), but they do indicate past concentrations of seabirds considerably greater than at present. The chief anomaly is the lack of recent phosphate deposits; if, as I have suggested, large colonies of ground-nesting seabirds were exterminated by introduced rats, where is the guano they deposited? In fact superficial deposits of quite high phosphate content are widespread on Aldabra, but are very thin and usually at the bottom of pockets or pits in the limestone (Baker 1963) and therefore not economic to extract; Hutchinson (1950) suggested that these deposits may be contemporary with those on Assumption and other islands in the region. It seems certain that there were fewer ground-nesting, guano-producing seabirds on Aldabra than on Assumption, even before rats came to Aldabra, for the possible reasons already suggested (§2a (ii)).

4. FUTURE CHANGES

Past communities have been reconstructed on the basis of the known physical structure of Aldabra in the past. Since we cannot predict its structure in the future, neither can we predict changes in the seabird communities with any confidence. The only change that seems inevitable is a reduction in the number of small lagoon islets for the ground-nesting birds to breed on. These islets are both destroyed, and produced from the lagoon shore of the land rim, by marine erosion; but whereas the lagoon shore is generally protected from erosion by mangroves, the islets in the open lagoon are not, so islets are probably destroyed faster than they are created. A substantial part of the seabird community, in terms of numbers if not biomass, will then have to seek alternative breeding sites elsewhere.

I thank R. Prŷs-Jones and B. Reville for permission to quote their observations on seabird distribution and numbers in the last few years.

240 A. W. DIAMOND

REFERENCES (Diamond)

Baker, B. H. 1963 Geology and mineral resources of the Seychelles archipelago. *Bull. geol. Surv. Kenya* **3**, 1–140.

Bayne, C. J., Cogan, B. H., Diamond, A. W., Frazier, J., Grubb, P., Hutson, A., Poore, M. E. D., Stoddart, D. R. & Taylor, J. D. 1970 Geography and ecology of Cosmoledo Atoll. *Atoll Res. Bull.* **136**, 37–56.

Braithwaite, C. J. R., Taylor, J. D. & Kennedy, W. J. 1973 The evolution of an atoll: the depositional and erosional history of Aldabra. *Phil. Trans. R. Soc. Lond.* B **266**, 307–340.

Diamond, A. W. 1971a Ecology of seabirds breeding at Aldabra Atoll, Indian Ocean. Ph.D. thesis, University of Aberdeen.

Diamond, A. W. 1971b The ecology of the sea birds of Aldabra. *Phil. Trans. R. Soc. Lond.* B **260**, 561–571.

Diamond, A. W. 1975a *Management plan for Cousin Island, Seychelles*. London: International Council for Bird Preservation (British Section).

Diamond, A. W. 1975b Biology and behaviour of frigatebirds (*Fregata* spp.) at Aldabra Atoll, Indian Ocean. *Ibis* **117**, 302–323.

Diamond, A. W. 1975c The tropicbirds (*Phaethon* spp.) of Aldabra Atoll, Indian Ocean. *Auk* **92**, 16–39.

Diamond, A. W. 1978 Population size and feeding strategies in tropical seabirds. *Am. Nat.* **112**, 215–223.

Gillham, M. E. 1977 Vegetation of sea and shore-bird colonies on Aldabra Atoll. *Atoll Res. Bull.* **200**, 1–19.

Houston, D. C. 1972 The ecology of Serengeti vultures. D.Phil. thesis, University of Oxford.

Hutchinson, G. E. 1950 The biogeochemistry of vertebrate excretion. *Bull. Am. Mus. nat. Hist.* **96**, 1–554.

MacArthur, R. H. 1957 On the relative abundance of bird species. *Proc. Natn. Acad. Sci. U.S.A.* **43**, 293–295.

Norman, F. I. 1975 The murine rodents *Rattus rattus exulans* and *norvegicus* as avian predators. *Atoll. Res. Bull.* **182**, 1–13.

Schreiber, R. W. & Ashmole, N. P. 1970 Sea-bird breeding seasons on Christmas Island, Pacific Ocean. *Ibis* **112**, 363–394.

Stoddart, D. R., Benson, C. W. & Peake, J. F. 1970 Ecological change and the effects of phosphate mining on Assumption Island. *Atoll Res. Bull.* **136**, 121–145.

Phil. Trans. R. Soc. Lond. B. **286**, 241–246 (1979)   [241]
Printed in Great Britain

A preliminary assessment of the rôle of the terrestrial decapod crustaceans in the Aldabran ecosystem

By H. G. L. ALEXANDER†
Royal Society Aldabra Research Station, Seychelles

Land crabs are the largest terrestrial invertebrates on Aldabra. The 12 species occupy most trophic levels, and some crabs are responsible for the transfer of energy from land to sea and vice versa. Some species may be responsible for preventing, or severely reducing colonization of Aldabra by exotic plant species. Other species are important in hastening leaf litter breakdown by digestion, while scavenging forms reduce the number of carrion-breeding flies. Burrowing forms may aerate the soil, and the littoral crab, *Grapsus tenuicrustatus*, by feeding on surface encrusting alga may speed erosion and aid soil formation. The hermit crabs form an important part of the diet of the flightless rail, and by depositing gastropod shells on land may provide drinking and breeding places for other animals.

INTRODUCTION

A working definition of terrestrial decapod crustaceans may be given as those crabs which habitually spend the greater part of their lives above water level. Thus defined, Aldabra is inhabited by 12 species of land crab, ranging from the littoral *Grapsus tenuicrustatus* through to well adapted terrestrial species like *Birgus latro*. Intermediate degrees of adaptation are shown by the other species: *Cardisoma carnifex*, *C. rotunda*, *Coenobita brevimana*, *C. cavipes*, *C. perlata*, *C. rugosa*, *Geograpsus crinipes*, *G. grayi*, *Ocypoda ceratophthalma* and *O. cordimana*.

The terrestrial decapod crustacea are an interesting group of animals owing to their secondary adaptation to life on land. Since all possess marine larvae it seems likely that initial colonization of Aldabra was achieved by larvae being brought from other regions of the Indian Ocean, presumably by the South Equatorial current. Nevertheless there exists the possibility that adult animals may have reached Aldabra on driftwood or similar flotsam, perhaps from the Malagasy region.

Hedley (1896) and Hesse, Allee & Schmidt (1937) have pointed out that coral atoll islands provide particularly suitable habitats for land crustaceans; thus it is not surprising that they should feature prominently in the Aldabran fauna. The land crabs are the largest invertebrates on Aldabra and occupy most trophic levels; consequently they are deeply involved in the energetics of the ecosystem.

ENERGY TRANSFER

Material of terrestrial origin may be transferred to the sea in a number of ways.

(1) Since all of the terrestrial decapods breed by means of marine larvae, the mortality of these larvae at sea represents a considerable energy loss to the terrestrial ecosystem. Some idea of the number of larvae lost may be gained from examining mean egg counts from two common and widely distributed species: *Birgus latro* 90 730 and *Cardisoma carnifex* 458 188. These very

† Present address: Department of Natural Sciences, South London College, Knight's Hill, London, SE27 0TX.

large figures suggest considerable larval mortality. However, it should be noted that the surviving larvae will feed at sea and on metamorphosis will return to land thus helping to offset the deficit.

(2) When shedding eggs the ovigerous female crabs are occasionally washed away. This is particularly the case with *Cardisoma carnifex*, whose exoskeletons were seen washed up on the beaches. Mortality among egg shedding females is not thought to be high but the observed incidences of *C. carnifex* carcases was proportionately higher during the breeding season than otherwise. It is not clear what feeds on the soft parts of the crabs but even if only bacteria are responsible it would still be a contribution to the marine budget.

(3) Marine predators also take land crabs. The most common example is predation on *Grapsus tenuicrustatus* by moray eels (*Muraena* spp.). The crabs showed a marked reluctance to enter pools and if they crossed water going from one rock to another the movement was so frantic that they 'ran' over the surface of the water. Sometimes the crabs sank which resulted in their seizure by any moray eel in the vicinity. However, *Grapsus tenuicrustatus* feeds principally on encrusting marine algae so the net energy loss is considerably reduced.

On one occasion the stomach contents of a larger grouper (*Epinephelus* sp.) was found to contain the remains of three adult *Cardisoma carnifex*. These animals may have been swept away during egg shedding, but since one was a male it is not clear how this prey was obtained.

Although no observations were made it appears likely that *Ocypoda ceratophthalma* would be taken by predatory fish since these crabs are frequently engulfed by waves when feeding at the water's edge. The same may also be true of coenobites.

So far consideration has been given to material which has been transferred from land into sea, but crabs are also responsible for the transfer of material of marine origin onto land. The rôle of returning metamorphosed larvae has been mentioned above. Unfortunately, no figures are available for percentage return but I believe it to be small. Crabs of the genus *Ocypoda* are important predators on turtle hatchlings and turtle eggs, thus preventing the return of material of marine origin to the sea. Details of this will be discussed later.

Although primarily predatory, ocypodes are also scavengers. They were frequently observed with *Coenobita perlata* and *C. rugosa*, feeding along the beach strand line. Much stranded organic material is eaten by these crabs and faeces deposited inland will not only contribute towards the terrestrial budget but hasten the breakdown of materials and the release of nutrients to plants. *Birgus latro* was also observed feeding on beaches at night but this is not thought to be a major feature of their feeding behaviour.

The terrestrial hermit crabs (*Coenobita* spp.) are responsible for dragging marine gastropod mollusc shells onto land. Out of a sample of 11976 adopted gastropod shells examined, only five were terrestrial forms and the rest marine. Although energy contribution is minimal, the abandoned shells sometimes fill with rainwater, thus providing drinking facilities for some animals and breeding grounds for others. Rails (*Dryolimnas cuvieri aldabranus*) were seen to drink from water-filled upturned shells, as were coenobites and *Birgus latro*. Mosquito larvae were seen in shells in places where no other standing fresh water was to be found.

Coenobita perlata were seen feeding on the bodies of a stranded turtle, various species of marine crabs and fish remains.

SCAVENGING

Several examples of scavenging by crabs have been cited above. It is necessary to emphasize this rôle, not only because of the energy turnover involved but the effect scavenging might have on population numbers of some other groups. Fosberg (1956) suggested that the scavenging effects of coenobites might explain the comparative scarcity of carrion-breeding flies on the Marshall Islands. No comparative figures are available at present, but subjectively, relatively few of these insects are found on Aldabra, presumably for the same reason. It would be interesting to observe the results of excluding crabs from an area where corpses of a variety of animals, e.g. tortoises, crabs, rats, washed-up fish and perhaps goats were present. This might be achieved experimentally by introducing a fixed quantity of carrion into two experimental plots; one on the main land mass, the other on an islet where the crab population is nil; and comparing insect larval numbers.

Cardisoma carnifex feeds extensively on fallen leaves and detritus. It undoubtedly plays an important part in the speeding up of leaf litter breakdown. This was especially noticeable in high-density *Cardisoma* areas where few leaves rested on the ground; in places where no or very few *Cardisoma* occur, such as the islets in west channels, the leaf litter was up to 10 cm deep.

Some experimental work was conducted to gain some idea of the turnover of food materials and energy uptake in *Cardisoma carnifex*. Two of the materials given were common foodstuffs; fallen leaves of *Casuarina equisetifolia* and tufts of the sedge *Fimbristylis cymosa*. Dry weight food consumption figures varied considerably, but values for energy assimilation for both groups of foods were similar, being $9.06 \, \mathrm{J \, g^{-1} \, d^{-1}}$ for *Casuarina* and $12.06 \, \mathrm{J \, g^{-1} \, d^{-1}}$ for *Fimbristylis*.

Population estimates based on burrow distribution in high-density *Cardisoma carnifex* areas gave a figure of 3683 crabs per ha. From data accumulated on *Cardisoma* populations, the mean mass of crabs was 322 g. Thus it may be calculated that the energy assimilation in high-density *Cardisoma* areas is in the order of $10.5–14.6 \, \mathrm{MJ \, ha^{-1} \, d^{-1}}$. These figures do, of course, apply to only one set of circumstances, but may be taken to indicate the scale of energy turnover by crabs.

Tortoise faeces were eagerly consumed by coenobites and hundreds of these crabs were to be found under bushes on the south coast which sheltered tortoises. Tortoise faeces 'sown' on beds of sterile soil often produced seedlings, demonstrating that seeds may pass through the digestive tract unharmed (D. Wood, personal communication). If this is a method of seed dispersal in the plants concerned, the coprophagous habits of the coenobites would prevent this, since the mouthpart and gastric mill mastication in these crabs is so efficient that no seeds were observed to have remained intact upon microscopic examination of the faeces.

Several crab species feed on decaying vegetation. It is likely that they lack a digestive cellulase and rely on bacteria and fungi to initiate the breakdown process. Some species of fish have been shown to have faster growth rates if fed on predigested food (J. R. H. Western, personal communication) and it may be that in these crabs a parallel situation exists.

HERBIVORY

Both *Cardisoma carnifex* and *C. rotunda* are herbivores, and plants known to be prominent in the diet of *Birgus latro*, *Coenobita perlata* and *C. rugosa*. Other crabs may be, but this was not observed. The most obvious effect is the consumption of seeds and seedlings thus exercising control over plant numbers. Many records were made of the consumption of ground level vegetation by *Cardisoma carnifex*. Especially favoured food plants were young *Colubrina asiatica*, *Euphorbia prostrata* and *Fimbristylis cymosa*, in addition to various grasses and sedges.

Coenobites often feed along the strand line on beaches and they may prevent the establishment or development of exotic plant species by consuming seeds and seedlings of plants washed up on the shore. The high degree of endemism among Aldabran plant species (Renvoize 1971) suggests restricted competition from more vigorous exogenous forms. It may well be that coenobites and perhaps other herbivorous crabs are responsible for this reduced competition. Newly arrived species of plant introduced as seeds in the faeces of migrant birds may suffer the same fate from the more 'inland' species of crab, such as *Cardisoma*, which have been observed eating bird faeces.

Coenobita rugosa eagerly consumes the terminal shoots of the alien *Catharanthus roseus* thereby substantially altering its growth form from an erect, rather spindly plant to a very bushy one. Since flowers are borne on the shoot tips the 'pruning' activities of the crab may increase the reproductive capacity of this plant considerably.

Another introduced plant, the coconut (*Cocos nucifera*) has a decided effect on the size and growth form of *Birgus latro*. Studies undertaken at six sites revealed that the mean mass of *Birgus* from coconut-dense areas was almost twice that of crabs from coconut-free areas. Details of this will be published elsewhere.

CARNIVORY

There are many examples of the capture and subsequent consumption of prey, in addition to the instances of carrion scavenging mentioned above.

The habitual carnivorous crabs are the genera *Geograpsus* and *Ocypoda*, although other species are known to take animal food occasionally. In tortoise nesting areas *Birgus* is said to be an important predator of hatchlings (I. R. Swingland, personal communication) but this was not observed by me, probably because the *Birgus* study areas were remote from tortoise breeding sites.

Ocypodes are important predators of turtle hatchlings and eggs and were seen digging into turtle nests for food, confirming the observations of Wiens (1962). There can be little doubt that this was deliberate, since burrows were dug in the middle of turtle nest depressions which were some distance from the crab's normal burrow sites. The Seychellois consider this habit commonplace and say that turtle eggs and hatchlings are brought to the surface for consumption. Yolk and other remnants are scavenged by coenobites. Large *Coenobita rugosa* have also been seen to dig down after turtle eggs, presumably attracted by scent (J. A. Stevenson, personal communication). On one occasion ocypodes accounted for 50% mortality of hatchling turtles out of observed emergences at Dune Jean Louis.

Geograpsus crinipes, together with *Ocypoda cordimana*, prey heavily on small coenobites, particularly *Coenobita rugosa*. Other, smaller, land crabs are taken from time to time, as are insects. Hughes (1966) considered that *Ocypoda ceratophthalma* is cannabalistic, but this was only rarely observed on Aldabra. However, many small *O. ceratophthalma* are consumed by *Geograpsus crinipes*, these two species exhibiting a considerable degree of habitat synchrony. Curiously, *Ocypoda ceratophthalma* was not observed eating small geograpsids.

On one occasion *Birgus latro* was seen consuming the coccid *Icerya seychellarum*. If this habit were a regular occurrence, it might provide the means for biological control of *Icerya*, whose presence has been associated with destruction of trees on the island. However, I believe this was an isolated case where the insect had fallen to the ground from a tree.

PREDATION

In addition to examples given of carnivory among crabs themselves, the crabs are preyed upon by several other groups.

Crabs were taken by several bird species. On the shore-line turnstones (*Arenaria interpres*) and crab plovers (*Dromas ardeola*) were seen to feed on *Ocypoda ceratophthalma*. Further inland pied crows (*Corvus alba*) were seen to feed on *Ocypoda cordimana*.

Small coenobites would appear to be important item of the flightless rail's diet and were seen to be consumed in quantity at Middle Camp. Rails would often run and grab the legs of coenobites, shaking them vigorously in order to snap them off. This prevents the hermit crab from forming the legs into the characteristic 'operculum' which blocks the entrance to the adopted shell. If the crabs were located when the limbs were withdrawn, then the rail would deliver a number of heavy blows with the beak in order to smash the 'operculum'. The soft abdomen was usually consumed first, followed by the rest of the body. Parent rails were seen to catch and break up coenobites to feed their young.

Records of stomach contents of feral cats shot on Aldabra showed *Grapsus tenuicrustatus* to be an important feature of the diet (J. A. Stevenson, personal communication). It is possible that feral cats and perhaps dogs might have died out from starvation but for the fact they were sustained by crabs.

Mosquitoes are known to feed on the heads and necks of tortoises, and although it was never observed it is possible that mosquitoes also feed on the fleshy abdomens of *Birgus latro*, particularly in areas such as Ile Michel where both *Birgus* and mosquitoes are abundant and tortoises almost non-existent. Furthermore, it is possible that the crabs may provide blood meals for other insect groups, notably members of the Ceratopogonidae.

EDAPHIC FACTORS

Although soil drainage is good, the activities of burrowing crabs further increase drainage and aeration. The 'tilling' activities are important in soil turnover, especially in view of the lack of earthworms which traditionally fill this rôle.

Tortoises often shelter under trees and shrubs and defecate there. Coenobites gather to feed on the faeces and also burrow down into the soil for shelter. The burrowing activities tend to dig in the tortoise faeces thus enriching the soil with humus and nutrients. Tortoise faeces not dug in tend to dry out and disintegrate, and are dispersed by the wind.

Macnae (1971) pointed out that *Grapsus tenuicrustatus* is important in the ecology of Aldabra since it eats blue-green algae growing on the surface of the limestone rock. The algae etch the outer few millimetres of the rock surface and this layer is removed during the crab's feeding activities. Thus *G. tenuicrustatus* is not only responsible for erosion of the limestone, but the resultant powder helps to form soil.

Erosion is hastened by the burrowing activities of crabs such as *Cardisoma carnifex* which make burrows in champignon crevices in solution pans.

Additional factors

Coenobites are good climbers and were found in a variety of bushes, with *Pemphis acidula* being the most commonly climbed. Bushes were sometimes literally festooned with them. It is not clear why they climb, perhaps to obtain food, perhaps to avoid predators; possibly both. In their wanderings, coenobites might be responsible for pollination of some of the plants they climb by transfer of pollen adhering to their appendages.

Birgus often drag coconuts back to their burrows for fibre stripping and subsequent consumption of the nut. Sometimes the nuts are abandoned before consumption and later germinate. *Birgus* may therefore be responsible for a wider distribution of this plant around the periphery of coconut plantations.

Although the crabs do not appear to compete directly with other groups, sympatric species of hermit crabs do compete for available shells (H. G. L. Alexander, unpublished data). However, one observation on Iles Moustique showed three *Coenobita cavipes* stealing fish regurgitated by a caspian tern (*Hydroprogne caspia*) for its chick.

One man-made hazard affecting crab populations on Aldabra is crude oil. During the period of the northwest monsoon (January–March), considerable quantities were washed up on beaches and many crabs which visit beaches were affected. Coenobites were particularly badly affected, the majority being contaminated with oil on their bodies and/or their adopted shells. This contamination was most noticeable on north coast pocket beaches where a number of dead oil-covered coenobites were found.

References (Alexander)

Fosberg, F. R. 1956 Military geography of the Northern Marshalls, prepared under the direction of the chief of Engineers, U.S. Army and the U.S. Geological Survey.

Hedley, C. 1896 General account of the atoll of Funafuti. *Australian Museum Memoir*, vol. 3. Sydney.

Hesse, R., Allee, W. C. & Schmidt, G. P. 1937 *Ecological animal geography*. London: John Wiley.

Hughes, D. A. 1966 Behavioural and ecological investigations of the crab *Ocypode ceratophthalmus* (Crustacea: Ocypodidae). *J. Zool., Lond.* **150**, 129–143.

Macnae, W. 1971 Mangroves on Aldabra. *Phil. Trans. R. Soc. Lond.* B **260**, 237–247.

Renvoize, S. 1971 The origin and distribution of the flora of Aldabra. *Phil. Trans. R. Soc. Lond.* B **260**, 227–236.

Wiens, H. J. 1962 *Atoll environment and ecology*. New Haven and London: Yale University Press.

Phil. Trans. R. Soc. Lond. B. **286**, 247–254 (1979)   [247]

Printed in Great Britain

Numbers of plant species on the islands of Aldabra Atoll

By Sarah H. Hnatiuk†

Royal Society Aldabra Research Station, Seychelles

The logarithm of island area accounts for 70 % of the variance in the number of plant species occurring on 100 lagoon islands. Two components of island altitude (altitude of the island rim and the logarithm of the island's inland altitude) are also of importance, and account for 9 % of the variation in species numbers. A further 13 variables account for only an extra 5 % of the variance in the mixed model. These results resemble the findings of other island studies. In the equation $S = K A^z$, $z = 0.345$ and falls within the range of expected values.

The species–area curve gives little indication of the 'small island effect' found for other small islands; this may reflect, among other factors, the richness of the Aldabran flora when compared with those of the small island ecosystems already studied. The curve is also compared with that compiled by Williams (1964) and a discrepancy between the two is discussed.

Woody plants are largely responsible for the increase of species numbers with increasing area. Species that are restricted to islands of particular sizes are listed and the characteristics of the frequencies of occurrence of the more common species are summarized.

Introduction

The study of island floras and faunas has formed an important part in the formulation of biogeographical theory (see, for example, MacArthur & Wilson 1967; Carlquist 1965, 1974). Many studies have attempted to elucidate the factors that determine the number of species occurring on islands, particularly the number of plants and of birds, and island area has usually been found to predict species number better than any other variable. The equation $S = K A^z$, where S is the number of species on an island, A the area, and K and z are constants, describes the general form of the relation between species number and island area. In some cases, however, area is not the best predictor of species number and some other factor has been found to provide a better indication of environmental diversity. For example, Hamilton, Rubinoff, Barth & Bush (1963) found that, by using a linear model, island altitude is the best predictor of plant species number in the Galápagos; and in the British Isles, the number of soil types per island predicted plant species number better than area (Johnson & Simberloff 1974). Latitude has been shown to be of some importance (Johnson, Mason & Raven 1968; Johnson & Simberloff 1974; Power 1972), and Abbott (1974) showed that plant species number on 19 sub-Antarctic and nearby islands were influenced more by the temperature of the coldest month of the year than by area.

In addition to the above variables that describe the habitat diversity of an island, there are others that relate to an island's potential for receiving immigrants. They include such factors as the isolation of an island from potential sources of immigrants and the richness of the source area. These factors are generally less important in determining species number than those describing island environmental diversity (see, for example, Abbott 1974; Hamilton *et al.* 1963; Johnson *et al.* 1968; Johnson & Simberloff 1974).

† Present address: 13 Eastfield Court, Ferndale, Western Australia 6155.

Aldabra Atoll (lat. 9° 24′ S, long. 46° 20′ E) consists of nearly 2000 islands, of which four large ones enclose a lagoon studded with many smaller ones. It is the smaller islands that are the focus of this study. They were formed from a single land mass when, 4000–5000 years ago, the atoll rim was breached by the sea, and lower-lying land within the rim was flooded (Braithwaite, Taylor & Kennedy 1973). Some of the islands have probably formed since then by erosion of the lagoon shores of the islands forming the atoll rim. The vegetation of the islands is derived from that on them when they were formed, plus immigrations, minus extinctions. They support a proportion of the approximately 250 species that make up Aldabra's terrestrial flora. They are situated in a lagoon measuring 30 × 10.5 km and none is more than 1060 m from the next island. They are low (mean altitude 1.44 m, range 0.25–8.50 m) and, but for a few sandy keys, consist almost entirely of limestones that compose the raised reef system of Aldabra. Soil is generally scarce and shallow, except for a few areas of deep sand. Thus, the main respect in which the islands differ from one another is in area, which was expected to account for most of the variation in species number. It was, however, deemed useful to include as many as possible of the factors that might affect species number so that their relative statistical importance could be determined.

METHODS

(a) Variables

Lists of the vascular plant species on 100 lagoon islands and the four large islands that form the atoll rim were made during 1973 and 1974. For the lagoon islands, estimates of the frequency of occurrence of each species were made during the wet season.

Measures on 19 independent variables were included in the analysis of determinants of plant species number. They consist of 12 that have been considered in other studies and seven others of potential importance.

(1) *Area.*

(2, 3) *Altitude.* This was considered as two components: the altitude of the island rim, that is, its shoreline above the high water level at spring tides (2), and the altitude from the top of the rim to the highest point inland (3).

(4) *Distance to nearest lagoon island.* This provides a measure of the island's isolation.

(5) *Distance to the nearest large island forming the atoll rim*, which was regarded as being the 'mainland' within the atoll ecosystem; another measure of the island's isolation.

(6–12) *Rock type*, as distinguished by Braithwaite *et al.* (1973). The types that were found on the islands consist of Picard Calcarenites (6), Esprit Limestone and Phosphorites (7), Takamaka Limestone (8) and Aldabra Limestone (9), as well as cavity fill (10) and beach deposits (11). A few islands consist partly or wholly of sand (12). In the absence of information on soil types for Aldabra, rock type provided the best available indication of the nature of the substrate on which the plants grew. As estimates of the proportions of each island composed of different rock types were unreliable, only presence or absence of a particular type was used in the analysis.

(13) *Percentage of the island on which soil occurred.*

(14) *Mean depth of soil.* Measures of variables (13) and (14) were obtained in the course of recording the incidence of plant species within 1 m² quadrats.

(15) *Presence of potholes.* It was thought that potholes might provide a sheltered microhabitat

with deeper soil than elsewhere on an island and that this might influence plant species number. Presence or absence of potholes was used in the analysis, as estimates of the abundance of potholes on each island could not be made reliably.

(16) *Distance to the nearest pass between the sea and the lagoon.* The passes represent the routes by which seaborne seeds originating from outside the Aldabran ecosystem would reach the lagoon islands; the nearer an island to a pass, the more likely it is to intercept foreign seeds.

(17) *Distance to Grande Passe.* As the largest of the atoll's passes and so the most likely route of entry of seaborne material, distance to Grande Passe was considered separately from the others.

(18, 19) *Position of the island in the lagoon on an east–west axis* (18) *and on a north–south axis* (19). As the main islands of the atoll rim show some geographic variation in the occurrence and abundance of plant species, it was thought that this variation might be apparent in the number of species on the lagoon islands as a function of position in the lagoon rather than as the result of any other factor.

A copy of all these data has been deposited with the Aldabra Data Recording Scheme at the Department of Geography, Downing Place, Cambridge CB2 3EN, U.K.

(b) Selection of islands

An island was defined as a piece of land that was always above high water level, even at the highest spring tides, and that was separated from all other pieces of land by every high tide. With the exception of a number of islands between La Gigi and Pointe Tanguin, for which data were collected in the course of developing the methods used in the study, the islands were selected on a restricted random basis. The guiding principle in choosing islands was to have as wide a range as possible of variation with respect to the independent variables. Large islands and islands isolated from one another and/or from the 'mainland' are relatively rare; all such islands were therefore included. The remaining islands were chosen randomly from the following areas: the eastern end of the lagoon, east of a line passing from Passe Houareau to a point at grid reference E 30, N 07; the eastern end of Ile Malabar; the group of islands south of Ile Esprit; and the islands south of Ile Polymnie. The only islands without representation in the study were those south of the middle and western portions of Ile Malabar.

(c) Analysis

Stepwise multiple regression was used to determine which of the independent variables were most important in determining species number on islands; the program employed was part of the Statistics Package for Social Sciences. The regressions were run on both untransformed and log-transformed data, and a mixed model was then constructed, using for each independent variable whichever of the linear or logarithmic variables accounted for the greater part of the variance.

RESULTS

Sixteen variables account for 84.16% of the variance in the number of plant species on the lagoon islands. From table 1, it can be seen that $\log_{10} A$ is by far the most important determinant of plant species number, although island altitude also contributes considerably to the total variance. The higher the island rim, the greater is the number of plant species supported by the island, whereas it is the logarithm of the inland altitude rather than the untransformed values, that shows a higher correlation with species number. These relations suggest that, once a certain height above sea level is reached, increased altitude is of less significance, presumably because the influence of sea water, either through wind-borne spray or percolation through the rock, diminishes. The presence of sand on an island has a small, but significant effect on the number of plant species present, probably because it provides a different environment from the limestones. The presence of Picard Calcarenites presumably increases the

TABLE 1. VARIABLES IN THE MIXED MODEL THAT CONTRIBUTE TO MORE THAN 1 % OF THE
VARIANCE IN THE NUMBERS OF PLANT SPECIES ON LAGOON ISLANDS

variable	percentage of variance for which variable accounts
$\log_{10} A$†	69.75**
$\log_{10} a$†	6.55**
altitude of island rim	2.87**
presence of Picard Calcarenites	1.39*
presence of sand	1.23*

**, Significant at $p < 0.01$, one-tailed; *, significant at $p < 0.05$, one-tailed.
† A, area; a, inland altitude.

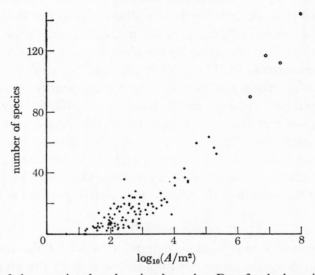

FIGURE 1. Number of plant species plotted against $\log_{10} A$. ○, Data for the large islands of the atoll rim.

number of plant species for the same reason, although it is not known what characteristics of this limestone type are particularly favourable to species diversity. None of the variables describing the isolation of the lagoon islands is of statistical importance; this is perhaps not surprising given the small distances between islands, and between islands and the 'mainland' of the atoll rim.

In the mixed model shown in table 1, $\log_{10} A$ accounts for 69.75% of the variance in the number of plant species (n) per island. If, however, area is to be used as a single variable in predicting species number, a better estimate is obtained by using $\log_{10} n$ and $\log_{10} A$, in which case $\log_{10} A$ accounts for 78.84% of the variance. The nature of the species–area relation is shown in figure 1. The curve climbs more steeply as $\log_{10} A$ increases but the regression coefficients for the lowest ($\log_{10} A < 2.0$) and highest ($\log_{10} A > 4.0$) portions of the curve are not significantly different from one another. Data for the four large islands of the atoll rim were not used in the multiple regression analysis because of their probable incompleteness but, as shown in figure 1, the points for these islands lie on the same curve as the lagoon islands. A plot of $\log_{10} n$ against $\log_{10} A$ (not illustrated) shows an almost linear relation for areas up to about 3.0 with a much less sharp increase in $\log_{10} n$ for the larger islands, including those of the atoll rim.

In the equation $S = K A^z$, $z = 0.345$.

In table 2 (see microfiche), where a mixture of physiognomic and taxonomic criteria are used to provide a convenient classification of the components of the island floras, it is shown that all elements of the floras contribute to the increased number of species with increasing area. Kruskal–Wallis one way analysis of variance indicates that the mean numbers of each type of plant are significantly different on islands of different sizes. The number of woody plant species increases more rapidly with area than the other categories of plants, suggesting that the major difference between large and small islands lies in the variety of woody plants that they support.

Examination of the species lists for the islands indicates that there are critical size limits for the occurrence of many species. Most of these species are, as expected, confined to the larger islands, but a few species of herbs and grasses are found only on the smaller islands. Table 3 (see microfiche) summarizes, for species of restricted occurrence, the sizes of islands on which they typically occur. The 52 species listed in table 3 represent nearly half of the 116 species of plants found on the islands; of the other 64 species, 35 occur on islands of all sizes and 29 are found rarely and show no clear preference for islands of particular dimensions.

Further information on the habitat requirements of individual species can be gained from the mean frequency with which they occur on islands belonging to the five $\log_{10} A$ classes. The mean frequencies were calculated for those islands on which the species occur, provided the species are found on 10 or more of the 100 islands studied. As shown in table 4 (see microfiche), the grasses tend to occur with greatest frequency on the smallest islands, with frequencies declining through the log area classes of increasing size. Of the 14 herbs that grow on 10 % or more of the islands, 9 show the same pattern as the grasses, but only 4 out of 19 woody plants do. From these figures, it can be seen that grasses and herbs are relatively common on small islands while shrubs are generally rarer on smaller than on larger islands. This picture bears out that obtained from the presence–absence data of table 3. It was expected that the frequency of occurrence of woody plants would increase with increasing island area, but this was found to be true for only three species. The majority of woody plants either showed peak frequencies on intermediate island sizes or, more rarely, varied little over the range of island areas studied. It would appear that, for all but three species, factors other than area are also important in determining their prevalence, although what these factors are have still to be established.

DISCUSSION

With the exception of the sub-Antarctic and nearby islands studied by Abbott (1974) and the British Isles (Johnson & Simberloff 1974), A or $\log_{10} A$ has been found to be the most important factor predicting plant species diversity on islands (references quoted in table 5 (see microfiche)). Hamilton *et al.* (1963), working with a linear model for the Galápagos islands' plants, found that altitude accounts for more of the variation in species number than area. However, when log-transformed data are used, $\log_{10} A$ is more important than any other variable, a view that Johnson & Raven's (1973) study with more recent data confirms. For Aldabra Atoll too, area is the most important variable in linear (66.68%), logarithmic (78.84%), and mixed (69.75%) models. As table 5 shows, the percentage variances in species number accounted for are comparable to values found by others. The two measures of island altitude together account for 9.4% of the variation in the number of plant species on Aldabra's lagoon islands, a figure very similar to that found for the low, sandy, northwest Hawaiian islands by Amerson (1975).

The value of z for Aldabra's lagoon islands is higher than that predicted from theoretical considerations for islands (Preston 1962), but is within the extremes of 0.15–0.39 reached by May (1975) from general considerations. At 0.345, it is not greatly different from values for the plants of the Galápagos calculated by Johnson & Raven (1973) and Preston and those for the Californian islands (Johnson *et al.* 1968). It has been suggested that high values of z can be expected for isolated areas (MacArthur & Wilson 1967), and the relatively high z for Aldabra may be taken to reflect its isolated position, 650 km off the east African coast and 390 km northwest of Madagascar. However, the reported values of z for land plants on true islands are similar (range 0.31–0.37), despite the varying degrees of isolation of the different islands. This observation supports Tepedino & Stanton's (1976) suggestion that z varies with the organism under study.

MacArthur & Wilson (1967) have drawn attention to the fact that, on very small islands, species number tends to remain constant over a range of island areas. They suggest that catastrophic events frequently denude such islands which therefore have area-independent extinction rates among their floras and faunas. While this may be true for some islands, such as the Florida Sand Keys, the 'small island effect' on Kapingamarangi Atoll is better explained by the observation that below an area of 1.42 ha or, more particularly, with an island width of less than 107 m, an island is probably not large enough to maintain a lens of fresh water (Niering 1956; Whitehead & Jones 1969). In the absence of such a lens, the only plants that establish on the islands are strand species, of which there are a limited number. The species–area curve for Kapingamarangi Atoll thus has an inflexion point at around island area of 1.42 ha, the curve climbing more steeply with islands of larger areas as non-strand species make their appearance.

As few of the species found on Aldabra's lagoon islands are introduced, a comparison can be made of Aldabra's species–$\log_{10} A$ curve (figure 1) with that for Kapingamarangi Atoll from which introduced plants are excluded. Aldabra's curve, like that for Kapingamarangi Atoll, climbs less steeply with increasing area among small than among large islands. There is, however, no significant difference between the flattest and steepest sections of Aldabra's curve. In fact, when the two curves are plotted on the same scale, the lower section of Aldabra's curve is seen to climb very much more steeply than the comparable section of Kapingamarangi's and there is no clear inflexion point in Aldabra's curve, although it is definitely steeper for areas greater than 10^4 m² (*ca.* 1 ha) than for smaller island areas. In other words, it appears that Aldabra's lagoon islands show only weakly, if at all, the small island effect. Furthermore, the entire curve for Aldabra's islands is displaced to the left of Kapingamarangi's, suggesting that Aldabra's islands support more species area for area than the sandy keys of Kapingamarangi.

They also support more species than the northwest Hawaiian islands (Amerson 1975) and the limestone islands west of Perth, Western Australia (Abbott 1977). Amerson quotes a mean of 3.6 species of vascular plants on islands with a mean area of 2.3 ha and a mean altitude of 2.4 m, and Abbott found that islands less than 4615 m² in area tend to be devoid of plants.

The difference of Aldabra's islands from these others may be explained in various ways. The Aldabran ecosystem may be floristically richer than these others because of its greater size and, in the cases of Kapingamarangi and the northwest Hawaiian islands, its lesser isolation from source areas of colonists. The temperature and rainfall régimes on Aldabra are probably more favourable for the evolution and maintenance of plant species diversity than those of Kapingamarangi and the Western Australian islands. The lagoon islands are sheltered from strong winds and heavy seas, and cyclones rarely reach Aldabra. These more sheltered conditions make it unlikely that the islands will be affected at all frequently by catastrophic events. Thus, while Amerson found that an island needs an altitude in excess of 1 m to support one species of plant, and Abbott that islands lower than 3.3 m tend to have no plants on them, many of the Aldabran islands with lower altitudes have more than one species. Furthermore, large colonies of nesting birds, which destroy the vegetation and reduce the number of plant species present, are found on only 10 % of the islands studied.

The upper section of the curve in figure 1 is a straight line, showing that the four large islands of the atoll rim have the same species–area relations as the lagoon islands. Comparison of the same data, on a log–log plot, with Williams's (1964) generalizations about the characteristics and interpretation of the species–area curve leads to an interesting conclusion. Williams found that, when $\log_{10} n$ is plotted against $\log_{10} A$, the first part of the curve rises steeply and then flattens out; he suggests that this curve corresponds to what is expected of species number within a single ecological association. At areas of about 4–8 ha ($\log_{10} A = 4.6$–4.9), the curve rises more steeply again, indicating the inclusion of new environments. The Aldabran curve shows the first steep climb followed by some flattening out, but there is no evidence of the second sharp rise. The absence of the second steep climb in the curve suggests that Aldabra's flora may be seen as forming one ecological association. This conclusion appears reasonable for the flora of most of the lagoon islands, but not for such islands of the atoll rim as Grande Terre where the platin formation provides a distinctive habitat characterized by tortoise turf (Grubb 1971), which is not found on the lagoon islands. One may question whether the inclusion of new habitats, as area sampled increases, necessarily shows up as an increase in $\log_{10} n$. On Aldabra, the mixed scrub that covers most of the atoll is species rich by comparison with the tortoise turf. Inclusion of the tortoise turf adds relatively few extra species to the total species count and does not show up in a log–log plot.

I thank the staff of the Royal Society Aldabra Research Station for making possible the efficient execution of the field work on which this paper is based, particularly H. Charles, A. Constance, D. Johnston, G. Larue, L. Topliffe and F. Topliffe. Much of the analysis was carried out at the Botany School, Oxford University, with the help of the University's Computing Centre. I am grateful to Professor Whatley for making the facilities of his department available to me. R. J. Hnatiuk discussed the work with me in all its stages and provided much helpful advice, and I. Abbott and P. Bridgewater commented on the manuscript.

REFERENCES (Hnatiuk)

Abbott, I. 1974 Numbers of plant, insect and land bird species on nineteen remote islands in the Southern Hemisphere. *Biol. J. Linn. Soc.* **6**, 143–152.

Abbott, I. 1977 Species richness, turnover and equilibrium in insular floras near Perth, Western Australia. *Aust. J. Bot.* **25**, 193–208.

Amerson, Jr, A. B. 1975 Species richness on the nondisturbed northwestern Hawaiian islands. *Ecology* **56**, 435–444.

Braithwaite, C. J. R., Taylor, J. D. & Kennedy, W. J. 1973 The evolution of an atoll: the depositional and erosional history of Aldabra. *Phil. Trans. R. Soc. Lond.* B **266**, 307–340.

Carlquist, S. 1965 *Island life*. Garden City, New York: The Natural History Press.

Carlquist, S. 1974 *Island biology*. New York: Columbia University Press.

Grubb, P. 1971 The growth, ecology and population structure of giant tortoises on Aldabra. *Phil. Trans. R. Soc. Lond.* B **260**, 327–372.

Hamilton, T. H., Rubinoff, I., Barth Jr, R. H. & Bush, G. L. 1963 Species abundance. *Science, N.Y.* **142**, 1575–1577.

Johnson, M. P., Mason, L. G. & Raven, P. H. 1968 Ecological parameters and plant species diversity. *Am. Nat.* **102**, 297–306.

Johnson, M. P. & Raven, P. H. 1973 Species number and endemism. *Science N.Y.* **179**, 893–895.

Johnson, M. P. & Simberloff, D. S. 1974 Environmental determinants of island species numbers in the British Isles. *J. Biogeogr.* **1**, 149–154.

MacArthur, R. H. & Wilson, E. O. 1967 *The theory of island biogeography*. Princeton, New Jersey: Princeton University Press.

May, R. M. 1975 Patterns of species abundance and diversity. In *Ecology and evolution of communities* (ed. M. L. Cody & J. M. Diamond), pp. 81–120. Cambridge, Massachusetts: Belknap Press of Harvard University.

Niering, W. A. 1956 Bioecology of Kapingamarangi Atoll, Caroline Islands. *Atoll Res. Bull.* **49**, 1–32.

Power, D. M. 1972 Numbers of bird species on the California islands. *Evolution* **26**, 451–463.

Preston, F. W. 1962 The canonical distribution of commonness and rarity. *Ecology* **43**, 185–215.

Renvoize, S. A. 1971 An annotated list of vascular plants growing on Aldabra and the neighbouring islands of Assumption, Astove and Cosmoledo. Unpublished manuscript.

Tepedino, V. J. & Stanton, N. L. 1976 Cushion plants as islands. *Oecologia* **25**, 243–256.

Whitehead, D. R. & Jones, C. E. 1969 Small islands and the equilibrium theory of insular biogeography. *Evolution* **23**, 171–179.

Wickens, G. E. 1974 A field guide to the flora of Aldabra. Unpublished manuscript.

Williams, C. B. 1964 *Patterns in the balance of nature*. London: Academic Press.

MICROFICHE

The relevant frames of the microfiche included with this publication contain the following tables referred to in the text of this paper.

TABLE 2. MEAN NUMBER AND RANGE OF PLANT SPECIES PER ISLAND ON ISLANDS OF DIFFERENT SIZES

TABLE 3. SPECIES WITH OCCURRENCE RESTRICTED TO ISLANDS OF CERTAIN SIZES

TABLE 4. CHANGE IN MEAN FREQUENCY OF OCCURRENCE OF SPECIES IN QUADRATS ON ISLANDS OF DIFFERENT SIZES

TABLE 5. COMPARISON OF THE PERCENTAGE VARIATION IN NUMBERS OF VASCULAR PLANT SPECIES ON ISLANDS ACCOUNTED FOR BY AREA AND ALTITUDE IN THIS AND OTHER STUDIES

Phil. Trans. R. Soc. Lond. B. **286**, 255–263 (1979)   [255]
Printed in Great Britain

Green turtle (*Chelonia mydas* (L.)) nesting activity at Aldabra Atoll

By T. S. H. Gibson†

Royal Society Aldabra Research Station, Seychelles

Green turtle (*Chelonia mydas*) nesting activity was indirectly monitored at the nesting sites at Aldabra by counting turtle tracks and nest pits during 11 months. Nesting activity took place throughout the year but a prolonged peak season was observed on southwest coast beaches between July and October, and less consistent peaks were observed for other beaches in February and March and from May to August.

Estimations based on track and pit counts suggest that about 700 turtles nested at Aldabra during the year. Although annual variations may occur, this is similar to earlier estimates and does not suggest any recent increase.

The distribution of turtle emergences among nesting beaches suggests that beaches fall into distinct nesting areas that are utilized to different extents.

The distribution of turtle emergences on the largest beach suggests that human settlements may be reducing nesting there.

1. INTRODUCTION

During the last decade it has been apparent to many visitors to Aldabra and the neighbouring islands that the number of green sea turtles (*Chelonia mydas*) nesting there is substantially less than during the early part of this century, when many hundreds of turtles were killed each year for human use (Hornell 1927). Recent estimates of the number of green turtles nesting at Aldabra (Hirth & Carr 1970; Frazier 1975) have been based on few published data. This paper presents data collected during an 11 month stay at Aldabra and offers a picture of the seasonality and distribution of nesting activity and an estimate of the numbers involved.

2. METHODS: TRACK AND PIT COUNTS

Green turtle nesting activity was monitored at Aldabra by counting turtle tracks and nest pits from May 1975 to April 1976. The whole set of marks made in a beach by a single turtle during nesting behaviour, including paths to and from the sea, was counted as one track and each track represents one emergence, whether or not egg-laying occurred. The method of assessment was to walk along the beach crest and count the number of crossings. The counts exclude emergences, apparently of an exploratory nature, that do not pass the beach crest; the majority of such tracks are obliterated by the succeeding high tides and would not be recorded. The positions of tracks were recorded in relation to beach marker posts so that tracks remaining visible from previous counts could be excluded. These counts were made at approximately fortnightly intervals at all the pocket beaches on the southwest coast of Grande Terre and irregularly about six times during the year at all the other important nesting sites (figure 1).

To relate the counted number of tracks to the actual number of emergences the proportion of tracks that remain visible must be known. The time taken for tracks to be eradicated by weathering was therefore estimated throughout the year on the southwest coast by monitoring

† Present address: School of Life Sciences, Leicester Polytechnic, P.O. Box 143, Leicester LE1 9BH, U.K.

the disappearance of marked fresh tracks. The results, though variable according to prevailing weather and exposure, averaged about 10 days from June to October and 14 days during other months and these measures of track longevity were used to convert the total number of tracks for each sample period into estimated numbers of emergences per day (figure 2a). For the north and south coasts fewer data were available and an average distribution of emergences is shown in figure 2 (b).

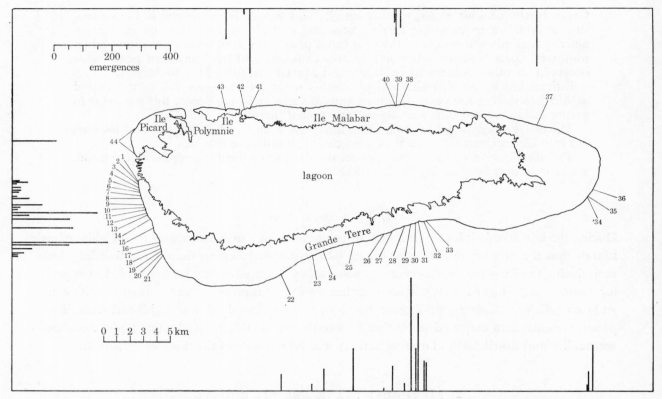

FIGURE 1. Outline map of Aldabra, showing locations of green turtle nesting beaches. The length of the line opposite each beach represents the estimated number of turtle emergences that occurred on that beach during the year of study. Locations: 1, beach 1; 2, Anse Anglais; 3, beach 3; 4, beach 4; 5, beach 5; 6, beach 6; 7, beach 7; 8, beach 8; 9, beach 9; 10, Deux Cèdres; 11, Trois Cèdres; 12, Anse Mais; 13, beach 13; 14, beach 14; 15, beach 15; 16, Anse Badamier; 17, Anse Rebise; 18, Anse Tamarind; 19, Force l'Anse Tamarind; 20, Anse Petit Tambalico; 21, Anse Tambalico; 22, Anse Quive; 23, Dune d'Messe; 24, Anse Imagination; 25, Entreboy; 26, Anse Cuivre; 27, Dune au Pic; 28, Dune Patates; 29, Dune Jean-Louis; 30, Dune Z (after Frazier 1971); 31, Dune Y (after Frazier 1971); 32, Anse Bigo; 33, Anse du Bois; 34, 'Cinq Cases (south)'; 35, Cinq Cases; 36, 'Cinq Cases (north)'; 37, Anse Cèdres; 38, Anse Badamier; 39, Anse Malabar; 40, 'Anse Malabar (west)'; 41, Anse Porche; 42, Anse Coco; 43, Anse Cèdres Polymnie; 44, 'Settlement Beach'.

The numbers of turtle nest pits on southwest coast beaches were also recorded at the beginning of the study and from September to April (figure 2a). These counts include all body pits remaining after nesting activity, both abortive nests not associated with eggs, and the 'leaving pits' that remain after deposited eggs are covered over. The average distribution of pits for the north and south coasts is shown in figure 2 (b).

The pattern of pit count distribution is similar to that of emergences but, particularly in figure 2 (b), tends to lag by 1 or 2 months; exploratory tracks precede nest digging activity and pits tend to persist longer than tracks. The longevity of pits on the southwest coast was estimated by recording positions of all new pits at each fortnightly survey and noting their eventual disappearance. There was a range of less than 2 weeks to over 6 months, mainly depending on the density of nesting; obliteration of pits by weathering takes many weeks, but most pits are eventually filled by spoil from adjacent nesting activity. The mean pit longevity on the southwest coast was about 13 weeks, and that for a sample of north and south coast beaches was about 11 weeks. In general, track counts provide the more sensitive indication of changes in nesting activity.

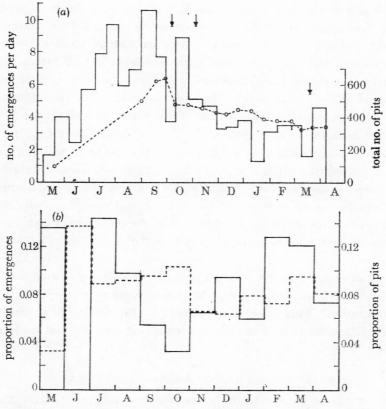

FIGURE 2. Temporal distribution of green turtle nesting activity. (a) Southwest coast beaches: cumulative data for beaches 1–18. ——, Mean estimated daily numbers of emergences occurring within fortnightly sample periods; – –, total numbers of pits visible on sample days. Arrows indicate exceptionally high tides; associated emergence rates are underestimates due to premature obliteration of some tracks. (b) North and south coast beaches: average proportion of the year's emergences or pits in each month, for 14 major beaches (June emergence data lacking). ——, Estimated emergences; – –, total pits.

3. SEASONAL PATTERNS OF NESTING ACTIVITY

The pattern of emergences in figure 2 (a) and (b) supports earlier reports (Hornell 1927; Frazier 1971) that nesting occurs throughout the year at Aldabra, although it is possible that the seasonal pattern of egg-laying differs slightly from that of emergence.

It is not clear why there should be different seasonal patterns for different coasts of Aldabra (figure 2 a, b) or how far they might vary from year to year. The difference does not seem to be spurious, for the pattern of figure 2 (a) is consistently shown in the separate records for nearly all the southwest coast beaches and in none of the others.

The seasonal distribution of Frazier's (1971) records of nesting activity, almost exclusively from the north and south coasts, is similar to that in figure 2(b), showing peaks from May to July and in February and March. Hornell (1927) reported monthly turtle fishery returns for turtles captured on unspecified beaches in 1925 and 1926, but the seasonal distribution (and total numbers) differed between the two years. The seasonal pattern in 1926 was similar to figure 2(b) and Frazier's data, but that for 1925 showed a single peak from April to July. The difference between Hornell's 2 years' data may partly reflect inconsistent turtle hunting effort, but Hornell thought the timing of the peak season was vulnerable to prevailing weather conditions. On the other hand, Hendrickson (1958), working on a Sarawak population of green turtles, found the timing of the peak to be unresponsive to changes in the timing of the monsoon.

It is possible that the difference in seasonality between the two areas of Aldabra (figure 2a, b) is indirectly associated with local weather differences by affecting turtles' choice of nesting locality. The finding by Bustard & Greenham (1969) that green turtles tended to nest on the lee side of an island in the Great Barrier Reef when strong winds were blowing supports this idea. On the southwest coast of Aldabra the peak season of emergence between July and October coincided with the most intense part of the season of southeast trade winds, which produce violent surf on the south coast. It is possible that the increased nesting activity on the relatively sheltered southwest coast was partly caused by turtles which might otherwise have emerged on the south coast. Such a response would not account in any simple way, however, for the lack of a pronounced peak of activity on the southwest coast during February and March or in the early part of the trade wind season. Again, there is no significant difference between the pattern on the south coast and that on the north coast, which is also relatively sheltered.

Hornell (1927) suggested that the separate peaks in numbers of nesting turtles that he noted between February and May and between May and September might be due to two overlapping turtle migrations. This might also account for the difference in nesting seasonality if the two populations tended to nest in different areas of coast, but this study offers no further evidence for this.

4. ANNUAL NUMBER OF NESTING TURTLES

Estimates were made of the total number of female green turtles that nested at Aldabra, based on both the counts of tracks and of nest pits from May 1975 to April 1976, described above (§2). These counts were used independently for estimations of the total number of egg clutches produced during that year (table 1) and the number of nesting turtles was inferred from this.

(a) Estimation of egg clutch production

(i) *Estimations based on tracks*

For the southwest coast, fortnightly track counts were converted to estimated numbers of emergences by using measures of track longevity (§2). These covered 11 months and the 12 month estimate (table 1) assumed three emergences per day (by interpolation in figure 2a) during the period when data are lacking.

For the north and south coasts the total number of emergences was more crudely estimated for each beach by computing the average number of track-days between successive track counts. The totals were divided by the measures of track longevity established on the southwest coast to give estimated numbers of emergences (table 1).

Estimated numbers of emergences were then converted to estimates of egg clutch production using the ratio of 82 emergences to 34 clutches ascertained by observation of individual turtles and by interpretation of fresh tracks at many beaches.

TABLE 1. ESTIMATION OF 12 MONTHS EGG CLUTCH PRODUCTION

	no. of tracks counted	estimated no. of emergences	estimated no. of clutches	no. of pits counted	estimated total no. of pits	estimated no. of clutches
			southwest coast			
8 months	—	—	—	878	—	—
11 months	1288	1670	—	—	—	—
12 months	—	1757	729	—	2183	707

	north and south coasts					
	estimated no. of track-days			estimated no. of pit-weeks		
June–Oct.	13 209	1321	548	19 176	1720	557
Nov.–May	16 755	1197	496	18 161	1629	527
	total no. of clutches		**1773**			**1791**

For explanation, see text (§4).

(ii) *Estimations based on pits*

For the southwest coast, the fortnightly counts of new pits, collected for 8 months, were summed. The number of pits produced in 12 months was derived from this by assuming that the ratio of 12 months' to 8 months' pits was the same as the ratio of 12 months' to 8 months' emergences.

For the north and south coasts, the number of pit-weeks were computed and converted to estimated numbers of pits produced in an analogous way to the calculation based on tracks.

Estimated numbers of pits were converted to estimates of egg clutch production by using the observed ratio of 105 pits to 34 clutches.

(b) *Interpretation of estimated egg clutch production*

The estimates of the total number of clutches separately derived from track and pit counts are in close agreement, especially in view of the approximations involved. However, it is possible that the estimate based on tracks is too low. For the calculation the track longevity on the south coast was taken as the same as on the southwest coast, whereas, owing to the exposed position of the beaches, it is probably less. Correction for this might increase the overall estimate based on tracks by *ca.* 10 %. To the total of about 1770–1950 clutches from these calculations must be added an estimate for 'Settlement Beach' (see §5*b*) and some allowance for the sporadic nesting that occurs on several rock strewn beaches and on the perched beach on the cliffs of the south coast. An overall figure of about 1950–2150 clutches is probable as the total nesting effort for the year.

There are no tagging records for Aldabran green turtles which might indicate the number of clutches produced each breeding season by each breeding turtle, or the length of the interval between seasons. Most turtles studied by other workers lay between three and seven times per

17-2

season (Hirth 1971). If the mean for Aldabran turtles were only three clutches per season the estimated total of about 1950–2150 clutches would imply that about 700 individuals laid eggs during the year of study. This estimate is similar to estimates by Frazier (1971) and Hirth & Carr (1967) who suggested that 1000 turtles or less nest each year at Aldabra.

Since green turtles do not normally nest every year (Hirth 1971) the individuals whose activity was recorded in this study represent only a proportion of the total population that nests at Aldabra, and it is possible that substantial variations may occur in the numbers nesting in successive years. Frazier (1975) noticed an apparent increase in nesting activity on some beaches at Aldabra in 1973 compared with the level observed in 1970. This study, however, offers no further evidence of a sustained increase in the number of nesting turtles.

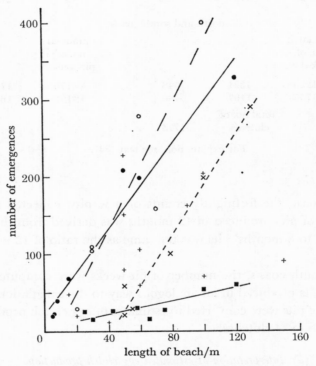

FIGURE 3. Relation between numbers of emergences and beach length. Lines are linear regressions of emergences on beach length for the following groups of beaches: ■, SW coast beaches 1–8, $y = 0.44x + 3.98$; ×, SW coast beaches 9–14, $y = 0.28x - 136.42$; ●, SW coast beaches 15–21, $y = 2.74x + 22.83$; ○, south coast beaches 28–33, $y = 4.07x - 31.12$; +, other beaches.

5. DISTRIBUTION OF NESTING ACTIVITY

(a) General observations

Apart from the 2 km long 'Settlement Beach', which supports only a small proportion of emergences at Aldabra (§5b), green turtle nesting is largely restricted to fewer than 50 short beaches scattered in the atoll perimeter of rocky cliffs and totalling only 2.5 km out of 83 km of coastline. The estimated numbers of green turtle emergences at each nesting beach during the year of study are illustrated in figure 1. The distribution is very uneven, half of all emergences occurring on the eight most favoured beaches.

It seems likely that the attractiveness of a beach might be related to its size as seen from the sea. The estimated number of emergences at each beach during the year is plotted in figure 3 against the beach length, approximately measured along the beach crest. Taken together, the points show only weak correlation ($r = 0.52$, $p = 0.001$) between the number of emergences and beach length, but there is a tendency for certain groups of beaches that are in close geographical proximity to show a much stronger relationship. Four such groups are differentiated in figure 3, three on the southwest coast and one on the south coast, and within each group the relation between frequency of emergences and beach length is approximately linear. The remaining beaches, on the north coast and at the east and west ends of the south coast, are mostly well separated from each other or are in small isolated groups and do not show any clear relation between frequency of emergences and beach length. Examination of sub-samples of the total number of emergences taken at different times of the year shows that the differentiation of beaches into these four groups remains constant despite the change that presumably takes place in the composition of the actively nesting population.

On the southwest coast the three beach groups occur within 8 km of coast and although sharply demarcated on the basis of figure 3, there is no obvious physical or topographical parameter which divides them up in the same manner. If not related to other simple features like beach length, these different emergence–length relations might alternatively be the result of a patchy distribution of nesting turtles around the coast, each group of beaches drawing on a differently sized stock of turtles. Such a distribution might arise either from the similar movements of all breeding turtles around the coast in response to a patchy marine habitat, or alternatively from active discrimination between the recognized features of several distinct target nesting areas. Unfortunately, very little is known about the factors that might influence the offshore movements of turtles, or about the extent of nest site fixity, if any, shown by Aldabran green turtles.

(b) 'Settlement Beach'

This beach on the sheltered west side of Ile Picard is virtually continuous for 2 km and accounts for two-fifths of the total length of green turtle nesting beach at Aldabra. It was possible to visit this beach more frequently than any other and nearly all emergences between September 1975 and April 1976 were recorded. The surprisingly small total of 88 emergences suggests that only 150 occurred during the whole year. This represents one of the lowest densities of emergence of all the beaches at Aldabra and, although it is possible that 'Settlement Beach' is naturally unfavoured by nesting turtles, it seems likely that the density is artificially low, possibly due to some effect of human presence, past or present, in settlements immediately behind the beach crest.

Between September and April the position of each emergence on the beach was recorded in relation to a series of numbered marker stakes at 50 m intervals from the northern end of 'Settlement Beach' to the Research Station at the southern end, and the numbers of emergences in each 50 m segment are plotted in figure 4. Although the total number of emergences is too small to reliably establish a detailed pattern of their distribution along the beach, it appears that the most favoured part is the $\frac{1}{2}$ km from the northern end and that the $\frac{1}{2}$ km nearest the settlement is much less favoured. No emergences were recorded on the end of the beach, near the research station, recently extended by wave action.

There are no obvious topographical features of the beach that might account for this uneven distribution of emergences. A similar distribution, showing areas of clumped nesting and an apparent reduction of nesting opposite a human settlement, has been reported by Carr & Carr (1972) for over 10 years' records of green turtle nesting at Costa Rica. Carr & Carr found no general explanation for this clumped distribution but argued that the deficiency of nests near the village could be either the result of turtles simply being scared away, or alternatively due to the steady loss of hatchlings having an imprinted tendency to return there after heavy human predation of emerging adults in the past. Of these two explanations, Carr & Carr regard the latter as 'more reasonable'. Although many more observations are required to

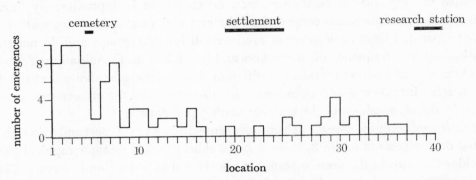

FIGURE 4. Distribution of turtle emergences on 'Settlement beach'. Numbers on the abscissa refer to beach marker posts at 50 m intervals, numbered from north to south. Heavy lines indicate the extent of buildings and artefacts.

clarify the distribution at Aldabra, it seems probable that similar considerations may apply at 'Settlement Beach'. It has not yet been shown that Aldabran green turtles return to their site of hatching in order to nest, nor that they repeatedly re-nest in the same locality, although it seems likely that they share this tendency with green turtles at Costa Rica and at Ascension Island (Carr & Carr 1972; Carr 1975). However, the data so far suggests a fairly sharp decline in emergences at the boundaries of the settlement, which itself occupies only a few hundred metres of beach (see figure 4). Carr & Carr's hypothesis would require an abrupt change in the predation rate along the beach and very precise site fixity indeed to account for such a distribution in this case. Further data are required to judge how large and abrupt the change in the density of emergences could be, but it remains a strong possibility that the presence of people and buildings within a few metres of the beach crest at the Settlement is currently inhibiting turtle emergence in the vicinity to some extent, despite the absence of bright lights, vibrating machinery and other common factors that often disturb green turtles.

I should like to thank all members of the Royal Society Aldabra Research Station who helped to collect track and pit counts at Aldabra, and particularly Mr R. Wilderspin. I should also like to thank Dr R. S. Oldham of Leicester Polytechnic for criticism of the manuscript.

REFERENCES (Gibson)

Bustard, H. R. & Greenham, P. M. 1969 Nesting behavior of the green sea turtle on a Great Barrier Reef island. *Herpetologica* **25**, 93–102.
Carr, A. 1975 The Ascension Island green turtle colony. *Copeia* **1975**, 547–555.
Carr, A. & Carr, M. H. 1972 Site fixity in the Caribbean green turtle. *Ecology* **53**, 425–429.
Frazier, J. 1971 Observations on sea turtles at Aldabra atoll. *Phil. Trans. R. Soc. Lond.* B **260**, 373–410.
Frazier, J. 1975 Marine turtles of the western Indian Ocean. *Oryx* **13**, 164–175.

Hendrickson, J. R. 1958 The green turtle, *Chelonia mydas* (L.), in Malaya and Sarawak. *Proc. zool. Soc. Lond.* **130**, 455–535.

Hirth, H. F. 1971 Synopsis of biological data on the green turtle *Chelonia mydas* (Linnaeus) 1758. *F.A.O. Fisheries Synopsis*, no. 85. Rome: United Nations F.A.O.

Hirth, H. & Carr, A. 1970 The green turtle in the Gulf of Aden and the Seychelle islands. *Verh. K. ned. Akad. Wet. (Aft. Nat., tweede Sect.)* **58**, 1–44.

Hornell, J. 1927 *The turtle fisheries of the Seychelle islands.* London: H.M.S.O.

INDEX OF PLACE NAMES

TAXONOMIC INDEX

GENERAL INDEX